TECHNOLOGY AND SOCIETY

TECHNOLOGY AND SOCIETY

BELL'S ELECTRIC

SPEAKING TELEPHONE:

ITS

INVENTION, CONSTRUCTION, APPLICATION,

MODIFICATION AND HISTORY.

BY

GEORGE B. PRESCOTT.

WITH 330 ILLUSTRATIONS.

NEW YORK:

D. APPLETON & COMPANY.

1884.

PREFACE.

The object which we have had in view, in preparing this work, has been to furnish the public with a clear and accurate description of the more recent and useful improvements in electrical science, and especially to explain the principles and operation of that marvellous production, the Speaking Telephone. In giving particular prominence to this part of the subject, however, we have by no means lost sight of another matter in connection therewith, of considerable historical importance, and which has also elicited an unusual amount of general interest. The question as to whom we are indebted for the telephone is one which, in consequence of the conflicting statements that have appeared from time to time, is, to say the least, extremely puzzling. We have, therefore, endeavored to give it the attention its importance demands, in order to arrive at a true solution of the problem, and, in doing so, have taken every opportunity to consult all available authorities on the subject. No effort has been spared in our investigation to obtain all the facts as they are; and these are now given as we have found them, without favor or prejudice. The reader will thus be enabled to judge for himself just what measure of credit to accord to each of the different experimenters who have been engaged with the problem of electrical transmission of articulate speech, and whose labors have been crowned with such abundant success.

INTRODUCTION.

WHEN Franklin drew from the clouds the electric spark upon the cord of his kite, it seemed obvious that electricity might be made use of for the purpose of telegraphy; and more than one hundred years ago Lesage established a telegraph in Geneva by the use of frictional electricity. But this force had very little power when transmitted over a long distance, and that little was practically uncontrollable, and therefore useless for telegraphy.

When galvanism was discovered, at the beginning of the present century, and the voltaic battery invented, it was at once supposed that this new form of electricity might work a telegraph, and ten years later the chemical telegraph was invented by Coxe, in Philadelphia. Under this system, the two wires from a galvanic battery were made to approach each other in a cell of water. When the galvanic circuit was closed, the water between the opposite poles, which were near each other, was decomposed, and a bubble of hydrogen rose to the surface, as the bubble from champagne does in the wine cup; and the observer, seeing it, knew that a current was passing, and that the bubble was the signal. But it was evanescent

" —— like snow falls in the river,
A moment white, then melts forever."

In 1820, Oersted discovered that an electric current would deflect a magnetic needle, and Arago and Davy simultaneously discovered that a piece of iron, surrounded by a spiral wire through which a current of galvanism passed, would become magnetic. From this fact Ampère deduced the hypothesis that magnetism is the circulation of currents of electricity at right angles to the axis joining the two poles of the magnet. That was a brilliant deduction; but no practical result was produced from it until 1825, when the first simple electro-magnet was made by Sturgeon, who bent a piece of wire into the shape of a horseshoe, and wound a fine wire around it in a helix, through which the galvanic current passed; and he found that the horseshoe wire was magnetic as long as the current flowed. Then at once an attempt was made with Sturgeon's magnet to produce the electro-magnetic telegraph, but without success. The difficulty was that the magnetic power could not be transmitted from the battery for more than fifty feet with Sturgeon's magnet, which was, therefore, entirely useless for the purposes of a telegraph; and, in 1829, Professor Barlow published a scientific demonstration in England, which was accepted by the scientific world, that an electro-magnetic telegraph was impossible; which was true in the then state of knowledge.

In 1830, Professor Henry deduced from the hypothesis of Ampère the invention now known as the compound electro-magnet. He also answered the demonstration of Barlow, and proved that the electro-magnetic telegraph was possible. In the same year he set up an electro-magnetic telegraph in Albany, over a line of a mile and a half in length, using a polarized relay, the armature of which was pivoted so as to vibrate between its poles as the current of electricity was reversed, thus transmitting intelligence by sound.

In 1831, Professor Faraday made known his discovery of the phenomenon of magnetic induction.

In 1834, Gauss and Weber constructed a line of telegraph, containing about 15,000 feet of wire, which was operated by the magneto-electric currents generated in a coil of wire when the latter was moved up or down upon a permanent magnet, around which it was placed. The slow oscillations of a magnetic needle, caused by the passage of the current, and which were observed through a glass, furnished the signals for correspondence. Sir William Thomson has since greatly improved the latter apparatus, and thereby given us the beautifully sensitive mirror galvanometer which bears his name.

In 1837, Steinheil discovered the important fact that the earth would serve as a conductor, thereby saving one wire in forming a circuit: Cooke invented his electro-magnetic semaphore, known as the needle telegraph, in which needles swing upon the face of a dial, just as the vanes of the old semaphores swung on the hill tops : Morse invented his electro-magnetic telegraph, which he put in operation between Baltimore and Washington in 1844 : and Page discovered that a musical sound accompanies the disturbance of the magnetic forces of a steel bar, when poised or suspended so as to exhibit acoustic vibrations.

In 1861, Reiss discovered that a vibrating diaphragm could be actuated by the human voice so as to cause the pitch and rhythm of vocal sounds to be transmitted to a distance, and reproduced by electro-magnetism.

In 1872, Stearns perfected a duplex system, whereby two communications could be simultaneously transmitted over one wire; and, in 1874, Edison invented a quadruplex system for the simultaneous transmission of four communications over the same conductor.

In 1874, Bell invented a method of electrical transmission by means of which the intensity of the tones, as well as their pitch and rhythm, could be reproduced at a distance; and subsequently conceived the idea of controlling the formation of electric waves by means of the vibrations of a diaphragm capable of responding to all the tones of the human voice, thus solving the problem of the transmission and reproduction of articulate speech over an electric conductor.

In 1876, Bell invented an improvement in the apparatus for the transmission and reproduction of articulate speech, in which magneto-electric currents were superposed upon a voltaic circuit, and actuated an iron diaphragm attached to a soft iron magnet.

During the same year, he also conceived the idea of substituting permanent magnets in place of the electro-magnets and battery previously employed, and of using the same instrument for both sending and receiving, instead of employing instruments of different construction, as had been previously done.

In 1877, Edison applied to the telephone the discovery made by himself a few years before, of the variation of resistance which carbon and certain other semiconductors undergo when subjected to a change of pressure. By this means he not only succeeded in varying the strength of the battery current in unison with the rise and fall of the vocal utterances, but, at the same time, also obtained louder articulation.

CONTENTS.

CHAPTER I.

THE SPEAKING TELEPHONE.

CHAPTER II.

BELL'S TELEPHONIC RESEARCHES.

CHAPTER III.

THE TELEPHONE ABROAD.

CHAPTER IX.

VARIOUS MODIFICATIONS OF THE BELL TELEPHONE.

CHAPTER X.

HISTORY OF THE INVENTION OF THE EDISON SPEAKING TELEPHONE.

CHAPTER I.

The Speaking Telephone, a recent American invention, which at the present moment is exciting the wonder and admiration of the civilized world, is a device for transmitting to a distance, over an electric circuit, and accurately reproducing at any desired place, various kinds of sounds, including those of the human voice. The function of the telephone is analogous to that of a speaking tube capable of almost infinite extension, through which conversation may be carried on as readily as with persons in the same room.

Before proceeding to give a description of the apparatus employed for communicating or reproducing articulate speech at a distance by the telephone, it will be well to devote some consideration to the process by which the ear distinguishes the vibrations of a particular tone, or the aggregate of the vibrations of all the tones which simultaneously act upon it, for by this means we may be enabled to ascertain the conditions under which the transmitting and receiving apparatus must act in order to effect the desired result.

It is well known that the sensation which we call sound is excited by the action of the vibrations of the atmosphere upon the tympanum or drum of the ear, and that these vibrations are conveyed from the tympanum to the auricular nerves in the interior parts of the ear, by means of a mechanical apparatus of wonderful delicacy and precision of action, consisting of a series of bones termed respectively the hammer, anvil and stirrup. In the process of reproducing tones by electro-magnetism, an artificial imitation of the mechanism of the human ear is employed, consisting of a stretched membrane or diaphragm corresponding to the tympanum, which by its vibrations generates and controls an electric circuit extended to a distant station by a metallic conductor.

If we analyze the process by which the ear distinguishes a simple sound, we find that a tone results from the alternate expansion and condensation of an elastic medium. If this process takes place in the medium in which the ear is situated, namely, the atmosphere, then at each recurring condensation the elastic membrane or tympanum will be pressed inward, and these vibrations will be transmitted, by the mechanism above referred to, to the auricular nerves.

The greater the degree of condensation of the elastic medium in a given time, the greater is the amplitude of the movement of the tympanum, and consequently of the mechanism which acts upon the nerves. Hence it follows that the function of the human ear is the mechanical transmission to the auditory nerves of each expansion and contraction which occurs in the surrounding medium, while that of the nerves is to convey to the brain the sensations thus produced. A series of vibrations, a definite number of which are produced in a given time, and of which we thus become cognizant, is called a tone.

The action which has thus reached our consciousness, being a purely mechanical one, may be rendered much more easy of comprehension by graphical delineation. If, for example, we assume the horizontal line $a\,b$ to represent a certain period of time, let the curves extending above the line $a\,b$ represent the

successive condensations (+), and the curves below the line the successive expansions (—), then each ordinate represents the degree of condensation or expansion at the moment of time corresponding to its position upon the line $a\,b$ and also the amplitude of the vibrations of the tympanum.

A simple musical tone results from a continuous, rapid and uniformly recurring series of vibrations, provided the number of complete vibrations per second falls within certain limits. If, for example, the vibrations number less than seven or eight per second, a series of successive noises are heard instead of a tone, while if their number exceeds forty thousand per second, the ear becomes incapable of appreciating the sound.

The ear distinguishes three distinct characteristics of sound:

1. The tone or pitch, by virtue of which sounds are high or low, and which depends upon the rapidity of the vibratory movement. The more rapid the vibrations the more acute will be the sound.

2. The intensity, by virtue of which sounds are loud or soft, and which depends upon the amplitude of the vibrations.

3. The quality, by which we are able to distinguish a note sounded upon, for example, a violin, from the same note when sounded upon a flute. By a remarkable series of experimental investigations Helmholtz succeeded in demonstrating that the different qualities of sounds depend altogether upon the number and intensity of the overtones which accompany the primary tones of those sounds. The different characteristics of sound may be graphically represented and the phenomena thus rendered more easy of comprehension.

In fig. 1, for example, let the lines $\bar{c}$ 8 represent a certain length of time, and the continuous curved line the successive vibrations producing a simple tone. The curves above the line represent the compression of the air, and those below the line its rarefaction; the air, an elastic medium, is thus thrown into vibrations which transmit the sound waves to the ear. The ear is unable to appreciate any sensations of sound other than those produced by vibrations, which may be represented by curves similar to that above described. Even if several tones are produced simultaneously, the elastic medium of transmission is under the influence of several forces acting at the same time, and which are subject to the ordinary laws of mechanics. If the different forces act in the same direction the total force is represented by their sum, while if they act in opposite directions, it is represented by the difference between them.

In fig. 1 three distinct simple tones, *c*, *g* and *e* are represented, the rapidity of the vibrations being in the proportion of 8, 6 and 5. The composite tone resulting from the simultaneous production of the three simple tones is represented graphically by the fourth line, which correctly exhibits to the eye the effect pro-

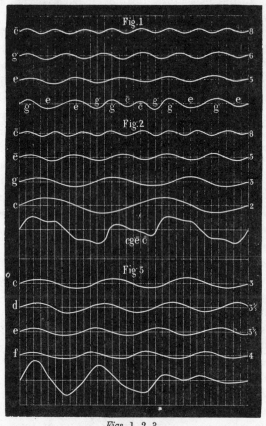

Figs. 1, 2, 3.

duced upon the ear by the three simultaneously acting simple tones.

Fig. 2 represents a curve formed of more than three tones, in which the relations do not appear so distinctly, but a musical

expert will readily recognize them, even when it would be difficult in practice for him to distinguish the simple tones in such a
chord.

This method of showing the action of tones upon the human
ear possesses the advantage of giving the clearest illustration
possible of the entire process.

We may even understand by reference to fig. 3 why it is that ·
the ear is so disagreeably affected by a discord.

It will be observed that the curves in the diagram represent
the three characteristics of sound which have been referred to.
The pitch is denoted by the number of vibrations or waves recurring within a given horizontal distance; the intensity by
the amplitude of the vibrations—that is their comparative
height above or depth below the horizontal line—and the
quality by the form of the waves themselves. It is, therefore,
easy to understand that if, by any means whatever, we can produce vibrations whose curves correspond to those of a given
tone or a given combination of tones, the same impression will be
produced upon the ear that would have been produced by the
original tone, whether simple or composite.

The earliest experiments in the production of musical sounds
at a distance, by means of electro-magnetism, appear to have
been made in 1861 by Philip Reiss, of Friedrichsdorf, Germany.
His apparatus was constructed in the manner shown in fig. 4.

A is the transmitting and B the receiving apparatus, which
are supposed to be situated at different stations. For the sake of
clearness, the appliances by which the apparatus is arranged for
reciprocal transmission in one direction or the other have been
omitted. Furthermore, it may be well to state that, as the apparatus was constructed merely for the purpose of making known
to a wider circle the discoveries which had thus far been made,
the possibility of extending the action of the apparatus to a distance beyond the limit of the direct action of the current had not
been taken into consideration. This is a mere question of mechanical construction, and has no especial bearing upon the phenomena under consideration. The tone transmitter A, figure 4,

is on the one hand connected by a metallic conductor with the tone receiver B at the distant station, and on the other with the battery C and the earth, or the return conductor. It consists of

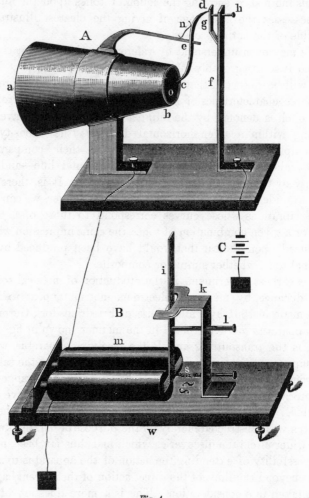

Fig. 4.

a conical tube, *a b*, about 6 inches in length, and having a diameter of 4 inches at the larger and 1½ inches at the smaller end.

It was found by experiment that the material of which the tube was constructed had no influence upon the action of the apparatus, and the same is true as to its length. An increase in the diameter of the tube was found to impair the effect. The inner surface of the tube should be made as smooth as possible. The smaller or rear end of the tube is closed by means of a collodion membrane, o, against the centre of which rests one extremity, c, of the lever c d, which lever is in electrical connection with the metallic conducting wire through its point e and supporting bracket. The proper length and proportion to be given to the respective arms c e and d e of the lever c e d is determined by mechanical considerations. It is advisable that the length of the arm c e should be greater than that of d e, so as to produce the necessary movement at c with the least possible exertion of force at d. The lever itself should be made as light as possible, in order that it may follow with certainty the movements of the membrane, as any inaccuracy in this respect will give rise to a false tone at the receiving station. When the apparatus is in a state of rest the contact at d g is closed; a delicate spring n maintains the lever in this position. The metallic standard f is connected with one pole of the battery C, the other pole of which is connected to the earth, or to the return wire leading to the other station. A flat spring g is attached to the standard f, and is provided with a contact point corresponding to that at d upon the lever c d. The position of this contact point may be adjusted by means of a screw h.

In order to prevent the interference occasioned by the action of the sonorous vibrations of the atmosphere upon the back side of the membrane, when making use of the apparatus, it is advisable to place a disk about twenty inches in diameter upon the tube a b, in the form of a collar or flange, at right angles to its longitudinal axis.

The tone receiver B, fig. 4, consists of an electro-magnet m, mounted upon a sounding box or resonator w, and included in the circuit of the electrical conductor from the transmitting station. Facing the poles of the electro-magnet is an armature which is attached to a broad but thin and light plate, i, which should be made as long as possible. The lever and armature are suspended from the upright support k, in the manner of a pendulum, its motion being regulated by the adjusting screw l and the spring s.

In order to increase the volume of sound, the tone receiver may be placed at one of the focal points of an elliptical chamber of suitable size, while the ear of the listener is placed at the other focal point.

The operation of the apparatus is as follows: When the different parts are in a state of rest the electric circuit is closed. If an alternate condensation and rarefaction of the air in the tube $a\ b$ is produced by speaking, singing, or playing upon a musical instrument, a corresponding motion is communicated to the membrane, and from thence to the lever $c\ d$, by which means the electric circuit is alternately opened and closed at $d\ g$, each condensation of the air in the tube causing the circuit to be broken, and each rarefaction in like manner causing it to be closed. Thus the electro-magnet $m\ m$, of the apparatus at B, becomes demagnetized or magnetized, according to the alternate condensations and rarefactions of the body of air contained in the tube $a\ b$, and consequently the armature of the electro-magnet is thrown into vibrations corresponding to those of the membrane in the transmitting apparatus. The plate i, to which the armature is attached, transmits the vibrations of the latter to the surrounding atmosphere, which in turn conveys them to the ear of the listener.

It must however be admitted, that while the apparatus which has been described reproduces the original vibrations with perfect fidelity, so far as their number and interval is concerned, it cannot transmit their intensity or amplitude. The accomplishment of this latter result had to await the further development of the invention.

It was in consequence of this defect in the apparatus that the more inconsiderable differences of the original vibrations were distinguished with great difficulty—that is to say, the vowel sounds were heard with more or less indistinctness, for the reason that the character of each tone depends not merely upon the number of the sonorous vibrations, but upon their intensity or amplitude also. This also accounts for the observed fact that while chords and melodies were transmitted and reproduced with a surprising degree of accuracy, single words, as pronounced in reading or speaking, were but indistinctly heard, although in this case, also, the inflections of the voice, interrogative, exclamatory, etc., could be distinguished without difficulty.

Figure 5 illustrates another form of Reiss's apparatus.

A is a hollow wooden box, provided with two apertures, one at the top and the other in front. The former is covered with a membrane S, such as a piece of bladder, tightly stretched in a

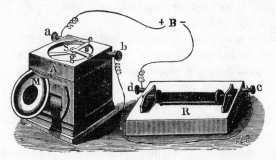

Fig. 5.

circular frame. When a person sings into the mouthpiece M, which is inserted in the front opening, the whole force of his voice is concentrated on the tight membrane, which is thrown into vibrations corresponding exactly with the vibrations of the air produced by the sound of the singing. A thin piece of platinum is glued to the centre of the membrane and connected with the binding screw *a*, in which a wire from the battery B is fixed. Upon the membrane rests a little tripod *e f g*, of which the feet *e* and *f* rest in metal cups upon the circular frame over which the skin is stretched. One of them, *f*, rests in a mercury cup connected with the binding screw *b*. The third foot, *g*, consisting of a platinum contact point, lies on the strip of platinum which is placed upon the centre of the vibrating membrane and hops up and down with it. By this means the closed circuit which passes through the apparatus from a to b is momentarily broken for every vibration of the membrane. The receiving instrument R consists of a coil or helix, enclosing an iron rod and fixed upon a hollow sounding box, and is founded on the fact, first investigated by Professor Joseph Henry, that iron bars, when magnetized by means of an electric current, become slightly elongated, and at the interruption of the current are restored to their normal length. In the receiving instrument these elongations and shortenings of the iron bar will succeed each other with precisely the same interval as the vibrations of the original tone, and the longitudinal vibrations of the bar will be communicated to the sounding box, thus being made distinctly audible at the receiving station.

It will be seen that the result produced by these devices is not the veritable transmission of sound by means of the electric current, but is simply a reproduction of the tones at some other point, by setting in action at this point a similar cause, and thereby producing a similar effect.

It is obvious that this apparatus, like the one previously described, is capable of producing only one of the three characteristics of sound, viz., its pitch. It cannot produce different degrees of intensity or other qualities of tones, but merely sings the melodies transmitted with its own voice, which is not very unlike that of a toy trumpet. Referring to the graphic representation of the composite tone in fig. 1, this apparatus would reproduce the waves at properly recurring intervals, but they would all be of precisely the same amplitude or intensity, for the reason that they are all produced by an electric current of the same strength.

In the spring of 1874 Mr. Elisha Gray, of Chicago, invented a method of electrical transmission by means of which the intensity of the tones, as well as their pitch, was properly reproduced at the receiving station. This was a very important discovery—in fact, an essential prerequisite to the development of the telephone, both in respect to the reproduction of harmonic musical tones and of articulate speech, as it enabled any required number of different tones to be reproduced simultaneously without destroying their individuality.

In this method the transmitters were so arranged that a separate series of electrical impulses of varying strength as well as rapidity passed into the line, thus reproducing at the distant end the intensities of the vibrations, corresponding to the graphic representation on the fourth or bottom line of fig. 1.   By this means a tune could be reproduced at any distance with perfect accuracy, including its pitch and varying intensity as well as quality of sound.   With a receiving instrument consist-

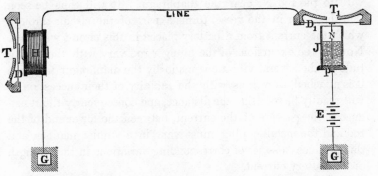

Fig. 6.

ing of an electro-magnet, having its armature rigidly fixed to one pole, and separated from the other by a space of $\frac{1}{64}$ of an inch, and mounted upon a hollow sounding box, which, like that of a violin, responded to all vibrations which were communicated to it, the tones became very loud and distinct.

Subsequently Mr. Gray conceived the idea of controlling the formation of what may be termed the electric waves, as represented in the diagram, figs. 1, 2 and 3, by means of the vibrations of a diaphragm capable of responding to sounds of every kind traversing the atmosphere, so arranged as to reproduce these vibrations at a distance.   When this was accomplished, the problem of the transmission and reproduction of articulate speech over an electric conductor was theoretically solved.

The principle and mode of operation of Gray's original telephone are shown in the accompanying fig. 6. The person transmitting sounds speaks into the mouthpiece T¹. D¹ is a diaphragm of some thin substance capable of responding to the various complex vibrations produced by the human voice. To the centre of the diaphragm one end of a light metallic rod, N, is rigidly attached, the other extending into a glass vessel J, placed beneath the chamber. This vessel, whose lower end is closed by a metallic plug, P, is filled with slightly acidulated water, or some other liquid of the same specific resistance, and the metallic plug or end placed in connection with one terminal of an electric circuit, the other end being joined by a very light wire to the rod N, near the diaphragm. It will thus be seen that the water in the vessel forms a part of the circuit through which the current from a battery placed in this circuit will pass. Now, as the excursions of the plunger rod vary with the amplitude of the several vibrations made by the diaphragm to which it is attached, as well as with the rapidity of their succession, it will readily be seen that the distance, and consequently the resistance to the passage of the current, between the lower end of the rod and the metallic plug, must vary in a similar manner, and this produces a series of corresponding variations in the strength of the battery current.

The receiving apparatus consists simply of an electro-magnet, H, and armature, a diaphragm, D, and a mouthpiece, T. The soft iron armature which is attached to the diaphragm stands just in front of the electro-magnet; consequently, when the latter acts, it does so in obedience to current pulsations, which have all the characteristics of the vibrating diaphragm D, and thus, through the additional intermediary of the soft iron, the vibrations produced by the voice in T are communicated to the diaphragm T of the receiving apparatus, and thus sounds of every character, including all the tones of the human voice, are reproduced with absolute fidelity and distinctness.

In the summer of 1876 Professor A. G. Bell, of the Boston University, exhibited at the Centennial Exhibition, in Philadelphia, a telephonic apparatus, differing somewhat in its details from that just described, by which articulate speech could be transmitted over an electric circuit, and reproduced at a distance with some degree of distinctness.

The principle of his method is illustrated in fig. 7. A represents the transmitting and B the receiving apparatus. When a person speaks into the tube T, in the direction of the arrow, the acoustic vibrations of the air are communicated to a membrane tightly stretched across the end of the tube, upon which is cemented a light permanent bar magnet *n s*. This is in close proximity to the poles of an electro-magnet M, in the circuit of the line, which is constantly charged by a current from the battery E. The vibrations of the magnet *n s* induce

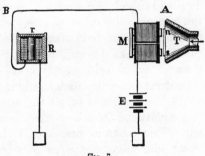

Fig. 7.

magneto-electric pulsations in the coils of the electro-magnet M, which traverse the circuit, and the magnitude of these pulsations is proportional to the rapidity and amplitude of the vibrations of the magnet; thus, for instance, when the small permanent magnet is made to move toward M, a current of electricity will be induced in the coils, which will traverse the whole circuit. This induced electricity will consist of a single wave or pulse, and its force will depend upon the velocity of the approach of *n s* to M. A like pulse of electricity will be induced in the coils when *n s* is made to move away from M; but this current will move through the circuit in an opposite direction, so that whether the pulsation goes from A to B or from B to A, depends simply upon the direction of the motion of *n s*.

The electricity thus generated in the wire by such vibratory movements varies in strength, as already observed, with the variations in the movement of the armature; the line wire between two places will, therefore, be filled with electrical pulsations exactly like the aerial pulsations in structure.

These induced electric currents are very transient, and their effect upon the receiver R is either to increase or decrease the power of the magnet there, as they are in one direction or the other, and consequently to vary the attractive power exercised upon the iron plate armature.

Let a simple sound be made in the tube, consisting of 256 vibrations per second; the membrane carrying the iron will vibrate as many times, and so many pulses of induced electricity will be imposed upon the constant current, which will each act upon the receiver, and cause so many vibrations of the armature upon it; and an ear held near r will hear the sound with the same pitch as that at the sending instrument. If two or more sound waves act simultaneously upon the membrane, its motions must correspond with such combined motion; that is, its motion will be the resultant of all the sound waves, and the corresponding pulsations in the current must reproduce at B the same effect. Now, when a person speaks in the tube, the membrane is thrown into vibrations more complex in structure than those just mentioned, differing only in number and intensity. The magnet will cause responses from even the minutest motion, and, therefore, an ear near r will hear what is said in the tube. Consequently, this apparatus is capable of transmitting both the pitch and intensity of the tones which enter the tube T. The receiving instrument consists simply of a tubular electro-magnet R, formed of a single helix with an external soft iron case, into the top of which is loosely fitted the iron plate r, which is thrown into vibrations by the action of the magnetizing helix. The sounds produced in this manner were quite weak, and could be transmitted but a short distance; but the mere accomplishment of the feat of transmitting electric impulses over a metallic wire which should reproduce articu-

late speech, even in an imperfect manner, at the farther end, excited great interest in a scientific as well as popular point of
view, throughout the civilized world.

During the ensuing autumn some important changes in the
telephone were effected, whereby its articulating properties
were greatly improved. Professor Bell, the inventor, having
observed that the actual function of the battery current with
which the line was electrically charged had simply the effect
of polarizing the soft iron cores of the transmitting and
receiving instruments; or of converting them into permanent
magnets, and that the mere passage of the constant voltaic current over the line had nothing to do with the result, conceived
the idea of maintaining the cores in a permanently magnetic or
polarized state by the inductive influence of a permanent mag-

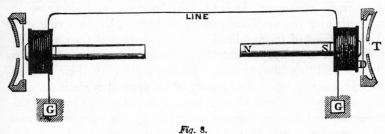

Fig. 8.

net instead of by a voltaic current. He therefore substituted
permanent magnets with small helices of insulated copper wire
surrounding one or both poles, in place of the electro-magnets
and battery previously employed.

Another important improvement made by him consisted in
using the same instrument for both sending and receiving instead
of employing instruments of different construction, as all previous
inventors had done.

The principle and mode of operation of the improved apparatus is represented in figure 8.

It consists of an ordinary permanent bar magnet, N S, a single
helix, H, of insulated copper wire placed upon one end of the
magnet, and a metallic diaphragm, D, consisting of a disk of thin

sheet iron, two and a quarter inches in diameter and one fiftieth of an inch thick, forming an armature to the magnet, N S. The vibratory motions of the air produced by the voice or other cause are directed towards and concentrated upon the diaphragm, D, by means of a mouthpiece, T. It will thus be seen that when vibrations are communicated to the air in front of the mouth-piece the impact of the waves of air against the elastic diaphragm will cause a corresponding movement of the latter. This in turn, by reacting upon the magnet, disturbs the normal magnetic con-dition of the bar, and since any change of magnetism in this tends to generate electrical currents in the surrounding helix, the circuit in which the helix may be placed will be traversed by a series of electrical pulsations or currents. Moreover, as these currents continue to be generated so long as the motion of the diaphragm continues, and as they increase and decrease in strength with the amplitude of its vibrations, thus varying with the variations of its amplitude, it is evident that they virtually possess all the physical characteristics of the agent acting upon the transmitting diaphragm. Consequently, by their electro-magnetic action upon the magnet of an apparatus identical with the one above described, and placed in the same circuit at the receiving end, they will cause its diaphragm to vibrate in exact correspondence with that of the transmitting apparatus.

During the past year many ingenious persons have turned their attention to the subject of telephones, and by the introduction of various modifications have succeeded in greatly improving the invention, so as to make it available for practical applica-tion. Prominent among these is Mr. G. M. Phelps, mechanician of the Western Union Telegraph Company, to whose ability in the invention of valuable improvements, as well as in the scien-tific arrangement of details in the construction of the apparatus, the public is indebted for some of the most effective telephones yet introduced. The peculiar excellence of these instruments consists in their distinct articulation, combined with a loudness of utterance that is not often met with in the numerous other forms that have appeared up to the present time. Both of these qualities, manifestly so desirable, are developed in these instruments in a very remarkable degree, while the distance over which they may be used is also another of their distinguishing characteristics, circuits of over one hundred miles having been worked by them with the most admirable results.

The most essential improvements introduced by Mr. Phelps consist in combining two or more vibrating diaphragms and two or more corresponding magnetic cores, enveloped in separate helices, connected in the same circuit, with a single mouthpiece or vocalizing chamber; in mounting two magnetic cores, when combined with separate diaphragms and coils, and a single mouthpiece, upon opposite poles of the same permanent magnet,

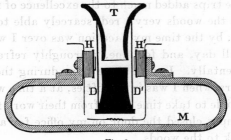

Fig. 9.

and in subdividing a single continuous induction plate into two or more separate and distinct areas of vibration, thus virtually forming two or more separate diaphragms, each of which acts or is acted upon by a separate magnetic core, to the consequent increased usefulness of the apparatus.

Figure 9 represents a form of the instrument constructed upon the above principles, which, both as regards distinctness of articulation and the facility with which it permits conversation to be carried on in consequence of the loudness of its tone, leaves little else to be desired. It consists of the permanent magnet M of hardened steel, which is bent into an oblong form, so as to occupy but little space, and also bring its poles conveniently near each other; two helices, H and H¹, of copper wire, placed respectively upon the north and south poles of the magnet; two metallic diaphragms, D and D¹, and the speaking tube or mouth-piece T, which may be made of wood, metal, or such other substance as fancy may suggest. The diaphragms are placed upon opposite sides of a short cylindrical piece of hard rubber, provided with a lateral opening for the insertion of the mouth-piece, and, together with it, form a sort of chamber, within which the air is alternately condensed and rarefied, in conse-quence of the motion or impulses communicated to its particles by the voice when directed toward the opening of the tube. Hence, it will be seen that each condensation exerts an outward pressure of its own upon the diaphragm, while each rarefaction causes a corresponding pressure from the external air, and thus a vibratory movement is imparted to both diaphragms at one and the same instant; consequently, if the helices are so con-nected that the direction of the current pulsations, which are inductively produced by the vibrations of the diaphragms in the manner already explained, are similar when they become united in the line, the magnetic force, as exhibited in the receiving ap-paratus at the distant station, will be augmented considerably above that produced by the action of a single coil and diaphragm alone, and thereby a corresponding increase in the loudness of the sound will be produced. The best effects are obtained when instruments of this form are employed both in transmitting and receiving, the advantages they possess for the latter purpose being quite as marked as for the former, as will appear obvious enough when we consider that every time a current passes through the helices the attractive forces thereby imparted to the cores or magnet poles are such as to cause the centres of the two diaphragms to be drawn directly from each other, thus produc-ing a much greater rarefaction of the air within the chamber than could be obtained by the action of a single diaphragm alone. A corresponding condensation, on the other hand, is pro-duced at each cessation of the current, owing to the return of the diaphragms, in virtue of their elasticity to their normal position.

The greater the degree of condensation and rarefaction, how-ever, the greater the amplitude of the sonorous vibrations—one expression being the equivalent of the other—and, therefore, the greater will be the intensity or loudness of the sound produced. We might add, in this connection, that the introduction of a second helix in the line circuits presents in itself a slight disadvantage. This arises from the inductive action of the pulsatory currents upon themselves in the coils and the reactive influence of the core, whereby other and opposing currents are produced, which tend to delay, and, in part, neutralize the effects of the former. The latter are termed extra currents, to distinguish them from those produced in circuits exterior to that in which

Fig. 10.

the inducing currents are passing. As they are found to accompany all electro-magnetic action whenever one part of a circuit is brought in proximity to another, as is the case in magnet helices, it will readily be seen that they must become the more troublesome as the number of stations are increased—it being necessary to keep the vibratory bells at each station in circuits, in order that calls may be heard. By the use of condensers, consisting of alternate sheets of tin foil and paraffined paper placed around the bell coils, we are enabled to overcome the difficulty these currents would otherwise present. Condensers, therefore, become almost indispensable in cases where many telephones are employed in one circuit.

The instrument we have just described is made separate by itself, to be used as a transmitting or receiving instrument, or it is combined in a box represented below, with a call bell and the oval shaped telephone to be considered presently.   In the latter case it is usually employed to transmit alone, while the oval form serves for receiving ; it can, however, be used for either purpose.

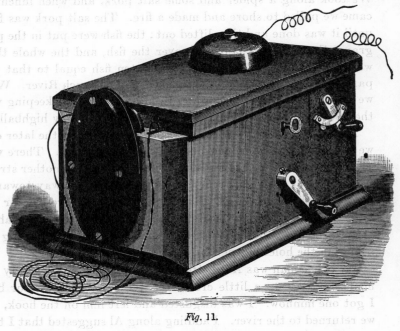

Fig. 11.

Mr. Phelps also found that the efficiency of the telephone for transmitting the human voice was much improved by reducing the cavity or chamber in which the diaphragm vibrates to the smallest practicable dimensions.   Further gain was also made by cushioning the bearings of the diaphragm on both sides with rings of paper.   In the form described below the diaphragms are still further cushioned on the side towards the magnets by a number of small spiral springs, placed under a hard rubber ring which supports the diaphragm.

The value of these last named improvements lies not so much in increasing the loudness of tone as in eliminating the reverberatory quality characteristic of most of the early telephones, and which gave an unnatural and hollow sound to the voice transmitted by them.

Fig. 12.

Another of the forms designed by Mr. Phelps, and now being extensively introduced by the American Telephone Company, is represented in fig. 10. It consists of a polished oval shaped case of hard rubber, with magnet, diaphragm and coils inside. In connection with this there is also a small magneto-electrical machine, contained in the oblong box shown in fig. 11, which is used for operating a call bell when the attention of the correspondent at the distant station is required. The currents generated by this machine, when the crank is turned, are conveyed by the conducting wires through the helices of a polarized magnet, shown on the under side of the cover, fig. 12, and cause the hammer attached to the armature lever to vibrate against the bell, thus producing a violent ringing during the time the crank is turned.

By the use of polarized magnets—the latter so named on account of their armatures being permanent magnets—the armature levers are retained in a definite position, depending upon the direction of the current last sent into the line, and no retractile spring whatever is required. At the same time, also, the alternating currents produced by the magneto-electrical machine are permitted to act with their maximum power, as the repelling force exercised in one pair of coils urges the armature in the same direction as that of the attractive force in the other, and the two effects are thus added.

It is usual to supply two telephones with this apparatus—two being preferable to one—as then one can be held to the ear while the other is being used to speak into. By this means any liability of losing a word while the instrument is being passed from the mouth to the ear, supposing one only to be used, is entirely prevented, and consequently the necessity for repetition avoided.

When the telephone is not in use it is placed in a slide, as shown in fig. 11, which causes a spring, shown at the end of the box in fig. 12, to be pressed inward and cut out the instrument, leaving only the magneto machine and call bell in circuit. The spring, when in its normal position, on the other hand, cuts out the machine and call bell and leaves the telephone alone in circuit.

Fig. 13 represents a somewhat more expensive but at the same time also a more desirable combination of the telephone and its accessories. The box is intended to be fastened permanently to the wall. It contains, in addition to the extra loud telephone with double diaphragms, which was described above, a call bell and a magneto-electric machine of improved construction. When not in use, only the call bell of this apparatus is in the main line circuit—the magneto machine, unlike that in the box just noticed, being cut out, so as to guard against accidental demagnetization of

Fig. 13.

the permanent magnet by lightning discharges, or by currents from telegraph lines when the latter are crossed or in contact with the telephone line, which is sometimes liable to occur. When we wish to send a signal, however, it is only necessary to turn the crank of the magneto machine, shown in front of the case, and at the same time press upon the push button C, which is visible on the left. The latter movement, by a change of connection to be more fully described presently, puts the magneto machine in circuit, and thus allows the currents generated by it to pass into the line and act upon the distant call bells.

The switch near the top of the case serves for cutting the apparatus in and out of circuit. When it is turned to the right, and the telephone is in the fork or holder, as represented in the figure—in which case it presses against a button corresponding to the spring in the former box and cuts itself out of circuit—only the call bell is left in with the main line. When it is

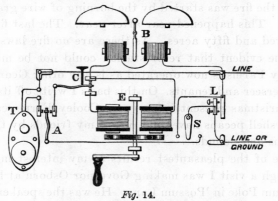

Fig. 14.

turned to the left hand or opposite side, which should always be done when left at night, all of the apparatus is cut out of circuit. A lightning arrester is provided in each box for the protection of the apparatus; but during thunder storms, and especially severe ones, it is best to cut the apparatus out of circuit altogether by means of the switch, as the best arresters sometimes fail. The accompanying diagrams, showing the internal arrangements of the different boxes, will give a much clearer understanding of the connections. Figure 14 represents the parts and connections of the improved apparatus, which is placed in a portable box, like the one shown in figure 11, without, however, the addition of what we have called the extra loud Speaking Telephone. In the ordinary working condition of the apparatus the switch S should be placed on the button contact, shown just to the right of it, and the telephone hung in its fork, which causes the spring A to be forced against the inside contact point. The telephone and magneto machine are thus cut out of circuit, as will be seen on tracing the connections, but the call currents arriving from a distant station on the line, find a ready path

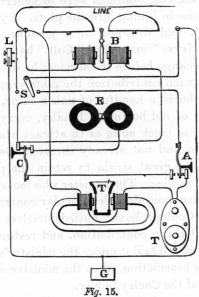

Fig. 15.

through the coils of the bell magnet B and spring below the push button C to the spring A, and thence by switch S to line again or ground, as the case may be, the final connection depending, of course, upon whether the station is located somewhere in the centre or at the terminal of the line. A call given by any one of the stations in the circuits will, therefore, be heard at all the others, as the connections at each are precisely similar. In giving the call, it is necessary, in addition to turning the crank of the magneto machine, to press against the push button

C, so as to bring the adjacent spring in contact with the little connecting piece which is metallically joined to the coils of the machine. Unless this is done no current will be sent into the line, because it is by this means alone that the inductive apparatus is placed in the circuit. When the button is down, the path opened for the current may be traced from the line terminal of the instrument by way of the bell and magneto coils to the spring beneath C; thence by way of spring A and switch S to line or ground.

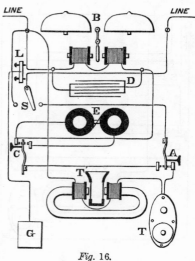

Fig. 16.

It will be obvious that the above arrangement supplies the means for giving a variety of calls in case there are several offices in one circuit; for, while turning the crank, the push button can be used, like a Morse key, to give different signals.

The removal of the telephone from its fork or holder puts it in circuit, and cuts everything else out, as will readily be seen by tracing the connections. The manner in which the apparatus is cut out of circuit, by turning the switch S on the left hand contact point, will also be seen on referring to the diagram.

Figures 15 and 16 show the internal connections and arrangement of the large box, figure 15, being the arrangement for a terminal, and figure 16 that for an intermediate station. The loud speaking instrument is shown in both. Figure 16 also shows the manner of connecting the condenser D around the bell coils, so as to avoid the previously noticed inductive difficulties which present themselves when many sets of the apparatus are placed in one circuit. The lightning arrester is represented at L. It will hardly be necessary to say anything further in regard to the connections in the last two figures, as the same letters that were used in the preceding figure have been retained for corresponding parts in these, and have, therefore, been already considered.

Fig. 17.

Figure 17 represents a form of Gray's Speaking Telephone manufactured by the Western Electric Telegraph Company, of Chicago.

Figure 18 shows a section of the same, reduced to about one third the natural size, and designed to show the internal mechanism.

By referring to the latter it will be seen that the core C is fastened to the upper end of the curved metallic bar H, which serves as the handle of the telephone. The lower end of the handle is in like manner attached to the metallic brace B. To this brace is secured, by means of a stout screw, the iron rim which holds the diaphragm; thus the core and the diaphragm form the two ends of a rigid metallic system, every part of which is of soft iron.

Around the core two helices of insulated copper wire are wound.   One of these—the polarizing helix—is somewhat longer than the other, and contains wire of larger gauge.   In using the telephone, this helix is connected in circuit with a local battery. The soft iron system is in consequence rendered magnetic, the end of the core exhibiting opposite polarity to that of the diaphragm confronting it.

By employing the battery current to charge the soft iron core,

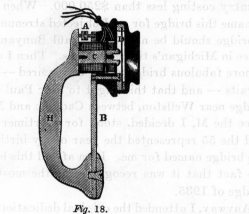

Fig. 18.

a greater degree of magnetism is thereby secured than could be obtained by the use of a permanent magnet of the same dimensions.

The difference also of magnetic potential existing between the diaphragm and the core is increased by making these respectively the opposite poles of the same magnet.

The other helix is made of very fine wire, and serves to convey to the line the undulating currents induced by the vibrating diaphragm.   At any point on the line these currents may be reconverted into sound by introducing an instrument similar to the above.

In adjusting this telephone advantage is taken of the elasticity of the brace B, which has a tendency to approach the handle H. This tendency is checked and regulated by the adjusting screw A, a turn of which will cause the brace to move towards or recede from the handle ; and, consequently, the diaphragm will also move to or recede from the core of the magnet.

Another of the forms devised by Mr. Gray is shown in fig. 19. In this there are two diaphragms, and no battery is used to charge the soft iron cores of the telephone, as is done in the original apparatus, the same result being obtained by the use of a permanent magnet, bent into a form like the letter U, as seen in the figure. The magnet also answers as a handle, by which

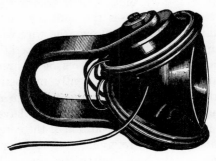

Fig. 19.

the instrument may be held conveniently. Two soft iron pieces are secured by screws to the poles of the magnet and carry helices of copper wire, which are joined together, and terminal wires leading therefrom serve to put the instrument in circuit.

The mouthpiece, which is of metal, has two divergent tubes connecting with narrow chambers, within which separate diaphragms of thin sheet iron are placed, so as to stand just opposite the pole pieces of the magnet and in close proximity thereto. Whenever, therefore, any movement is produced in the air at the opening of the tube the resultant impulse is readily conveyed through it and its branches to the chambers, and thus communicates motion to the diaphragms. The principle of the action in this apparatus is, of course, the same as that in the other forms of magneto telephones.

It will be observed that all the Speaking Telephones which we have described, possess certain common characteristics embodied in Bell's original discovery, and are essentially the same in principle although differing somewhat in matters of detail. All, for example, employ a diaphragm at the transmitting end capable of responding to the acoustic vibrations of the air; all employ a diaphragm at the receiving end capable of being thrown into vibrations by the action of the magnetizing helix, corresponding to the vibrations of the transmitting diaphragm; all depend for their action upon undulating electric currents produced by the vibratory motion of a transmitting diaphragm, which increases and decreases the number and amplitude of the electric impulses transmitted over the wire without breaking the circuit; and, finally, in all practically operative telephones, whether vocal or harmonic, the cores of the receiving instrument are maintained in a permanently magnetic state by the inductive action, either of a permanent voltaic current or of a permanent magnet. Repeated experiments have shown, also, that this permanent magnetic condition of the cores is absolutely essential, in order that the receiving magnet may become properly responsive to telephonic vibrations, especially when these are of great rapidity and comparatively small amplitude.

Mr. Thomas A. Edison, of Menlo Park, New Jersey, has invented a telephone, which, like that of Gray, shown in figure **6**, is based upon the principle of varying the strength of a battery current in unison with the rise and fall of the vocal utterance. The problem of practically varying the resistance controlled by the diaphragm, so as to accomplish this result, was by no means an easy one. By constant experimenting, however, Mr. Edison at length made the discovery that, when properly prepared, carbon possessed the remarkable property of changing its resistance with pressure, and that the ratios of these changes moreover corresponded exactly with the pressure. Fig. 20 represents a convenient and ready way of showing the decrease in resistance of this substance when so subjected. The device consists of a carbon disk, two or three cells of battery, and a tangent or other form of galvanometer. The carbon C is placed between two metallic plates which are joined with the galvanometer and battery in one circuit, through which the battery current is made to pass. When a given weight is placed upon the upper plate the carbon is subjected to a definite amount of pressure, which is shown by the deflection of the galvanometer needle through a certain number of degrees. As additional weight is added, the deflection increases more and more, so that by carefully noting the deflections corresponding to the gradual increase of pressure we can thus follow the various changes of resistance at our leisure. Here, then, was the solution ; for,

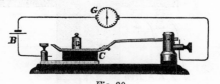

Fig. 20.

by vibrating a diaphragm with varying degrees of pressure against a disk of carbon, which is made to form a portion of an electric circuit, the resistance of the disk would vary in precise accordance with the degree of pressure, and consequently a proportionate variation would be occasioned in the strength of the current. The latter would thus possess all the characteristics of the vocal waves, and by its reaction through the medium of an electro-magnet, might then transfer them to another disk, causing the latter to vibrate, and thus reproduce audible speech.

Fig. 21 shows the telephone as constructed by Mr. Edison. The carbon disk is represented by the black portion, E, near the diaphragm, AA, placed between two platinum plates, D and G, which are connected in the battery circuit, as shown by the lines. A small piece of rubber tubing, B, is attached to the centre of the metallic diaphragm, and presses lightly against an ivory piece, C, which is placed directly over one of the platinum plates. Whenever, therefore, any motion is given to the diaphragm, it is immediately followed by a corresponding pressure upon the carbon and by a change of resistance in the latter, as described above. The object in using the rubber just mentioned is to dampen the movement of the disk, so as to bring it to rest almost immediately after the cause which put it in motion has ceased to act; interference with articulation, which the prolonged vibration of the metal tends to produce in consequence of its

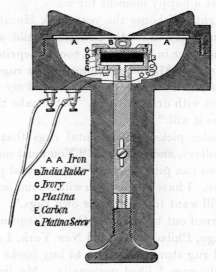

A A *Iron*
B *India Rubber*
C *Ivory*
D *Platina*
E *Carbon*
G *Platina Screw*

Fig. 21.

elasticity, is thus prevented, and the sound comes out clear and distinct. It is obvious that any electro-magnet, properly fitted with an iron diaphragm, will answer for a receiving instrument in connection with this apparatus.

Fig. 22 shows a sending and receiving telephone and a box containing the battery.

In the latest form of transmitter which Mr. Edison has introduced the vibrating diaphragm is done away with altogether, it having been found that much better results are obtained when a rigid plate of metal is substituted in its place. With the old vibrating diaphragm the articulation produced in the receiver is more or less muffled, owing to slight changes which the vibrating disk occasions in the pressure, and which probably results from tardy dampening of the vibrations after having been once started. In the new arrangement, however, the articulation is

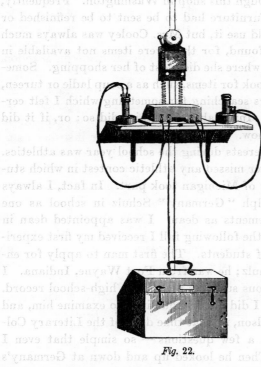

Fig. 22.

so clear and exceedingly well rendered that a whisper even may readily be transmitted and understood. The inflexible plate, of course, merely serves, in consequence of its comparatively large area, to concentrate a considerable portion of the sonorous waves upon the small carbon disk or button; a much greater degree of pressure for any given effort on the part of the speaker is thus brought to bear on the disk than could be obtained if only its small surface alone were used.

The best substance so far discovered for these disks is lampblack, such as is produced by the burning of any of the lighter hydrocarbons. Mr. Edison has found, however, that plumbago, hyperoxide of lead, iodide of copper, powdered gas retort carbon, black oxide of manganese, amorphous phosphorus, finely divided metals, and many sulphides may be used; indeed, tufts of fibre, coated with various metals by chemical means and pressed into buttons have also been employed, but they are all less sensitive than the lampblack, and have consequently been abandoned for the latter substance.

With the telephone, as with the ordinary telegraphic instruments, there is of course a limit beyond which the apparatus cannot be rendered practically serviceable, but in most cases this limit is sooner reached for the telephone than for other instruments that are employed for the transmission of telegraphic matter.   One reason why this is so is probably due to the fact that the current pulsations generated by the vibrating diaphragm are made to follow each other with so much greater rapidity than those that are sent into the line by the ordinary hand manipulation, that less time is allowed for charging and discharging the line, and the phenomenon of inductive retardation thus becomes soonest manifest in the former case.

Another reason, however, and perhaps the principal one, is that the disturbances created by the inductive action of electrical currents in neighboring·wires combine with the signals, and so confuse the latter in many cases, that it becomes altogether impossible to distinguish them.   It is necessary, therefore, when we wish to speak over long distances, or over wires in close proximity to Morse lines, either to employ some means for neutralizing these disturbances, or to so increase the loudness of the articulation that it can be heard above this confused mingling of many sounds.

One of the best means so far suggested for overcoming the difficulty is the employment of metallic circuits throughout for the telephone, placing the two wires forming a single circuit very close together, so as to render the inductive action practically the same in each. The resulting currents would thus neutralize each other and leave the telephone quite free.

It is claimed that the inductive disturbances just noticed are much less marked with Mr. Edison's telephone than with any of the other forms, owing to the fact that the signals or sounds in the former are produced by stronger currents, and the receiving instruments are made less sensitive to those fugitive currents that are always met with in telegraph lines.

Mr. Edison has recently invented a telephonic repeater, which is designed to be used in connection with his apparatus for increasing the distance over which it may be made available. The principal parts are shown in fig. **23**. I is an induction coil, whose

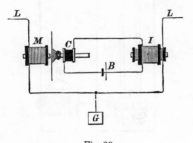

Fig. 23.

secondary is connected in the main line L′, into which the repeating is to be done; C is a carbon transmitter, included with battery B in the primary circuit, and operated by the magnet M instead of by the voice. The variations in the current produced by speaking against the disk of the instrument at the transmitting end of the line, cause this magnet to act on the repeater diaphragm, and thus produce different degrees of pressure on the carbon disk and thereby change its resistance. A corresponding change consequently takes place in the current of the primary coil, and thus gives rise to a series of induced currents in the secondary, which pass into the line, and, on reaching the receiver at the opposite terminal, are there transformed into audible sound.

We have not yet personally experimented with this apparatus, but if it can be made only in a slight degree as effective as the ordinary carbon telephones, which already have permitted conversation to be carried on over five hundred miles of actual telegraph line, its advantage must sooner or later be made serviceable.

Instead of the magneto machine and call bell, which have already been described in connection with the telephone, a bat-

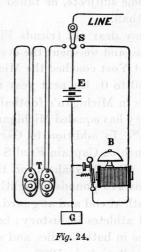

Fig. 24.

tery and vibrating bell may be, and sometimes are used for signaling purposes. Fig. 24 represents the connections for an arrangement of this kind. The line wire is joined to the back end of a four point button switch, S. The right hand front contact leads to one end of the helices which surround the bell magnet, and whose opposite end is in metallic connection with the armature lever. In its normal position this lever is held by a spiral spring against the back stop, which is joined to a wire leading to the ground. The middle front point of the switch communicates with one pole of a battery, E, whose opposite pole is in connection with the ground wire, and the left hand point is connected to one or two telephones, T, also in communication with the ground.

When the apparatus is not being used the switch is left on the right hand contact, so that a current coming from the line has a free path through the helices, armature lever and back stop to earth. The soft iron core is thus rendered magnetic and attracts the armature, but after the latter has moved a short distance it leaves the spring forming part of the back stop, and in so doing breaks the circuit. The magnetism of the cores consequently disappears, and the armature is drawn back so as to complete the circuit once more, when another attraction follows, and so the process goes on alternating as long as battery is kept on at the distant station. Each attraction, therefore, occasions a distinct tap upon the bell, and as the magnetization and demagnetization are exceedingly rapid, the taps consequently succeed each other with sufficient rapidity to keep up a continuous ringing.

If the attendant at the distant station is wanted, the switch is placed on the middle contact, which allows the current from battery E to pass into the line, causing the distant bell to ring. The switch is then turned to the right again, when, if the signal has been observed, an acknowledgment to that effect is given by the distant correspondent placing his battery in circuit, and thereby in turn causing the bell at the station which originally gave the signal to ring. Both switches are then turned to the left hand side, by which means the telephones are put in circuit and made available for the interchange of correspondence.

Fig. 25 shows an arrangement for a Morse and telephone combination, which in many cases it is very convenient to have. When the switch is turned on to the right hand contact point the Morse apparatus is in circuit, and can then be used for the exchange of business in the ordinary way. The Morse apparatus answers also for a call to attract the attention of a correspondent when wanted; the local battery has been omitted in the diagram. When the switch is turned to the left the telephones alone are in circuit.

Before leaving the subject we must more particularly mention
one point in connection therewith that is of too much interest to
be overlooked.   This is in relation to the various characteristics
or forms of action that take place in the transmission of articulate speech, and which furnish us, in the operation of the
Speaking Telephone, with a most beautiful illustration of the
correlation of forces, or of their mutual convertibility from
one form into another.   When we speak into a telephone
the muscular efforts exerted upon the lungs force the air
through the larynx, within which are situated two membranes
called the vocal chords.   These can be tightened or relaxed at

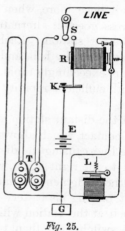

Fig. 25.

will by the use of certain muscles, and, being thrown into vibration by the passage of the air, give rise to a series of sonorous
waves or aerial pulsations, varying in pitch with the tension or
laxity of the chords.   The impact of these pulsations against the
metallic diaphragm produces, in turn, corresponding vibrations
of the latter, which, as we have seen, is in close proximity to the
poles of a permanent magnet.   By this means, therefore, the
inductive action of the diaphragm on the magnet is called into
play, and there is consequently generated in the surrounding
helix a series of electrical currents, which the intervening con-

ductor conveys to the distant station, where their further action is then spent in the production of magnetism. The receiving diaphragm, being then thrown into vibration by the resulting attractions, responds with faithful accuracy to the vibrations originally produced at the transmitting end of the line, and thus

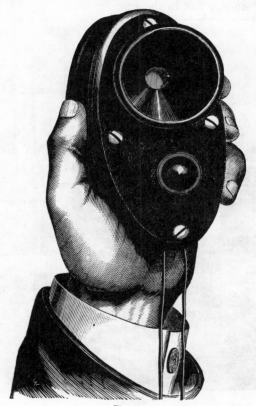

Fig. 26.

also reproduces those sonorous waves which reach the ear and give us the sensation of sound. Here, then, we have, first, the mechanical effects of muscular action converted into electricity, then into magnetism, and finally back again into mechanical action. At each transformation, however, a portion of the energy is lost, so far as its available usefulness is concerned; and, therefore, the sound waves which reach the ear, although precisely similar in pitch and quality to those first produced by the vocal organs, are nevertheless much enfeebled—their amplitude, on which alone loudness depends, being diminished by the amount of energy lost in the transformation.

Fig. 27.

During the past year the articulating or Speaking Telephone has attracted very general interest and attention, not only in this country but also in Europe. It has already been extensively introduced here upon many of our short lines, and bids fair to become of almost universal application in a very short time, its extreme simplicity and the reliability of its operation rendering it one of the most convenient of the many electrical appliances in use.   In Germany it has been adopted as a part of the telegraph system of the country, and there, as well as in other foreign countries, it is also being generally introduced for various private purposes, for establishing communication with the interior of coal

POSITIVELY
NO
ADMITTANCE

C. WRIGHT N.Y.

Fig. 28.

and iron mines, and for facilitating the carrying on of a multitude of industries of various kinds.

The innumerable uses to which the telephone has already been applied shows more forcibly than anything else its practical importance, and the advantages it affords for communicating between places separated even by comparatively long distances ; no more convenient or serviceable instrument for this purpose has ever been produced, while at the same time it is capable of being used by every one.   It can also be united with the District Telegraph system, so extensively developed here, and thereby the range of the latter system, which is now limited to a few special calls, such as police, fire, hack, etc., may be very much extended and improved.   In addition to this again, its connection with the general telegraph system will soon greatly increase the usefulness of that service, by bringing many villages and hamlets that are now destitute of any telegraphic facilities whatever into communication with the rest of the world.   Hitherto the great obstacle in the way of accomplishing this object has been the expense of keeping skilled employés at such places, where the business receipts are usually less than would be required to pay the salary of an operator.   The application of the telephone, however, now provides the means of connecting these places to the nearest telegraph office with very little trouble and with little or no outlay for running expenses. We may therefore confidently expect that another year or two will suffice to establish telegraph communication with nearly every place in the country.

The apparatus, as at present furnished to the public by the American Speaking Telephone Co., is all contained in a neatly finished oblong box, which has already been described on pages 25 and 26. Figs. 11 and 12 show the outfit complete.

Fig. 26 gives a large size front view of the telephone, and also shows the manner of holding it when in use.   Manufacturers and others, whose works are situated at some distance from their offices, will hardly need to be told of the advantages that may be derived from the use of the telephone, whereby they are at all times practically enabled to oversee and personally superintend the details of affairs at the works ; these must be evident to every one.   It will also appear equally obvious that large and expensive warehouses may in many cases be dispensed with in cities where rents are always high, the telephone rendering it possible to fill orders at a moment's notice directly from the factory or works quite as readily as from the warehouse, and at much less expense. Figs. 27 and 28 clearly illustrate the facility with which communication may be maintained between office and factory, and plainly show to what extent personal supervision may be exercised without at all necessitating the presence of the managing director at the place itself. In the former figure the manager at his desk in the city is seen giving instructions to his foreman, who is shown at the works in the latter, carefully noting everything that is being said.

As a matter of prophetic interest in connection with the telephone we feel constrained to reproduce here an extract from a popular little work, published a few years ago in France.[1] The author, as will be seen, strikingly foreshadows the realization of the Speaking Telephone as it exists to-day, complete in everything but loudness of articulation. Speaking of the marvels in telegraphy, he says :

" Wonderful as are these achievements, the inventions in telegraphy have gone still further. To be able to transmit thought to a distance is a triumph which was formerly astonishing ; but we are now accustomed to it, and continue to practice it without its creating the slightest wonder. To be able to transmit handwriting, and even drawings, appeared to be more difficult ; but this problem has also been resolved, and we now hardly wonder that this feat is accomplished by means so simple. Mankind ever requires a new stimulus to its curiosity, and already it is looking forward to the discovery of more marvels in telegraphy. Some years hence, for all we know, we may be able to transmit the vocal message itself, with the very inflection, tone and accent of the speaker. Already has the acoustic telegraph been invented ; the principle has been discovered, and it only remains to render the invention practicable and useful—a result which, in these days of science, does not appear to be impossible.

Sound, of whatever kind, is produced by a series of vibrations, more or less rapid, which, setting out from a sonorous

---

[1] *Les Merveilles de l' Electricité, par J. Baille.* Paris, 1871.

body, traverse the air and reach our ear. Just as a stone, dropped into a pond, throws off a succession of circular undulations or water rings, so a concussion, acting on the air, produces analogous vibrations, though they are invisible, and it is when these vibrations reach the ear that we become sensible of sound. Helmholtz, an eminent German scientist, has analyzed the human voice and determined its musical value. According to him each simple vowel is formed by one or more notes of the scale, accompanied by other and feebler notes which are harmonics of these. He demonstrates that it is the union of all these notes that give quality to the voice. Every syllable is formed by the notes of the vowel accomplished by different movements of the organs of the mouth. Helmholtz, reflecting upon this, thinks it would be possible to construct a human voice by artificially producing and combining the elementary sounds of which it is composed. This is not the place to discuss such theories, but if we grant that there is any truth in them, we can understand that the acoustic telegraph can be invented and can transmit the living voice. Already experiments have been made in this direction.

A vibrating plate produces a sound, and, according to the rapidity of the vibrations, these sounds are sharp or flat. At each of the vibrations the plate touches a small point placed in front of it, and this contact suffices to throw the current into the line. When the plate ceases to vibrate and returns to its position of equilibrium, it no longer touches the metal point and the current is consequently interrupted. By this means is obtained a series of interruptions, more or less rapid, according to the sound, the current being thrown into the line and interrupted once for each of the vibrations.

At the extremity of the line the current enters an electromagnet, which attracts another vibrating plate of size and quality identical with the former. Attracted and repelled very rapidly, exactly, and as rapidly in fact as the plate mentioned above, this second plate gives forth a sound which will have the same musical value as that of the other, as the number of vibrations per second is the same in both cases.

Should this process be perfected it will be possible to transmit sound by means of the telegraph—to transmit a series of sounds, a tune, or spoken sentence and conversation.   This consummation has not, however, been yet attained.   Many experiments have been made, the principle has been applied in divers ways, and everything makes us hope that we will yet arrive at a perfect system of acoustic telegraphy.   Advances have been made very far upon the road to success.   A series of vibrating plates, answering to the strings of a harp, has been arranged, each of which vibrates when struck by a particular sound, and sends off electricity to create at the end of a line the same vibrations in a corresponding plate, or, in other words, to reproduce the same sound.

This system, it must be admitted, is at least very ingenious. Experiments have been made in laboratories, that is to say under conditions entirely favorable, and such as we would not often find in actual practice.   Under these conditions a musical air has actually been successfully transmitted by this acoustic telegraph.   All must admit that this is a promising beginning; but we must not make too much haste to exalt the miracle and to extol the advantages of the future machine, or to abandon ourselves to the indulgence in indiscriminate laudation on the strength of this new discovery.   That would be a gross mistake and an injury to science.   True scientific faith is doubt, until the truth appears in uncontrovertible clearness.   Care must be taken not to take for reality that which is merely a desire on our part.   We must guard against all premature exultation, because it weakens us in the search for truth, and because even one deception is cruel.   Let us therefore give to doubt, to patience and to perseverance, the place which some too readily give to congratulation."

CHAPTER II.

IN a lecture delivered before the Society of Telegraph Engineers, in London, October 31st, 1877, Prof. A. G. Bell gave a history of his researches in telephony, together with the experiments that he was led to undertake in his endeavors to produce a practical system of multiple telegraphy, and to realize also the transmission of articulate speech. As the subject has now become of great interest, both in a scientific and popular point of view, we feel warranted in reproducing the lecture in full. After the usual introduction, Professor Bell said:

"It is to-night my pleasure, as well as duty, to give you some account of the telephonic researches in which I have been so long engaged. Many years ago my attention was directed to the mechanism of speech by my father, Alexander Melville Bell, of Edinburgh, who has made a life-long study of the subject. Many of those present may recollect the invention by my father of a means of representing, in a wonderfully accurate manner, the positions of the vocal organs in forming sounds. Together we carried on quite a number of experiments, seeking to discover the correct mechanism of English and foreign elements of speech, and I remember especially an investigation in which we were engaged concerning the musical relations of vowel sounds. When vowel sounds are whispered, each vowel seems to possess a particular pitch of its own, and by whispering certain vowels in succession a musical scale can be distinctly perceived. Our aim was to determine the natural pitch of each vowel; but unexpected difficulties made their appearance, for many of the vowels seemed to possess a double pitch—one due, probably, to the resonance of the air in the mouth, and the other to the resonance of the air contained in the cavity behind the tongue, comprehending the pharynx and larynx.

I hit upon an expedient for determining the pitch, which, at that time, I thought to be original with myself. It consisted in vibrating a tuning fork in front of the mouth while the positions of the vocal organs for the various vowel sounds were silently taken. It was found that each vowel position caused the reinforcement of some particular fork or forks.

I wrote an account of these researches to Mr. Alex. J. Ellis, of London, whom I have very great pleasure in seeing here tonight. In reply, he informed me that the experiments related had already been performed by Helmholtz, and in a much more perfect manner than I had done. Indeed, he said that Helmholtz had not only analyzed the vowel sounds into their constituent musical elements, but had actually performed the synthesis of them.

He had succeeded in producing, artificially, certain of the vowel sounds by causing tuning forks of different pitch to vibrate simultaneously by means of an electric current. Mr. Ellis was kind enough to grant me an interview for the purpose of explaining the apparatus employed by Helmholtz in producing these extraordinary effects, and I spent the greater part of a delightful day with him in investigating the subject. At that time, however, I was too slightly acquainted with the laws of electricity fully to understand the explanations given ; but the interview had the effect of arousing my interest in the subjects of sound and electricity, and I did not rest until I had obtained possession of a copy of Helmholtz's great work,[1] and had attempted, in a crude and imperfect manner it is true, to reproduce his results. While reflecting upon the possibilities of the production of sound by electrical means, it struck me that the principle of vibrating a tuning fork by the intermittent attraction of an electro-magnet might be applied to the electrical production of music.

I imagined to myself a series of tuning forks of different pitches, arranged to vibrate automatically in the manner shown

---

[1] *Helmholtz.* Die Lehre von dem Tonempfindungen. (English translation, by Alexander J. Ellis, Theory of Tone.)

by Helmholtz—each fork interrupting, at every vibration, a voltaic current—and the thought occurred, Why should not the depression of a key like that of a piano direct the interrupted current from any one of these forks, through a telegraph wire, to a series of electro-magnets operating the strings of a piano or other musical instrument, in which case a person might play the tuning fork piano in one place and the music be audible from the electro-magnetic piano in a distant city ?

The more I reflected upon this arrangement the more feasible did it seem to me ; indeed, I saw no reason why the depression of a number of keys at the tuning fork end of the circuit should not be followed by the audible production of a full chord from the piano in the distant city, each tuning fork affecting at the receiving end that string of the piano with which it was in unison. At this time the interest which I felt in electricity led me to study the various systems of telegraphy in use in this country and in America. I was much struck with the simplicity of the Morse alphabet, and with the fact that it could be read by sound. Instead of having the dots and dashes recorded upon paper, the operators were in the habit of observing the duration of the click of the instruments, and in this way were enabled to distinguish by ear the various signals.

It struck me that in a similar manner the duration of a musical note might be made to represent the dot or dash of the telegraph code, so that a person might operate one of the keys of the tuning fork piano referred to above, and the duration of the sound proceeding from the corresponding string of the distant piano be observed by an operator stationed there. It seemed to me that in this way a number of distinct telegraph messages might be sent simultaneously from the tuning fork piano to the other end of the circuit by operators, each manipulating a different key of the instrument. These messages would be read by operators stationed at the distant piano, each receiving operator listening for signals of a certain definite pitch, and ignoring all others. In this way could be accomplished the simultaneous transmission of a number of telegraphic messages along a single wire, the number being limited only by the delicacy of the listener's ear. The idea of increasing the carrying power of a telegraph wire in this way took complete possession of my mind, and it was this practical end that I had in view when I commenced my researches in electric telephony.

In the progress of science it is universally found that complexity leads to simplicity, and in narrating the history of scientific research it is often advisable to begin at the end.

In glancing back over my own researches, I find it necessary to designate, by distinct names, a variety of electrical currents by means of which sounds can be produced, and I shall direct your attention to several distinct species of what may be termed telephonic currents of electricity. In order that the peculiarities of these currents may be clearly understood, I shall ask Mr. Frost

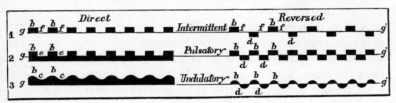

Fig. 29.

to project upon the screen a graphical illustration of the different varieties.

The graphical method of representing electrical currents shown in fig. 29 is the best means I have been able to devise of studying, in an accurate manner, the effects produced by various forms of telephonic apparatus, and it has led me to the conception of that peculiar species of telephonic current, here designated as *undulatory*, which has rendered feasible the artificial production of articulate speech by electrical means.

A horizontal line (*g g'*) is taken as the zero of current, and impulses of positive electricity are represented above the zero line, and negative impulses below it, or *vice versa*.

The vertical thickness of any electrical impulse (*b* or *d*), measured from the zero line, indicates the intensity of the electrical current at the point observed, and the horizontal extension of the electric line (b or d) indicates the duration of the impulse.

Nine varieties of telephonic currents may be distinguished, but it will only be necessary to show you six of these. The three primary varieties designated as intermittent, pulsatory and undulatory, are represented in lines 1, 2 and 3.

Sub-varieties of these can be distinguished as direct or reversed currents, according as the electrical impulses are all of one kind or are alternately positive and negative. Direct currents may still further be distinguished as positive or negative, according as the impulses are of one kind or of the other.

An intermittent current is characterized by the alternate presence and absence of electricity upon the circuit;

A pulsatory current results from sudden or instantaneous changes in the intensity of a continuous current; and

An undulatory current is a current of electricity, the intensity of which varies in a manner proportional to the velocity of the motion of a particle of air during the production of a sound: thus the curve representing graphically the undulatory current for a simple musical tone is the curve expressive of a simple pendulous vibration—that is, a sinusoidal curve.

	Intermittent	Direct	Positive	1	Positive intermittent current.	
			Negative	2	Negative	"	"
		——	Reversed	3	Reversed	"	"
Telephonic currents of electricity may be	Pulsatory	Direct	Positive	4	Positive pulsatory current.	
			Negative	5	Negative	"	"
		——	Reversed	6	Reversed	"	"
	Undulatory	Direct	Positive	7	Positive undulatory current.	
			Negative	8	Negative	"	"
		——	Reversed	9	Reversed	"	"

And here I may remark, that, although the conception of the undulatory current of electricity is entirely original with myself, methods of producing sound by means of intermittent and pulsatory currents have long been known. For instance, it was long since discovered that an electro-magnet gives forth a de-

cided sound when it is suddenly magnetized or demagnetized.
When the circuit upon which it is placed is rapidly made and
broken, a succession of explosive noises proceeds from the magnet. These sounds produce upon the ear the effect of a musical
note when the current is interrupted a sufficient number of
times per second. The discovery of Galvanic Music by Page,[1]
in 1837, led inquirers in different parts of the world almost
simultaneously to enter into the field of telephonic research;
and the acoustical effects produced by magnetization were
carefully studied by Marrian,[2] Beatson,[3] Gassiot,[4] De la
Rive,[5] Matteucci,[6] Guillemin,[7] Wertheim,[8] Wartmann,[9] Jan-
niar,[10] Joule,[11] Laborde,[12] Legat,[13] Reis,[14] Poggendorff,[15]

---

[1] *C. G. Page.* "The Production of Galvanic Music." Silliman's Journ., 1837,
xxxii. p. 396; Silliman's Journ., 1838, xxxiii. p. 118; Bibl. Univ. (new series), 1839,
ii. p. 398.

[2] *J. P. Marrian.* Phil. Mag., xxv. p. 382; Inst., 1845, p. 20; Arch. de l'Électr.,
v. p. 195.

[3] *W. Beatson.* Arch. de l'Électr., v. p. 197; Arch. de Sc. Phys. et Nat. (2d series),
ii. p. 113.

[4] *Gassiot.* See "Treatise on Electricity," by De la Rive, i. p. 300.

[5] *De la Rive.* "Treatise on Electricity," i. p. 300; Phil. Mag., xxxv. p. 422;
Arch. de l'Électr. v. p. 200; Inst. 1846, p. 83; Comptes Rendus, xx. p. 1287; Comp.
Rend. xxii. p. 432; Pogg. Ann. lxxv. p. 637; Ann. de Chim. et de Phys. xxvi.
p. 158.

[6] *Matteucci.* Inst., 1845, p. 315; Arch. de l'Électr., v. 389.

[7] *Guillemin.* Comp. Rend. xxii. p. 264; Inst. 1846, p. 30; Arch. d. Sc. Phys. (2d
series), i. p. 191.

[8] *G. Wertheim.* Comp. Rend. xxii. pp. 336, 544; Inst. 1846, pp. 65, 100; Pogg.
Ann. lxviii. p. 140; Comp. Rend. xxvi. p. 505; Inst. 1848, p. 142; Ann. de Chim.
et de Phys. xxiii. p. 302; Arch. d. Sc. Phys. et Nat. viii. p. 206; Pogg. Ann. lxx ii.
p. 43; Berl. Ber. iv. p. 121.

[9] *Elie Wartmann.* Comp. Rend. xxii. p. 544; Phil. Mag. (3d series), xxviii. p.
544; Arch. d. Sc. Phys. et Nat. (2d series), i. p. 419; Inst. 1846, p. 290; Monatscher.
d. Berl. Akad. 1846, p. 111.

[10] *Jannair.* Comp. Rend. xxiii. p. 319; Inst. 1846, p. 269; Arch. d. Sc. Phys. et
Nat. (2d series), ii. p. 394.

[11] *J. P. Joule.* Phil. Mag. xxv. pp. 76, 225; Berl. Ber. iii. p. 489.

[12] *Laborde.* Comp. Rend. l. p. 692; Cosmos, xvii. p. 514.

[13] *Legat.* Brix. Z. S. ix. p. 125

[14] *Reis.* "Téléphonie." Polytechnic Journ. clxviii, p. 185; Böttger's Notizbl.
1863, No. 6.

[15] *J. C. Poggendorff.* Pogg. Ann. xcviii. p. 198; Berliner Monatsber, 1856, p. 133;
Cosmos, ix. p. 49; Berl. Ber. xii. p. 241; Pogg. Ann. lxxxvii. p. 139.

Du Moncel,[1] Delezenne[2] and others.[3] It should also be mentioned that Gore[4] obtained loud musical notes from mercury, accompanied by singularly beautiful crispations of the surface, during the course of experiments in electrolysis; Page[5] produced musical tones from Trevelyan's bars by the action of the galvanic current; and further it was discovered by Sullivan[6] that a current of electricity is generated by the vibration of a wire composed partly of one metal and partly of another. The current was produced so long as the wire emitted a musical note, but stopped immediately upon the cessation of the sound.

For several years my attention was almost exclusively directed to the production of an instrument for making and breaking a voltaic circuit with extreme rapidity, to take the place of the transmitting tuning fork used in Helmholtz' researches. I will not trouble you with the description of all the various forms of apparatus that were devised, but will merely direct your attention to one of the best of them, shown in fig. 30. In the transmitting instrument T a steel reed a is employed, which is kept in continuous vibration by the action of an electro-magnet e and local battery. In the course of its vibration the reed strikes alternately against two fixed points m, l, and thus completes alternately a local and a main circuit. When the key K is depressed, an intermittent current from the main battery B is directed to the line wire W, and passes through the electro-magnet E of a receiving instrument R at the distant end of the circuit, and thence to the ground G. The steel reed A is placed

---

[1] *Du Moncel.* Exposé, ii. p. 125; also, iii. p. 83.

[2] *Delezenne.* "Sound produced by magnetization," Bibl. Univ. (new series), 1841, xvi. p. 406.

[3] See London Journ. xxxii. p. 402; Polytechnic Journ. cx. p. 16; Cosmos, iv. p. 43; Glösener——Traité général, &c. p. 350; Dove.-Repert. vi. p. 58; Pogg. Ann. xliii. p. 411; Berl. Ber. i. p. 144; Arch. d. Sc. Phys. et Nat. xvi. p. 406; Kuhn's Encyclopædia der Physik, pp. 1014–1021.

[4] *Gore.* Proceedings of Royal Society, xii. p. 217.

[5] *C. G. Page.* "Vibration of Trevelyan's bars by the galvanic current." Silliman's Journal, 1850, ix. pp. 105–108.

[6] *Sullivan.* "Currents of Electricity produced by the vibration of Metals," Phil. Mag. 1845, p. 261; Arch. de l'Électr. x. p. 480.

in front of the receiving magnet, and when its normal rate of vibration is the same as the reed of the transmitting instrument it is thrown into powerful vibration, emitting a musical tone of a similar pitch to that produced by the reed of the transmitting instrument, but if it is normally of a different pitch it remains silent.

A glance at figs. 31, 32 and 33 will show the arrangement of such instruments upon a telegraphic circuit, designed to enable a number of telegraphic despatches to be transmitted simultaneously

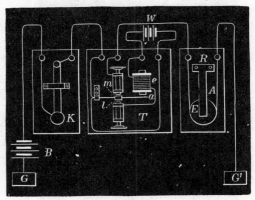

Fig. 30.

along the same wire. The transmitters and receivers that are numbered alike have the same pitch or rate of vibration. Thus the reed of T′ is in unison with the reeds T′ and R′ at all the stations upon the circuit, so that a telegraphic despatch sent by the manipulation of the key K′ at the station shown in fig. 31, will be received upon the receiving instruments R′ at all the other stations upon the circuit. Without going into details, I shall merely say that the great defects of this plan of multiple telegraphy were found to consist, firstly, in the fact that the receiving operators were required to possess a good musical ear in order to discriminate the signals; and secondly, that the signals could only pass in one direction along the line (so that two wires would be necessary in order to complete communication in both direc-

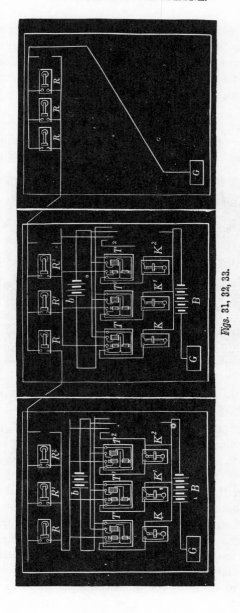

Figs. 31, 32, 33.

tions). The first objection was got over by employing the device which I term a "vibratory circuit breaker," shown in the next diagram, whereby musical signals can be automatically·recorded.

Fig. 34 shows a receiving instrument, R, with a vibratory circuit breaker V attached. The light spring lever V overlaps the free end of the steel reed A, and normally closes a local circuit, in which may be placed a Morse sounder or other telegraphic apparatus. When the reed A is thrown into vibration by the passage of a musical signal, the spring arm V is thrown upwards, opening the local circuit at the point C. When the spring arm V is so arranged as to have normally a much slower rate of vibration than the reed A, the local circuit is found to remain perma-

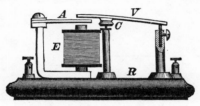

Fig. 34.

nently open during the vibration of A, the spring arm V coming into contact with the point C only upon the cessation of the receiver's vibration. Thus the signals produced by the vibration of the reed A are reproduced upon an ordinary telegraphic instrument in the local circuit.

Fig. 35 shows the application of electric telephony to autographic telegraphy. q, q represent the reeds of transmitting instruments of different pitch, s, s the receivers at the distant station of corresponding pitch, and u, u, etc., the vibratory circuit breakers attached to the receiving instruments, and connected with metallic bristles resting upon chemically prepared paper w. The message or picture to be copied is written upon a metallic surface, p, with non-metallic ink, and placed upon a metallic cylinder connected with the main battery, c; and the chemically prepared paper, upon which the message is to be received, is placed upon a metallic cylinder connected with the local battery d at the receiving station. When the cylinders at either end of the circuit are rotated—but not necessarily at the same rate of speed— a *fac simile* of whatever is written or drawn upon the metallic surface p appears upon the chemically prepared paper w.

The method by means of which musical signals may be sent simultaneously in both directions along the same circuit is shown in our next illustration, figs. 36, 37 and 38. The arrangement is similar to that shown in figures 31, 32 and 33, excepting that the intermittent current from the transmitting instruments is passed

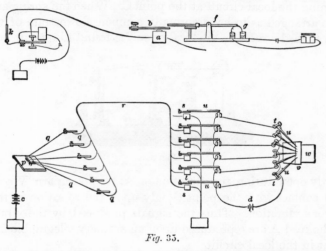

Fig. 35.

through the primary wires of an induction coil, and the receiving instruments are placed in circuit with the secondary wire. In this way free earth communication is secured at either end of the circuit, and the musical signals produced by the manipulation of any key are received at all the stations upon the line. The great objection to this plan is the extreme complication of the parts and the necessity of employing local and main batteries at every station. It was also found by practical experiment that it was difficult, if not impossible, upon either of the plans here shown, to transmit simultaneously the number of musical tones

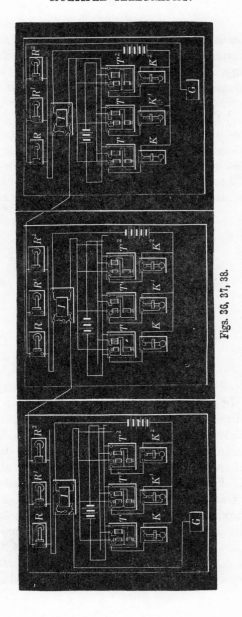

Figs. 36, 37, 38.

that theory showed to be feasible. Mature consideration revealed the fact that this difficulty lay in the nature of the electrical
current employed, and was finally obviated by the invention of
the undulatory current.

It is a strange fact that important inventions are often made
almost simultaneously by different persons in different parts of
the world, and the idea of multiple telegraphy, as developed in
the preceding diagrams, seems to have occurred independently
to no less than four other inventors in America and Europe.
Even the details of the arrangements upon circuit—shown in
figs. 31, 32, 33 and 36, 37, 38—are extremely similar in the plans
proposed by Mr. Cromwell Varley, of London, Mr. Elisha Gray,

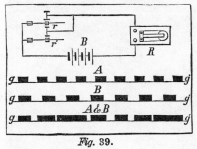

Fig. 39.

of Chicago, Mr. Paul La Cour, of Copenhagen, and Mr. Thomas
Edison, of Newark, New Jersey. Into the question of priority
of invention, of course, it is not my intention to go to-night.

That the difficulty in the use of an intermittent current may
be more clearly understood, I shall ask you to accompany me
in my explanation of the effect produced when two musical
signals of different pitch are simultaneously directed along the
same circuit. Fig. 39 shows an arrangement whereby the reeds
r r' of two transmitting instruments are caused to interrupt
the current from the same battery, B. We shall suppose the
musical interval between the two reeds to be a major third, in
which case their vibrations are in the ratio of **4** to **5**, *i. e.*, 4
vibrations of *r* are made in the same time as 5 vibrations of *r'*.
A and B represent the intermittent currents produced, 4 im-

pulses of B being made in the same time as 5 impulses of A.
The line A + B represents the resultant effect upon the main
line when the reeds r and r' are simultaneously caused to make
and break the same circuit, and from the illustration you will
perceive that the resultant current, whilst retaining a uniform
intensity, is less interrupted when both reeds are in operation
than when one alone is employed. By carrying your thoughts
still further, you will understand that when a large number of
reeds of different pitch or of different rates of vibration are simultaneously making and breaking the same circuit, the resultant
effect upon the main line is practically equivalent to one continuous current.

It will also be understood that the maximum number of

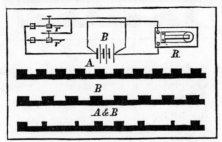

Fig. 40.

musical signals that can be simultaneously directed along a
single wire without conflict, depends very much upon the ratio
which the "make" bears to the "break;" the shorter the contact made, and the longer the break, the greater the number of
signals that can be transmitted without confusion, and *vice versa.*
The apparatus by means of which this theoretical conclusion has
been verified is here to-night, and consists of an ordinary parlor
harmonium, the reeds of which are operated by wind in the
usual manner. In front of each reed is arranged a metal screw,
against which the reed strikes in the course of its vibration. By
adjusting the screw, the duration of the contact can be made
long or short. The reeds are connected with one pole of a
battery, and the screws against which they strike communicate

with the line wire, so that intermittent impulses from the battery are transmitted along the line wire during the vibration of the reeds.

We now proceed to the next illustration. Without entering into the details of the calculation you will see that with a pulsa-

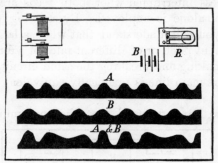

Fig. 41.

tory current the effect of transmitting musical signals simultaneously is nearly equivalent to a continuous current of minimum intensity—see A + B, fig. 40; but when undulatory currents are employed the effect is different—see fig. 41. The current

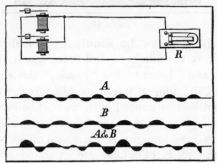

Fig. 42.

from the battery B is thrown into waves by the inductive action of iron or steel reeds vibrated in front of electro-magnets placed in circuit with the battery; A and B represent the undulations caused in the current by the vibration of the magnetized bodies, and it will be seen that there are four undulations of B in the same time as five undulations of A. The resultant effect upon the main line is expressed by the curve A+B, which is the algebraical sum of the sinusoidal curves A and B. A similar effect is produced when reversed undulatory currents are employed, as shown in fig. 42, where the current is produced by the vibration of permanent magnets in front of electro-magnets united upon a circuit without a voltaic battery. It will be understood from figs. 41 and 42 that the effect of transmitting musical signals of different pitches simultaneously along a single wire is not to obliterate the vibratory character of the current, as in the case of intermittent and pulsatory currents, but to change the shapes of

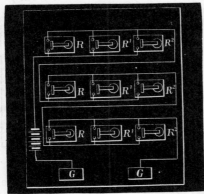

Fig. 43.

the electrical undulations. In fact, the effect produced upon the current is precisely analogous to the effect produced in the air by the vibration of the inducing bodies. Hence it should be possible to transmit as many musical tones simultaneously through a telegraph wire as through the air. The possibility of using undulatory currents for the purposes of multiple telegraphy enabled me to dispense entirely with the complicated arrangements of the circuit shown in figs. 31, 32, 33 and 36, 37, 38, and to employ a single battery for the whole circuit, retaining only the receiving instruments formerly shown. This arrangement is represented in fig. 43. Upon vibrating the steel reed of a receiver R, R′, at any station by any mechanical means, the corresponding reeds at all the other stations are thrown into vibration, reproducing the signal. By attaching the steel reeds to the poles of a powerful permanent magnet, as shown in fig. 45, the signals can be produced without the aid of a battery.

I have formerly stated that Helmholtz was enabled to produce vowel sounds artificially by combining musical tones of different pitches and intensities. His apparatus is shown in fig 44. Tuning forks of different pitch are placed between the poles of electro-magnets ($a′$, a^2, &c.), and are kept in continuous vibration by the action of an intermittent current from the fork b. Reso-

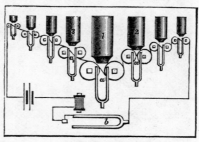

Fig. 44

nators 1, 2, 3, etc., are arranged so as to reinforce the sounds in a greater or less degree, according as the exterior orifices are enlarged or contracted.

Thus it will be seen that upon Helmholtz's plan the tuning forks themselves produce tones of uniform intensity, the loudness being varied by an external reinforcement; but it struck me that the same results would be obtained, and in a much more perfect manner, by causing the tuning forks themselves to vibrate with different degrees of amplitude. I therefore devised the apparatus shown in fig. 45, which was my first form of articulating telephone. In this figure a harp of steel rods is employed,

---

[1] The full description of this figure will be found in Mr. Alexander J. Ellis's translation of Helmholtz's work, " Theory of Tone."

attached to the poles of a permanent magnet, N. S.   When any
one of the rods is thrown into vibration an undulatory current
is produced in the coils of the electro-magnet E, and the electro-
magnet E′ attracts the rods of the harp H′ with a varying force,
throwing into vibration that rod which is in unison with that
vibrated at the other end of the circuit.   Not only so, but the
amplitude of vibration in the one will determine the amplitude
of vibration in the other, for the intensity of the induced current
is determined by the amplitude of the inducing vibration, and
the amplitude of the vibration at the receiving end depends
upon the intensity of the attractive impulses.   When we sing
into a piano, certain of the strings of the instrument are set in
vibration sympathetically by the action of the voice with differ-

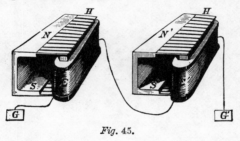

Fig. 45.

ent degrees of amplitude, and a sound, which is an approximation to the vowel uttered, is produced from the piano.   Theory
shows that, had the piano a very much larger number of strings
to the octave, the vowel sounds would be perfectly reproduced.
My idea of the action of the apparatus, shown in fig. 45, was
this : Utter a sound in the neighborhood of the harp H, and
certain of the rods would be thrown into vibration with different amplitudes.   At the other end of the circuit the corresponding rods of the harp H′ would vibrate with their proper relations
of force, and the *timbre* of the sound would be reproduced.   The
expense of constructing such an apparatus as that shown in fig.
45 deterred me from making the attempt, and I sought to simplify the apparatus before venturing to have it made.
     I have before alluded to the invention by my father of a sys-

tem of physiological symbols for representing the action of the vocal organs, and I had been invited by the Boston Board of Education to conduct a series of experiments with the system in the Boston school for the deaf and dumb. It is well known that deaf mutes are dumb merely because they are deaf, and that there is no defect in their vocal organs to incapacitate them from utterance. Hence it was thought that my father's system of pictorial symbols, popularly known as visible speech, might prove a means whereby we could teach the deaf and dumb to use their vocal organs and to speak. The great success of these experiments urged upon me the advisability of devising methods of exhibiting the vibrations of sound optically, for use in teaching the

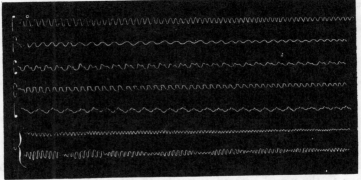

Fig. 46.

deaf and dumb. For some time I carried on experiments with the manometric capsule of Köenig and with the phonautograph of Léon Scott. The scientific apparatus in the Institute of Technology in Boston was freely placed at my disposal for these experiments, and it happened that at that time a student of the Institute of Technology, Mr. Maurey, had invented an improvement upon the phonautograph. He had succeeded in vibrating by the voice a stylus of wood about a foot in length, which was attached to the membrane of the phonautograph, and in this way he had been enabled to obtain enlarged tracings upon a plane surface of smoked glass. With this apparatus I succeeded

in producing very beautiful tracings of the vibrations of the air
for vowel sounds. Some of these tracings are shown in fig. 46.
I was much struck with this improved form of apparatus, and it
occurred to me that there was a remarkable likeness between
the manner in which this piece of wood was vibrated by the
membrane of the phonautograph and the manner in which the
ossiculæ of the human ear were moved by the tympanic mem-

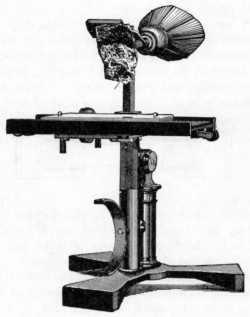

Fig. 47.

brane. I determined, therefore, to construct a phonautograph
modelled still more closely upon the mechanism of the human
ear, and for this purpose I sought the assistance of a distinguished aurist in Boston, Dr. Clarence J. Blake. He suggested
the use of the human ear itself as a phonautograph, instead of
making an artificial imitation of it. The idea was novel and
struck me accordingly, and I requested my friend to prepare

a specimen for me, which he did. The apparatus, as finally constructed, is shown in fig. 47. The *stapes* was removed and a
stylus of hay about an inch in length was attached to the end
of the incus. Upon moistening the membrana tympani and the
ossiculæ with a mixture of glycerine and water the necessary
mobility of the parts was obtained, and upon singing into the
external artificial ear the stylus of hay was thrown into vibration,
and tracings were obtained upon a plane surface of smoked
glass passed rapidly underneath. While engaged in these experiments I was struck with the remarkable disproportion in
weight between the membrane and the bones that were vibrated
by it. It occurred to me that if a membrane as thin as tissue
paper could control the vibration of bones that were, compared
to it, of immense size and weight, why should not a larger and
thicker membrane be able to vibrate a piece of iron in front of

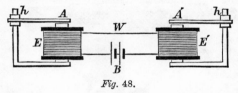

Fig. 48.

an electro-magnet, in which case the complication of steel rods
shown in my first form of telephone, fig. 45, could be done
away with, and a simple piece of iron attached to a membrane
be placed at either end of the telegraphic circuit.

Fig. 48 shows the form of apparatus that I was then employing for producing undulatory currents of electricity for the purposes of multiple telegraphy. A steel reed, A, was clamped
firmly by one extremity to the uncovered leg *h* of an electro-
magnet E, and the free end of the reed projected above the
covered leg. When the reed A was vibrated in any mechanical
way the battery current was thrown into waves, and electrical
undulations traversed the circuit B E W E′, throwing into vibration the corresponding reed A at the other end of the circuit.
I immediately proceeded to put my new idea to the test of
practical experiment, and for this purpose I attached the reed

A (fig. 49) loosely by one extremity to the uncovered pole h of
the magnet, and fastened the other extremity to the centre of a
stretched membrane of goldbeaters' skin n.   I presumed that
upon speaking in the neighborhood of the membrane n it would
be thrown into vibration and cause the steel reed A to move in
a similar manner, occasioning undulations in the electrical current that would correspond to the changes in the density of the
air during the production of the sound; and I further thought
that the change of the intensity of the current at the receiving
end would cause the magnet there to attract the reed A′ in such
a manner that it should copy the motion of the reed A, in which
case its movements would occasion a sound from the membrane
$n′$ similar in *timbre* to that which had occasioned the original
vibration.

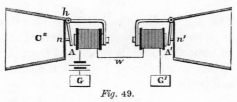

Fig. 49.

The results, however, were unsatisfactory and discouraging.
My friend, Mr. Thomas A. Watson, who assisted me in this first
experiment, declared that he heard a faint sound proceed from
the telephone at his end of the circuit, but I was unable to
verify his assertion.   After many experiments, attended by the
same only partially successful results, I determined to reduce
the size and weight of the spring as much as possible.   For this
purpose I glued a piece of clock spring, about the size and shape
of my thumb nail, firmly to the centre of the diaphragm, and
had a similar instrument at the other end (fig. 50); we were
then enabled to obtain distinctly audible effects.[1]   I remember

---

[1] In a suit tried in the Circuit Court of the United States, District of Massachusetts, for an infringement of the patents issued to Alexander Graham Bell, Judge
Lowell, in his decision sustaining the validity of the patents, says: The defendants insist that the instrument represented [Fig. 49] will not transmit articulate
speech; that this great result has been reached by Mr. Bell entirely through the

an experiment made with this telephone, which at the time gave
me great satisfaction and delight. One of the telephones was
placed in my lecture room in the Boston University, and the
other in the basement of the adjoining building. One of my
students repaired to the distant telephone to observe the effects
of articulate speech, while I uttered the sentence, 'Do you

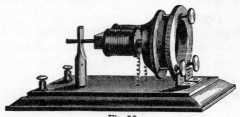

Fig. 50.

understand what I say?' into the telephone placed in the lecture
hall. To my delight an answer was returned through the instrument itself, articulate sounds proceeded from the steel spring
attached to the membrane, and I heard the sentence, "Yes, I
understand you perfectly." It is a mistake, however, to suppose

Fig. 51.

that the articulation was by any means perfect, and expectancy
no doubt had a great deal to do with my recognition of the
sentence; still, the articulation was there, and I recognized the
fact that the indistinctness was entirely due to the imperfection
of the instrument. I will not trouble you by detailing the

---

improvements described in his second patent, such as the substitution of a metal
plate for the stretched membrane, and some others.

The importance of the point is, that if Bell, who is admitted in this case to be
the original and first inventor of any mode of transmitting speech, had not com-

various stages through which the apparatus passed, but shall merely say that after a time I produced the form of instrument shown in fig. 51, which served very well as a receiving telephone. In this condition my invention was exhibited at the Centennial Exhibition in Philadelphia. The telephone shown in fig. 50 was used as a transmitting instrument, and that in fig. 51 as a receiver, so that vocal communication was only established in one direction.

Another form of transmitting telephone exhibited in Philadelphia, intended for use with the receiving telephone (fig. 51), is represented by fig. 52.

A platinum wire attached to a stretched membrane completed a voltaic circuit by dipping into water. Upon speaking to the

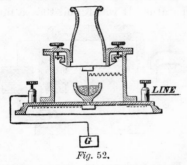

Fig. 52.

membrane articulate sounds proceeded from the telephone in the distant room. The sounds produced by the telephone became louder when dilute sulphuric acid, or a saturated solution of salt, was substituted for the water. Audible effects were also produced by the vibration of plumbago in mercury, in a solution

---

pleted his method, and put it into a working form when he took out his first patent, he may lose the benefit of his invention; because in his second patent, he makes no broad claim to the method or process, but only to the improvements upon a process assumed to have been sufficiently described in his first patent.

There is some evidence that Bell's experiments with the instrument described [Fig. 49], before he took out his patent, were not entirely successful; but this is now immaterial; for it is proved that the instrument will do the work, whether the inventor knew it or not, and in the mode pointed out by the specification.

of bichromate of potash, in salt and water, in diluted sulphuric acid, and in pure water.

The articulation produced from the instrument shown in fig. 51 was remarkably distinct, but its great defect consisted in the fact that it could not be used as a transmitting instrument, and thus two telephones were required at each station, one for transmitting and one for receiving spoken messages.

It was determined to vary the construction of the telephone shown in fig. 50, and I sought, by changing the size and tension of the membrane, the diameter and thickness of the steel spring, the size and power of the magnet, and the coils of insulated wire around their poles, to discover empirically the exact effect of each element of the combination, and thus to deduce a more perfect form of apparatus. It was found that a marked increase in

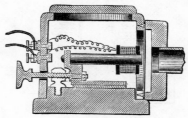

Fig. 53.

the loudness of the sounds resulted from shortening the length of the coils of wire, and by enlarging the iron diaphragm which was glued to the membrane. In the latter case, also, the distinctness of the articulation was improved. Finally, the membrane of gold beaters' skin was discarded entirely, and a simple iron plate was used instead, and at once intelligible articulation was obtained. The new form of instrument is that shown in fig. 53, and, as had been long anticipated, it was proved that the only use of the battery was to magnetize the iron core of the magnet, for the effects were equally audible when the battery was omitted and a rod of magnetized steel substituted for the iron core of the magnet.

It was my original intention, as shown in fig. 45, and it was always claimed by me, that the final form of telephone would be operated by permanent magnets in place of batteries, and numerous experiments had been carried on by Mr. Watson and myself privately for the purpose of producing this effect.

At the time the instruments were first exhibited in public the results obtained with permanent magnets were not nearly so striking as when a voltaic battery was employed, wherefore we thought it best to exhibit only the latter form of instrument.

The interest excited by the first published accounts of the operation of the telephone led many persons to investigate the subject, and I doubt not that numbers of experimenters have independently discovered that permanent magnets might be employed instead of voltaic batteries. Indeed, one gentleman, Professor Dolbear, of Tufts College, not only claims to have

Fig. 54.

discovered the magneto-electric telephone, but, I understand, charges me with having obtained the idea from him through the medium of a mutual friend.

A still more powerful form of apparatus was constructed by using a powerful compound horse shoe magnet in place of the straight rod which had been previously used (see fig. 54). Indeed, the sounds produced by means of this instrument were of sufficient loudness to be faintly audible to a large audience, and in this condition the instrument was exhibited in the Essex Institute, in Salem, Massachusetts, on the 12th February, 1877, on which occasion a short speech shouted into a similar telephone in Boston, sixteen miles away, was heard by the audience in Salem. The tones of the speaker's voice were distinctly audible to an audience of six hundred people, but the articulation was only distinct at a distance of about six feet. On the same occasion, also, a report of the lecture was transmitted by word of mouth from Salem to Boston, and published in the papers the next morning.

From the form of telephone shown in fig. 53 to the present form of the instrument (fig. 55) is but a step. It is, in fact, the arrangement of fig. 53 in a portable form, the magnet F H being placed inside the handle and a more convenient form of mouthpiece provided. The arrangement of these instruments upon a telegraphic circuit is shown in fig. 56.

And here I wish to express my indebtedness to several scientific friends in America for their coöperation and assistance. I would specially mention Professor Peirce and Professor Blake, of Brown University, Dr. Channing, Mr. Clarke and Mr. Jones. In Providence, Rhode Island, these gentleman have been carrying on together experiments seeking to perfect the form of apparatus required, and I am happy to record the fact that they communicated to me each new discovery as it was made, and every new step in their investigations. It was, of course, almost inevitable that these gentlemen should retrace much of the ground that had been gone over by me, and so it has happened that many of their discoveries had been anticipated by my own researches ; still, the very honorable way in which they, from time to time, placed before me the results of their discoveries, entitles them to my warmest thanks and to my highest esteem. It was always my belief that a certain ratio would be found between the several parts of a telephone, and that the size of the instrument was immaterial ; but Professor Peirce was the first to demonstrate the extreme smallness of the magnets which might be employed. And here, in order to show the parallel lines in which we were working, I may mention the fact that two or three days after I had constructed a telephone of the portable form (fig. 55), containing the magnet inside the handle, Dr. Channing was kind enough to send me a pair of telephones of a similar pattern, which had been invented by the Providence experimenters. The convenient form of mouthpiece shown in fig. 55, now adopted by me, was invented solely by my friend, Professor Peirce. I must also express my obligations to my friend and associate, Mr. Thomas A. Watson, of Salem, Massachusetts, who has for two years past given me his personal assistance in carrying on my researches.

In pursuing my investigations I have ever had one end in view—the practical improvement of electric telegraphy—but I have come across many facts which, while having no direct bearing upon the subject of telegraphy, may yet possess an interest for you.[1]

For instance, I have found that a musical tone proceeds from a piece of plumbago or retort carbon when an intermittent current of electricity is passed through it, and I have observed the most curious audible effects produced by the passage of reversed intermittent currents through the human body. A rheotome was placed in circuit with the primary wires of an induction coil, and the fine wires were connected with two strips of brass. One of these strips was held closely against the ear, and a loud sound proceeded from it whenever the other slip was touched with the other hand. The strips of brass were next held one in each hand. The induced currents occasioned a muscular tremor in the fingers. Upon placing my forefinger to my ear a loud crackling noise was audible, seemingly proceeding from the finger itself. A friend who was present placed my finger to his ear, but heard nothing. I requested him to hold the strips himself. He was then distinctly conscious of a noise (which I was unable to perceive) proceeding from his finger. In this case a portion of the induced currents passed through the head of the observer when he placed his ear against his own finger, and it is possible that the sound was occasioned by a vibration of the surfaces of the ear and finger in contact.

When two persons receive a shock from a Ruhmkorff's coil by clasping hands, each taking hold of one wire of the coil with the free hand, a sound proceeds from the clasped hands. The

---

[1] See *Researches in Telephony.* Trans. of American Acad. of Arts and Sciences, vol. xii, p. 1.

effect is not produced when the hands are moist. When either of the two touches the body of the other a loud sound comes from the parts in contact. When the arm of one is placed against the arm of the other, the noise produced can be heard at a distance of several feet. In all these cases a slight shock is experienced so long as the contact is preserved. The introduction of a piece of paper between the parts in contact does not materially interfere with the production of the sounds, but the unpleasant effects of the shock are avoided.

When an intermittent current from a Ruhmkorff's coil is passed through the arms a musical note can be perceived when the ear is closely applied to the arm of the person experimented upon. The sound seems to proceed from the muscles of the fore-arm and from the biceps muscle. Mr. Elisha Gray[1] has

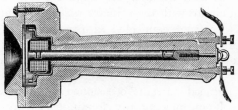

Fig. 55.

also produced audible effects by the passage of electricity through the human body.

An extremely loud musical note is occasioned by the spark of a Ruhmkorff's coil when the primary circuit is made and broken with sufficient rapidity. When two rheotomes of different pitch are caused simultaneously to open and close the primary circuit a double tone proceeds from the spark.

A curious discovery, which may be of interest to you, has been made by Professor Blake. He constructed a telephone in which a rod of soft iron, about six feet in length, was used instead of a permanent magnet. A friend sang a continuous musical tone into the mouthpiece of a telephone, like that shown

---

[1] *Elisha Gray.* Eng. Pat. Spec., No. 2646, Aug., 1874.

in fig. 55, which was connected with the soft iron instrument alluded to above.   It was found that the loudness of the sound produced in this telephone varied with the direction in which the iron rod was held, and that the maximum effect was produced when the rod was in the position of the dipping needle. This curious discovery of Professor Blake has been verified by myself.

When a telephone is placed in circuit with a telegraph line the telephone is found seemingly to emit sounds on its own account.   The most extraordinary noises are often produced, the causes of which are at present very obscure.   One class of sounds is produced by the inductive influence of neighboring wires and by leakage from them, the signals of the Morse alphabet passing over neighboring wires being audible in the telephone, and another class can be traced to earth currents upon the wire, a curious modification of this sound revealing the presence of defective joints in the wire.

Professor Blake informs me that he has been able to use the railroad track for conversational purposes in place of a telegraph wire, and he further states that when only one telephone was connected with the track the sounds of Morse operating were distinctly audible in the telephone, although the nearest telegraph wires were at least forty feet distant.

Professor Peirce has observed the most curious sounds produced from a telephone in connection with a telegraph wire during the aurora borealis, and I have just heard of a curious phenomenon lately observed by Dr. Channing.   In the city of Providence, Rhode Island, there is an overhouse wire about one mile in extent with a telephone at either end.   On one occasion the sound of music and singing was faintly audible in one of the telephones.   It seemed as if some one was practicing vocal music with a pianoforte accompaniment.   The natural supposition was that experiments were being made with the telephone at the other end of the circuit, but upon inquiry this proved not to have been the case.   Attention having thus been directed to the phenomenon, a watch was kept upon the instruments, and upon a subsequent occasion the same fact was observed at both ends of the line by Dr. Channing and his friends. It was proved that the sounds continued for about two hours, and usually commenced about the same time. A searching examination of the line disclosed nothing abnormal in its condition, and I am unable to give you any explanation of this curious phenomenon. Dr. Channing has, however, addressed a letter upon the subject to the editor of one of the Providence papers, giving the names of such songs as were recognized, with full details of the observations, in the hope that publicity may lead to the discovery of the performer, and thus afford a solution of the mystery.

My friend Mr. Frederick A. Gower communicated to me a curious observation made by him regarding the slight earth connection required to establish a circuit for the telephone, and together we carried on a series of experiments with rather startling results. We took a couple of telephones and an insulated wire about 100 yards in length into a garden, and were enabled to carry on conversation with the greatest ease when we held in our hands what should have been the earth wire, so that the connection with the ground was formed at either end through our bodies, our feet being clothed with cotton socks and leather boots. The day was fine, and the grass upon which we stood was seemingly perfectly dry. Upon standing upon a gravel walk the vocal sounds, though much diminished, were still perfectly intelligible, and the same result occurred when standing upon a brick wall one foot in height, but no sound was audible when one of us stood upon a block of freestone.

One experiment which we made is so very interesting that I must speak of it in detail. Mr. Gower made earth connection at his end of the line by standing upon a grass plot, whilst at the other end of the line I stood upon a wooden board. I requested Mr. Gower to sing a continuous musical note, and to my surprise the sound was very distinctly audible from the telephone in my hand. Upon examining my feet I discovered that a single blade of grass was bent over the edge of the board, and that my foot touched it. The removal of this blade of grass was followed by the cessation of the sound from the telephone, and I found that the moment I touched with the toe of my boot a blade of grass or the petal of a daisy the sound was again audible.

The question will naturally arise, Through what length of wire can the telephone be used? In reply to this I may say that the maximum amount of resistance through which the undulatory current will pass, and yet retain sufficient force to produce an audible sound at the distant end, has yet to be determined; no difficulty, has, however, been experienced in laboratory experiments in conversing through a resistance of 60,000 ohms, which has been the maximum at my disposal. On one occasion, not having a rheostat at hand, I may mention having passed the current through the bodies of sixteen persons, who stood hand in hand. The longest length of real telegraph line through which I have attempted to converse has been about 250

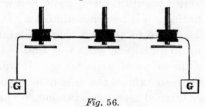

Fig. 56.

miles. On this occasion no difficulty was experienced so long as parallel lines were not in operation. Sunday was chosen as the day on which it was probable other circuits would be at rest. Conversation was carried on between myself, in New York, and Mr. Thomas A. Watson, in Boston, until the opening of business upon the other wires. When this happened the vocal sounds were very much diminished, but still audible. It seemed, indeed, like talking through a storm. Conversation, though possible, could be carried on with difficulty, owing to the distracting nature of the interfering currents.

I am informed by my friend Mr. Preece that conversation has been successfully carried on through a submarine cable, sixty miles in length, extending from Dartmouth to the Island of

Guernsey, by means of hand telephones similar to that shown in fig. 56."

At the conclusion of the lecture complimentary remarks were made by the President and various other members who were present, and a cordial vote of thanks was extended to Professor Bell for his very philosophical and entertaining discourse. We reproduce a portion of the remarks made by Mr. Preece :

" While on the one part Professor Bell has placed in our hands, to a certain extent, a new power, he has, on the other hand, thrown upon our shoulders an extra weight. The poor telegraph engineer has now to master many sciences. Not only must he know something of electricity and magnetism—not only must he know a good deal of chemistry—not only must he pass through various stages of mathematical knowledge, but now, thanks to Professor Bell, he is obliged to be master of the intricacies of acoustics. I do not blame him, because the study of sound is in itself a beautiful occupation, and when it becomes linked to one's profession it becomes almost a luxury.

Professor Bell alluded to the fact that expectancy led him in his first telephone to anticipate what was said. I will give you an illustration of the effect of expectancy. It was my pleasure, on a recent occasion, to exhibit the telephone before a very large audience. Many learned men were present. There is one very remarkable feature of a learned meeting. When you call upon a learned member to make a learned remark he frequently makes a foolish one. Now, I selected one of the leading scientific men of the day, and placed the telephone in his hand. It was in connection with a similar instrument fifty-five miles away. Of course we expected to hear from him some learned axiom, some sage aphorism or some wonderful statement ; but, after some hesitation, he said : ' Hey diddle diddle—follow that up,' He rapidly put the telephone up to his ear and announced with much glee, ' He says, cat and the fiddle.' Fifty miles off my assistant was answering the question. I asked him next day if he understood ' Hey diddle diddle.' He said ' No.' ' What did you say?' ' I asked him to repeat!' "

CHAPTER III.

[1] OF all modern inventions connected with the transmission of telegraphic signals, the telephone, devised by Mr. Alexander Graham Bell, has excited the most widespread interest and wonder. Wherever Mr. Bell has appeared before the public to give an account of his invention and the researches which have led up to it, crowds have assembled to hear him. Nor is this astonishing; for the telephone professes not only to convey intelligible signals to great distances without the use of a battery, but to transmit in fac-simile the tones of the human voice, so that a voice shall be as certainly recognized when heard over a distance of a few hundreds of miles as if its owner were speaking in the room by our side. And the telephone does not fall short of its profession. Scientific men have had their wonder and curiosity aroused even more than the unscientific public, since a scientific man appreciates the enormous difficulties to be overcome before such an instrument can be realized. Had any hardy speculator a few years ago proposed a telephone which should act on the principle, and be constructed in the form, of Mr. Bell's instrument, he would probably have been considered a lunatic. [2] The effects are so marvellous; the exciting causes at first sight so entirely inadequate to produce them. For a telephonic message differs as widely from an ordinary telegraphic message as a highly finished oil painting differs from a page of print. In the one you have only white and black—black symbols on a white ground—the symbols being limited in number, and recurring again and again with mere differences of order. The painting, on the other hand, discloses every variety of color and arrangement. No sharp lines of discontinuity offend the eye; on the contrary, the tints shade off gradually and softly

---

[1] From the *Westminster Review*.   [2] See Baille's prediction, page 47.

into each other, presenting tone and depth in endless variety. The page of print is unintelligible without the aid of a key ; the painting tells its story plainly enough to any one who has eyes to see.

Let us inquire for a moment what is the nature of the apparatus which we have been using for the last thirty or forty years for the transmission of telegraphic signals. The instruments chiefly employed have been the single needle telegraph and the Morse instrument. In the former a coil of wire surrounds a magnetized needle, which is suspended in a vertical position. When an electrical current passes through the coil, the needle is deflected to right or left, according to the direction of the current. The sender, by means of a handle, can pass either positive or negative currents into the circuit. The right and left deflections of the needle are combined in various ways to form the letters of the alphabet, and the letters form words. Thus, at the sending station a message is broken up into little bits, each bit or part of a bit transmitted separately, and the process of building these up again performed at the receiving station. Some of the letters of the alphabet are indicated by a single movement of the needle, that is, by a single current ; for others, as many as four are required.

In the Morse instrument only one current is utilized, which may be either positive or negative, and the requisite variety is obtained by allowing the current to pass through the circuit for a longer or shorter interval. The essential part of the instrument consists of an electro-magnet with an iron armature attached to one end of a lever. At the other end of the lever is a pointer or pencil, and a paper ribbon moves at a constant rate in front of the end of the pointer. When the coils of the electro-magnet are traversed by a current, the iron armature is attracted, and the pointer comes in contact with the paper ribbon, on which it makes a mark, long or short, according to the duration of the current. Thus are produced the dots and dashes. These are combined in a similar way to the right and left movements of the needle in the needle instrument. In some of the more refined instruments letters are indicated and even printed directly at the receiving station. This is, of course, a great simplification ; but with such arrangements we cannot have more than this. The page of print represents the limit of what such instruments and methods can do for us. It is true that a skilled operator with the Morse instrument can interpret the signals as they arrive without looking at the marks on the paper, simply by using his ears. Every time the circuit is made or broken a click is heard, and long practice has taught him to rely on the evidence of his ears with as much confidence as one less accustomed to the work would trust his eyes. Nevertheless, he hears only a succession of clicks, which must be interpreted before they become intelligible to any one but himself.

In these forms of apparatus, it will be observed, the currents are intermittent; each current, circulating through the coil, is followed by an interval of rest. They begin and end abruptly, and all perform the same kind of work ; that is, they deflect a needle, or produce marks on a piece of paper. Telephonic currents, on the other hand, rise and fall, ebb and flow, change in intensity within comparatively wide limits, but preserve their continuity so long as continuous sounds are being uttered in the neighborhood of the telephone. They are called undulatory currents, to distinguish them from the intermittent currents of the ordinary telegraphic apparatus ; and their peculiar character is an essential feature of the telephone.

No skill or training is required for the effective use of the telephone. The operator has merely to press the instrument to his ear to hear distinctly every sound transmitted from the distant end. For this, it is true, an effort of attention is required, and some persons use the instrument at the first trial with more success than others. Individuals differ in the facility with which they are able to concentrate their attention on one ear, so as to be practically insensible to what goes on around them. But this habit of attention is readily acquired, and when it is once acquired the telephone may be used by any one who has ears to hear and a tongue to speak. In sending a message, the instrument is held about an inch in front of the mouth, and the sender merely talks into the mouthpiece in his ordinary, natural manner. The words are repeated by the instrument at the other end of the circuit with the same pitch, the same cadences, and the same relative loudness. But what strikes one the most is that the character of the speaker's voice is faithfully preserved and reproduced. Thus one voice is readily distinguished from another. No peculiarity of inflection is lost. Nor is this result effected over short distances only. No doubt a sentence will be heard with diminishing distinctness as it comes over an increasing distance. In this country experiments have not yet been made, so far as we know, over very long distances; but Mr. Bell states that he carried on a conversation without any difficulty between Boston and New York, two hundred and fifty-eight miles apart, through an ordinary telegraph wire. A man's breathing was distinctly heard one hundred and forty-nine miles away. At the Newport torpedo station, in Rhode Island, speaking was carried on through a line including five miles of submerged cable and an equal length of land wire. Resistance coils were added two thousand ohms at a time, until twelve thousand ohms were introduced into the circuit, without interfering with the transmission of speech. The importance of this test will be understood when it is remembered that the resistance of the Atlantic cable is equal to seven thousand ohms only.[1] The experiments at Newport were continued by the addition of a total resistance of thirty thousand ohms, but beyond twelve thousand ohms, the sound was found to diminish in intensity. Mr. Bell states that the maximum amount of resistance through which the undulating current will pass, and yet retain sufficient force to produce an audible sound at the distant end,

---

[1] It by no means follows, as the writer would lead us to infer, that the telephone can be used to transmit articulate speech through extended lengths of cable simply because it has served well, under very dissimilar circumstances, to communicate through an equivalent resistance of artificial line. The laws regarding the phenomenon of inductive retardation in long ocean cables, like those across the Atlantic, hold good for currents produced by the telephone as well as for currents derived from any other source whatever.

has yet to be determined. In the laboratory he has conversed through a resistance of sixty thousand ohms. There is a practical difficulty in transmitting telephonic signals through a telegraph wire running parallel to a number of other wires which are being used for ordinary telegraphic purposes. Induction currents are produced in the telephone wire, which greatly interfere with the distinctness of the sounds. The difficulty is said to be overcome by having an extra return wire, instead of utilizing the earth for a part of the circuit, as is ordinarily done. The two wires are put side by side in close proximity, and the detrimental effect of the inductive currents is thus partially or entirely disposed of. The following extract from a letter which appeared in the Daily News a few weeks ago shows that inductive action, when the parallel circuits are not numerous, does not seriously interfere with the transmission of speech:

The experiments with the telephone were made by me upon the cable lying between Dover and Calais, which is twenty-one and three-quarter miles long. Several gentlemen and ladies were present, and conversed in French and English with a second party in France for upwards of two hours. There was not the slightest failure during the whole time. I was only using one wire. The other three (it is a four-wire cable) were working direct with London and Paris, Calais and Lille. I could distinctly hear the signals by the three wires on the telephone and at times, when but one of the three wires was working, I could decipher the Morse signals, and read a message that was passing from Glasgow to Paris. Yet when all the three wires were working simultaneously, the telephone sounds were easily and clearly distinguishable above the click of the signals. I happened to know several of the party in France, and was able to recognize their voices. They also recognized mine, and told us immediately a lady spoke that it was a female voice. When making some trials upon a line three fourths of a mile long, I arranged a musical box (the tones of which are very feeble) under the receiver of an air-pump, the top of the receiver being open. Upon this opening I placed the telephone, and every note came out at the second end so clearly as to enable those who were present to name the tune that was played.   Unfortunately we had not the same means in France, but simply held the mouth of the telephone close to the box, and some of the notes were audible, but not so perfect as on the short line.   One young lady burst out laughing the moment she placed the instrument to her ear, and exclaimed, "Some one is whistling, 'Tommy, make way for your uncle!'"   As my correspondent and myself had had a little practice, we were, without the slightest difficulty, able to talk in our usual manner, without any strain upon the voice or any unnatural lengthening of syllables.   We were not able to hear breathing, in consequence of the continued pecking caused by induction from other wires.

The construction of the telephone (fig. 57) is remarkably simple.

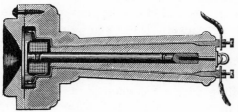

Fig. 57.

It consists of a steel cylindrical magnet, about five inches long and three eighths of an inch in diameter, encircled at one extremity by a short bobbin of wood or ebonite, on which is wound a quantity of very fine insulated copper wire.   The magnet and coil are contained in a wooden cylindrical case.   The two ends of the coil are soldered to thicker pieces of copper wire, which traverse the wooden envelope from one end to the other, and terminate in the binding screws at its extremity.   Immediately in front of the magnet is a thin circular iron plate, which is kept in its place by being jammed between the main portion of the wooden case, and a wooden cap carrying the mouth or ear trumpet.   These two parts are screwed together.   The latter is cut away at the centre, so as to expose a portion of the iron plate,

about half an inch in diameter.   In the experiments which **Mr.**
Bell has carried out in order to determine the influence of the various parts of the telephone on the results produced, and their relations to each other when the best effects are obtained, he employed
iron plates of various areas and thicknesses, from boiler plate
three-eighths of an inch in thickness to the thinnest plate pro-
curable.   Wonderful to relate, it appears that scarcely any plate
is too thin or too thick for the purpose, but the best thickness is
that of the ferrotype plate used by photographers.   Thin tin
plate also answers very well.   The iron plate is cut into the form
of a disk, about two inches in diameter, and is placed as near as
possible to the extremity of the steel magnet without actually
touching it; the effect of this position being that, while the induced magnetism of the plate is considerable, it is susceptible to
very rapid changes. owing to the freedom with which the plate
can vibrate.   The dimensions of the various parts of the instrument here given are found to be convenient, but they are by
no means essential.   Good results have been obtained by means
of a magnet only an inch and a half long, and a working instrument need not be too large for the waistcoat pocket.   There is no
difference between the transmitting and the receiving telephone;
each instrument serves both purposes.   Nevertheless, in order to
avoid the inconvenience of shifting the instrument backwards
and forwards between the ear and the mouth, it is better to have
two on the circuit at each station.   The operator then holds one
permanently to his ear, while he talks with the other.

It will not be supposed that the idea of this marvellously
simple piece of apparatus was evolved ready formed from the
inventor's brain : very far otherwise.   It is the final outcome of a
long series of patient researches carried out by Mr. Bell in the
most skilful and philosophical manner, in which one modification suggested another, accessory after accessory was discarded,
and finally the instrument was pruned down to its present form
and dimensions.   Telephones have been long known.   A few
years ago a simple arrangement whereby articulate sounds could
be transmitted over a distance of fifty or sixty yards, or even fur-

ther, could be bought in the streets for a penny. It consisted of a pair of pill boxes, the bottoms of which were connected by a piece of string stretched tight, while over the mouth of each was pasted tissue paper. On speaking to one of the pill boxes the tissue paper and enclosed air were set in vibration. The vibrations so produced were communicated to the thread and transmitted to the distant pill box, which was held close to the ear, where they affected the air in such a way as to reproduce the original sounds. The simple apparatus was more effective than would be at first imagined. Electric telephones were devised in this country about the same time that the telegraph was introduced, but the best of them differed widely from the modern instrument. They were capable of conveying to a distance sounds of various pitch, so that the succession of notes constituting a melody could be reproduced many miles away, but the special character of the voice by which the melody was originated was entirely lost.[1] Now the great interest which attaches to Mr. Bell's telephone, and the intense wonder and curiosity it has aroused, are due to its power of conveying absolutely unaltered every peculiarity of voice or musical instrument. A violin note reappears as a violin note; it cannot be mistaken for anything else. And in the case of a human voice, it is not less easy to distinguish one speaker from another than it would be if the speakers were in the room close by instead of being miles or even hundreds of miles away. This is the charm of the new telephone; this it is which renders it immeasurably superior to anything of the kind which preceded it.

Mr. Bell's researches in electric telephony began with the artificial production of musical sounds, suggested by the work in which he was then engaged in Boston, viz: teaching the deaf and dumb to speak. Deaf mutes are dumb merely because they are deaf. There is no local defect to prevent utterance, and Mr. Bell has practically demonstrated by two thousand of

---

[1] Reiss's telephone was the first invention which could accomplish the result here stated, and this was invented in Germany, in 1861. See description of Reiss's telephone, page 9.

his own pupils that when the deaf and dumb know how to control the action of their vocal organs, they can articulate with comparative facility. Striving to perfect his system of teaching, it occurred to Mr. Bell that if, instead of presenting to the eye of the deaf mute a system of symbols, he could make visible the vibrations of the air, the apparatus might be used as a means of teaching articulation. In this part of his investigations Mr. Bell derived great assistance from the phonautograph. He succeeded in vibrating by the voice a style of wood, about a foot in length, attached to the membrane of the phonautograph; and with this he obtained enlarged tracings of the vibrations of the air, produced by the vowel sounds, upon a plane surface of smoked glass. Mr. Bell traced a similarity between the manner in which this piece of wood was vibrated by the membrane of the phonautograph and the manner in which the ossiculæ of the human ear were moved by the tympanic membrane. Wishing to construct an apparatus closely resembling the human ear, it was suggested to him by Dr. Clarence J. Blake, a distinguished aurist of Boston, that the human ear itself would be still better, and a specimen was prepared. Our readers are aware that the tympanic membrane of the ear is connected with the internal ear by a series of little bones called respectively the malleus, the incus and the stapes, from their peculiar shapes, and that by their means the vibrations of the tympanic membrane are communicated to the internal ear and the auditory nerves. Mr. Bell removed the stapes and attached to the end of the incus a style of hay about an inch in length. Upon singing into the external artificial ear, the style of hay was thrown into vibration, and tracings were obtained upon a plane surface of smoked glass passed rapidly underneath. The curves so obtained are of great interest, each showing peculiarities of its own dependent upon the vowel sound that is sung. Whilst engaged in these experiments Mr. Bell's attention was arrested by observing the wonderful disproportion which exists between the size and weight of the membrane—no thicker than tissue paper—and the weight of the bones vibrated by it, and he was led to inquire whether a thicker membrane might not be able to vibrate a piece of iron in front of an electro-magnet. The experiment was at once tried. A piece of steel spring was attached to a stretched membrane of gold beater's skin and placed in front of the pole of the magnet. This answered very well, but it was found that the action of the instrument was improved by increasing the area of metal, and thus the membrane was done away with and an iron plate substituted for it. It was important at the same time to determine the effect produced by altering the strength of the magnet; that is, of the current which passed round the coils. The battery was gradually reduced from fifty cells to none at all, and still the effects were observed, but in a less marked degree. The action was in this latter case doubtless due to residual magnetism: hence, in the present form of apparatus a permanent magnet is employed. Lastly, the effect of varying the dimensions of the coil was studied, when it was found that the sounds became louder as its length was diminished; a certain length was, however, ultimately reached, beyond which no improvement was effected, and it was found to be only necessary to enclose one end of the magnet in the coil of wire.

Such was the instrument that Mr. Bell sent to the Centennial Exhibition at Philadelphia. The following is the official report of it, signed by Sir William Thomson and others:

Mr. Alexander Graham Bell exhibits an apparatus by which he has achieved a result of transcendent scientific interest—a transmission of spoken words by electric currents through a telegraph wire. To obtain this result Mr. Bell perceived that he must produce a variation of strength of current as nearly as may be in exact proportion to the velocity of a particle of air moved by the sound, and he invented a method of doing so—a piece of iron attached to a membrane (fig. 58), and thus moved to and fro in the neighborhood of an electro-magnet, which has proved perfectly successful. The battery and wire of this electro-magnet are in circuit with the telegraph wire and the wire of another electro-magnet at the receiving station. This second electro-magnet has a solid bar of iron for core which is connected at one end by a thick disk of iron to an iron tube surrounding the coil and bar. The free circular end of the tube constitutes one pole of the electro-magnet, and the adjacent free end of the bar core the other.   A thin circular iron disk, held pressed against the end of the tube by the electro-magnetic attraction and free to vibrate through a very small space without touching the central pole, constitutes the sounder by which the electric effect is reconverted

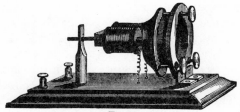

Fig. 58.

into sound (fig. 59).   With my ear pressed against this disk, I heard it speak distinctly several sentences.   I need scarcely say I was astonished and delighted.   So were others, including some judges of our group, who witnessed the experiments and verified with their own ears the electric transmission of speech.   This, perhaps, the greatest marvel hitherto achieved by the electric

Fig. 59.

telegraph, has been obtained by appliances of quite a homespun and rudimentary character.   With somewhat more advanced plans and more powerful apparatus, we may confidently expect that Mr. Bell will give us the means of making the voice and spoken words audible through the electric wire to an ear hundreds of miles distant.

The present form of instrument, which is now being manufactured in large numbers by the Silvertown Company, does not essentially differ from that reported on so enthusiastically by Sir William Thomson. Only it is more simple in construction and more handy.

Before attempting any explanation of the action of the telephone, it may be well to draw the attention of our readers to the special characteristics of the human voice, and to those peculiarities which distinguish one musical note from another. Whatever the differences in question may depend upon, it is certain that they are transmitted and reproduced in the telephone with unerring fidelity, and it is, therefore, important that we should understand their nature and origin. Take a tuning fork and set it in vibration by striking or drawing a violoncello bow across its prongs. The fork yields its own proper note, which will be loud or the reverse, according as the fork has been struck energetically or lightly. So long as we use one fork only it is obvious that the only variation which can be produced in the sound is a variation of intensity. If the extent of vibration be small, the resulting sound is feeble ; its loudness increases with the excursion of the prongs. What is true of the tuning fork is true of any other musical instrument, and hence, generally, the loudness of a musical sound depends upon the amplitude of vibration of that which produced it. Now, take two similar tuning forks of different pitch, and suppose that one is exactly an octave above the other. They may be excited in such a way that the notes emitted are of equal loudness, and then the only respect in which they differ from each other is in pitch. The pitch of a fork depends upon its rate of vibration. It is comparatively easy with suitable apparatus to measure the rate of vibration of a tuning fork, and were we to test the two forks in question, it would be found that that giving the higher note vibrates exactly twice as fast as the other. If the one performs a hundred oscillations in a second, the other which is an octave above, completes two hundred in the same interval of time. Thus, the pitch of a note yielded by a tuning fork depends upon its rate of vibration, and on nothing else, and the same is true of a piano-forte wire, the air in an organ pipe, a harmonium reed, etc. We have now ac-counted for two of the characteristics of a musical note, its loud-ness and its pitch; but there is a third, equally, if not more im-portant, and by no means so simple of explanation. We refer to what is usually spoken of in English books on acoustics as the quality of the note; the French call it timbre and the Ger-mans klangfarbe. It is that which constitutes the difference be-tween a violin and an organ, or between an organ and a piano-forte, or between two human voices; indeed between any two musical sounds which are of the same pitch and loudness, but are still distinguishable from each other. In order to explain the physical cause of quality, we will suppose we have a thin metallic wire about a yard long stretched between two points over a sounding board. When plucked at its centre the wire vibrates as a whole, the two ends are points of rest, and a loop is formed between them. The note emitted by the wire when vibrating in this manner is called its fundamental note. If the wire be damped at its centre, by laying on it with slight pressure the feather of a quill pen, and plucked at a point half way between the centre and one end, both halves will vibrate in the same manner, and independently of each other. That is to say, there will be two equal vibrating segments and a point of rest or node at the centre. But the rapidity of vibration of each segment will be twice as great as that of the wire when vibrating as a whole, and consequently the note emitted will be the octave of the fun-damental. When damped at a point one third of the length from either extremity, and plucked half way between that point and the nearer extremity. the wire will vibrate in three equal divi-sions, just as it vibrates in two divisions in the previous case. The rate of vibration will be now three times as great as at first, and the note produced will be a twelfth above the funda mental. Similarly, by damping and plucking at suitable points the wire may be made to vibrate in four parts, five parts, six parts, etc., the rate of vibration increasing to four, five, six, etc., times what it was at first. Let us suppose that when the wire was swinging as a whole, and sounding its fundamental note, the number of oscillations performed in a second was one hundred. Then we see that by taking suitable precautions the wire can be made to break up into two, three, four, five, six, etc., vibrating segments, the rates of vibration being respectively two hundred, three hundred, four hundred, five hundred, six hundred, etc., and the series of notes emitted being the octave above the fundamental, the fifth above the octave, the double octave, the third and fifth above the double octave, and so on. We now come to an important point, which is this—that, the wire being free, it is practically impossible to strike or pluck it in such a way as to make it vibrate according to one of the above systems only. It will vibrate as a whole wherever and however it be struck, but this mode has always associated with it or superposed upon it some of the other modes of vibration to which we have just referred. In other words, the fundamental note is never heard alone, but always in combination with a certain number of its overtones, as they are called. Each form of vibration called into existence sings, as it were, its own song, without heeding what is being done by its fellows, and the consequence is that the sound which reaches the ears is not simple but highly composite in its character. The word clang has been suggested to denote such a composite sound, the constituent simple sounds, of which it is the aggregate, being called its first, second, third, etc., partial tones. All the possible partial tones are not necessarily present in a clang, nor of those which are present are the intensities all the same. For instance, if the wire be struck at the centre, that point cannot be a node, but must be a point of maximum disturbance; hence all the even partial tones are excluded and only the odd ones, the first, third, fifth, and so on, are heard.

That characteristic of a musical note or clang, which is called its quality, depends upon the number and relative intensities of the partial tones which go to form it. The tone of a tuning fork is approximately simple; so is that of a stopped wooden organ pipe of large aperture blown by only a slight pressure of wind. Such tones sound sweet and mild, but also tame and spiritless. In the clang of the violin, on the other hand, a large number of partial tones are represented; hence the vivacious and brilliant character of this instrument. The sounds of the human voice are produced by the vibrations of the vocal chords, aided by the resonance of the mouth. The size and shape of the cavity of the mouth may be altered by opening and closing the jaws, and by tightening or loosening the lips. We should expect that these movements would not be without effect on the resonance of the contained air, and such proves on experiment to be the fact. Hence, when the vocal chords have originated a clang containing numerous well developed partial tones, the mouth cavity, by successively throwing itself into different postures, can favor by its resonance first one overtone and then another; at one moment this group of partial tones, at another that. In this manner endless varieties of quality are rendered possible. Any one may prove to himself, by making the experiment, that when singing on a given note he can only change from one vowel sound to another by altering the shape and size of his mouth cavity.

Having thus briefly indicated the physical causes of the various differences in musical notes, and the production of sounds by the organ of voice, we will devote a few moments to consider how these sounds are propagated through the air and reach the plate of the telephone. When a disturbance is produced at any point in an aërial medium. the particles of which are initially at rest, sonorous undulations spread out from that point in all directions. These undulations are the effect of the rapid vibratory motions of the air particles. The analogy of water waves will help us to understand what is taking place under these circum stances. If a stone be dropped into the still water of a pond, a series of concentric circular waves is produced, each wave con sisting of a crest and a hollow. The waves travel onwards and outwards from the centre of disturbance along the surface of the water, while the drops of water which constitute them have an oscillatory motion in a vertical direction. That is to say, fol- lowing any radial line, the water particles vibrate in a direction at right angles to that in which the wave is propagated. The distance between two successive crests or two successive hollows is called the length of the wave; the amplitude of vibration is the vertical distance through which an individual drop moves. In a similar manner sonorous undulations are propagated through air by the oscillatory motion of the air particles. But there is this important difference between the two cases, that, in the latter, the vibrating particles move in the same direction in which the sound is being propagated. Consequently such waves are not distinguished by alternate crests and hollows, but by alternate condensations and rarefactions of the air, the transmission of which constitutes the transmission of sound. The wave length is the distance between two consecutive condensations or rarefactions. It depends upon the pitch of the transmitted sound, being shorter as the sound is more acute, while the extent of vibration of the air particles increases with the loudness. Such are the peculiarities of the vibratory motion in air corresponding to the pitch and loudness of the transmitted sound. But what is there in the character of the motion to account for difference in quality? A little consideration will show that there is only one thing left to account for these, and that is the form of the vibration. Let us mentally isolate a particle of air, and follow its movements as the sound passes. If the disturbance is a simple one, produced, say, by the vibration of a tuning fork, the motion of the air particle will be simple also, that is, it will vibrate to and fro like the bob of a pendulum, coming to rest at each end of its excursion, and from these points increasing in velocity until it passes its neutral point. Such, however, is clearly not the only mode of vibration possible. If the disturbance be produced by a clang comprising a number of partial tones of various intensities, all excited simultaneously, it is obvious that the air particle must vibrate in obedience to every one of these. Its motion will be the resultant of all the motions due to the separate partial tones. We may imagine it, starting from its position of rest, to move forward, then stop short, and turn back for an instant, then on again until it reaches the end of its excursion. In returning it may perform the same series of to-

and-fro motions in the opposite direction, or it may move in a totally different way. Nevertheless, however complex its motion may be—and, as a rule, it will be exceedingly complex—its periodic character will be maintained. All the tremors and perturbations in one wave length will recur in all the others.

When sonorous undulations impinge upon the iron plate of the telephone, the latter is set in vibration. Its particles move to and fro in some way or other. The complexity of their motion will depend upon that of the air from which it was derived. But for the sake of simplicity we will assume that the plate has a simple pendulous motion. It will be remembered that the iron plate is placed quite close to, but not quite in contact with, the extremity of the steel magnet. It becomes, therefore, itself a magnet by induction; and, as it vibrates, its magnetic power is constantly changing, being strengthened when it approaches the magnetic core, enfeebled as it recedes. Again, when a magnet moves in the neighborhood of a coil of wire, the ends of which are connected together, an electrical current is developed in the coil, whose strength depends upon the rapidity with which, and the distance through which, the magnet moves. In the telephone then, as the plate moves towards the coil, a current is induced in the latter which traverses the whole length of wire connecting it with the distant instrument; the plate returning, another current with reversed sign follows the first. The intensity of these currents depends, as we have said, on the rapidity with which these movements are effected, but is largely influenced also by the fact that the plate does not retain a constant magnetic strength throughout its excursions. Under the assumption we have made with respect to the simplicity of the plate's motion, it follows that the induced currents, alternately positive and negative, follow each other in a uniform manner, and with a rapidity corresponding to the pitch of the exciting note. These currents pass along the circuit, and circulate round the coil of the distant telephone. There they modify the magnetic relations between the steel magnetic core and the iron plate in such a way that one current—say the positive—attracts the plate, while the other

—the negative—repels it. And since the arriving currents follow each other, first positive and then negative, with perfect regularity, the plate will also vibrate in a uniform manner, and will perform the same number of vibrations per second as did the plate of the sending instrument. Hence the sound heard will be an exact copy, except as to loudness, of that produced at the sending station. Having thus followed the sequence of phenomena in this simple case, we are enabled to extend our explanation to the case in which composite sounds of more or less complexity—-vowel sounds and speech—are transmitted. We are compelled to admit that every detail in the motion of an air particle, every turn and twist, must be passed on unaltered to the iron membrane, and that every modification of the motion of the membrane must have its counterpart in a modification of the induced currents. These, in their turn, affecting the iron plate of the receiving telephone, it follows that the plates of the two telephones must be vibrating in an absolutely identical manner.

We can thus follow in a general manner the course of the phenomena, and explain how air vibrations are connected with the vibrations of a magnetic plate—how these latter give rise to electrical currents, which, passing over a circuit of hundreds of miles, cause another magnetic plate to vibrate, every tremor in the first being reproduced in fac-simile in the second, and thus excite sonorous undulations which pass on to the ear. We can understand all this in a general way, but we are not the less lost in wonder that the sequence of events should be what it is. That a succession of currents could be transmitted along a telegraph wire without the aid of a battery, that, by simply talking to a magnetic membrane in front of a coil of wire, the relations of the magnetic field between the two could be so far modified as to produce in the coil a succession of electrical currents of sufficient power to traverse a long circuit, and to reproduce a series of phenomena identical with those by which the currents were brought into existence, would have been a few years ago pronounced an impossibility. A man would have been derided who proposed an instrument constructed on such principles.

Nevertheless, here it is realized in our hands. We can no longer doubt, we can only wonder, and admire the sagacity and patience with which Mr. Bell has worked out his problem to a successful issue.

CHAPTER IV.

IMPROVEMENTS OF CHANNING, BLAKE AND OTHERS.

In the winter and spring of 1877 a notable series of experiments were made by a few scientific gentlemen in Providence, R. I., which resulted in making the telephone portable, and in giving to it distinct articulation. Every step leading to these important results was communicated to Prof. Bell, and the principal improvements thus originating, especially the handle instrument and the mouth-piece, were at once adopted by him, and form part of what is now commonly known as the handle telephone.

In March, 1877, the speaking telephone, in its most practical form, consisted of a box resembling a photographer's camera, with a two inch tube for mouth-piece, opening into a cavernous air chamber in front of a plate of sheet iron about $4\frac{1}{2}$ inches in diameter. Behind this plate was a large U magnet, with a soft iron core clamped to each pole, surrounded with a spool of fine insulated wire. These instruments were unwieldy, and their articulation defective, for three reasons: First, the mouth-piece did not converge the air on the centre of the plate, and the cavernous air chamber produced reverberation; second, the magnet did not react symmetrically with the centre of the plate, but the two poles or cores of the U magnet reacted with the parts of the plate which were opposite to them on each side of the centre; third, the plate was too large and heavy to respond perfectly and promptly to the average voice.

Experiments, commencing in the physical laboratory of Brown University, and continued several months by Prof. Eli W. Blake, Prof. John Peirce, and others, culminated, in April, in the construction, by Dr. William F. Channing, of the first portable telephone. This consisted of two small blocks of wood fastened to each other at right angles—one perforated for the mouth-piece and holding a ferrotype plate, $2\frac{1}{4}$ inches in diameter; the other supporting a compound U magnet (made of two three inch toy magnets) with a single soft iron core, carrying a spool of fine insulated wire, clamped to one of its poles and opposed to the centre of the ferrotype plate. The other pole of the compound magnet was either brought in contact with the outer edge of the plate or left free.

This little instrument, weighing about twelve ounces and easily held in the hand, especially when mounted on a handle, talked more distinctly than the large instruments, even over long circuits, though not quite so loud. It was followed later in April by a telephone made by Prof. Peirce, in which a small compound U magnet was enclosed in a cubical block of wood, on the top of which he placed for the first time his converging mouth-piece—an acoustic apparatus which deserves special description.

Fig. **60.**

This is shown in section in fig. **60.** The sound waves converge upon the centre of the plate through the aperture a, usually about $\frac{7}{16}$ inch diameter.

The sound waves also spread symmetrically from the centre, and act upon the plate through the very flat air chamber $b\ b$. To prevent resonance and ensure the prompt response of the plate, this air chamber is usually made only from $\frac{1}{32}$ to $\frac{1}{16}$ inch in depth, and about $1\frac{3}{4}$ inches in diameter when a ferrotype plate ($c\ c$) is used. This mouth-piece made distinct and natural the previously obscure articulation of the telephone.

At the time Prof. Peirce's mouth-piece was made, Prof. Bell had arrived at the discovery that the instruments talked better if the air chamber, usually made deeper than that shown in fig. 53, was stuffed with paper. The reason will be sufficiently obvious from the above.

Prof. Peirce's upright block was followed naturally by the "handle telephone," now in general use, which was made by Dr. Channing early in May, 1877. Figs. 61 and 62 show both a sectional and perspective view of the instrument. In this a small straight magnet, simple or compound, carrying a single soft iron core and spool, is enclosed in a light and elegant handle, and the

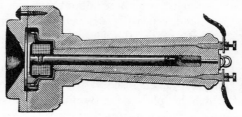

Fig. 61.

ferrotype plate is mounted in the circular head, of which the mouth-piece forms part. The design and style of the instrument is due to Mr. Edson S. Jones, another of the Providence experimenters.

After a competitive test with the box telephones, as at that time made, the handle telephone was adopted and sent out early

Fig. 62.

in June by the Telephone Company; and its portability, elegance and superior articulation contributed largely to the rapid diffusion of the telephone in this country and in Europe which immediately followed.

Prof. Bell was familiar with the preceding Providence experiments which had already made the telephone portable, and which suggested the handle form. In May, shortly after the construction of the handle instrument in Providence, and before it reached Boston, Prof. Bell, working in the same direction, had put a U magnet, each pole armed with a core and a spool, inside of a handle. The instrument was too cumbrous and inelegant for adoption, as well as defective in construction. Prof. Bell's desire to put both poles of the magnet to visible use was especially unfortunate in this case, as the smallness of the plates in the portable telephones makes it impossible that the two poles of the U magnet should act anywhere near the centre of the plate. The instrument was not adopted, and it could not have accomplished for the diffusion and commercial success of the telephone what was done by the original handle instrument.

Yet, with no other basis than this experiment, Prof. Bell, in his lecture in London, before the Society of Telegraph Engineers (see page 76), says : " Two or three days after I had constructed a telephone of the portable form, containing the magnet inside the handle, Dr. Channing was kind enough to send me a pair of telephones of a similar pattern, which had been invented by the Providence experimenters." As already stated, the instrument thus referred to is an accurate representation of the handle telephone of Dr. Channing and Mr. Jones, which has had so wide a career, and differs broadly in type from the experimental instrument of Prof. Bell, which never passed into use. Prof. Bell, in the above extract, not only claims the origination of the handle telephone, which has gone round the world and has a recognized place in the history of speaking telephony, but he also implies that he gave to the telephone portable form, thus ignoring one of the principal contributions of the Providence experimenters.

It happened with the telephone as with the Morse telegraph. In the beginning it was supposed that the power of the instruments was proportioned to their size. Later experiments have shown in both that more delicate instruments are the most effective.

It will be observed that Professor Bell is criticised here, not for claiming that he had made a straight magnet telephone, but for claiming this in combination with the handle, and figuring this combination, which constitutes the well known handle instrument, as his own. His real claim is to the independent experiment of putting a U magnet in a handle, subsequent to the construction of the genuine handle instrument in Providence.

Another practical result obtained in Providence as early as June, was the glass plate telephone of Henry W. Vaughan, State assayer. A disk of soft iron, about the size and shape of a nickel cent, was cemented with shellac to the centre of a very thin glass plate, 2¼ inches in diameter. This, with Peirce's mouth-piece and the usual magnets, gave the loudest and clearest articulation attained at that or at a later time, and may be the germ of important improvements. Mr. Vaughan also made, before the telephone had been seen in France, what has since been described as the multiple telephone of M. Trouvé. In this telephone, plates form the sides and ends of a cubical or poly hedral chamber, a magnet and coil being behind each plate.

Among other scientific observations with the telephone, Prof. Peirce heard the auroral sounds early in the summer of 1877, and Dr. Channing noticed the characteristic telephonic sound of lightning, even when distant, preceding the visible flash. Prof. E. W. Blake made the capital experiment, imperfectly reported in Prof. Bell's lecture, of substituting a soft iron bar for the magnet of the telephone. Whenever this bar was turned in the direction of the dipping needle, the telephone would talk by the earth's magnetism; but when swung up into a position at right angles with the dipping needle, the telephone became perfectly silent. Prof. Blake also talked with a friend by telephone for a short distance, using the parallel rails of the same railroad track as conductors, and hearing at the same time, by induction, the Morse operating from the telegraph wires overhead. This illustrates the apparent indifference of the telephone, at times, to insulation. Prof. Blake also originated the responsive tuning forks, in which two forks of the same musical pitch are magnetized ; a short iron core, surrounded with a spool of wire, is supported between the poles or prongs of each. The wires being connected, if one tuning fork is struck the other responds at a distance.

The names of Messrs. Louis W. Clarke and Charles E. Austin should be mentioned among the corps of Providence experimenters as contributors to this chapter of telephonic progress.

[1] With the object of stimulating inquiry into the means of improving the telephone, which is the most beautiful adaptation

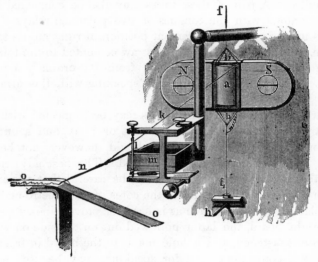

Fig. 63.

of telegraphy ever made, I desire to draw attention to a few simple methods by which any one may satisfy himself of its practicability ; for no one having witnessed its performance can fail to see a great future before it.

The recorder of Sir W. Thomson, shown in fig. 132, affords a ready means of speaking, and gives out such clear tones as to make the listener at first involuntarily look behind the instrument for the speaker (who may be miles away). It suffices to

---

[1] John Gott. *Journal Society Telegraph Engineers.* Nos. XV. and XVI. 1877.

take a tube two inches in diameter, and stretch over one end a membrane of parchment or thin gutta percha (the latter is less affected by the breath, the former becoming somewhat flaccid after a time). To the centre of the membrane cement a straw, and fix the tube in front of the instrument, about six inches from the movable coil b; cement the other end of the straw to the coil at the point where the silk fibre k is usually fixed. This is all that is necessary for both speaking and receiving. Six or eight cells of battery connected in circuit with the electro-magnets suffice. A pair of these tubes may also be connected in a similar manner with the tongues of two polarized relays. The tube is to be fixed in a convenient position, at right angles to the tongue, and the free end of the straw cemented to the tongue, taking care that the latter is free from its ordinary contact points. No battery is required for speaking with this arrangement.

Or a pair of these speaking tubes may be connected with the ordinary armatures of any instrument or relay, and a current kept on the line. The armature should, however, not be too heavy, and should be carefully adjusted. The best adjustment gives the loudest sound. In sending, be careful that the armature in vibrating does not touch the cores of the electro-magnet.

A plate of thin iron, such as is used for stove pipes, fixed to an upright board, the latter hollowed out on the side on which the plate is fastened, and a hole made in the board in front for inserting a convenient tube for speaking, may be used as an armature, and a pair of coils placed in front of the iron plate through which a current from a battery is flowing, the cores to be adjusted as close as possible to the plate; this answers for sending and receiving. The battery need not be strong; if it be so, the armatures have to be removed further away from the coils. On a short line the resistance of the coils, with a suitable battery, is of little importance. I have spoken as well with small coils of three ohms as with 400 ohms.

If a pair of coils at the receiving end be placed on a violin, and connected to the line on which there is a permanent current and a sending instrument as described, singing and speaking into the tube at the distant end can be heard by placing the ear to the violin. The effect is exalted by laying a plate of iron on the poles of the electro-magnet.

By these simple means—and they are selected as being within the reach of many—may be demonstrated the possibility of speaking over miles of telegraph line. The sound of the voice in the tube is not that of a whisper, but of a voice at a distance ; and the nearer you seem to bring the sound the better your adjustment, and vice versa.

I have spoken through four knots of buried cable without sensible diminution of effect.

When the instruments are not well adjusted, some words will come clear when others do not ; and I have found the sentence, Are you ready ? pronounced deliberately, intelligible when others were not.

The object to be sought for is to augment the strength of the variations of current. At present it is limited by the power of the voice to move an armature or coil ; and unless it can be magnified by putting in play a reserve of force, as compressed air, etc., improvement cannot go far.

The most hopeful field seems to be the effecting a variation, through a sensible range of resistance at the sending end, to vary the strength of current in a primary coil by shunting or varying the resistance of a battery circuit ; as, for example, a fine wire inserted more or less in mercury.

CHAPTER V.

EDISON'S TELEPHONIC RESEARCHES.

THE following communication from Mr. Thomas A. Edison gives a detailed account of his researches in telephony, and is a valuable contribution to the history of the development of the speaking telephone.

Some time in or about the month of July, 1875, I began experimenting with a system of multiple telegraphy, which had for its basis the transmission of acoustic vibrations. Being furnished, at the same time, by Hon. William Orton, President of the Western Union Telegraph Company, with a translated description from a foreign scientific journal of Reiss's[1] telephone, I also began a series of experiments, with the view of producing an articulating telephone, carrying on both series simultaneously, by the aid of my two assistants, Messrs. Batchelor and Adams.

With regard to the multiple telegraph I will say that many methods were devised, among which may be mentioned the transfer system. This consisted in combining a large tuning fork with multiple forks, so arranged at two terminal stations, with contact springs leading to different Morse instruments, that the synchronous vibrations of the forks would change the main line wires from one set of instruments to other sets at both stations, at a rate of 120 times per second. With this rate of vibration the wire would be simultaneously disconnected at both terminal stations from one set of Morse signalling apparatus, and momentarily placed in alternate connection with three other similar sets of apparatus, and then again returned to the first set, without causing the apparatus to mark the absence of the current otherwise than by a perceptible weakening of the same.

---

1 Zeitschrift des Deutsch-Oesterreichischen Telegraphen-Vereins, herausgegeben in dessen Auftrage von der Königlich Preussischen Telegraphen-Direction. Redigirt von Dr. P. Wilhelm Brix. Vol. ix., 1862, page 125. (For a description of Reiss's apparatus see pages 9 to 13, inclusive.)

By this means, therefore, four perfectly independent wires were practically created, upon which signalling could be carried on with any system which was worked no faster than the ordinary Morse system. Each of these wires was also duplexed and found to work perfectly upon a line of artificial resistance, thus allowing, with the ordinary apparatus, of the simultaneous transmission of eight different messages.

Notwithstanding the perfect success of the system upon an artificial line, however, which possessed little or no electrostatic capacity, I have never, in practice, been able to produce a sufficiently perfect compensation for the effects of the static charge

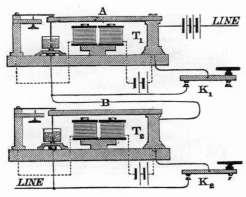

Fig. 64.

to allow of the successful use of the system on a line of over forty miles in length, although I have put the line to earth at both stations after it leaves one set of instruments and before it is placed in contact with another set; have sent reversed currents into it, and have also used magnetic and condenser compensation in various ways, known to experts in static compensation, but all without avail. By vibrating the line wire between two sets of apparatus, however, good satisfaction has been obtained on lines of about 200 miles in length.

In my system of acoustic transmission, which was devised in September, 1875, and is shown in fig. **64**, two tuning forks, A and B, vibrating from 100 to 500 times per second, were kept in continuous motion by a local magnet and battery, and the short circuiting was controlled by the signalling keys K_1 and K_2.

As will be seen on reference to the figure, this system, like that shown in my patent of 1873, is dependent upon the varying resistance occasioned by employing a movable electrode in water, and which thus produces corresponding variations of the battery current in the line.

The receivers R_1 and R_2, fig. 65, were formed of telescopic tubes of metal, by lengthening or shortening of which the column of air in either could be adjusted to vibrate in unison with the

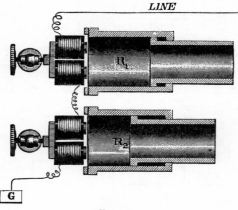

Fig. 65.

proper tone of the fork, whose signals were to be received by each particular instrument. An iron diaphragm was soldered to one end of these tubes, and the latter placed in such a manner as to bring the diaphragm of each respectively just in front of an electro-magnet, which, in action, would cause them to vibrate. When the column of air in either receiver was properly adjusted to a given tone, the signals due to stopping and starting the vibrations by the distant key were very loud, as compared to other tones not in harmony with the column of air. Flexible rubber tubes, with ear pieces, were connected to the receivers, so that, in using the instruments, the head of the operator was not required to be held in an unnatural or strained position.

This system worked very well; but one defect in it was apparent from the first, and that was its continual tendency to give the operator what is termed the back-stroke, even from the slightest cause, such as the opening of a door or the moving of the head, and also occurred on the slightest inattention whatever.

With a Morse sounder, as is well known, every dot is made apparent to the ear by two sounds, the first being produced when the lever strikes the anvil, and the other when it strikes the upper or back contact. A dash, like the dot, is also composed of two sounds, but the interval of time between the production of the first, the downward stroke or sound and the upward stroke, is what determines its character. It frequently happens, however, when a sounder is so adjusted that the sound produced by the down stroke is of the same volume or loudness as the one given by the up stroke, that the order of reading becomes reversed on the slightest disturbance or inattention and the ear mistakes the up sound for the down sound, and *vice versa*. The signals consequently become unintelligible, and the operator can only restore the proper order by closing both ears and watching the motion of the sounder lever, or by deadening the back sound by placing the finger on the lever until the ear again catches a word or two.

Similarly with the musical signals, the dots and dashes are formed by the relative short or long duration of a continuous tone, but in this case the pitch is always the same, and this constitutes an element of confusion that is quite as bad as the back stroke of the sounder above referred to. I therefore arranged my keys so as to transmit two short tones close together to form a dot, and two tones separated by an interval to form a dash ; but there was still so little distinctive difference between one and the other that I was led to defer further experiment with the apparatus for a time. It is probable that some means will be found for producing a greater degree of difference between the two elements of the signals, such, for instance, as the employment of two forks of slightly different pitch, which, at least, promises well. When this is done the system will be of some value.

It will be noticed that the receiving instrument shown in fig. 104 contains the diaphragm magnet and chamber of the magneto-speaking telephone; and I may say here that I believe I was the first to devise apparatus of this kind, which I intended for use in connection with acoustic telegraphs. I can, however, lay no claim to having discovered that conversation could be carried on between one receiver and the other upon the magneto principle by causing the voice to vibrate the diaphragm.

Another system of multiple transmission consisted, partly, in the use of reeds for receivers, and has been exceedingly well developed in the hands of Mr. Elisha Gray, but I forbear explaining it here, owing to its complexity and lack of practical merit.

My first attempt at constructing an articulating telephone was made with the Reiss transmitter and one of my resonant receivers described above, and my experiments in this direction, which continued until the production of my present carbon telephone, cover many thousand pages of manuscript. I shall, however, describe here only a few of the more important ones.

In one of the first experiments I included a simplified Reiss transmitter, having a platinum screw facing the diaphragm, in a circuit containing twenty cells of battery and the resonant receiver, and then placed a drop of water between the points; the results, however, when the apparatus was in action, were unsatisfactory—rapid decomposition of the water took place and a deposit of sediment was left on the platinum. I afterwards used disks attached both to the diaphragm and to the screw, with several drops of water placed between and held there by capillary attraction, but rapid decomposition of the water, which was impure, continued, and the words came out at the receiver very much confused. Various acidulated solutions were then tried, but the confused sounds and decompositions were the only results obtained.

With distilled water I could get nothing, probably because, at that time, I used very thick iron diaphragms, as I have since frequently obtained good results; or, possibly, it was because the ear was not yet educated for this duty, and therefore I did not know what to look for. If this was the case, it furnishes a good illustration of the fact observed by Professor Mayer, that we often fail to distinguish weak sounds in certain cases when we do not know what to expect.

Sponge, paper and felting, saturated with various solutions, were also used between the disks, and knife edges were substituted for the latter with no better results. Points immersed in electrolytic cells were also tried, and the experiments with various solutions, devices, etc., continued until February, 1876, when I abandoned the decomposable fluids and endeavored to vary the resistance of the circuit proportionately with the amplitude of vibration of the diaphragm by the use of a multiplicity of platinum points, springs and resistance coils—all of which were designed to be controlled by the movements of the diaphragm, but none of the devices were successful.

In the spring of 1876, and during the ensuing summer, I endeavored to utilize the great resistance of thin films of plumbago and white Arkansas oil stone, on ground glass, and it was here that I first succeeded in conveying over wires many articulated sentences. Springs attached to the diaphragm and numerous other devices were made to cut in and out of circuit more or less of the plumbago film, but the disturbances which the devices themselves caused in the true vibrations of the diaphragm prevented the realization of any practical results. One of my assistants, however, continued the experiments without interruption until January, 1877, when I applied the peculiar property which semi-conductors have of varying their resistance with pressure, a fact discovered by myself in 1873, while constructing some rheostats for artificial cables, in which were employed powdered carbon, plumbago and other materials, in glass tubes.

For the purpose of making this application, I constructed an apparatus provided with a diaphragm carrying at its centre a yielding spring, which was faced with platinum, and in front of this I placed, in a cup secured to an adjusting screw, sticks of crude plumbago, combined in various proportions with dry powders, resins, etc. By this means I succeeded in producing a telephone which gave great volume of sound, but its articulation was rather poor; when once familiar with its peculiar sound, however, one experienced but little difficulty in understanding ordinary conversation.

After conducting a long series of experiments with solid materials, I finally abandoned them all and substituted therefor tufts of conducting fibre, consisting of floss silk coated with plumbago and other semi-conductors. The results were then very much better, but while the volume of sound was still great, the articulation was not so clear as that of the magneto telephone of Prof. Bell. The instrument, besides, required very frequent adjustment, which constituted an objectionable feature.

Upon investigation, the difference of resistance produced by the varying pressure upon the semi-conductor was found to be exceedingly small, and it occurred to me that as so small a change in a circuit of large resistance was only a small factor, in the primary circuit of an induction coil, where a slight change of resistance would be an important factor, it would thus enable me to obtain decidedly better results at once. The experiment, however, failed, owing to the great resistance of the semi-conductors then used.

After further experimenting in various directions, I was led to believe, if I could by any means reduce the normal resistance of the semi-conductor to a few ohms, and still effect a difference in its resistance by the pressure due to the vibrating diaphragm, that I could use it in the primary circuit of an induction coil. Having arrived at this conclusion, I constructed a transmitter in which a button of some semi-conducting substance was placed between two platinum disks, in a kind of cup or small containing vessel. Electrical connection between the button and disks was maintained by the slight pressure of a piece of rubber tubing, $\frac{1}{4}$ inch in diameter and $\frac{1}{2}$ inch long, which was secured to the diaphragm, and also made to rest against the outside disk. The vibrations of the diaphragm were thus able to produce the requisite pressure on the platinum disk, and thereby vary the resistance of the button included in the primary circuit of the induction coil.

At first a button of solid plumbago, such as is employed by electrotypers, was used, and the results obtained were considered excellent, everything transmitted coming out moderately distinct, but the volume of sound was no greater than that of the magneto telephone.

In order, therefore, to obtain disks or buttons, which, with a low normal resistance, could also be made, by a slight pressure, to vary greatly in this respect, I at once tried a great variety of substances, such as conducting oxides, sulphides and other partial conductors, among which was a small quantity of lamp-black that had been taken from a smoking petroleum lamp and preserved as a curiosity on account of its intense black color.

A small disk made of this substance, when placed in the telephone, gave splendid results, the articulation being distinct, and the volume of sound several times greater than with telephones worked on the magneto principle. It was soon found upon investigation, that the resistance of the disk could be varied from three hundred ohms to the fractional part of a single ohm by pressure alone, and that the best results were obtained when the resistance of the primary coil, in which the carbon disk was included, was $\frac{6}{10}$ of an ohm, and the normal resistance of the disk itself three ohms.

Mr. Henry Bentley, president of the Local Telegraph Company, at Philadelphia, who has made an exhaustive series of experiments with a complete set of this apparatus upon the wires of the Western Union Telegraph Company, has actually succeeded in working with it over a wire of 720 miles in length, and has found it a practicable instrument upon wires of 100 to 200 miles in length, notwithstanding the fact that the latter were placed upon poles with numerous other wires, which occasioned sufficiently powerful induced currents in them to entirely destroy the articulation of the magneto telephone. I also learn that he has found the instrument practicable, when included in a Morse circuit, with a battery and eight or ten stations provided with the ordinary Morse apparatus; and that several way stations could exchange business telephonically upon a wire which was being worked quadruplex without disturbing the latter, and notwithstanding, also, the action of the powerful reversed currents of the quadruplex on the diaphragms of the receiver. It would thus seem as though the volume of sound produced by the voice with this apparatus more than compensates for the noise caused by such actions.

While engaged in experimenting with my telephone for the purpose of ascertaining whether it might not be possible to dispense with the rubber tube which connected the diaphragm with the rheostatic disk, and was objectionable on account of its tendency to become flattened by continued vibrations, and thus necessitate the readjustment of the instrument, I discovered that my principle, unlike all other acoustical devices for the transmission of speech, did not require any vibration of the diaphragm—that, in fact, the sound waves could be transformed into electrical pulsations without the movement of any intervening mechanism.

The manner in which I arrived at this result was as follows: I first substituted a spiral spring of about a quarter inch in length, containing four turns of wire, for the rubber tube which connected the diaphragm with the disks. I found, however, that this spring gave out a musical tone which interfered somewhat with the effects produced by the voice; but, in the hope of overcoming the defect, I kept on substituting spiral springs of thicker wire, and as I did so I found that the articulation became both clearer and louder. At last I substituted a solid substance for the springs that had gradually been made more and more inelastic, and then I obtained very marked improvements in the results. It then occurred to me that the whole question was one of pressure only, and that it was not necessary that the diaphragm should vibrate at all. I consequently put in a heavy diaphragm, one and three quarter inches in diameter and one sixteenth inch thick, and fastened the carbon disk and plate tightly together, so that the latter showed no vibration with the loudest tones.

Upon testing it I found my surmises verified; the articulation was perfect and the volume of sound so great that conversation carried on in a whisper three feet from the telephone was clearly heard and understood at the other end of the line.

This, therefore, is the arrangement I have adopted in my present form of apparatus, which I call the carbon telephone, to distinguish it from others. It is fully described in another part of this work.

The accessories and connections of this apparatus for long circuits are shown in fig. 66. A is an induction coil, whose primary

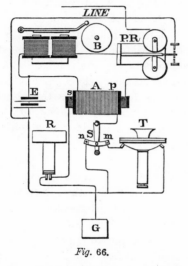

Fig. 66.

wire *p*, having a resistance of several ohms, is placed around the secondary, instead of within it, as in the usual manner of construction. The secondary coil *s*, of finer wire, has a resistance of from 150 to 200 ohms, according to the degree of tension required; and the receiving telephone R consists simply of a magnet, coil and diaphragm. One pole of the magnet is connected to the outer edge of the diaphragm, and the other, which carries the wire bobbin of about 75 ohms resistance, and is included in the main line, is placed just opposite its centre.

P R is the signalling relay, generally a Siemens' polarized instrument, which has been given a bias towards one side, and consequently is capable of responding to currents of one definite direction only.

The lever of this relay, when actuated by the current from a distant station on the line in which the instrument is included, closes a local circuit containing the vibrating call bell B, and thus gives warning when speaking communication is desired.

Besides serving to operate the call bell, the local battery E is also used for sending the call signal. S is a switch, the lever of which, when placed at o, between m and n, disconnects the transmitter T and local battery E from the coil A, and in this position leaves the polarized relay P R free to respond to currents from the distant station. When this station is wanted, however, the lever S is turned to the left on n, and depressed several times in rapid succession. The current from the local battery, by this means, is made to pass through the primary coil of A, and thus for each make and break of the circuit induces powerful currents in the secondary s, which pass into the line and actuate the distant call bell.

When the call signals have been exchanged, both terminal stations place their switches to the right on m, and thus introduce the carbon transmitter into their respective circuits. The changes of pressure, produced by speaking against the diaphragm of either transmitter, then serve, as already shown, to vary the resistance of the carbon, and thus produce corresponding variations in the induced currents, which, acting through the receiving instrument, reproduce at the distant station whatever has been spoken into the transmitting instrument.

For lines of moderate lengths, say from one to thirty miles, another arrangement, shown in fig. 67, may be used advantageously. The induction coil, key, battery, and receiving and transmitting telephones, are lettered the same as in the previous figure, and are similar in every respect to the apparatus there shown; the switch S, however, differs somewhat in construction from the one already described, but is made to serve a similar purpose.

When a plug is inserted between 3 and 4, the relay or sounder R′, battery E, and key K only are included in the main line circuit, and this is the normal arrangement of the apparatus for signalling purposes. The battery, usually about three cells of the Daniell form, serves also both for a local and main battery. When a plug is inserted between 1, 2 and 4, the apparatus is available for telephonic communication.

I have also found, on lines of from one to twenty miles in length, that the ordinary call can be dispensed with, and a simplified arrangement substituted. This latter consists simply

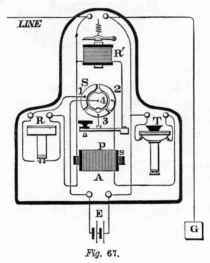

Fig. 67.

of the ordinary receiving telephone, upon the diaphragm of which a free lever, L, is made to rest, as shown in fig. 68. When the induced currents from the distant station act upon the receiver R, the diaphragm of the latter is thrown into vibration, but by itself is capable of giving only a comparatively weak sound; with the lever resting upon its centre, however, a sharp, penetrating noise is produced by the constant and rapid rebounds of the lever, which thus answers very well for calling purposes at stations where there is comparatively but little noise.

Among the various other methods for signalling purposes which I have experimented with, I may mention the sounding of a note, by the voice, in a small Reiss's telephone; the employment of a self-vibrating reed in the local circuit; and a break wheel with many cogs, so arranged as to interrupt the circuit when set in motion.

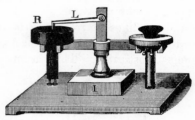

Fig. 68.

I have also used direct and induced currents to release clock work, and thus operate a call, and in some of my earlier acoustic experiments tuning forks were used, whose vibrations in front of magnets caused electrical currents to be generated in the coils surrounding the latter.

By the further action of these currents on similar forks at a distant station, bells were caused to be rung, and signals thus

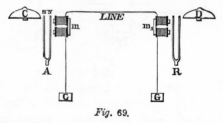

Fig. 69.

given. Fig. 69 shows an arrangement of this kind. A and B are two magnetized tuning forks, having the same rate of vibration and placed at two terminal stations. Electro-magnets m and m^1 are placed opposite one of the prongs of the forks at each station, while a bell, C or D, stands opposite to the other. The coils of the magnet are connected respectively to the line

wire and to earth. When one of the forks is set in vibration by
a starting key provided for the purpose, the currents produced
by the approach of one of its magnetized prongs towards the
magnet, and its recession therefrom, pass into the line and to the
further station, where their action soon causes the second fork
to vibrate with constantly increasing amplitude, until the bell is
struck and the signal given.

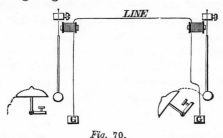

Fig. 70.

For telephonic calls the call bells are so arranged that the one
opposite to the fork, which generates the currents, is thrown out
of the way of the latter's vibrations.

Another call apparatus, which I have used, is represented in
fig. 70. In this arrangement two small magnetic pendulums,
whose rates of vibration are the same, are placed in front of

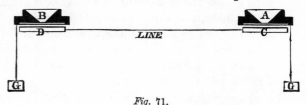

Fig. 71.

separate electro-magnets, the helices of which join in the main
line circuit. When one of the pendulums is put in motion, the
currents generated by its forward and backward swings in front
of the electro-magnet pass into the line, and at the opposite terminal, acting through the helix there, cause the second pendulum
to vibrate in unison with the former.

Fig. 71 shows a form of electrophorous telephone which acts

by the approach of the diaphragm contained in A or B towards or its recession from a highly charged electrophorous, C or D. The vibrations of the transmitting diaphragm cause a disturbance of the charge at both ends of the line, and thus give rise to faint sounds. Perfect insulation, however, is necessary, and either apparatus can be used both for transmitting and receiving, but the results are necessarily very weak.

Another form of electro-static telephone is shown in fig. 72. In this arrangement Deluc piles of some 20,000 disks each are contained in glass tubes A and B, and conveniently mounted on glass, wood or metal stands. The diaphragms, which are in electrical connection with the earth, are also placed opposite to one pole of each of the piles, while the opposite poles are joined together by the line conductor. Any vibration of either dia-

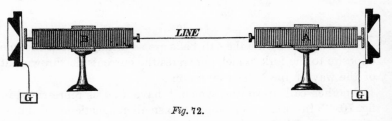

Fig. 72.

phragm is thus capable of disturbing the electrical condition of the neighboring disks, the same as in the electrophorous telephones; and consequently the vibrations, when produced by the voice in one instrument, will give rise to corresponding electrical changes in the other, and thereby reproduce in it what has been spoken into the mouthpiece of the former.

With this arrangement fair results may be obtained, and it is not necessary that the insulation should be so perfect as for the electrophorous apparatus. Fig. 73 shows a form of electro-mechanical telephone, referred to near the beginning of this communication, by means of which I attempted to transmit electrical impulses of variable strength, so as to reproduce spoken words at a distance. Small resistance coils—1, 2, 3, etc.—were so arranged with connecting springs near a platinum faced lever

B, in connection with the diaphragm in A, that any movement
of the latter caused one or more of the coils to be cut in or out
of the primary circuit of an induction coil C, the number, of
course, varying with the amplitude of the vibrating diaphragm.
Induced currents corresponding in strength with the variations
of resistance were thus sent into the line, and could then be made
to act upon an ordinary receiving telephone.   By arranging the

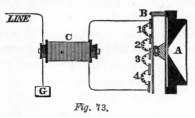

Fig. 73.

springs in a sunflower pattern about a circular lever, I have succeeded in transmitting articulate sentences by this method, but
the results were very harsh and disagreeable.

Fig. **73** shows a form of the water telephone previously referred to, in which a double cell was used, so as to afford considerable variation of resistance for the very slight movements

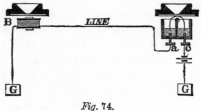

Fig. 74.

of the diaphragm.   The action of the apparatus will readily be
understood from the figure, where a wire in the form of the
letter U is shown, with the bend attached to the diaphragm, and
its ends dipping into the separate cells, and thus made to form
part of the circuit when the line is joined to the instrument at *a*
and *c.*

CHAPTER VI.

The most important advance that has been made in the application of the telephone to business, manufactures and medical science dates from the discovery of the varying electrical resistance of certain bodies when submitted to pressure. The carbon telephone is based on this fact, and more recent discoveries prove that any mass of metal that is not continuous, like a heap of shot, a coil of chain, or charcoal impregnated with iron, will produce changes in an electrical current when submitted to pressure. This pressure may be the impact of sonorous waves of all kinds, and thus such a mass of metal may become the transmitter of a telephonic circuit.

In Chapter V. we have already described a few of the discoveries and inventions made by Mr. Edison in his researches which culminated in the invention of the carbon telephone. We now propose to present a more complete description of the important forms of telephone upon which he then experimented, as well as to describe his more recent acoustic inventions. The carbon telephone is only one of many contrivances for reproducing articulate speech at a distance, but owing to its clear and truthful articulation, its simplicity of construction, and the far greater volume of sound which it creates, it is likely to be the most extensively used. Other instruments of Mr. Edison's invention, however, are not far behind it, and may by improvement be made equally effective. As a rule, Mr. Edison has succeeded better with those telephones which produce a variation in the resistance of the circuit than with such as depend for their action upon a variation of the electromotive force or static charge.

An instrument very similar to the carbon transmitting telephone is shown in fig. 75 (devised November 19, 1877), the essential difference being that the carbon is replaced by bibulous paper, moistened with water. This semi-conductor, like the carbon, changes its resistance under the influence of varying pressure. The paper is kept moist by capillary action, a strip being used, one end of which dips into a reservoir of water. In fig. 96 (devised June 27, 1877) is shown a form of the carbon transmitting telephone, requiring no adjustment whatever, and which operates well, notwithstanding the simplicity of its construction. It consists essentially of a plate of metal resting on the bottom of a hollow vessel, and carrying a block of prepared

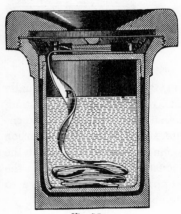

Fig. 75.

Fig. 76.

carbon, upon which a second and light metallic plate is laid. The weight of the upper plate affords an initial pressure, which is varied by speaking into the mouth of the vessel. The carbon block may be replaced by a disk of cloth, the pores of which have been filled with pulverized black lead. By this treatment the cloth becomes slightly conductive. The instrument thus modified is shown in fig. 77 (devised Sept. 20, 1877). In fig. 78 (devised August 12, 1877) the pulverized plumbago P is floated upon mercury, M, and is compressed between the surface of the mercury and a metallic block fastened to the centre of the diaphragm.

Still another form of the Edison transmitter is shown in fig. 79 (devised July 5, 1877). The carbon C rests upon the diaphragm, which, in this instrument, is a horizontal plate forming the top of a vocalizing chamber, the mouth piece being at the side. Three fine cords attach the carbon to the framework of the diaphragm, and prevent it from being displaced when the diaphragm is vibrating. In appearance this instrument resembles the Reiss telephone, and in principle it would be much the

Fig. 77.   *Fig.* 78.

same were it not that, in vibrating, the carbon never actually leaves the plate upon which it rests, but simply, for an instant, releases its pressure. It is evident that the resistance of the circuit depends upon the electric connection between the carbon and the diaphragm, and that this connection depends upon the pressure of the carbon, which is constantly changing when the diaphragm is in vibration. This apparatus is too sensitive to extraneous sounds to be useful in telephony.

Fig. 79.

Another form acting on much the same principle is illustrated by fig. 80 (devised Sept. 30, 1877); it is called the inertia telephone, though it is hardly certain that its action is to be attributed solely to inertia. The carbon C is placed between two metallic plates, one of which is fastened to the diaphragm, and the other is held by a screw bearing in a framework, attached to the diaphragm by insulating supports. When vibrating, the whole system moves, instead of the plate P alone, as in the ordinary carbon transmitter. Mr. Edison's explanation of its mode of action is, that the degree of pressure with which the carbon rests against the plates is varied during the vibration. Thus, after a movement toward the right, the diaphragm suddenly stops, and the carbon presses in virtue of its inertia on the plate P.

An advantage which the magneto-telephone has over the earlier forms of Mr. Edison's telephone is, that its diaphragm

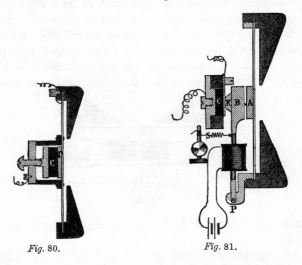

Fig. 80.   *Fig.* 81.

does not touch anything, and can therefore vibrate with perfect freedom. On the other hand, the diaphragm of the carbon telephone, used before his adoption of the present non-vibrating rigid plate, presses with considerable force upon the carbon, and thus causes it to make false vibration. In the form shown in fig. 81 (devised June 25, 1877), this difficulty is not encountered. The diaphragm carries an armature, A, of soft iron, which confronts but does not touch the magnet B. A and B are opposite poles of the same magnet, being connected at P, and polarized by a local circuit. The magnet B presses upon the carbon at C, the pressure being regulated by the screw S. The attraction between A and B varies with the distance between them. When, in vibrating, A moves toward B, the attraction rapidly increases, and B lessens its pressure upon C. During a motion in the opposite direction, the attraction diminishes, and B, drawn by the spring S, increases its pressure upon C.

A similar contrivance is illustrated in fig. 82. (Devised April 10, 1877.) The diaphragm carries an armature, A, which, by its motion, changes the potential of two electro-magnets. These changes in magnetism cause a bar, situated in their magnetic field, to reproduce the original vibrations. The ends of the bar are held by the magnetic force against two pieces of carbon, c and c. These and the bar are included in the primary circuit of an induction coil. The resistance of the circuit

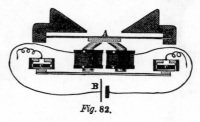

Fig. 82.

decreases when the bar is drawn up, and increases as the bar descends.

Of all substances which have thus been tested in the telephone for increasing and decreasing the resistance of the circuit by the effect of the sonorous vibrations, lamp black from the lighter hydrocarbons proves the best. It is very essential that the lamp black should be deposited at the lowest temperature possible, and the flame of the lamp should not be allowed to play upon the deposit; otherwise the product is of high resistance and wholly unsuitable for this purpose. Commercial lamp black of the best quality, scarcely allows a current to pass through it, while that obtained by the process herein described offers but slight resistance.

The lamp black as it comes from the burning apparatus is

laid upon a white slab, and those portions which have a brown tinge are picked from the mass ; the remainder is then ground in a mortar and placed in a large mould and subjected to a pressure of several thousand pounds. The cake thus pressed is re-powdered and re-pressed several times. Finally, it is weighed out in divisions of three hundred milligrammes and moulded into buttons as seen in the telephone.

The reason why lamp black thus moulded is superior to any other material is satisfactorily explained, when we consider that of all finely divided substances obtained either by mechanical action or chemical precipitation, it is seen, when under the microscope, to have the greatest number of particles, or in other words, to be the most finely divided. Now it is well known that the increase and decrease of the resistance of any button of finely divided conducting matter, when subject to pressure, is due entirely to the contact of a greater or less number of particles at the junction or surfaces.

Again, it is known that the telephone is exquisitely sensitive to the slightest change of resistance in the circuit; hence, if a button of gas retort carbon composed of inelastic particles, few in number (as compared to lamp black), is used in a telephone, the production of a wave by gradually increasing pressure is obtained by the gradually increasing number of particles which are brought in contact with the surface plates. Now these particles are so few and large, and in many cases several particles aggregated in the retort carbon, that the wave instead of being pure is harsh and grating. This wave may be graphically represented by a serrated line inclined at an angle of 45°, the points representing the disturbance of the current by the effect of the particles themselves. Now if the button of gas retort carbon be replaced by one of graphite, which is composed of much smaller particles with no aggregations as with the first, the waves will be represented by the line as above, but the points will be scarcely perceptible, and these gaps being so minute, are beyond the power of the telephone to detect; hence we obtain a pure wave, but these gaps weaken the wave as a whole by their effect on the self-induction of the telephone receiver.   But in the case of lamp black, the particles are infinitely finer than graphite, and, moreover, the button is somewhat elastic; hence the line representing the form of the wave will be perfectly straight, although theoretically there are gaps. They are infinitely small as compared to graphite or other conducting material, therefore we not only prevent harsh sounds, but obtain a stronger wave, owing to the absence of gaps and their effect on the self-induction of the magnet.   Lamp black when moulded into buttons possesses another property differing from all other conducting material, and that is its elasticity.   For instance, if we subject buttons of different materials to pressure, the greatest difference of resistance with a given weight will be produced on the lamp black button; again, if we increase the weight on all the buttons, a point will be reached where any additional weight ceases to reduce the resistance appreciably, except in the case of the lamp black, which continues to show decrease of resistance by additional weight placed upon it long after the other buttons cease to be affected, as all the particles that can come in contact will be brought in contact by a slight weight owing to the inelastic nature.   Mr. Edison has endeavored to obtain an approximation as to the number of points of contact on the lamp black button now used.   In order to accomplish this purpose he first placed a Rutherford diffraction grating under the microscope having 17,291 lines ruled on speculum metal within a space of one inch, and by the side of this a button of lamp black, then by changing from one to the other, he calculated that there were not less than 10,000,000 of points upon the surface of the button, nearly all of which were constantly in use when subjected to the sonorous vibrations.   Had the Rutherford grating been ruled both ways there would have been 298,000,000 of points, and there is little doubt that a button of platina ruled double in this manner would give good results in the telephone, but would not equal the lamp black, owing to its want of elasticity.

The elasticity of the lamp black button has another advantage, insomuch that it allows a considerable initial pressure to be placed upon it without materially reducing its sensibility; hence the apparatus is not so liable to be thrown out of adjustment as those employing an inelastic button, where the initial pressure must be exceedingly light to retain its sensibility.   When adjusted in this manner, a loud sound causes a break in the circuit, and the sounds are harsh and disagreeable, and allow sparks to occur, which in time coats the metallic armature and renders it unfit for use.   The only defect, if so it may be called, in the button made of lamp-black, is that it is somewhat friable; but Mr. Edison's experience goes to prove that if the telephone is made in a proper manner, so that no part of it will, when under the effect of the sonorous waves, vibrate and hammer the button, it will last for months, and as far as can be seen, will continue to last as long as the instrument that holds it; but if the instrument is so devised that the armatures are allowed to hammer the button, or if the initial pressure is very light and the instrument receives a violent concussion (for instance, by being dropped on the floor), the button is liable to crack, but even in this case the volume of sound is not materially lessened. Mr. Edison has attempted to harden these buttons by mixing the lamp-black with sugar, tar and other substances previous to moulding, and after moulding subjecting them to a high temperature.   This treatment makes them hard but inelastic, and yet far superior to any other substance which he has tried.

The value of different substances to be used as buttons in the telephone are given below, the first mentioned being the best, and the others in the order given:

Lamp-black,
Hyperoxide of lead,
Iodide of copper,
Graphite,
Gas carbon,
Platinum black.

Finely divided materials which do not oxidize in the air, such as osmium, ruthenium, silicon, boron, iridium and platinum, give results proportionate to this minute division, but many of them are such good conductors that it is necessary to mix some very fine non-conducting material with them before moulding. All the conducting oxides, sulphides, iodides, and nearly every metal finely divided has been tried by Mr. Edison, in various states of divisibility and mixed with various substances. Liquids in porous buttons of finely divided non-conducting material, render these particles conducting, and they, consequently, act in the same manner, but, of course, owing to the formation of gas, polarization, etc., they are objectionable.

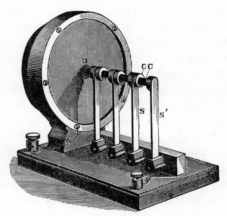

Fig. 83.

THE MICROPHONE.

The device of using several pieces of the semi-conductor instead of one was early tried by Mr. Edison. He found, in general, that the loudness of the sound was increased by thus multiplying the number of contact surfaces, but also that the articulation was impaired. Instruments of this nature have since become known as microphones, though it is not probable that faint sounds were ever augmented through their agency so that they could be easily recognized at a distance from their source. Fig. 83 shows one of the first forms, invented by Mr.

Edison, April 1, 1877. Four pieces of charcoal are used, C C, etc., each supported by an upright spring, as at S and S'. The piece of charcoal nearest the diaphragm impinges upon a disk of carbon, which is fastened to the centre of the diaphragm. The primary wires of an induction coil are attached to the diaphragm and the spring S. The circuit is then completed through the semi-conductors.

Other forms are shown in figs. 84 and 85. The former has two carbons, separated by a plate of metal. The latter has three contiguous pieces of carbon.

Fig. 86 (devised Sept. 21, 1877) illustrates a microphone,

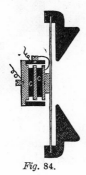

Fig. 84. *Fig.* 85.

having ten plates of silk; a mixture of dextrine and lamp-black having been previously worked into the pores.

In fig. 87 (devised June 7, 1877), fifty disks, D, with iron protoxidized on the surface, are shown inclosed in a glass tube.

A novel form of transmitter used by Mr. Edison in his experiments is shown in fig. 88 (devised Aug. 12, 1877). The semi-conductor is a collection of small fragments of cork covered with plumbago. It can be used with or without a diaphragm. The instrument shown in fig. 89, (devised Aug. 24, 1877) acts both as a transmitter and receiver, the latter fact being discovered by Mr. Chas. Batchelor, Mr. Edison's assistant. The solid carbon of the transmitter is here replaced by silk fibres coated with graphite. Its action as a receiver is probably due to the attraction of parallel currents; the volume of the whole being contracted during the passage of a current through F.

In May, 1878, Mr. Hughes, of London, published some interesting experiments, based upon Mr. Edison's discovery of the variable resistance of solid conductors when subjected to pressure.

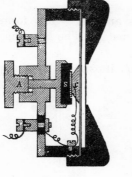

Fig. 86.

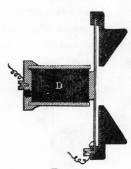

Fig. 87.

In fig. 90, A is a glass tube filled with a mixture of metallic tin and zinc, commonly known as white silver powder. This powder is slightly compressed by two plugs of gas car-

Fig. 88.

Fig. 89.

bon inserted at the ends, to which are attached wires, having a battery, B, and galvanometer, G, in circuit. The plugs are cemented in their place by being covered over with ordinary sealing wax. Upon grasping this tube by the two ends, and giving it a tensile strain by pulling them in contrary directions, but in a line with its length, the galvanometer needle is deflected in one direction, and on pushing the ends towards one another, so as to put on a strain of compression, the needle of the galvanometer is instantly deflected in the opposite direction. In this case the finely divided metallic particles forming the contents of the tube are brought into more intimate connection by compression, and are more separated during the operation of extension, and thus the resistance of the circuit is varied, increasing the current in the first instance, and decreasing it in the second. If this view be correct, the movement of the galvanometer needle in the reverse direction cannot be called a

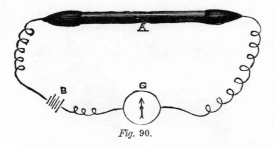

Fig. 90.

deflection, but a returning to zero, stopping at that position which represents the strength of the current flowing through its coils when the tube is being extended. This experiment alone would be a remarkable example of the marvellous sensitiveness of the telephone as a detector of minute variations of electrical force, for it is hardly possible to conceive the minute increment that takes place in the length or capacity of a glass tube, some three inches long, when extended by pulling with the fingers. But this sensitive tube is far more delicate than is shown by the last named experiment. So sensitive is it, that it is capable of taking up sonorous vibrations, and by its own vibrations under their influence it transmits through an electric wire to a distant telephone, undulatory currents capable of reproducing therein all the sounds by which they were produced, and with even greater perfection than would be attained if a telephone were the transmitting instrument. By attaching one of these tubes to a small resonating box, as shown in fig. 91, we have one of the very simplest electric articulating telephones that has ever been produced. It consists of nothing more than a tube of glass filled with a powder whose electric conductivity can be varied by variations of compression, wires being led from the two ends, and this little apparatus attached to a little box opened at one end, which serves as the mouth piece of the instrument. The wires are attached to a distant telephone, and have a battery of three

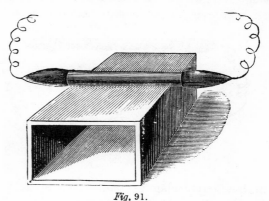

Fig. 91.

small Daniell cells in circuit. With this simple telephone the sounds are so loud that it is possible to sing into one instrument, and hear at the same time singing from a distant station in another. This duplex arrangement with a single circuit works perfectly, the one communication in no way interfering with the other.

When a stick of pure vegetable carbon, such as is used by artists, is employed instead of the tube, no effect is produced, because of its very high resistance making it to all intents and purposes a perfect non-conductor ; but by heating it to incandescence, and suddenly plunging it into a bath of mercury, it

becomes impregnated with minute particles of that metal, and
in that state can be used almost as well as the tube of
compound metallic powder.   Similarly, charcoal impregnated
with platinum perchloride may be used with advantage, whether
in the form of a stick or as powder contained in a tube.

Mr. Hughes, in experimenting with various substances,
arrived at the conclusion that whatever conductor is employed, it must not be homogeneous in its nature, so that
increase or decrease of pressure, by producing closer or more
distant union between its conducting particles, has the property
of varying the strength of the current transmitted, giving to it

Fig. 92.

an undulatory character.   A tube containing clean lead shot
will exhibit the phenomena, but after a time, in consequence of
an insulating oxide being formed on the surface of each shot, it
ceases to convey the current.   Possibly by immersing the shot
in a non-oxidizing medium, such as naphtha, the defect might
be remedied, but far better substances for the experiments can
be found than shot.

Fig. 92   represents a perspective view of a small wooden box
open at one end, and resembling the boxes used as resonators for
tuning forks.   A convenient size is ten inches wide, eighteen inches
long and seven inches deep.   On this is a small glass tube
open at both ends, and fastened down with sealing wax.   In the

tube are a number of pieces of willow charcoal that have been metallized with iron.   To prepare this charcoal, take sticks (pencils) of charcoal and pack them loosely in an iron box with a loose cover, and bring the box slowly to a white heat. This tends to drive out the water that may be held in the pores of the charcoal, and it is replaced by the vapor of iron, so that, when cool, the sticks of charcoal are loaded with iron and have a decided metallic ring.   Small pieces of the metallized charcoal are placed in the glass tube and closely pressed together till it is full and a portion of the charcoal projects at either end, as shown in the figure.   The wires of a telephonic circuit are wound round these projecting ends, and the ends of the tube

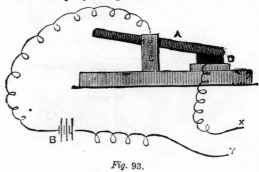

Fig. 93.

are then closed with sealing wax.   This apparatus, simple as it is, makes a telephonic transmitter of most remarkable sensitiveness.   On holding an ordinary magneto-electric telephone to the ear (with a battery in the line), the mere rubbing of the finger on the box, the trace of a pencil, or the footsteps of a house fly walking on or near the box will be heard with perfect distinctness.   So sensitive is this instrument that sounds that cannot be heard by the ear become clear in the telephone.

A watch placed on the box gives all the sounds of its works— the grinding of the wheels, the sonorous ring of the spring and the minutest tick of the gearing.   Words spoken in the box sound with the power of a trumpet in the telephone, and the blowing of the breath resembles the roar of the wind in a forest.

Fig. 93 represents another form of transmitter based on the same principles. A is a short piece of a carbon point, such as is used in the electric light, mounted by a metallic arm pivoted on

Fig. 94.

the upright C. There are two of these uprights secured to the wooden plate, one on each side of the stick of carbon. At D is

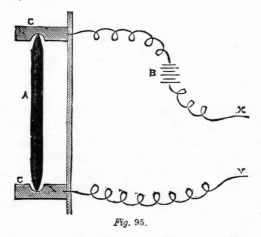

Fig. 95.

a small block of the metallized charcoal resting on an insulator (sealing wax). X and Y are the two wires of a telephonic line.

This apparatus shows the effect of varying pressure on electrical resistance.   On lifting the lower end from the mass of charcoal the circuit is broken.   On pressing it down on the charcoal the electrical resistance will vary with the pressure, however minute it may be.   The pressure exerted by sonorous vibrations, even though they may be caused by the tread of a fly or the pressure of a finger, cause so great changes in the electrical status of the line that when the telephone receiver is placed at the ear these minute movements are distinctly heard.

Fig. 94 represents a thin pine board about six inches square, placed upright on a suitable support.   To this are attached, by

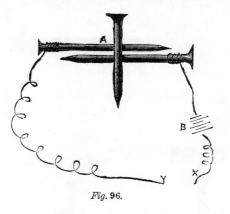

Fig. 96.

means of sealing wax, two pieces of common gas carbon, C, C. (See detail sketch, fig. 95.)   In each piece is hollowed out a shallow cup, and supported between them is an upright spindle of gas carbon, A, the pointed ends just touching the cups.   This spindle is placed in a telephonic circuit by twisting the wires round the carbon cups, as shown in the drawing.   Words spoken before this sounding board, even at a distance of several yards, are distinctly heard in the telephone.   These transmitters, rough and crude as they may appear, plainly show that a most important advance has been made in telephony.   With instruments of more delicate construction, even more remarkable results may yet be obtained. Ordinary mechanical structures which contain a good many joints, such as a small machine or a small chain made into a little heap, act almost as well as the substances to which we have referred. In these special cases the phenomena· are probably due to the electric current having imparted to it an undulatory character through being transmitted through a circuit containing a number of what the telegraph engineer would call faults, which are variable in their faultiness, through variations of pressure between the separate parts of the conducting structure. It must seem strange, and yet it is never-theless a fact, that if we place two common nails in a telephonic circuit and insulate them from each other, and then place a third nail upon them so as to close the circuit, a capital trans-mitter is at once made. The sonorous vibrations, falling on the nail, will be reproduced in the telephone with startling distinct-ness. Fig. 96 shows such a transmitter. Two common nails, A, are fastened down to a horizontal board ; wires X and Y are attached to them, leading to a battery, B, and a telephone in such a manner that the nails form the only break in the circuit, which can be closed by laying any conducting material across them. When a third nail is laid across the other two, it is clear that (as a cylinder can only touch another cylinder whose axis is not parallel with it in a single point) the electric circuit has a very imperfect connection at the points of contact between the nails, and it is to this faulty connection that the sensitiveness of this arrangement is due.

In the accounts which have been published of experiments with the microphone, the statement has frequently been made, that minute sounds are actually magnified by it, in the same sense that minute objects are magnified by the microscope. A little reflection will show, however, that there is no real analogy in the action of the two instruments. The sound that is heard in the receiving instrument of the microphone, when a fly is walking across the board on which the transmitter is placed, is not the sound of the fly's footsteps, any more than the stroke of a powerful electric bell, or sounder, is the magnified sound of the operator's fingers tapping lightly and, it may be, inaudibly upon the key. This view of the subject readily explains why the microphone has failed to realize the expectations of many persons, who, upon its first exhibition, enthusiastically announced that by its aid, we should be able to hear many sounds in nature which had hitherto remained wholly inaudible.

SHORT CIRCUITING TELEPHONES.

A number of the telephones invented by Mr. Edison may be classed together as short circuiting, or cut out telephones. The principle upon which they act might thus be briefly stated : In vibrating, the diaphragm cuts from the circuit resistances, which

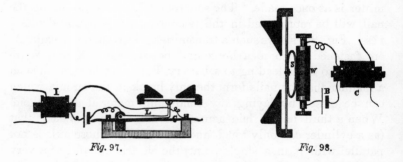

Fig. 97.   *Fig.* 98.

are proportional to the amplitude of the vibrations. A transmitter constructed upon this principle is shown in fig. 97 (devised March 20, 1877). A lever, L, of metal, vibrating in a vertical plane, rests at one end upon a strip of carbonized silk, C, which is part of the primary circuit of the induction coil I. In the course of its vibrations the lever cuts from the circuit parts of the silk, the current passing temporarily through the lever.

Another, acting on the same principle, but differing considerably in construction, is shown in fig. 98 (devised August 21, 1877). A fine wire, W, of high resistance, is wrapped around a cylinder in a spiral groove. The wire forms part of the primary circuit of the coil C. A spring, S, of metal, in the form of an ellipse, is fastened at one side to the diaphragm, while the other side presses against the uninsulated wire upon the cylinder. The diaphragm, in moving toward the right, flattens the spring, making it impinge upon a greater number of convolutions than it would if the motion were in the opposite direction. The resistance of the circuit depends, therefore, upon the position of the centre of the diaphragm. The disadvantage of this arrangement is, that either a whole convolution or none at all is suppressed from the circuit, rendering the current rather more intermittent than pulsatory.

In fig. 99 (devised October 21, 1877), a similar spring rests upon a narrow strip of metal, on the surface of a glass plate.

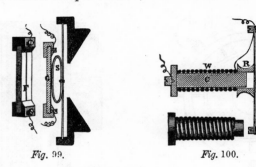

Fig. 99.   *Fig.* 100.

The film is shown in perspective at F, and consists of a fine strip of the silvered surface of a mirror ; the rest of the burnished metal having been removed.

The action of this instrument is similar to that of the instrument shown in fig. 274.

Still another form of short circuiting telephone is shown in fig. 100 (devised Nov. 1, 1877). A spiral spring, W, is wrapped around a cylinder, the diaphragm pressing against the last turn, so that, in vibrating, the convolutions approach or recede from each other. A very slight motion of the diaphragm is sufficient to cause the first few coils to come together ; and, in general, the number of coils that thus touch each other is dependent upon the amplitude of the diaphragm's motion. The wire is included

in the primary circuit of an induction coil, so that the resistance
of the circuit fluctuates as the diaphragm vibrates.   This wire
has also been used as the primary of the induction coil itself
with better results.

CONDENSER TELEPHONES.

Telephones in which static charge, instead of current strength,
is made to vary in unison with the vocal utterances, have also
been tried with success by Mr. Edison.   The forms shown in
figs. 101 and 102 (devised February 9 and December 10, 1877)
differ only in construction, not in principle.

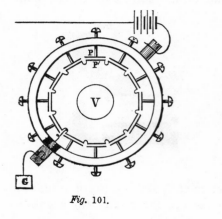
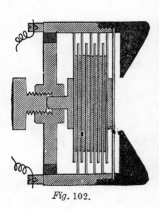

Fig. 101.   *Fig.* 102.

The former consists of a circular vocalizing chamber with
mouth piece at V.   The chamber is surrounded with plates,
which are connected with each other and with the ground.
These plates are free to vibrate, and are shown in the figure in
section, as at P'.   Immediately behind each of these stands a
similar plate as at P, held at its centre by an adjusting screw.
The outside row of plates are electrically connected with each
other and with the battery which goes to line.   When the inside
row of plates vibrates under the influence of a sound, the distance
between the plate varies and changes their static capacity.

In fig. 102 the plates are arranged as in the ordinary form of condenser. An initial pressure is put upon them by a screw bearing in the solid frame of the instrument. The diaphragm, in vibrating, varies the distance between the plates; this alters their static charge and affects also the electric tension of the line.

The resistance of a conductor is dependent upon its shape. If an isometric block of metal be drawn out into a wire, its resistance may be indefinitely increased. This fact lies at the basis of several ingenious telephones invented by Mr. Edison.

The one shown in fig. 103 (devised August 17, 1877) is of exceedingly simple construction. A globule of mercury, M, rests upon a slightly concave plate of metal. A needle from the diaphragm indents its upper surface, and as it vibrates

Fig. 103.   Fig. 104.

slightly alters the shape of the globule. This alteration, though exceedingly small, is sufficient to vary the resistance of the telephonic current considerably.

It is a peculiar characteristic of a globule of mercury that it changes its original shape during the passage of a current through it. Mr. Edison has made an application of this phenomena in the telephone receiver shown in fig. 104 (devised August 19, 1877). The globule of mercury, M, is placed, together with a conducting solution, in a U shaped tube. The currents from a transmitter, passing through the contents of the tube, elongate the mercury. This agitates the liquid and vibrates the float F, which is fastened to the centre of the diaphragm.

THE VOLTAIC PILE TELEPHONE.

We have shown in fig. 105 (devised August 25, 1877) an instrument known as the pile telephone. A piece of cork, K, fastened to the diaphragm, presses upon a strip of platinum which is attached to a plate of copper. The latter is one of the terminal plates of an ordinary voltaic pile. The other terminal plate presses against the metallic frame of the instrument. When the pile is included in a closed telephonic circuit it furnishes a continuous current. The strength of this current depends upon the internal resistance of the pile and its polarization, and these are varied by vibrating the diaphragm.

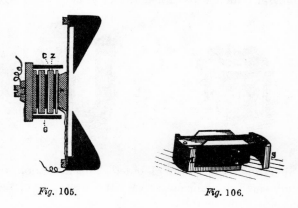

Fig. 105.   *Fig.* 106.

A convenient and peculiar form of receiver used by **Mr. Edison** is shown in fig. 106 (devised August 30, 1877). It is like the ordinary magneto telephone, except that the circular diaphragm is replaced by a strip of thin iron, the edges having been bent so as to render it stiff. We mention it simply because it demonstrates the fact that it is not essential that a circular diaphragm be used.

A novel and purely mechanical telephone is illustrated by fig. 107 (devised August, 1877). In place of a line wire, the illuminating gas contained in gas pipes is used. It is calculated for short distances only, as it is essential that the gas used in communicating offices should be drawn from the same main pipe. In the figure, P is the main pipe. The telephones are represented at T and T′. The instrument is merely a cone fastened by its apex to the gas pipe in place of the burner. The larger end is closed by a thin circular diaphragm. The vibrations are conveyed from one diaphragm to another through the medium of the gas.

The phonograph and telephone, when combined, form an instrument known as the telephonograph, of which fig. 108 (devised August 17, 1877) is a representation. The drum of the phonograph is shown in section. The diaphragm, instead of being vibrated by the voice, is vibrated by the currents which traverse the helix H, and which originate at a distant station.

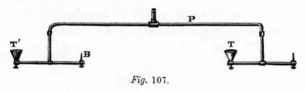

Fig. 107.

The object of the instrument is to obtain a record of what is said at the distant office, which can be converted into sound when desired.

THE MOTOGRAPH.

The motograph receiver, from which we have been accustomed to hear sounds almost destitute of quality, has by a little modification become an articulating telephone.

It works quite well in conjunction with the Edison carbon transmitter. In fig. 109 (the form shown was devised November 23, 1877) the back of the motograph receiver has been removed, showing its construction. Within the drum D is contained the decomposing solution, and the covering surrounding the drum is kept constantly moist by capillary action. A metallic spring attached to the centre of the diaphragm rests upon the drum. While receiving, the drum is revolved by turning the milled screw at A.

Mr. Edison's musical transmitter is shown in fig. 110. The

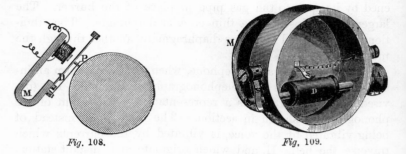

Fig. 108.

Fig. 109.

point P, projecting from the centre of the diaphragm, impinges upon a wrapping of platina foil covering a small drum of rubber, capable of adjustment by a thumb screw.

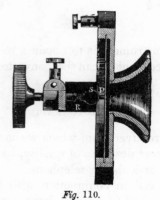

Fig. 110.

THE CARBON RHEOSTAT.

A very important application of the property possessed by semi-conductors, of changing their resistance under varying pressure, is shown in fig. 111. The cuts represent the new Edison carbon rheostat. The instrument is designed to replace the ordinary adjustable rheostats whenever a resistance is to be inserted in a telegraph line, as, for example, in balancing quadruplex circuits, and where accuracy is not required.

Fig. 112 is a vertical section. It shows a hollow cylinder of vulcanite, containing fifty disks of silk that have been saturated with sizing, and well filled with fine plumbago and dried. These are surmounted by a plate of metal, C, which can be raised or lowered by turning the screw D. The carbon disks can thus be

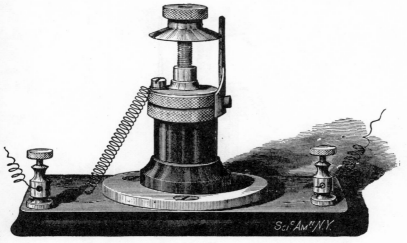

Fig. 111

subjected to any degree of pressure at pleasure. When inserted in the line, it is a matter involving no loss of time to obtain any desired resistance. The resistance can be varied from four hundred to six thousand ohms.

THE MICRO-TASIMETER.

The micro-tasimeter is the outcome of Edison's experiments with his carbon telephone. Having experimented with diaphragms of various thickness, he ascertained that the best results were secured by using the thicker diaphragms. At this stage he experienced a new difficulty. So sensitive was the carbon button to changes of condition, that the expansion of the rubber telephone handle rendered the instrument inarticulate, and finally inoperative. Iron handles were substituted, with a similar result, but with the additional feature of musical and creaky tones distinctly audible in the receiving instrument. These sounds Edison attributed to the movement of the molecules of iron among themselves during expansion. He calls them molecular music. To avoid these disturbances in the

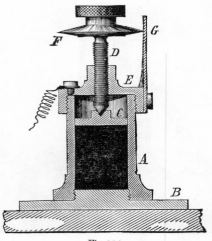

Fig. 112.

telephone, the handle was dispensed with, but it had done a great service in revealing the extreme sensitiveness of the carbon button, and this discovery opened the way for the invention of the new and wonderful instrument.

The micro-tasimeter is represented in perspective in figs. 113 and 114, in section in fig. 115, and the plan upon which it is arranged in the electric circuit is shown in fig. 116.

The instrument consists essentially in a rigid iron frame for holding the carbon button, which is placed between two platinum surfaces, one of which is fixed and the other movable, and in a

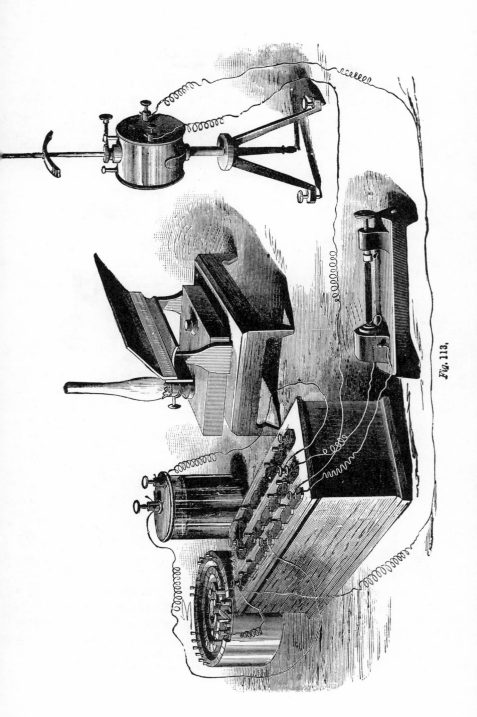

Fig. 113.

device for holding the object to be tested, so that the pressure resulting from the expansion of the object acts upon the carbon button.

Two stout posts, A, B, project from the rigid base piece C. A vulcanite disk, D, is secured to the post A, by the platinum

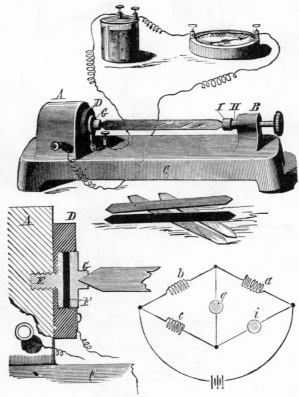

Figs. 114, 115, 116.

headed screw E, the head of which rests in the bottom of a shallow circular cavity in the centre of the disk. In this cavity, and in contact with the head of the screw E, the carbon button F is placed. Upon the outer face of the button there is a disk of platinum foil, which is in electrical communication with the battery. A metallic cup, G, is placed in contact with the platinum disk to receive one end of the strip of whatever material is employed to operate the instrument.

The post B is about four inches from the post A, and contains a screw acted follower, H, that carries a cup, I, between which and the cup G is placed a strip of any substance whose expansibility it is desired to exhibit. The post A is in electrical communication with a galvanometer, and the galvanometer is connected with the battery. The strip of the substance to be tested is put under a small initial pressure, which deflects the galvanometer needle à few degrees from the neutral point. When the needle comes to rest, its position is noted. The slightest subsequent expansion or contraction of the strip will be indicated by the movement of the galvanometer needle. A thin strip of hard rubber, placed in the instrument, exhibits extreme sensitiveness, being expanded by heat from the hand, so as to move through several degrees the needle of a very ordinary galvanometer, which is not affected in the slightest degree by a thermopile facing and near a red hot iron. The hand, in this experiment, is held a few inches from the rubber strip. A strip of mica is sensibly affected by the heat of the hand, and a strip of gelatine, placed in the instrument, is instantly expanded by moisture from a dampened piece of paper held two or three inches away.

For these experiments the instrument is arranged as in fig. 291, but for more delicate operations it is connected with a Thomson's reflecting galvanometer, and the current is regulated by a Wheatstone's bridge and a rheostat, so that the resistance on both sides of the galvanometer is equal, and the light pencil from the reflector falls on 0° of the scale. This arrangement is shown in fig. 290, and the principle is illustrated by the diagram, fig. 293. Here the galvanometer is at g, and the instrument which is at i is adjusted, say, for example, to ten ohms resistance. At a, b and c the resistance is the same. An increase or diminution of the pressure on the carbon button by an infinitesimal expansion or contraction of the substance under test is indicated on the scale of the galvanometer.

The carbon button may be compared to a valve, for, when it is compressed in the slightest degree, its electrical conductivity is increased, and when it is allowed to expand it partly loses its conducting power.

The heat from the hand, held six or eight inches from a strip of vulcanite placed in the instrument—when arranged as last described—is sufficient to deflect the galvanometer mirror so as

Fig. 117.

to throw the light beam completely off the scale. A cold body placed near the vulcanite strip will carry the light beam in the opposite direction.

Pressure that is inappreciable and undiscoverable by other means is distinctly indicated by this instrument.

Mr. Edison proposes to make application of the principle of this instrument to numberless purposes, among which are delicate thermometers, barometers and hygrometers.

Fig. 117 shows in perspective the latest form of the Edison

micro-tasimeter, or measurer of infinitesimal pressure. The value of the instrument lies in its ability to detect small variations of temperature.

This is accomplished indirectly. The change of temperature causes expansion or contraction of a rod of vulcanite, or other material which changes the resistance of an electric circuit, by varying the pressure it exerts upon a carbon button included in the circuit. During the total eclipse of the sun, July 29, 1878, it successfully demonstrated the existence of heat in the corona. It is also of service in ascertaining the relative expansion of substance due to rise of temperature.

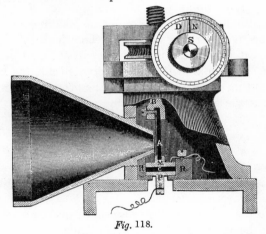

Fig. 118.

In fig. 118 the important parts are represented in section, affording an insight into its construction and mode of operation.

The substance whose expansion is to be measured is shown at A. It is firmly clamped at B, its lower end fitting into a slot in the metal plate M, which rests upon the carbon button. The latter is in an electric circuit, which includes also a delicate galvanometer. Any variation in the length of the rod changes the pressure upon the carbon and alters the resistance of the circuit. This causes a deflection of the galvanometer needle; a movement in one direction denoting expansion of A, while an opposite

motion signifies contraction.   To avoid any deflection which
might arise from change in strength of battery, the tasimeter
is inserted in an arm of the Wheatstone bridge, while the
galvanometer is used in the bridge wire of the same.

In order to ascertain the exact amount of expansion in deci-
mals of an inch, the screw S, seen in front of the dial, is turned
until the deflection previously caused by the change of temperature is reproduced.   The screw works a second screw, causing
the rod to ascend or descend, and the exact distance through
which the rod moves is indicated by the needle N, on the dial.

The instrument can also be advantageously used to measure
changes in the humidity of the atmosphere.   In this case the
strip of vulcanite is replaced by one of gelatine, which changes
its volume by absorbing moisture.   The delicacy of the apparatus to heat is remarkable, and far exceeds that of any other
apparatus.   When adjusted moderately delicate, the heat of the
hand placed in line with the cone of the tasimeter thirty feet distant, causes the spot of light of the galvanometer to leave the
scale.

THE AEROPHONE.

The aerophone, an invention of Mr. Edison's for amplifying
sound, has already attracted considerable attention, though as
yet it has not been perfected.

Its object is to increase the loudness of spoken words without
impairing the distinctness of the articulation.

The working of the instrument is as follows:

The magnified sound proceeds from a large diaphragm, which
is vibrated by steam or compressed air.   The source of power is
controlled by the motion of a second diaphragm vibrating under
the influence of the sound to be magnified.

There are three distinct parts to the instrument:

A source of power.

An instrument to control the power.

A diaphragm vibrating under the influence of the power.

The first of these is usually compressed air, supplied from a

tank. It is necessary that it should be of constant pressure.
The second, shown in section at fig. 119, consists of a diaphragm and mouth piece like those used in the telephone. A
hollow cylinder is attached by a rod to the centre of the diaphragm. The cylinder and its chamber E will, therefore, vibrate

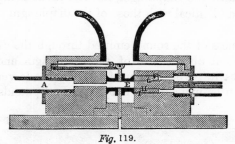

Fig. 119.

with the diaphragm. A downward movement lets the chamber
communicate with the outlet H, an upward movement with the
outlet G. The compressed air enters at A and fills the chamber,
which in its normal position has no outlet. Every downward
vibration of the diaphragm will thus condense the air in the

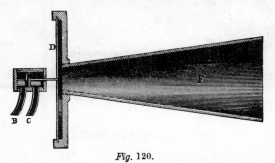

Fig. 120.

pipe C, at the same time allowing the air in B to escape via F.
An upward movement condenses the air in B, but opens I.

The third and last part is shown in section in fig. 120. It
consists of a cylinder and piston, P, like that employed in an
ordinary engine. The piston rod is attached to the centre of a

large diaphragm, D. The pipes C and B are continuations of those designated in fig. 34 by the same letters. The pipe C communicates with one chamber of the cylinder and B with the other. The piston, moving under the influence of the compressed air, moves also the diaphragm, its vibrations being in number and duration identical with those of the diaphragm in the mouth piece.

The loudness of the sound emitted through the directing tube F is dependent on the size of the diaphragm and the power which moves it. The former of them is made very large, and the latter can be increased to many hundred pounds pressure.

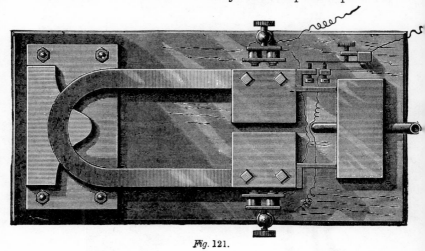

Fig. 121.

THE HARMONIC ENGINE.

This instrument is shown in fig. 121. Mr. Edison claims that ninety per cent. of the power derived from the battery is utilized through its agency. The chief part of the machine is a tuning fork of large dimensions, vibrating about thirty-five times a second, and carrying on each arm a weight of thirty-five pounds. The amplitude of the vibration is about one eighth of an inch, and the vibrations are sustained by means of two very small electro-magnets placed near the end of each arm. These magnets are connected in circuit with each other and with a commutator worked by one of the arms.

Small branches extend from the fork arms into a box containing a miniature pump having two pistons, one attached to each arm. Each stroke of the pump raises a very small quantity of water, but this is compensated for by the rapidity of the strokes. Mr. Edison's proposal is to compress air with the har-

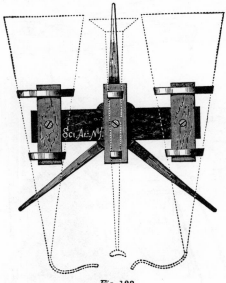

Fig. 122.

monic engine, and use it as a motor for propelling sewing machines and other light machinery. It appears to be considerably in advance of other electric engines, and through its agency electricity may yet become a valuable motive power.

THE MEGAPHONE.

One of the most interesting experiments made by Mr. Edison in his researches on sound is that of conversing through a

Fig. 123.

distance of one and a half to two miles, with no other apparatus than a few paper funnels. These funnels constitute the megaphone, figs. 122 and 123, an instrument wonderful both for its simplicity and effectiveness. The two larger funnels are six feet eight inches long, and twenty-seven and a half inches in diameter at the larger end. They are each provided with a flexible ear tube, the end of which is placed in the ear.

The speaking trumpet in the middle does not differ materially from the ordinary ones. It is a little longer and has a larger bell mouth. With this instrument conversation has been carried on through a distance of one and a half to two miles in an ordinary tone of voice. A low whisper, uttered without using the speaking trumpet, is distinctly audible at a distance of a thousand feet, and walking through grass and weeds may be heard at a much greater distance.

Mr. Edison is experimenting upon an apparatus for the benefit of the deaf. The results thus far have been quite satisfactory, and he hopes soon to have a practical apparatus for introduction to the public. The principal drawback at present is the large size of the apparatus.

NEW STETHOSCOPIC MICROPHONE.

By means of this apparatus of MM. Ducretet & Co., of Paris, the feeblest pulsations of the heart, pulse and arteries may be heard in several telephones placed in circuit. It is a very delicate instrument, and exquisitely sensitive, and this is its fault, if it has any.

Two tambours, such as devised by M. Mavey, are coupled to a microphone (fig. 124); one of these, T, acts, through the medium of the india rubber tube which unites them, upon the tambour T, and, consequently, on the lever microphone L, the sensitiveness of which can be regulated by the counterpoise P O. The microphone terminates in a pencil, C, formed of retort carbon or of plumbago, which rests on a disk of the same material fixed on the receiving tambour. The whole forms a complete circuit, in which is a Daniell or Leclanché battery of one to three elements, and the telephones through which are heard the pulsation from the searching tambour T.

This microphone is susceptible of modification, and will undoubtedly be the means of more extended physiological observations. By substituting a small funnel for the tambour T, speech may be transmitted.

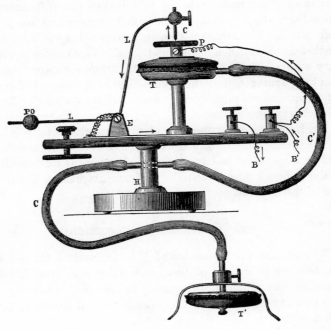

Fig. 124.

Mr. Edison, in his telephonic experiments, discovered that the vibrations of the vocal organs were capable of producing considerable dynamic effect. Acting on this hint, he began experiments on a phonomoter, or instrument for measuring the mechanical force of sound waves produced by the human voice. In the course of these experiments he constructed the machine shown in fig. 125, which exhibits the dynamic force of the voice. The instrument has a diaphragm and mouth piece similar to a phonograph. A spring, which is secured to the bed piece, rests on a piece of rubber tubing placed against the diaphragm. This spring carries a pawl that acts on a ratchet or roughened wheel on the fly wheel shaft. A sound made in the mouth piece creates vibrations in the diaphragm, which are sufficient to propel the fly wheel with considerable velocity. It requires a surprising amount of pressure on the fly wheel shaft to stop the machine while a continuous sound is made in the mouth piece.

We have already referred, on page 36 and elsewhere, to the later improvements made by Mr. Edison in the carbon telephone. The subject, however, has by no means been exhausted, and we, therefore, return to its reconsideration the more willingly now, as the opportunity thus afforded enables us to say a few words also in regard to the improved magneto telephones which Mr. Phelps constructs for working in connection with the carbon transmitter.

The continued use of these improved transmitters, in a practical way, for a number of months past, has shown them to be the best adapted of any of the forms now in use for real effective service ; and if the necessary use of a battery in connection with them is, after all, so much of an inconvenience as some would imagine, their rapid introduction, in spite of this fact, and to the exclusion of other instruments, is sufficient evidence that the above mentioned drawback is fully compensated for by corresponding advantages in other directions.

On page 36 it has been stated that in the more recent forms of the carbon telephone Mr. Edison had done away with the vibrating diaphragm altogether, replacing the same by an inflexible plate of metal, whose sole function was to collect and concentrate a larger portion of the sonorous waves upon the limited carbon surface.

This form of transmitter is shown in fig. 126. The prepared carbon, represented at C, is contained in a hard rubber block, open clear through, so that one side of the former is made to

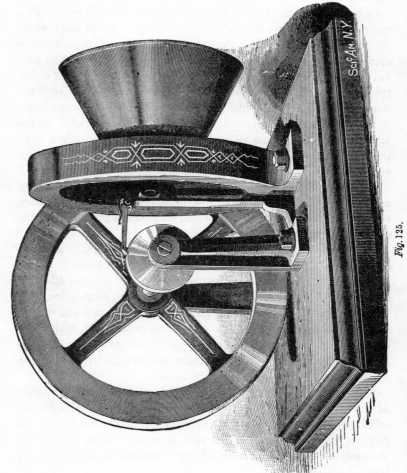

Fig. 125.

rest upon the metallic part of the frame which forms one of the connections of the circuit. The opposite side of the carbon is covered with a circular piece of platinum foil, P, which leads to a binding post insulated from the frame, and forming the other connection for placing the instrument in circuit. A glass disk, G, upon which is placed a projecting knob, A, of aluminum, is glued to the foil; and the diaphragm D, connecting with the knob, serves, when spoken against, to communicate the resulting pressure to the carbon. A substantial metallic frame surrounds the carbon and its connections, and their complete protection against injury, to which they are liable from careless handling, is thereby secured.

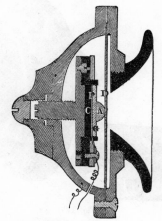

Fig. 126.

The same instrument, in perspective, is shown in fig. 127, mounted upon a projecting arm with a joint at each end, only one of which, however, is shown in the cut. The lower end of the arm is secured by means of the joints to a desk shown in fig. 128, and thus, as will readily be seen—the motion being in a vertical direction — permits of placing the telephone in a convenient position for speaking purposes, and, consequently, rendering it easily adapted for the accommodation of persons of various heights.

The Edison telephone, it should be distinctly understood, relies wholly upon the battery for its power, and not upon the voice, as is the case with other telephones. Consequently, it is unnecessary to shout into the apparatus, and thus destroy the privacy of conversation. All that is required is that the words should be spoken distinctly and in an ordinary tone of voice.

One great drawback to the universal introduction of the telephone, that has thus far been experienced, is the disturbing influence of current pulsations in neighboring conductors when the latter are in use, and which produces a rattling noise within the telephone. This phenomenon, to which we have before

Fig. 127.

referred, under the head of induction, page 23, and elsewhere, is effectually overcome by using the Edison telephone, as the power of this instrument is so great that it can be operated with perfect success on lines having the greatest amount of inductive action, and where no other form could be used.

Figs. 129 and 130 represent two forms of the magneto telephone, as devised by Mr. Phelps, which give surprisingly good results, both when used singly and in combination with the Edison transmitter. In shape they somewhat resemble a single and double crown, and owing to this fact, have been designated respectively single and double crown instruments.

The single crown telephone, fig. 129, is composed of the ordinary diaphragm, electro-magnet, or soft iron pole piece, and several steel bars that have previously been rendered permanently magnetic. Six (being the usual number) of these permanent magnets, bent into a circular form, are used in this instrument in place of the single magnet employed in other magneto telephones. These have their like poles joined to one end of the core which carries the magnetizing helix, and radiate from it in

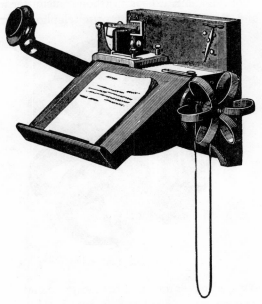

Fig. 128.

as many different directions. The opposite poles are joined to the periphery of the diaphragm, which is contained in a polished case of hard rubber, and faces the free end of the soft iron core.

The double crown instrument is shown in fig. 130, and, as will be seen, consists of two single crown telephones joined together, with a common vocalizing chamber between them. The coils on each of the cores are connected in such a way that the currents generated in them, when the diaphragms are made to vibrate, mutually strengthen each other, or, when used in combination with the Edison transmitter, that the action of the pulsating current in each coil contributes to a single result, and thus enhances the effectiveness of the apparatus.

Some idea of the performance of these improved instruments will be conveyed by mentioning the results obtained at a recent exhibition of them in the Sunday school room of Dr. Wells' church, Brooklyn. Mr. Edison's carbon transmitter was used for sending and Mr. Phelps' single crown telephone for receiving.

Fig. 129.

The sound was also reënforced at the receiving end by the use of a large paper cone, whose smaller extremity was held to the mouth piece of the instrument. The circuit extended from the residence of Dr. Wells, near the church, to the lecture room. Speech from the telephone was distinctly heard in all parts of the room by an audience of about three hundred persons, while the singing of a vocal quartette, solo singing, and guitar playing were transmitted with surprising clearness and loudness. It should be observed, moreover, that the performance in this case was very different from the so called musical telephones, by means of which only the pitch and rhythm of the notes are distinguished, the tone always resembling that of a penny trumpet. In this instance, the quality of the tone, which is the real life of music, was exactly reproduced. This is one of the characteristics of the magneto telephone — everything is faithfully reproduced. Dr. Wells addressed the audience from his parlors through the telephone, and not only was he clearly understood, but his voice was also instantly recognized.

Fig. 131 shows a convenient way of arranging the telephone

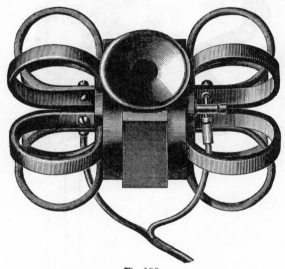

Fig. 130.

apparatus for shop, counting room, and various other purposes. An Edison carbon telephone jointed to a projecting arm, so as to be capable of movement in different directions to suit the operator, serves as the transmitter, and the Phelps crown instrument as the receiver, the call being given by an ordinary telegraph sounder and a key for interrupting the circuit.

The switch shown at the back serves for putting the telephone in and out of circuit. The small induction coil used with the apparatus is placed beneath the desk and in a position where it is not liable to damage.   When the switch is turned as represented in the cut, the apparatus is in the proper condition for speaking purposes.   When it is turned to the opposite buttons, which is its normal position when not in use, the telephones are cut out of circuit, the sounder, battery and key alone being then included.   By depressing the key now, which in the normal position keeps the circuits closed through a back contact, the battery current is interrupted and the sounder armature released,

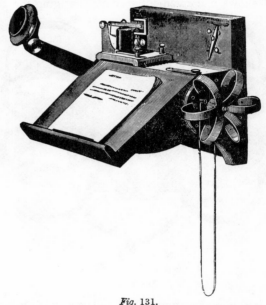

Fig. 131.

thus furnishing the call, to indicate that telephonic communication is desired.

It will be understood, of course, that the same battery is used both for signalling and talking purposes.   In the former case the battery current traverses the line and produces the signal directly, while in the latter it merely passes through the telephone and primary wire of the induction coil and the induced currents, produced in the secondary coil by the variations of the battery current when the telephone is spoken into, traverses the line and produces the articulation heard in the receiver at the distant station. This apparatus, mounted as in fig. 131, is much used, in fact, almost universally, in the merchants' exchange system, to which we shall refer presently.

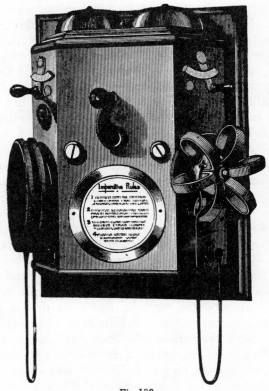

Fig. 132.

The form of call here shown, however, is intended only for short lines, as the current from the small battery employed would not be sufficiently powerful to operate a sounder placed some miles away. For long lines the magneto machine is used to generate the call currents. The combination shown in fig. 132, and which contains a machine of this kind, is somewhat similar in arrangement to the one given on page 27, but of a more improved pattern. The call bell and duplex telephone are the same, and the principal difference consists only in the arrangement of circuit connections, within the box, and in the addition of the single crown instrument, by which greater effectiveness is obtained. The switch at the upper right hand side of the box is used to put the apparatus in and out of circuit, as desired, while that on the left serves for connecting or disconnecting the bell magnets. When placed as represented in the figure, the latter is in circuit, and will cause the bell to ring both at the home and distant stations, if the button marked C is pushed in repeatedly, while the crank shown in front, and which operates the magneto machine, is turned at the same time.

Fig. 133 represents the same form of call box, with an Edison transmitter attached to replace the duplex instrument in the combination just described. The internal connections are the same in both, so that it will be unnecessary to describe them again.

Fig. 134 shows a call box, devised by Mr. Gray, and much used in the Western States in combination with the bipolar telephone.

A still later form has been arranged by Mr. Phelps. This also contains the magneto call apparatus and switch connections of the combinations referred to above, and in addition to these it is provided with an ingenious device, first suggested and applied by Mr. Henry Bentley, of Philadelphia, by means of which the carbon telephone, and, consequently, the battery also, is cut out of circuit at all times, except when actually in use for transmitting purposes. This device consists of a small spring placed on top of the handle of the instrument, or at the side, as the case may be, and which, in its normal position, keeps the telephone circuit disconnected, but immediately establishes it whenever the handle is grasped by the hand, being then pressed down upon the contact button, and thus allowing the battery current to pass through the telephone and primary wire of the induction coil. As the result of this arrangement, Mr.

Bentley has been enabled to introduce the Leclanché battery for speaking purposes in the telephone system, in place of the gravity battery heretofore used, and thereby has paved the way for greatly reducing the expense of maintenance in larger systems, like that of which we intend to speak directly, as the

Fig. 133.

consumption of battery material may be reduced to a minimum at the outset and no expense need be incurred for attendance, except at very long intervals. Altogether this seems to be the most economical and practical combination that has yet been brought out, and its very general introduction would appear to be all but assured.

CHAPTER VII.

THE Talking Phonograph, invented by Mr. Thomas A. Edison, is a purely mechanical invention, no electricity being used. It is, however, somewhat allied to the telephone, for, like the latter, its action depends upon the vibratory motions of a metallic diaphragm, capable of receiving from and transmitting to the air sound vibrations.

The term phonograph, or sound-recorder, includes, besides Mr. Edison's, a large number of instruments, which, though they are not able to reproduce sound, are capable of graphically representing it.

Before treating of these instruments, it might be well to recall what has been said in an earlier part of this work on the nature of sound.

Bearing in mind that sound is and has for its origin motion, we will see that a vibrating body, situated in an elastic medium like our atmosphere, becomes the central source of a peculiar form of action, which is ever propagated outward. This is known as wave motion, and if the number of vibrations causing it be within certain limits, the wave motion becomes perceptible to the ear, and is called sound.

Any change in the original vibrations will cause a change in the nature of the sound emitted. Thus, if their amplitude be increased, the sound becomes louder, and can be heard at a greater distance, or, in other words, intensity is dependent on the extent of the vibrations.

Again, should the number of vibrations in equal portions of time be varied, the note will rise or fall in the musical scale; or, pitch depends on the number of vibrations occurring in a given time.

A third and, in this connection, more important characteristic of sound is that, while an unchanging fundamental tone is emitted, other and more rapid vibrations may accompany it, on the same principle that the surface of large ocean waves is covered with smaller and independent ripples.   It is the accompaniment and predominance of certain of these harmonics, as they are called, that gives to a note that peculiar property whereby it may be distinguished from another of equal intensity and pitch.   This characteristic is often called the timbre or color of the note, but is known equally well as its quality.

The human voice is the most perfect of all musical instruments.   Certain parts of its mechanism can at will be thrown into vibration, and these vibrations can be varied in amplitude and number at pleasure.   Associated with the apparatus for effecting this, is a hollow cavity, which serves, as does the resonant chamber of an organ pipe, to reinforce the sound.   The shape of this cavity may be so varied that it will resound to vibrations of any pitch.   By means of this latter power we are able to produce the vowel sounds.   Accompanying the original vibrations are others which are multiples of it, and it is by reinforcing one or more of these that the quality of each vowel is secured.   Thus the forcible expulsion of air from the mouth may give rise to articulate speech or sounds, whose shadings and degrees of loudness vary with the number and pressure of the resulting impulses, and also with the degree of suddenness with which they commence and terminate.

So rapid are the vibrations of a body when emitting a sound, that the eye and ear cannot discern all the phenomena which accompany them.   This has led students of acoustics to devise means of representing graphically the movements which the sounding body undergoes; and it is through the study of these drawings that much of our knowledge of the nature of sound has been obtained.

One of the simplest ways of producing what we shall hereafter call the record of a sound is to draw a vibrating tuning fork over a sheet of paper, so that a pencil attached to one prong of the fork shall leave behind it a waving line, as shown in fig. 134.

With this crude arrangement the energy is wasted in over-coming friction, and the fork soon comes to rest. To lessen the friction it is usual to employ paper covered with a layer of lampblack. Instead of the pencil is substituted a small pointed bristle,

Fig. 134.

the weight of which is so slight that it will not modify the motion of the prong. With very little force the black can be removed, leaving a white line on a dark ground.

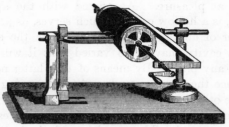

Fig. 135.

The use of a revolving cylinder, around which the paper is wrapped, early suggested itself, and in the hands of Duhamel the apparatus assumed the form shown in fig. 135. The axis upon which the drum revolves is a screw, which turns in a fixed nut,

Fig. 136.

causing the drum to advance at each revolution through the distance between two consecutive turns of the thread, which is sufficient to prevent one portion of the record from being super-placed upon that which precedes it. Fig. 136 shows the paper after it has been removed from the cylinder and spread out. The dots, a, b, c, etc., are made by a clock which usually accompanies the apparatus. The distance between them represents the duration of one second. The amplitude and peculiar character of each vibration are clearly shown, and to ascertain the rate of vibration it is only necessary to count the number of undulations between two consecutive dots.

Devices have also been made by König, with which the resultant vibrations arising from two or more notes emitted simultaneously may be recorded directly from the vibrating bodies.

The phonograph invented by M. Léon Scott does not require that tracing shall be made at the place where the sound originates, but wherever it can be heard. It consists of a hollow chamber, made sufficiently large to respond to sounds of the lowest audible pitch, mounted before a cylinder, similar to that shown in fig. 135. One end of this resonator is left open, and the other is terminated by a ring, on which is fixed an elastic membrane. The air within the resonator is easily thrown into vibration, which is shared by the membrane. The latter carries a stylus, which also participates in the motion, and records it upon the blackened paper. The human voice, the tones from musical instruments, and even the rumbling of distant thunder are thus graphically presented on paper.

For recording vocal impulses one of the most sensitive instruments is the logograph, invented by W. H. Barlow, F. R. S.

The pressure of the air in speaking is directed against a membrane, which vibrates and carries with it a delicate marker, which traces a line on a travelling ribbon. The excursions of the tracer are great or small from the base line which represents the quiet membrane, according to the force of the impulse, and are prolonged according to the duration of the pressure, different articulate sounds varying greatly in length as well as in intensity ; another great difference in them also consists in the relative abruptness of the rising and falling inflections, which makes curves of various shapes. The smoothness or ruggedness of a sound has thus its own graphic character, independent both of its actual intensity and its length. The logograph consists of a small speaking trumpet, having an ordinary mouth-piece connected to a tube, the other end of which is widened out and covered with a thin membrane of gold beater's skin or gutta percha. A spring presses slightly against the membrane, and has a light arm of aluminium, which carries the marker, consisting of a small sable brush inserted in a glass tube containing a colored liquid. An endless strip of paper is

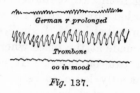

German r prolonged

Trombone

oo in mood

Fig. 137.

caused to travel beneath the pencil, and is marked with an irregular curved line, the elevations and depressions of which correspond to the force, duration and other characteristics of the vocal impulses. The lines thus traced exhibit remarkable uniformity when the same phrases are successively pronounced.

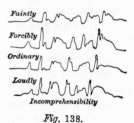

Faintly

Forcibly

Ordinary

Loudly

Incomprehensibility

Fig. 138.

Fig. 137 shows curves obtained by the interposition of a light lever between the membrane and the smoked glass, which is drawn along beneath the style, whose excursions are much magnified by the lever. The curves show respectively the tongue trill or German r prolonged, the mark produced by the sound of a trombone, and by the sound of oo in mood.

Fig. 138 shows a tracing from the utterance of the word incomprehensibility, with different degrees of effort. It will be noticed that while a certain variation occurs, due to the energy, each sound preserves a specific character.

Fig. 139 shows in the upper portion the effect of words of quantity which require a large volume of air, and are maintained a relatively longer time than the more explosive or intense kind.

The lower diagram is what the tracer wrote when the familiar stanza from Hohenlinden was repeated.

A much more delicate instrument for recording sonorous

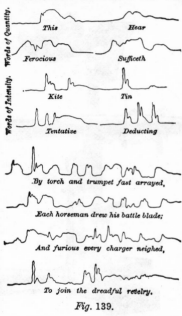

Fig. 139.

vibrations has been made by using the membrana tympani of the human ear as a logograph. This is represented in fig. 140.

The stapes was removed, and a short stylus of hay substituted, of about the same weight, so as to increase the amplitude of the vibrations and afford means of obtaining tracings upon smoked glass, as in the logograph experiments. The membrane is kept moist by a mixture of glycerine and water, and the specimen attached to a perpendicular bar sliding in an upright post, and

moved by a ratchet wheel.   To the upright is attached, horizontally, a metallic stage six inches in length, upon which slides a
carriage with a glass plate, and having a regular movement given
to it by wheel and cord.   A bell-shaped mouth-piece is inserted
in the external auditory meatus and luted in position.

The vibrations of the membrane, due to a musical tone sounded
in the bell, may be observed by means of a ray of light thrown

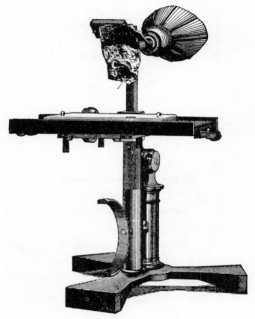

Fig. 140.

upon small specula of foil attached to the malleus, incus, or to
different portions of the membrana tympani, or may be recorded
on smoked glass by a stylus fastened to the descending process
of the malleus or incus by means of glue, in a line with the long
axis of the process, and extending downward, so as to reach the
plate of smoked glass, which is moved at a right angle to the
excursion of the stylus; the latter then traces a wave line cor-

responding to the character and pitch of the musical tone sounded into the ear.

As the glass plates present plane surfaces, and as the point of the vibrating style sweeps through the segment of a circle, the curves obtained are apt to be discontinuous, especially when the amplitude is great. To obviate this difficulty a sheet of glass is employed, having a curved surface, the concavity being presented to the stylus. The sheet of glass is a section of a cylinder whose semi-diameter is equivalent to the length of the style. In this way the point of the stylus never leaves the surface of the glass, and the curve resulting from its vibration is continuous. The carbon film is preserved by pouring collodion upon it. As soon as this is dry, the film may be floated off with water, and placed upon a plane sheet of glass, or upon paper, and varnished in the ordinary way.

Numerous other methods of rendering sound-vibrations visible to the eye might be cited. In general these methods are of two kinds. They either aim at producing a lasting record on paper, glass, etc., which may be preserved and examined at leisure, or they present to the eye in a vivid way the sound vibrations as they are actually transpiring. Of the latter class, one devised by König deserves a passing notice. A hollow chamber is divided by a thin membrane of caoutchouc into two compartments : one of which communicates through a tube to the mouth-piece, in front of which the sounds are generated; the other is supplied from a pipe with ordinary coal gas, which issues from the compartment through a fine burner, where it is ignited. Any motion of the diaphragm will change the pressure on the gas, and either lengthen or shorten the jet. The movements of the flame when viewed directly are scarcely perceptible. To render them distinct, they are received on a four-sided mirror, which is made to revolve. The image of the flame is thus lengthened out into a luminous band. When the membrane vibrates, the upper edge of the band becomes serrated, each elevation being due to one sound-vibration.

The instruments thus far described, while able to produce

records undoubtedly correct, could go no farther. The records thus made suggested no way of reproducing the sound. Nor was this effected until Mr. Edison produced his wonderful talking phonograph.

In its simplest form the talking phonograph consists of a mounted diaphragm (fig. 141), so arranged as to operate a small steel stylus placed just below and opposite its centre, and a brass cylinder, six or more inches long by three or four in diameter, which is mounted on a horizontal axis, extending, each way, beyond its ends for a distance about equal to its own length.

A spiral groove is cut in the circumference of the cylinder from one end to the other, each spire of the groove being separated from its neighbor by about one tenth of an inch. The

Fig. 141.

shaft, or axis, is also cut by a screw thread corresponding to the spiral groove of the cylinder, and works in screw bearings; consequently, when the cylinder is caused to revolve by means of a crank that is fitted to the axis for the purpose, it receives a forward or backward movement of about one tenth of an inch for every turn of the same—the direction, of course, depending upon the way the crank is turned. The diaphragm is supported by an upright casting capable of adjustment (fig. 142), and so arranged that it may be removed altogether when necessary; when in use, however, it is clamped in a fixed position above or in front of the cylinder, thus bringing the stylus always opposite the groove as the cylinder is turned. A small flat spring attached to the casting

extends underneath the diaphragm as far as its centre, and carries the stylus; and between the diaphragm and spring a small
piece of india rubber is placed to modify the action, it having
been found that better results are obtained by this means than
when the stylus is rigidly attached to the diaphragm itself. The
action of the apparatus will now be readily understood from
what follows. The cylinder is first very smoothly covered with
tinfoil, and the diaphragm securely fastened in place by clamping its support to the base of the instrument. When this has
been properly done, the stylus should lightly press against that
part of the foil over the groove. The crank is now turned,
while, at the same time, some one speaks into the mouth-piece of

Fig. 142.

the instrument, which will cause the diaphragm to vibrate; and,
as the vibrations of the latter correspond with the movements of
the air producing them, the soft and yielding foil will become
marked along the line of the groove by a series of indentations
of different depths, varying with the amplitude of the vibrations
of the diaphragm; or, in other words, with the inflections or
modulations of the speaker's voice. These inflections may, therefore, be looked upon as a sort of visible speech, which, in fact,
they really are. If now the diaphragm is removed by loosening
the clamp, and the cylinder then turned back to the starting

point, we have only to replace the diaphragm and turn in the same direction as at first to hear repeated all that has been spoken into the mouth-piece of the apparatus, the stylus, by this means, being caused to traverse its former path; and, consequently, rising and falling with the depressions in the foil, its motion is communicated to the diaphragm, and thence through the intervening air to the ear, where the sensation of sound is produced.

As the faithful reproduction of a sound is, in reality, nothing more than a reproduction of similar acoustic vibrations in a given time, it at once becomes evident that the cylinder should be made to revolve with absolute uniformity at all times, otherwise a difference, more or less marked, between the original sound and the reproduction will become manifest. To secure this uniformity of motion, and produce a practically working machine for automatically recording speeches, vocal and instrumental music, and perfectly reproducing the same, the inventor has devised an apparatus in which a plate replaces the cylinder. This plate, which is ten inches in diameter, has a volute spiral groove cut in its surface, on both sides, from its centre to within one inch of its outer edge. An arm, guided by the spiral upon the under side of the plate, carries a diaphragm and mouth-piece at its extreme end. If the arm be placed near the centre of the plate, and the latter rotated, the motion will cause the arm to follow the spiral outward to the edge. A spring and train of wheel-work regulated by a friction-governor, serves to give uniform motion to the plate. The sheet upon which the record is made is of tinfoil. This is fastened to a paper frame, made by cutting a nine-inch disk from a square piece of paper of the same dimensions as the plate. Four pins upon the plate pass through corresponding eyelet-holes punched in the four corners of the paper when the latter is laid upon it, and thus secure accurate registration, while a clamping-frame hinged to the plate fastens the foil and its paper frame securely to the latter. The mechanism is so arranged that the plate may be started and stopped instantly, or its motion reversed at will, thus giving the greatest convenience to both speaker and copyist.

Mr. Edison has found that the clearness of the instrument's articulation depends considerably upon the size and shape of the opening in the mouth-piece.   When words are spoken against the whole diaphragm, the hissing sounds, as in shall, fleece, etc., are lost.   These sounds are rendered clearly when the hole is small and provided with sharp edges, or when made in the form of a slot surrounded by artificial teeth.

Beside tinfoil other metals have been used.   Impressions have been made upon sheets of copper, and even upon soft iron. With the copper foil the instrument spoke with sufficient force to be heard at a distance of two hundred and seventy-five feet in the open air.

By using a form of pantograph, Prof. A. M. Mayer has obtained magnified tracings on smoked glass of the record on the

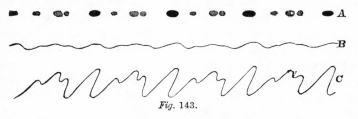

Fig. 143.

foil.   The apparatus he used consisted of a delicate lever, on the under side of which is a point, made as nearly as possible like the point under the thin iron plate in the phonograph.   Cemented to the end of the longer arm of this lever is a pointed slip of thin copper foil, which just touches the vertical surface of a smoked glass plate.   The point on the short arm of the lever rests in the furrow, in which are the depressions and elevations made in the foil on the cylinder.   Rotating the cylinder with a slow and uniform motion, while the plate of glass is slid along, the point of copper foil scrapes the lampblack off the smoked glass plate and traces on it the magnified profile of the depressions and elevations in the foil on the cylinder.   In fig. 143, A represents the appearance to the eye of the impressions on the foil, when the sound of *a* in *bat* is sung against the iron plate of the phonograph. B is the magnified profile of these impressions on the smoked glass obtained as just described. C gives the appearance of König's flame when the same sound is sung quite close to its membrane. It will be seen that the profile of the impressions made on the phonograph, and the contours of the flames of König, when vibrated by the same compound sound, bear a close resemblance.

Mr. Mayer finds that the form of the trace obtained from a point attached to a membrane vibrating under the influence of a compound sound, depends on the distance of the source of the sound from the membrane, and the same compound sound will form an infinite number of different traces as the distance of its place of origin from the membrane is gradually increased; for, as you increase this distance, the waves of the components of the compound sound are made to strike on the membrane at different periods of their swings. For example, if the compound sound is formed of six harmonics, the removal of the source of the sonorous vibrations, from the membrane to a distance equal to $\frac{1}{4}$ of a wave length of the 1st harmonic, will remove the 2d, 3d, 4th, 5th and 6th harmonics to distances from the membrane equal, respectively, to $\frac{1}{2}$, $\frac{3}{4}$, 1, $1\frac{1}{4}$ and $1\frac{1}{2}$ wave-lengths. The consequence evidently is, that the resultant wave-form is entirely changed by this motion of the source of the sound, though the sonorous sensation of the compound sound remains unchanged. This is readily proved experimentally by sending a constant compound sound into the cone of König's apparatus, while we gradually lengthen the tube between the mouth-piece and the membrane.

The articulation and quality of the phonograph, although not yet perfect, is full as good as the telephone was six months ago. The instrument, when perfected and moved by clock work, will undoubtedly reproduce every condition of the human voice, including the whole world of expression in speech and song. The sheet of tinfoil or other plastic material receiving the impressions of sound will be stereotyped or electrotyped, so as to be multiplied and made durable; or the cylinder will be made of a material plastic when used, and hardening afterward. Thin sheets of papier-maché, or of various substances which soften by heat, would be of this character. Having provided thus for the durability of the phonograph plate, it will be very easy to make it separable from the cylinder producing it, and attachable to a corresponding cylinder anywhere and at any time. There will doubtless be a standard of diameter and pitch of screw for phonograph cylinders. Friends at a distance will then send to each other phonograph letters, which will talk at any time in the friend's voice when put upon the instrument. How startling, also, it will be to reproduce and hear at pleasure the voice of the dead! All of these things are to be common, every-day experiences within a few years. It will be possible a generation hence to take a file of phonograph letters, spoken at different ages by the same person, and hear the early prattle, the changing voice, the manly tones, and also the varying manner and moods of the speaker—so expressive of character—from childhood up!

These are some of the private applications. For public uses, we shall have galleries where phonograph sheets will be preserved as photographs and books now are. The utterances of great speakers and singers will there be kept for a thousand years. In these galleries spoken languages will be preserved from century to century with all peculiarities of pronunciation, dialect or brogue. As we go now to see the stereopticon, we shall go to public halls to hear these treasures of speech and song brought out and reproduced as loud, or louder, than when first spoken or sung by the truly great ones of earth. Certainly, within a dozen years, some of the great singers will be induced to sing into the ear of the phonograph, and the electrotyped cylinders thence obtained will be put into the hand organs of the streets, and we shall hear the actual voice of Christine Nilsson or Miss Cary ground out at every corner.

In public exhibitions, also, we shall have reproductions of the sounds of nature, and of noises familiar and unfamiliar. Nothing will be easier than to catch the sounds of the waves on the beach, the roar of Niagara, the discords of the streets, the noises of animals, the puffing and rush of the railroad train, of the rolling thunder, or even the tumult of a battle.

When popular airs are sung into the phonograph and the notes are then reproduced in reverse order, very curious and beautiful musical effects are oftentimes produced, having no apparent resemblance to those contained in their originals. The instrument may thus be used as a sort of musical kaleidoscope, by means of which an infinite variety of new combinations may be produced from the musical compositions now in existence.

The talking phonograph will doubtless be applied to bell-punches, clocks, complaint boxes in public conveyances, and to toys of all kinds. It will supersede the shorthand writer in taking letters by dictation, and in the taking of testimony before referees. Phonographic letters will be sent by mail, the foil being wound on paper cylinders of the size of a finger. It will recite poems in the voice of the author, and reproduce the speeches of celebrated orators. Dramas will be produced in which all the parts will be "well spoken—with good accent and good discretion;" the original matrice being prepared on one machine provided with a rubber tube having several mouth-pieces: and Madame Tussaud's figures will hereafter talk, as well as look, like their great prototypes!

CHAPTER VIII.

THE TELEPHONE EXCHANGE.

A marked impetus was given to the already widely extended and continually increasing application of the telephone to business and domestic purposes, by the establishment of the Telephone Exchange—a system of telephone correspondence carried on through a central office, by means of wires radiating from it to the houses, offices, counting rooms, etc., of the subscribers to the exchange, a separate wire, as a general thing, being used for each subscriber, who is also provided with a list of all the other subscribers to the system, and when, at any time, desiring to communicate with any one of them, has merely to notify the central office, and the two corresponding wires are immediately connected, and direct correspondence is established. Attendants, sufficiently numerous, are kept on duty at the central office to attend to the switching, and to keep everything in proper working condition.

The central offices are equipped with switch boards similar in construction and operation to those employed in telegraph offices. In the beginning, simple devices answered the requirements of the service, but, in the larger cities, as the number of subscribers increased, these simple devices became inadequate, and new and more complicated ones had to be devised. The various exchanges were owned and managed by distinct organizations, and each one sought to solve the problem of providing a perfect exchange system in his own way, and, as a natural consequence, when the telephone exchanges in this country alone had increased to upward of seven hundred, the number of distinct types had become very large.

We propose to describe each of the distinctive varieties which the evolution of the system has thus far produced, in order to facilitate the creation and adoption of a thoroughly practical and perfect system. In doing this, we shall make no attempt to describe the various types by the order of their invention or efficiency, but so far as practicable, by their distinctive characteristics. We shall begin by describing the past and present telephone systems of Paris.

THE GOWER SYSTEM.

In 1880 there were two telephone companies in Paris, one using the Gower telephone, the other the Edison. A third company introduced the Blake transmitter, but was soon con-

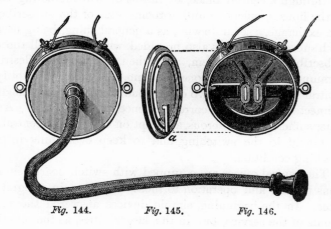

Fig. 144.   Fig. 145.   Fig. 146.

solidated with the Gower Company, who were the first to introduce telephonic communication in Paris. The Gower telephone, of which an exterior view and sections are shown in Figs. 144, 145 and 146 of the annexed engravings, requires no battery, as the currents for transmission of sound are generated by the instrument, and it is provided with a peculiarly arranged magnet, by means of which a sound resembling that of a trumpet can be produced for signaling. Each subscriber was provided with a telephone connected with the main central office by means of an insulated wire, which was laid underground. A great difficulty was experienced in insulating the wires sufficiently to avoid the effects of induction. When several wires ran in the same direction they were united in a cable, and the covering of the wires was of different colors, so that a wire could be traced very readily in case of accidents. At the central office the cable was separated, and each wire was conducted to its special office connection. To better explain the operation of this telephone system, we will describe it in action. Each sub-

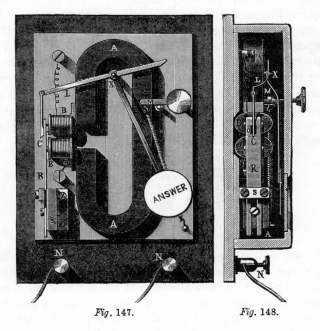

Fig. 147.   Fig. 148.

scriber is known by a certain number. Assuming that **No. 5** desires to communicate with another subscriber, he gives the signal by blowing into the tube of his telephone.

The Gower Company, desiring to maintain the simplicity of the instrument, adopted a signaling device invented by Mr. Ader. It is illustrated in Figs. 147 and 148. A is the magnet of a telephone, and the subscriber's wire communicates with the bobbins, B B. R is the vibratory tongue, fixed at its lower end. The signal consists of a white disk with the word 'Answer' printed on it, and it may also bear the number of the corresponding subscriber. This disk is attached to a pivoted lever, which can be locked in an inclined position, so as to keep the disk out of sight by means of a rod attached to it and terminating in a triangular stud, which passes into a slot in the upper end of the vibratory tongue, R. The signal disk will drop until its lever arm is perpendicular, when released by the vibration of the tongue, R, and it will then be visible through an opening in the box of the apparatus. When the sound signal is given the plate, R, vibrates, and at each vibration the triangular stud, C, will slip out of the slot in the plate a very short distance and finally leave it altogether when the disk shows. The sound signal is required to operate this visible signal, as the vibrations produced by the ordinary speaking are not powerful enough to operate this mechanism.

Fig. 149.

A call bell is sometimes arranged so as to sound when the disk drops, and it is of great service in case the switchman is not at his post, as it calls attention to the fact that he is wanted. Generally, six signaling devices are arranged in one box, as shown in Fig. 149, and the signal box with the call bell is arranged above the switch, as shown in Fig. 150.

The subscribers' wires are arranged in groups of about thirty, those persons communicating with each other very frequently being united in one group. Each switchman has charge of a signal box and switch, represented in Fig. 150, which shows only ten subscribers, whereas there are twenty to thirty or more in each division, as before stated. A box containing the Ader signals is represented in the upper part of the cut, the white circles, with the numerals above them, representing the small windows or openings through which the disks can be seen when they have dropped. The call bell, which can be brought into action when required by means of a commutator, I, is mounted on the top of the signal box. The plug switch, which is arranged below the signal box, consists of a series of vertical bars of metal, one for each subscriber, and a series of horizontal bars of metal arranged behind the vertical bars in such a manner

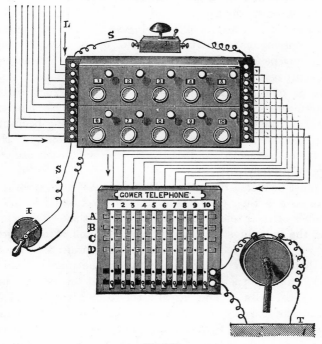

Fig. 150.

that the two series do not touch each other, but are perforated at the crossings, so that a communication between a vertical and a horizontal bar can be established by passing a plug through the said perforations at the intersection of the bars. Each vertical bar is provided with a pin, and in Fig. 150 all the pins are represented as connecting the vertical bars with the lowest hori-

zontal bar connected with a ground wire. Supposing the subscriber to have given his signal, and thus notified the switchman
that he desires to communicate with another subscriber, the
switchman takes the plug from the transverse bar and places it
into the aperture at the crossing of the bar, No. 5, with the
second horizontal bar, and he is now in communication with
No. 5, and asks him with whom he desires to communicate. No.
5 replies that he desires to be connected with No. 9. The employé then resets the signal of No. 5, and connects No. 9 with
the second bar by means of the plug in the manner described,
and is thus in communication with No. 9, and gives the signal,
which may be a simple sound signal, the Ader visible signal,
or the call bell, as the subscriber may have arranged it at his
house or office. No. 9 is then notified that No. 5 wishes to
communicate with him, and No. 5 is notified that No. 9 is ready;
the pins of the vertical bars, Nos. 5 and 9, having been placed
above one and the same transverse bar, for instance, A, Nos. 5
and 9 are connected, and can converse with each other with
complete privacy.

It must be stated that the disks of 5 and 9 have been raised,
and as soon as their conversation is over, Nos. 5 and 9 blow into
the tubes of their telephones, thus notifying the switchman, who
places the two plugs back in the bar connected with the ground
wire. But if Nos. 3 and 7 wish to communicate at the same
time that 5 and 9 are in communication, the pins belonging to
3 and 7 must be passed into the apertures at the intersection of
the vertical bars, 3 and 7, with the second transverse bar, B,
and in like manner, the next two subscribers are connected
by means of the bar, C, and so on. These connections, however,
only relate to subscribers of one and the same group or division.
If the subscribers belong to separate divisions the connections
are a little more complicated. If, for instance, No. 5 notifies
the switchman that he desires to converse with No. 83, who is
not in his group, which may be designated by A, and comprises
the subscribers from 1 to 30, but probably will be found in
group C, comprising the subscribers from 60 to 90, the switch-

man passes the pin of No. 5 through one of a number of horizontal bars located between the bar, D, and the second bar, not shown in drawings, and then writes on a slip of paper: "The subscriber 5, group A, line 6 (for example), desires to be connected with No. 83, group C," and sends this slip to the group C. The switchman in charge of this group notifies No. 83, and then connects him with the line 6. He then sends the slip

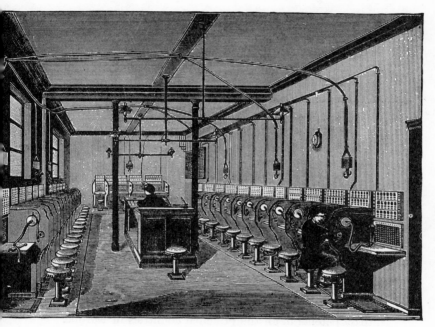

Fig. 151.

to the employé in charge of the grand commutator, where the groups A and C are connected in the line 6, thus permitting No. 5 to converse with 83. As soon as they have completed their conversation they give the signals, and all the pins are replaced into their former position.

Figure 151 gives an exact representation of the central station as it existed in 1880, showing the cases of each group arranged along the wall, and the grand commutator which connects 50 lines in the rear.

This system requires no batteries either for calling or transmitting. There were in 1880 one hundred subscribers connected in Paris, and five hundred applications had been received.

In 1881 the two telephone companies in Paris were united, when a new exchange system was adopted.

THE LARTIGUE–BROWN SYSTEM.

The Central Telephone System in Paris, established by *La Société Générale des Téléphones*, is one of the most complete and practically perfect telephone exchange systems in the world. For the details of this establishment we are indebted to Mr. R. G. Brown, electrical engineer of the company, and to Mr. A. L. Ternant, who has recently published an exceedingly interesting and exhaustive account of it in the *Journal Télégraphique*, the official publication of the *Bureau International des Administrations Télégraphique*.

The central office is situated at No. 27 Avenue de l'Opera. The arrangements of the office, including the establishment of the great rosettes, Fig. 152, to which all the wires from every quarter converge, to expand anew to the indicating boards and the connecting apparatus (and which it was necessary, so to speak, to wholly create in every part, and of which the elements have been constructed in the workshops of the company), constitute by their uniformity, a system of organization absolutely new, and of which the *Société Générale des Téléphones* has secured the ownership by patents in all the principal countries in Europe.

This system, which has been highly commended by the telephone engineers of the entire world, not excepting those of our own country, the birthplace, not only of the telephone, but of the telephone exchange as well, is due to the combined efforts of Mr. Lartigue, director; Mr. R. G. Brown, electrical engineer, in charge of the working service; Mr. Berthon, engineer of the technical service; and of Mr. Gilquin, foreman of the company's factory. The central office exchange, which forms the basis of

Fig. 152.

the establishment of the Paris system, is of American origin, having been introduced by General Marshall Lefferts, President of the Gold and Stock Telegraph Company, in the City of New York, in 187J, in connection with the printing telegraph instruments.

London has since had its "Telegraph Exchange" (copied after its New York originator, from whom it procured its first instruments), a system of private telegraph communications, distributing from a central office to the houses or offices of its subscribers, arranged in groups of five or six upon each wire, the quotations of the stock and produce markets, and other information of a similar character. The stock and market report telegraph, established in Paris in 1872, was also based upon this system; but it was reserved to the telephone to perfect it and make it practically useful for all purposes, not only of business, but of a domestic character. America not only preceded Europe in the establishment of the telephone exchange—the first telephone exchange having been established in Boston, in 1877—but in the application of new combinations, many of which have been adopted in the establishment of the Central Telephone Office in Paris; besides which, it should be remarked, that a great many of the recently invented apparatus in use there are due to Mr. R. G. Brown, a young and intelligent American engineer attached to the company.

As we have said, the function of the central office is to serve as an intermediary between the subscribers, by means of wires radiating to them. In order to accomplish this, it is necessary that the subscriber who desires to talk with another shall be able to give to the central office a tangible sign of his desire, and that the communication may be established in such a manner that the termination of the conversation may be similarly signaled to the central office by the subscribers.

All of these conditions, as well as many others besides, are fulfilled by the central office in Paris. Before describing the apparatus which it contains, we must say a word of the central office and of the favorable position which it occupies in the very heart of the capital. In the rear of a store room, serving as a sales room of apparatus, and also as that of a waiting room, is a long gallery, divided longitudinally by a double partition, forming two offices. A space of about a yard in width between the partitions is utilized by the inspector of communications, who enters through a panel in front (figure 153).

Let us see, first, by descending into the basement, how 'the subscribers are connected with this office. The wires which arrive at the central office are enclosed in cables manufactured at the works of Besons, which formerly belonged to M. Rattier. This manufactory has been united with the new *Société Générale des Téléphones et de Constructions Electriques*, with a capital of $5,000,000, for the purpose, so to speak, of monopolizing the manufacture of these cables. These telephone cables are placed in the city sewers, under the care of the technical service of the administration of the state telegraphs. The technical service of the *Société des Téléphones* furnishes to the state a plan of the sewers, which the cables must follow, with the indication of their location. These cables are suspended by hooks fastened into the stones of the sewer vaults.

Each of the wires contained in the cable is formed of a copper conductor consisting of three strands, covered with a layer of gutta-percha, and afterward by an envelope of colored cotton. Each cable contains fourteen conductors thus composed. They are formed into a rope, covered first by strong linen tape, and then by a sheath of lead. The wires are of various colors, to the number of seven, each pair of wires of the same color serving for a single subscriber. These colors are white, blue, yellow, maroon, black, red and green. Each cable is numbered throughout its entire length, and it is thus easy to find the wire when it is necessary to make repairs, as well as to change communication.

The telephone company generally lay a new cable only after having grouped seven subscribers in the same neighborhood. In the meantime, new subscribers are served by temporary cables of two conductors.

Fig. 153.

These cables are afterward replaced, as soon as it has been possible to group seven subscribers in the same cable of fourteen wires. The branches to houses are made by means of small special cables of two wires, bound to the principal cables by means of a ligature upon a lead cover. The positions of wires not utilized remain unconnected in the cable of fourteen conductors. Figure 154 shows how the operation of entering the house of a subscriber is accomplished.

The following is the mode adopted for connecting the houses or offices of the subscribers with the cables in the sewers :

First.—In case they have one or two subscribers only in a block, they run a cable of two wires from the nearest central office direct to each. This is very rarely done nowadays.

Second.—In case they have, for instance, three hundred or four hundred subscribers waiting for lines, they select seven of

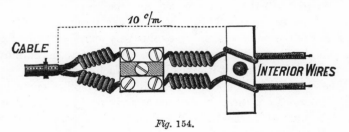

Fig. 154.

these subscribers who are next door neighbors, and run a cable of fourteen wires direct from the central office to the front of their house. Here they branch off the fourteen wires, by using the little cables of two conductors, and run one of these little cables to each of the subscribers.

Third.—This little cable stops at the window of the room where the telephone apparatus is to be placed; the apparatus is connected with the little cable in the American manner—that is, with wooden supports and insulated office wire.

Fourth—Every house in Paris has what is known as its particular sewer. This is simply an archway made under the sidewalk, and commences at the side of the house itself and stops at.

the main sewer. All sewers in Paris, except the main collectors, are under the sidewalks near the curb. The collectors are under the roadway; but they are, in fact, small rivers, into which all the main sewers empty.

Fifth.—To get the little cable from the particular sewer to the outside, they would simply make a hole close to the side of the house, and directly over the roof of the particular sewer, through the sidewalk, and into this sewer. In this hole they insert a perpendicular gas pipe, which projects six or seven feet out of the hole, and through this gas pipe they run the little cable.

It sometimes happens that they have to reach a subscriber who has no sewer in his street. In that case they run the little cable up the side of a house, after getting as near it by way of the sewers as possible, and from the top of this house they build an air line to the subscriber's house, by attaching fixtures to the roofs, as in America. This, however, very rarely occurs.

The double wire system is exclusively employed in Paris. The single wire system, with a return, by the earth, is employed in provincial towns, but it gives less satisfactory results.

The cables which connect with the central office enter by a short branch from the principal sewer arriving upon a level with the basement of the central office. A plate of copper, fastened to the wall by means of bolts, is pierced by a sufficient number of holes to permit of the admission of the cables into the establishment. 250 cables, furnishing 1750 circuits, are thus brought into the basement of the central office. These cables are carried upward and downward to the back of a switch board, similar to that in the Central Telegraph Office, *rue de Grenelle St. Germain.* This switch board, or system of commutators in the form of a rosette, has frequently been described by Mr. Berthon. These rosettes (Fig. 152) are about three yards in height, and have an interior space of about one and a half yards in diameter. There are seven of them in the basement of the Central Telephone Office, forming two groups, one of three and the other of four, and arranged in a rectangle, with doors in front, permitting of access

to the interior as well as to the exterior. The cables attached
to the interior are arranged in equal numbers above and below.
The fourteen conductors, which are long enough to reach to the
exterior circumference of the rosette, are carried upon the anterior surface, where they can be concentrated in perfect order.
Each pair of wires, corresponding to the circuit of a subscriber,
is connected with screws to a small commutator, consisting of
two copper bars, insulated from each other by a piece of ebonite.
Each cable supplies seven of these circuits, forming a section of
the rosette. Figure 155 represents one of these sections. Each
rosette can altogether accommodate thirty-four, corresponding to
two hundred and thirty-eight subscribers. The small commutators are attached at the other end to some insulated wires, covered with cotton and saturated with paraffine, which are (by the
interior circumference of the rosette) directly connected to the
commutators called jack knives, situated in the panels of the
central office. Each cable carries the indication of its number,
engraved upon an ivory counter. Each pair of wires bears a
similar indication of the address of the subscriber, and a number corresponding to this indication is attached to the two extremities of the interior wires connecting by the jack knife with
the indicator of this subscriber.

The double wire system has been adopted by the *Société Générale* upon the special recommendation of Mr. R. G. Brown, and
they were obliged accordingly to modify the ordinary jack
knife switch, which was brought from America. This new
commutator being formed, so to speak, from two simple jack
knife switches placed side by side, it is necessary that we should
first describe the simple jack knife switch, which is still employed upon all the provincial systems where they employ the
single wire system. Like the Swiss commutator, the jack knife
switch is a commutator of double entry, but it permits of other
combinations. It is composed of a piece of copper (fig. 156) of
rectangular form, and is attached to the panel by two nut screws.
The first screw, L, is terminated by a bolt which serves, at the
same time, to fasten the jack knife switch to the panel, and as

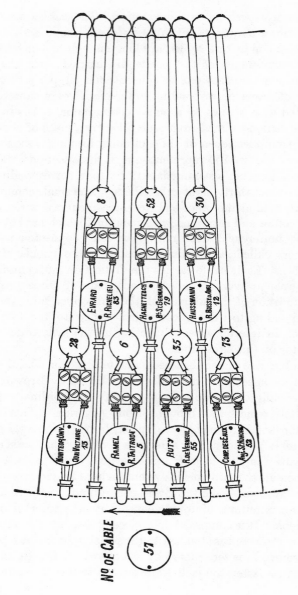

Fig. 155.

a conductor between the subscriber's wire, which is attached to it, and the metallic mass of the commutator. The second nut screw, I, is put in communication with the wire of the indicator of which the other extremity is connected to the earth. Still further, this bolt is insulated from the mass of metal of the jack knife switch, and is also provided with a small gudgeon of metal, projecting toward the superior part, but with which it is not metallically connected. This gudgeon communicates with the extremity of a rigid spring, R, R, fastened at one end by a screw to the metallic mass of the jack knife switch. This spring is itself put in play by a small brass pin, which is attached to it, and penetrates into the orifice 2 of our figure, and of which we shall presently see the action. In the position in-

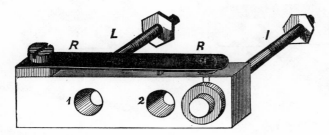

Fig. 156.

dicated by figure 156, the jack knife switch is in waiting, ready for service. The line communicates with the indicator. If the subscriber calls and sends the current from his battery, the indicator falls, a bell, placed in the local circuit of this indicator, is set ringing, and the central office is " called ;" that is, apprized that the subscriber wishes to communicate with it. As you perceive, the jack knife switch has two orifices marked 1 and 2. The operator then pushes in orifice 2 a brass peg attached to a flexible metallic cord coming from a telephone. The peg raises the pin placed under the spring, R, and immediately breaks the contact existing between the mass of the jack knife switch and the indicator. That simple introduction of the peg

makes consequently two changes; it detaches the indicator from
the line, and connects the line with the telephone. The operator then takes the instructions of the subscriber, who indicates
the person whom he desires to speak with. In order to establish the connection between two jack knife switches (figure 157)
they make use of a flexible metallic cord, terminated by two
brass pegs, which they insert in the orifices 1 and 2. If they
wish to put one of the indicators in derivation (that is to say, to
let a portion of the current pass to earth through the indicator
at the central office, while two subscribers are communicating),
they put the pin corresponding in the orifices number 1, the
spring is not lifted, and the metallic mass of the jack knife

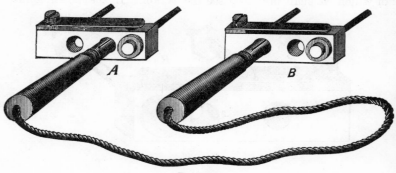

Fig. 157.

switch, which constitutes a part of the line of correspondence, is
still connected to the indicator and to the earth. Experience
has proved that there is no appreciable difference in the telephonic reception, whether they suppress all derivation, or put in
one of 300 ohms resistance. Now the two bobbins of the indicator form a circuit of which the resistance has about 200 ohms.
Other combinations are possible with the jack knife switch.
They can make use of special calling indicators, which may be
introduced into the circuit of the subscribers who are conversing.
This operation is made by means of two flexible cords, of which
one goes to the jack knife switch, A, at the point of entry

of the indicator, and the other at the point of exit of this indicator in the jack knife switch, B. The double jack knife switch employed at the central office in Paris gives precisely this combination with a single apparatus. Figure 158 shows the design seen in front and in perspective.

This double jack knife switch is the result of the combined efforts of Messrs. Lartigue, Brown and Berthon. It is formed of two metallic parts, placed back to back, and separated from each other by a thin plate of ebonite. The anterior plate is per-

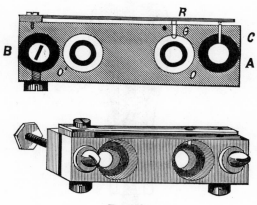

Fig. 158.

forated by two orifices, which extend across the ebonite into the posterior plate, where they are of a little smaller size. These two plates are tightly fastened together by two screws, A and B, which extend to the back in order to fasten the jack knife switch to the table by means of two bolts, which come out near the two borders of the indicator. The screw, A, is completely insulated from the metal of the two plates, except at the point, C, where a small pin can be seen upon it, insulated from the plate, permitting of the establishment of communication at this point, C, with the spring, R, of the ordinary jack knife switch. The two plates each communicate with one of the wires of the double line, and the indicator remains in the circuit of this dou-

ble line, so long as the spring maintains the contact between the
anterior plate and the indicator.   But this apparatus will be put
out of the circuit, as soon as the contact of C and of R shall be
broken by the introduction of a pin in the orifice, O. The pegs*
which must be introduced in the orifices, O, and O', are likewise
intended for double wires. The part *a* (figure 159) is very much

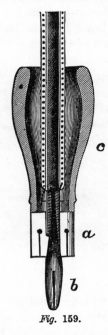

Fig. 159.

larger than the part *b*, and these two parts of the peg are carefully insulated from one another by means of the ebonite handle, *c;* each of them communicating besides with one of the
wires contained in the flexible cord, to which the peg is attached.
These flexible double conductor cords are thus formed: The
central conductor is a wire continuously wound into a small
spiral, and covered by a silk netting thick enough to completely

---

* The pegs and double conducting cords were designed by Mr. Lartigue.

insulate this wire from the second, which is wound in the same
manner into a spiral, upon it. A second netting of floss silk
covers the whole, forming a very flexible, easily handled, cord.
The central wire gives passage to the solid part, *b*, of the double
pin which it surrounds, and presses upon it in such a manner as
to form an excellent contact, which is still further assured by being soldered to it. The second wire is soldered to the ring of
the pin, *a*, and the two parts of the pin are constructed in such

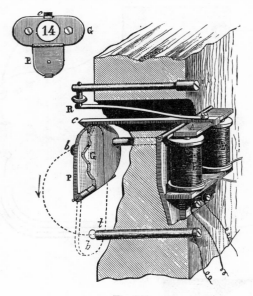

Fig. 160.

a manner as to each produce a good independent contact when
they are introduced together in the orifices, O, O', of the jack
knife switch. When this operation is made, the spring is raised
and the wire of the indicator corresponding to the insulated
point, C, is put out of contact. This indicator (Fig. 160) is
formed of two electro-magnets, E E, of which the helices
have a combined resistance of about 200 ohms. The movement of the detent. *c*, raises the latch of a small shutter,

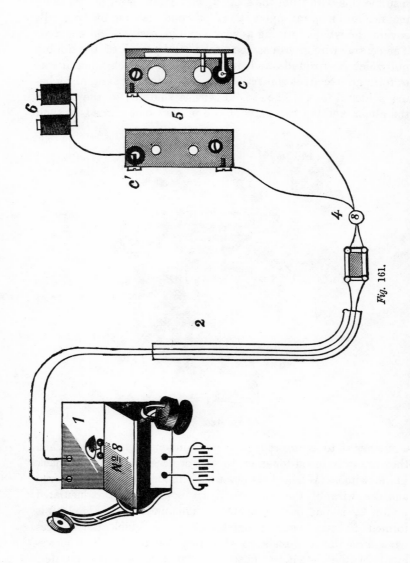

Fig. 161.

G, which, in falling, uncovers the number corresponding
with the subscriber who calls. Figure 161 shows the complete circuit. The jack knife switch being formed of two
distinct parts, these parts are indicated separately, in order to
be seen more clearly. We see that if the subscriber pushes
his call button, the current of his battery goes upon the line,
traverses the rosette in order to arrive at the anterior plate of

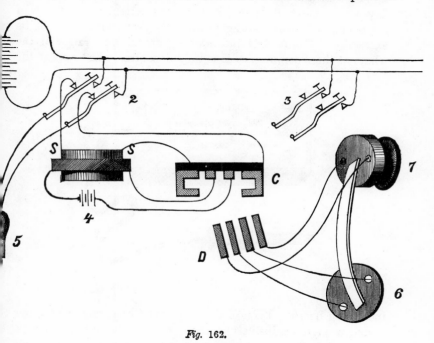

Fig. 162.

the jack knife switch, gains the insulated point by the spring,
then the indicator, and returns by the point, c, and the posterior
plate in the second wire of the line, where the circuit is completed at the opposite pole of the battery of the subscriber. The
central office responds to this call by means of the whole apparatus, of which figure 162 gives the diagram. It is composed of
a combined telephone, which is connected with a commutator,

C, of a special form, designed by Mr. Brown, of a call key (figure 163), of an induction coil, and of two series of Leclanché battery calls, of which the larger is employed in connection with the calling apparatus, and the other is used to engender an inductive current in the bobbin of the induction coil. These apparatus are not at all seen in the office; they are arranged at the back of the panels. The flexible cord attached to the call key, by the two corresponding set screws, extends to the rear of the panel, and comes out again upon the front with a peg at its extremity. Figure 164 indicates the actual appearance of the whole of these communications in the central office and of the

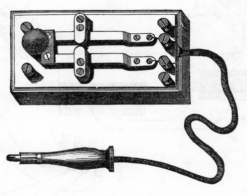

Fig. 163.

indicating boards. Each of the employés (the company employs young women exclusively) carries with her her combined telephone, of which figure 165 indicates the arrangement. This apparatus ought always to be kept in a perfect state of cleanliness and good order. We will suppose that Number 10 calls. Immediately the employé pushes at first the piece, D, of four contacts of figure 162 in the commutator, C. Figure 166 shows the details of this piece, D. In making this change the telephone transmitter is put in communication with the small battery of the inductor and of the primary coil of the induction ma-

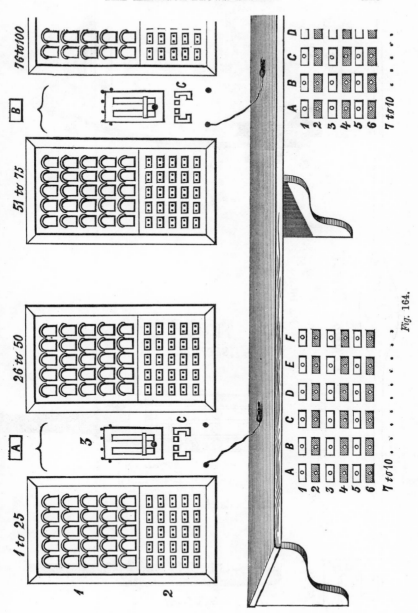

Fig. 164.

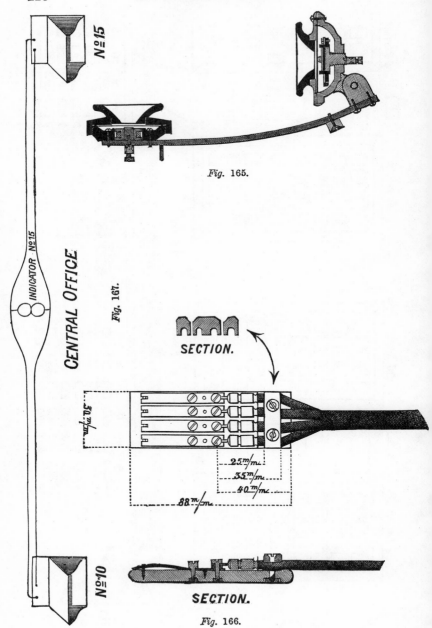

Fig. 165.

Fig. 167.

INDICATOR Nº 15

CENTRAL OFFICE

Nº 15

Nº 10

SECTION.

SECTION.

Fig. 166.

chine, while the receiver is put in communication, on one side, with the contact of the key connected with the double peg of the jack knife switch and consequently with the line, and, on the other, with the secondary circuit of the induction coil. In pushing, then, the peg into the orifice to the right of the jack knife switch, the indicator is put out of the circuit, and the communication with the subscriber is established. One or two taps of the key notifies the correspondent that he has been heard, and that they will speak with him. The subscriber replies that he wishes to communicate with Number 15. The employé responds: "Well, sir," and, after having removed the peg from the call key of the circuit of Number 10, she repeats the preceding operation with Number 15, by introducing the peg into the orifice to the left of his jack knife switch, rings two or three times, and awaits the response of that subscriber, having obtained which she informs him that Number 10 wants him, and then, by means of a flexible junction cord, of which the two extremities are terminated by a peg, she establishes the communication between the subscribers Numbers 10 and 15, by introducing one of the pegs into the orifice at the right of the jack knife switch Number 10, and the other peg into the orifice at the left of the jack knife switch Number 15. In these conditions she can speak to each of the subscribers, and put them in correspondence. She can then remove from the commutator, C, the connection piece attached to her telephone, and then devote herself to other occupations. It is proper to remark, that the arrangement of the jack knife switch Number 15 leaves the indicator of the subscriber corresponding in the derived circuit of the two wires over which the communication is being held (figure 167). This arrangement will permit the subscribers to delay to the very latest moment the announcement that their conversation is terminated, by pressing their call button, because the indicator remains always in the circuit. This arrangement does not weaken the sounds of the telephone, and we shall see, further on, that the circuit will even admit of two of these derivations without affecting the conversation.

In order to facilitate the operations, they have given distinct colors to the junction cords and to the communication cords. The first are green and the others red. In figure 164, there will be seen a series of commutators arranged under the shelf which runs along the panels. These are of the jack knife switches of a special form, and are composed of two metallic plates perforated and separated by a thick sheet of ebonite. The whole constitutes a sort of Swiss commutator permitting the establishment of communications between the subscribers whose connecting boards are too distant from each other for the ordinary junction cords, which are only five feet in length, to reach. Figure 168 gives a specimen of communications of the general commutator which connect between these series of jack knife switches. All the jack knife switches, A, B, C, etc., of 1 ; A, B, C, etc., of 2, are connected by the wires from one end of the office to the other in the manner indicated for A and F of 1, and for C and D of 2. So that, in supposing the extreme case where subscriber Number 1 of the first group of 50, formed of the two first connecting boards, desires to speak to Number 500, who is found in the second connecting boards of the tenth group, it will be necessary to utilize the general commutator to connect them, since the ordinary junction cord is not long enough for the purpose. Each group of two connecting boards is provided with sixty of the jack knife switches, but each of the groups has only a right to employ of the series of six corresponding by his row to the number of the group of the 50 jack knife switches comprised in two connecting boards. * Thus, in order to place Number 1 in communication with Number 500, we must take an elastic green cord of which one extremity will be inserted into the right hand orifice of the jack knife switch Number 1 and the other into one of the six jack knife switches of the first row, say B ; we then insert another elastic red cord into the left hand orifice of the jack

---

* The even rows of the jack knife switches are painted black, in order to facilitate the finding of the commutator desired.

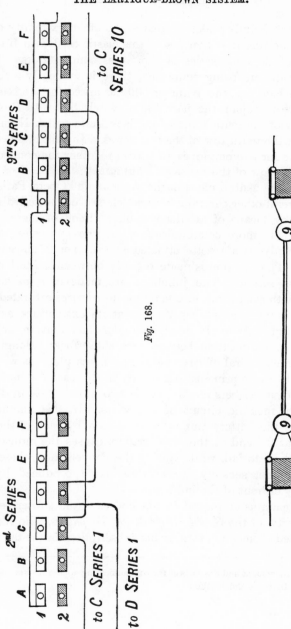

Fig. 168.

Fig. 169.

knife switch Number 500, situated at the other extremity of the office, connecting the other peg of this elastic cord with B of the first row of the tenth series of the Swiss commutators. These two commutators being connected, there is evidently a circuit. If, on the contrary, the Number 500 has asked for the Number 1, we have to rejoin the jack knife switch 500 with B of the tenth row of the tenth series of the jack knife switch Number 1 with B of the tenth row of the first series. In this manner it is impossible for two employés to utilize together the connections of the same row of the Swiss commutators.*

Besides the central office in the Avenue de l'Opera, Paris possesses several other central offices which are connected directly together by means of auxiliary cables. Each of these offices has one or more communications of these species which come directly to a rosette situated at Number 27 Avenue de l'Opera. The junction is made directly between central offices upon this rosette. The junctions are made in a permanent manner with the central rosette by means of wires saturated with paraffine carrying a number of order at its extremities, as indicated in figure 169. It must be understood that in order to establish communication between two subscribers belonging to two different central offices, everything takes place as we have explained for the principal office, only in this case the indicators of the two subscribers remain, at the two extremities, in derivation in the metallic circuit of the wires. In this manner the current of the battery put into circulation by each of the subscribers, at the end of the conversation, causes the indicator of each of them to fall, while, during the conversation, these derivations do not sensibly diminish the force produced by the secondary current of the induction coil.

The apparatus employed in the houses of the subscribers are the property of the *Société Générale des Téléphones*, who likewise constructed them. On signing his subscription for the telephone

---

* This arrangement and the parts of the communicating apparatus were designed by Messrs. Lartigue and Berthon.

service, the subscriber chooses his apparatus from the following: Ader, Gower, Bell, Crossley, Blake and Edison transformed.

The Ader telephone is most employed in Paris. It contains a microphone with ten crayons, forming twenty points of contact arranged *en grille* (Fig. 170). There is scarcely a dozen of Gower-

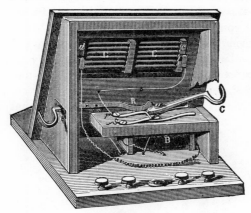

Fig. 170.

Fig. 171.

Bell in use. They consist of a sort of microphonic transmitter of Crossley with six crayons radiating from a central piece and forming twelve points of contact; the receiver is a Gower placed at the further end of a small tube hung upon an iron rest. However, they do not find it very satisfactory in Paris, on

account of the tube, which brings the sound to the ear and stifles
it. The Crossley is also much employed; but the system of
apparatus of Mr. Ader being preferred by the company and by
the subscribers, there are more of them constructed than of the
others. The Crossley (Figs. 171 and 172) is, as it were, the exclusive apparatus of the provinces, and we find it everywhere, at
Marseilles, Lyons and Bordeaux.

The Edison transmitter has been discarded, because the
diaphragm enlarges by the expansion caused by the heat of the
mouth, in consequence of which the pressure of the plate on the
button varies, being sometimes too great and sometimes too
feeble; the result being the need of too frequent regulating,

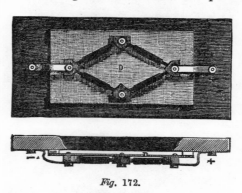

Fig. 172.

which fatigues the subscriber. The Edison transmitter has only
been retained in the combination telephone of Mr. Brown, which
is employed in the central offices of Paris and of the provinces·
They have, besides, transformed the old desk sets of the Edison
telephone pattern into Ader telephones. The arm of the transmitter has been taken off, and the diaphragm of the Ader microphone has been substituted for it on the desk (Fig. 173). The
apparatus thus transformed presents a very good appearance. The
company is making this change in such a manner as to gradually remove all the Edison telephones, which the subscribers do
not like; first, because they feel a repugnance to putting the

mouth into the instrument even to speak, and second, because
the apparatus becomes so easily deranged, as we have already
explained.   The Ader cannot get out of adjustment, for the simple reason that it has no adjustment.

It results from the preceding that the system of the old telephone company, which did not employ a battery, has been completely discarded   The actual apparatus in use are in great part
those of the American system, and their attention was called to
this system upon the proposition of Mr. Brown, who had presented to the directors of the company, in 1880, a remarkable
report, which served as a starting point to the organization finally
adopted.   This system requires the employment of a battery at

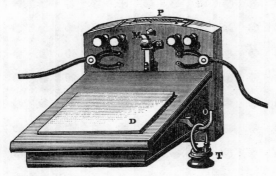

Fig. 173.

the house of the subscriber, and the *Société Générale* has organized
the service in such a manner that this element can never become
defective.   A special covered wagon visits each day from thirty
to forty subscribers, and completely changes their batteries.   The
six Leclanché elements placed at the service of the subscribers
are contained in a closed box, which is placed in a convenient
place in the subscriber's office.   The employé in charge of the
service replaces the old battery by a new one and carries all the
old batteries to the service rooms situated at Number 10 *Place
de la République.*   The next day these batteries are examined,
the jar is repainted anew and the manganese plates are replaced,

if that is necessary ; in a word, the battery is completely renewed.
The batteries employed at the central offices are the same as
those of the subscribers; that is a form of the Leclanché in
which the zinc element is a cylindrical plate surrounding the

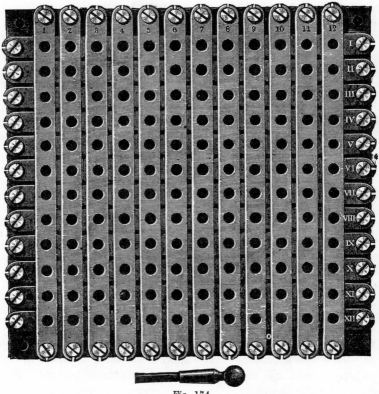

Fig. 174.

agglomerated manganese.   There are four in the circuit of each
of the bells and four others upon each of the microphones, but
half only are utilized each time, the two others remaining in
repose, in order to recover the force lost by polarization.

Figure 174 shows the construction of the Swiss commutator,

which forms the base of all the switch boards used in telephone exchanges.

There are at present ten central offices in regular service in Paris. Here is a list of them:

A. 27 Avenue de l'Opera.
B. Parc Monceaux.
C. La Villette.
D. Chateau d'Eau.
E. Rue de Lyon.
F. Gobelins.
G. Rue de Bac.
H. Grenelle.
I. Passy.
S. Rue des Petits-Champs, 66.

The number of communications made during the week ending Tuesday, December 27, 1881, was as follows:

Bureau.						Number of Subscribers.
A,	communications from the 21st to the 27th,				38,783	535
B,	"	"	"	"	6,803	132
C,	"	"	"	"	6,246	77
D,	.	"	"	"	12,269	201
E,	"	"	"	"	755	12
F,	"	"	"	"	800	12
G,	"	"	"	"	10,318	124
I,	"	"	"	"	639	26
S,	"	"	"	"	10,862	208
	Total,				87,475	1,327

At the same date the number of auxiliary wires in service increased to seventy-seven.

Each of the auxiliary offices has a directress, and the day service is divided between the young women, who take their turns of service from half past eight o'clock in the morning until seven o'clock in the evening. They are then relieved by young men, who perform the night service from seven o'clock in the evening until half-past eight o'clock in the morning. The calls in the night are less frequent, and vary from 200 to 250. The call bell, which is employed in the call circuit of the indicators, is replaced at night by a clock.

The central office, at Number 27 Avenue de l'Opera, is directed by Miss Hattie Lordon, who is also general overseer of the female service. The following are, in addition, some details regarding the *personnel* of the service, which appears very well organized. It is placed under the general direction of Mr. Lartigue, and comprises a working service, of which Mr. R. G. Brown is the Electrical Engineer, and a Chief Engineer of the Technical Service, which office is filled by Mr. Berthon. Mr. Gilquin is the head of the factory. The working service of the Paris system comprises five inspectors and seventeen overseers in charge of maintenance and repairs; seven workmen for setting up batteries in the central offices and of those of the subscribers, and four for keeping them in repair. The active service of the communication in the central offices comprises seventy young women for the day and thirty young men for the night. The offices are visited day and night by the inspectors, who come to examine the communications.

The organization of the telephonic service in the provinces is far from being as perfect as in Paris. Nevertheless they work regularly in Lille, Rouen, Havre, Nantes, Bordeaux, Lyons, Marseilles and other important centres. The double wire system is not yet uniformly established in France, and the system of a single wire, with a return by the earth, exists in nearly all the cities aside from Paris. The induction which is produced at times between two wires, which follow the same course, or which are situated upon the same poles, causes a good deal of annoyance in the single wire system. The apparatus of the provinces are not yet perfected; except at Lyons (where they use the jack knife switch with a wire of Mr. Brown), the Swiss commutator is altogether in use. They are gradually introducing the combination telephone in the central offices, and the apparatus of the subscribers are, in general, of the Crossley pattern.

The lines are insulated in various ways; at Marseilles they are entirely upon double poles, forming gibbets, and placed upon the ridge poles of the houses.

At Bordeaux, in the suspended part, the poles are formed of two iron U, very light, which they fasten against the walls, or which are attached to the ridge poles. They employ upon these lines a steel wire of 1 mm., 8 (about Number 15 Birmingham wire gauge, weighing seventy pounds to the mile). The best part of the Bordeaux system is carried under the earth in tubes, made of cement, placed at a depth of three feet. They start from the central office, situated at the Baths south of the Quinconces. The cables confined in these pipes are formed of a sheath of gutta-percha, recovered by an envelope of tarred hemp. A small metallic wire, wound over this, maintains the hemp in place, and lessens the effects of the induction.

The following tables show the whole number of subscribers to the *Société Générale des Téléphones.* The statements are made up to the 21st of October, 1881, and to 14th of February, 1883.

Statistics of the Société Générale des Téléphones for the week ended December 27, 1881.

CITIES.	No. of Subscribers.	No. of Communications for the week.
Paris	1,327	87,475
Bordeaux	86	....
Havre	55	....
Lille	....	....
Lyons	161	....
Marseilles	121	....
Nantes	58	....
	1,808	....

Statistics of the Société Générale des Téléphones, for the week ended February 14, 1883.

CITIES.	No. of Subscribers.	No. of Communications for the Week.
Paris, France...................	2,722	100,358
Algiers, Africa.................	4	. . . .
Bordeaux, France..............	252	3,876
Le Havre, "	181	5,122
Lille, "	121	846
Lyons, "	442	31,018
Marseilles, "	292	11,331
Nantes, "	104	1,095
Oran, Africa.................	25	. . . .
Rouen, France.................	57	. . . .
St. Pierre-Calais..............	22	. . . .
Total to the 14th February, 1883,	4,222	153,646
" " 27th December, 1881,	1,808	. . . .
Increase.................	2,414	. . . .

The telephonic service in the provinces is still in a period of transformation, which has followed the amalgamation of the *Compagnie Générale* with the *Société des Téléphones.* This *Société* has come, besides, to take an important position in France as a company of electrical construction, and has increased its capital to the amount of $5,000,000. The Paris system does great honor to the *Société Générale* and to its competent agents. Some serious efforts permit us to hope that with the increase of the subscribers the provincial service can be in the future established in the same perfect condition which distinguishes its establishment in the capital.

THE SCOTT-ELLSWORTH SYSTEM.

In 1880 there were three telephone exchanges in operation in the City of New York, viz.: those of the Bell Telephone Company, the Law Telegraph Company, and the Gold and Stock

Telegraph Company. The two former used the Blake transmitter and the Bell receiver; the latter used the Edison transmitter and the Phelps receiver. During the summer of 1880 the exchanges of the Gold and Stock Telegraph Company and of the Bell Telephone Company were purchased by the Metropolitan Telephone and Telegraph Company, and united under one management and system, those of the Bell Company being adopted.

The Telephone Exchange of the Gold and Stock Telegraph Company—which played a very important part in the early development of the enterprise—was due to the combined efforts of Mr. George B. Scott, the superintendent of the company, and Mr. T. G. Ellsworth, the manager of the central office. Fig. 175 represents the Central Telephone Exchange office, situated at No. 198 Broadway, New York, as it existed in 1880, before the consolidation with the Bell system into that of the Metropolitan Telephone and Telegraph Company. Near the centre of the room an enclosed oblong frame is erected, and within this all the wires of the system are connected and separately led to sections of a switch board. These sections are arranged alongside of each other, facing outward and in four parallel rows, one above the other, but all within convenient reach of an attendant standing upon the floor. Referring to a single section (Fig. 176), as the connections are similar in all, the line wire, after its introduction within the frame or back of the switch, is connected to a screw passing through the section and in electrical connection with a jack knife switch in front, provided with both front and back contacts. In its normal position, the jack knife switch is held on the back contact, which is simply a slight projection from a metallic plate, and thus establishes a good electrical path for a current arriving from the line to this plate, and a brass disk beneath it, which is also in electrical connection, through a small relay, with the earth, and thus the circuit for the call current is completed. A catch on the end of the armature lever, which extends through the wooden part of the section, engages with an annunciator disk and keeps it in a vertical position so long as the armature remains unattracted, or during the normal condition of the line when idle. If, however, a current is sent into the line from the other terminal station, by the depression of a key like the one shown in Fig. 177, the armature lever is at-

Fig. 176.

tracted, and thus releases the annunciator disk, which, being hinged below, now falls by its own weight, and indicates not only that a call has been sent, but also at what particular station it originated. On seeing the number, the switchman connects his portable telephone with the subscriber's line, by inserting the plug at the end of the flexible telephone cord in the jack knife switch (Fig. 176). This operation not only connects the switchman with the line, but it also breaks the connection between the subscriber's line and the annunciator. The switch-

Fig. 177.

man's telephone being already connected with a battery and induction coil, and in condition to talk over the subscriber's line, he says to the subscriber (whom we will call No. 10), "Well, sir?" No. 10 replies, "No. 30." The switchman then connects the jack knife switch of No. 10 with one of the long horizontal bars, seen at the lower part of Figs. 175 and 176, which he turns slightly, to indicate that it is occupied. He then inserts one end of a flexible cord in the jack knife switch of No. 30, and taps with the other end on a long brass strip connected with a sig-

Fig. 178.

naling battery, thus sending electrical impulses through the line wire connecting with No. 30 and ringing his bell, when No. 30 removes his receiving telephone from its switch (Fig. 177), and listens while the switchman connects the jack knife switch of No. 30 with the same horizontal rod that is connected with

No. 10.   He then removes the connection of No. 10 from the rod, and tells No. 10 to go ahead, when the conversation between No. 10 and No. 30 proceeds.

The clearing out relays shown in Fig. 178, and at the further end of the office in Fig. 175, indicate to the central office when the subscribers have finished talking. These relays, which are of comparatively high resistance, are each arranged to work a local circuit, in which there is an annunciator representing one of the switch rods.

Each horizontal switch rod is connected with one of the relays, and all of the relays are grounded. Now, No. 10, having begun the conversation through the telephone, must indicate when it is ended; therefore, upon hanging up his receiving telephone, he pushes the button four or five times, working the relay, and consequently, the annunciator connected with it, indicating that whatever is connected with the horizontal switch rod whose number corresponds with that of the annunciator, may be removed, and the switch rod may be used for any one else.

This idea of putting the subscribers' line to ground in the central office through a resistance, for the purpose of enabling the subscribers to notify the central office when they had finished their conversation, originated with Mr. R. G. Brown, then chief operator of the Gold and Stock Exchange, and now electrical engineer of the General Telephone Company, in Paris, where this ingenious device is still in use, and proves a valuable auxiliary to the service.

Mr. Brown first conceived this idea in November, 1878. The plan of employing spring jacks and other looping devices was not only expensive, but, with the kind of switch boards then in use, required the employment of two connecting bars—one for each line—which took up valuable space ; and looking about for some substitute for the looping in devices, Mr. Brown ascertained that a telephone, or high resistance electro-magnet, could be attached between a telephone line and the ground without perceptibly interfering with the transmission of speech, and hence adopted this plan, with very excellent results.

Fig. 177 shows the apparatus in the subscriber's office. The adjustable arm carries an Edison carbon button transmitter, connected with the primary wire of an induction coil concealed beneath the desk. A receiving telephone, known as the pony crown, which is connected with the line wire, hangs upon a switch at the opposite end of the desk. Removing and replacing the telephone operates the switch. Above the desk there is an

Fig. 179.

ordinary single stroke electric bell, and below it are two cells of Leclanché battery (Fig. 179).

One wire from the subscriber's battery is grounded; the other connects with the push button seen at the side of the desk. When this button is pressed the current passes through the line wire to the switch at the central office, and thence through the magnet of the annunciator to the ground.

Among the peculiar devices originated for use in this office are the portable switchman's telephone, which is shown in Figs. 175 and 176, and the switch rods, shown in the same view. The latter are the invention of Mr. T. G. Ellsworth, the manager of the central office.

The boys attending the switches become expert and rarely make mistakes.

There were no less than six thousand calls per day in this office ; yet there was no delay, no mistakes, no trouble, save from the occasional breaking of a wire or the crossing and interference of one wire with another.

An idea of the activity of a telephone central office may be obtained from the larger view. The actual condition of things is far from being exaggerated.

The desk, seen at the left of Fig. 175, is the chief operator's desk, and the line men, whose business it is to rectify troubles, got their orders at this desk.

There were upwards of 600 wires entering this office alone, and it required over a thousand cells of battery to work them.

Persons desiring to avail themselves of this means of communication subscribed to certain conditions, which required, among other things, the payment of a monthly rental, and the observance of the rules of the company. Men were then sent from the central office to place the telephone and battery, and to run a wire from the subscriber's telephone to the central office, supporting it at intervals by poles and fixtures, as in the case of telegraph lines. The line and the instrument were kept in order by the company. Any imperfection in the action of either reported to the chief operator's desk at the central office received immediate attention, men being sent out at once to find and remedy the trouble.

An alphabetically arranged list of subscribers was furnished with each telephone, and as new subscriptions were made, supplementary lists were furnished to all subscribers.

THE LAW SYSTEM.

The experience of the various Telephone Exchanges in the larger cities throughout the country, shows that as the number of subscribers increases, the number of their communications increase in a twofold ratio. For example, if with one hundred subscribers there are five hundred communications per day, then with five hundred subscribers there will be at least five thousand communications per day.

To make the necessary connections and disconnections at the central office, or offices, for these communications quickly, reliably, with uniformity as to time, and without confusion, has been a problem of difficult solution.

Various plans of working and an endless variety of apparatus have been devised, tried, found inadequate and abandoned; and many of the large exchanges in the country are now operating their second or third systems, which are not entirely satisfactory.

The systems referred to are all essentially alike, although differing more or less in their apparatus or details, and operate substantially as follows: A subscriber wishing communication with another, signals the central office, by dropping there an indicator, or ringing a bell. The central office then connects with him by telephone, and asks the name of the party with whom he wishes to communicate, and, on being informed, rings up the party wanted and connects the two. The central office usually ascertains when to disconnect, either by listening to the whole communication, or by listening from time to time; but sometimes an indicator or bell is left in circuit, which may be dropped or rung, as the case may be, by either subscriber, when the conversation is ended. This would seem to be simple enough; but when it sometimes happens that these indicators drop, or bells ring faster than the desired connections can be made, even with the best apparatus and operators, it can be understood why these systems are still regarded as imperfect.

The system invented by Frank Shaw, engineer of the Law Telegraph Company, of New York, and in operation by that company, and known as the Law System, is said to require the least possible time in which to make connection, and to be superior to all others.

The Law Telegraph Company operates exchange systems in New York and Brooklyn, and its central offices are connected by trunk or connecting wires with those of the Metropolitan Telephone and Telegraph Company, thus enabling the subscribers of the two companies to intercommunicate.

The telephone instruments used by the Law Telegraph Company are the same as those used by the Metropolitan Company, that is, the Blake Transmitter and Bell Receiver.

Nearly all the rest of the apparatus, however, as well as the *modus operandi*, is radically different, and merits a full description.

In addition to the usual wire (the individual wire) connecting the subscriber with the central office, he is provided, in common with about 130 other subscribers, with a circuit wire, styled the "calling wire," which is used exclusively in giving the orders to the central office for connecting and disconnecting the individual wires.

The use of this calling wire enables the company to do away with annunciator cases, switch boards, local and trunk tables, etc., in the central offices, and to substitute therefor, as the sole apparatus of the office, a table thirty-four inches square, on which are concentrated no fewer than 400 individual wires, 75 to 100 trunk wires and 4 calling wires. Around this table are seated four operators, each of whom has a transmitter and a receiver in the circuit of a separate calling wire. The transmitter is placed on an upright rod at his right, and the receiver is held constantly at his ear by means of a steel band passed over the head, which band serves also as the magnet of the telephone. He is therefore always in readiness to receive an order, without the necessity of a preliminary call or signal, and both his hands are left free to fill the orders.

Each of three of these calling wires connects with the premises of about 133 subscribers, and the fourth connects with all the other tables in the system, whether located in the same or in other central offices. The former are styled subscribers' calling wires, and the latter, "trunk line calling wires," because used for transmitting orders to connect and disconnect the trunk lines. All tables in the system are exactly alike in every respect, and each has a certain number of trunk lines in direct connection with each other.

Figure 180 is a cut of the table and figure 181 of the top. Its construction is as follows :

Each individual wire enters the box in the centre from the floor below it, and connects with a vertical brass tube, about two feet in height and half an inch in diameter. A brass rod, about a foot long and carrying a little flat spring, is suspended in each tube (see Figure 182) by a stout, flexible cord, which terminates in a brass cap bearing a steel pin and resting on a ground plate set just above the tubes, but separated from them.

The rod is made to move freely through the tube, and the spring maintains an electrical connection between them, which is never broken.

This box of tubes opens in the centre of the table top, all parts of which can be easily reached from any side, and of which the ground plate forms a portion of the surface, the rest being composed of 75 to 100 square brass bars drilled with holes to receive the steel pins.

Portions of these bars are connected with trunk wires leading to similar bars on similar tables (either in the same office or other offices), and the rest are used for local connections.

The tubes are arranged in four sections of 100 each, each section ten tubes square, and numbered from 0 to 9 on all four sides, so that the figures can be read equally well from all sides of the table.

The figures on either of the two parallel sides may stand for tens, and those on the other two sides will stand for the units— the hundreds are understood.

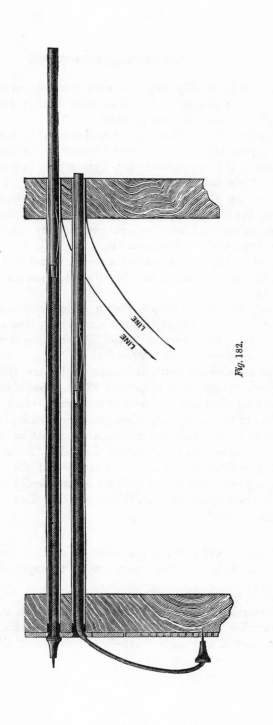

Fig. 182.

It must be readily seen that with this system of numbering, the operator can select any plug more quickly and surely than if each plug bore its own number.

The plate bearing the figures is connected with a battery having a pole changer or circuit breaker in its wire—or with a generator, if preferred—so that when a plug is touched to it the subscriber's bell is given a continuous ring. A small key is inserted in each square bar, which, when depressed by the finger, bears against a plate underneath similarly connected. When subscribers have been connected, they can be rung up by these keys without disconnecting.

Another plate, that next to the one numbered, is connected with the same battery, but directly, and used for giving single strokes.

The push button switch, shown underneath each transmitter, is used to switch the telephones temporarily into a trunk calling wire coming from another table. When there is more than one such wire there is a switch for each.

The subscribers' outfit is shown in Figure 183. The usual magneto generator is dispensed with. The black knob seen projecting through the door is the same switch shown at the corners of the table, and, when held pressed in, it connects the entire apparatus with the calling wire; in its normal condition the apparatus is in the circuit of the individual wire.

The box contains, besides this switch and the gravity switch (holding the receiver and used for automatically switching from the call bell to the telephone), one cell of " Law " battery and a simple call bell.

Figure 184 shows the combination of the circuits, and will serve to illustrate the operation of the system, which is as follows :

Subscriber 113 wishing to communicate with subscriber 394, he switches into his call wire (C¹) by holding his finger on his push button and calls "113–394." Operator S¹ immediately selects these pins, one with each hand, holds them an instant on the continuous ring-up plate, inserts them in a bar and the work is finished. Whole time occupied—about three seconds. The conversation ended, 113 calls, "113 off," and the operator S immediately withdraws pins 113 and 394, one with each hand, touches them to the single stroke plate, thereby giving a disconnect signal to each subscriber, releases them, and they

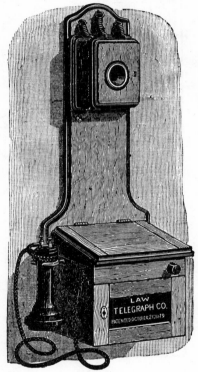

Fig. 183.

run back to their places. Whole time occupied—about two seconds.

If the call had been "113–782," 782 being a subscriber connected with another table (either in the same or another central

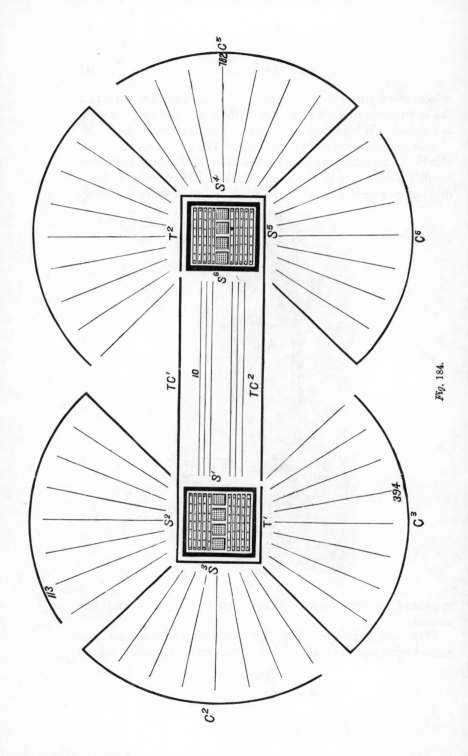

Fig. 184.

office), the operator S^1 would then have selected a trunk line bar leading to that table, say bar connecting with trunk line 10, with one hand rung and connected 113 with that bar, and with the other hand pressed his push button switch and called over wire $T\ C^1$ to the distant operator, 782–10, and T^2 would immediately ring and connect 782 with the bar similarly numbered in his table. Whole time occupied—about five seconds.

The disconnection is similarly accomplished. It will be observed that the operators at the same table work entirely independent of each other, and they never speak, except over a trunk call wire, to a distant operator.

Should subscriber 782 give the order to disconnect, it would be received by operator S^5, who would withdraw pin 782, switch into wire $T\ C^2$, say to operator T^1—" 10 off," whereupon operator T^1 would withdraw pin 113 from bar 10.

All subscribers are numbered, and names are not used at all.

Subscribers do not interrupt or interfere with one another on the calling wire, because they distinctly hear each other, and each order is but a word or two, and is filled at once.

Under this system a subscriber can connect and disconnect at will with other subscribers in rapid succession ; an invaluable feature for giving quotations to customers, ascertaining the whereabouts of a party, and for many other purposes.

Some of the calling wires are metallic circuits, and some of them ground circuits. Usually they loop into the subscriber's office, although they sometimes merely branch or tap in.

The following advantages are claimed for the Law System :

The expense of constructing and establishing' it is less than any other, because the cost of the calling circuit is less than the cost of the usual apparatus of annunciators, spring-jacks and batteries, in the central office, and batteries or magneto bells in the subscribers' offices, none of which are required ; and the cost of maintaining and operating is very much less, because,

1st. But one third to one quarter the usual number of operators are needed.

2d. The calling wire gets out of order less than the usual annunciators and batteries, and, of course, for the same reason, the service is better to subscribers.

3d. The system requires a much less number of inspectors and adjusters, as the calling wire is a corps of inspectors in itself, and its service as such alone pays for its cost.

4th. But about one tenth the usual number of cells of battery are used.

5th. The usual and inevitable expense of changing the apparatus with the view to improving it, is avoided, because there is little or none to change.

The calling wire may be either a metallic or a ground circuit, although the former is preferable, and it should loop back into the central office frequently, so that in case of trouble it can be immediately traced to a particular loop and quickly found and removed. This looping back is without any material waste of wire, because subscribers are always so numerous near the central office, that both parts of each loop can be used advantageously. In the preceding comparison of costs of construction provision is made for running the calling wire entirely of No. 13 iron wire, with Kerite insulation, but in many cities and places this insulation would not be necessary or advisable.

On pole routes the top pin should always be given to the call wire.

The call wire may either loop into each subscriber's office, or it may branch in. The former is preferable in large or active exchanges and with more than 50 in a circuit, and the latter in small exchanges and with but a few on a circuit, but both plans are sometimes advantageous for different circuits from the same central office.

Whenever calls are comparatively few, in order to avoid the necessity of an operator holding the telephone constantly to his ear, a branch in the central office from the calling wire, with a battery and bell in circuit to the ground, may be provided, and

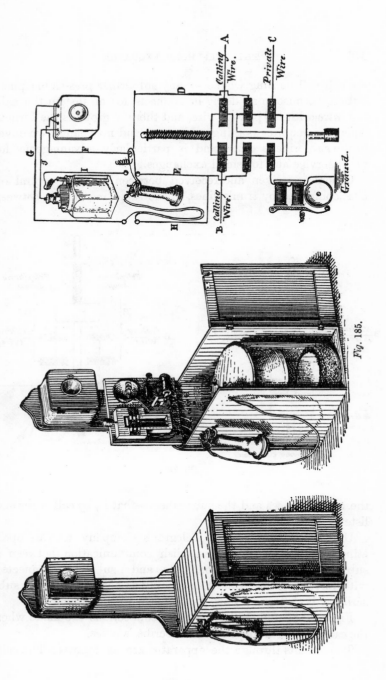

Calling Wire. A

Private C Wire.

D

Ground.

Calling B Wire.

H

Fig. 185.

the bell will be rung whenever any subscriber presses his push-button, because in so doing he connects for an instant the calling wire with his private wire, and thereby grounds the former. This plan requires nothing additional, and no change whatever in the subscriber's office, and is particularly advantageous for night service and for small exchanges.

Orders are given and received between different central offices connected by trunk lines, in the same manner as between

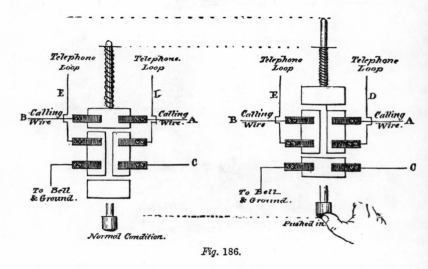

Fig. 186.

the central offices and the subscribers—that is, by call wires and listening operators.

Under this plan the Law Telegraph Company, who are operating five central offices, establish communication between a subscriber connected with one office and a subscriber connected with another office almost as quickly as between the two subscribers, both of whom are connected with the same office.

Figures 185 and 186 show how connections are made when the calling wire is looped into subscriber's office.

The circuits through the apparatus are as follows: The calling wire enters at A, and goes directly out at B. No resistance is in this circuit, therefore, at the subscriber's station when the telephone is not in use. The private wire enters at C, and by way of D and E goes to the bell and then to the ground; hence the station is in condition to be called. When the telephone is removed from its hook and the push button switch is pushed and held in, the private wire entering at C goes over the plate next to

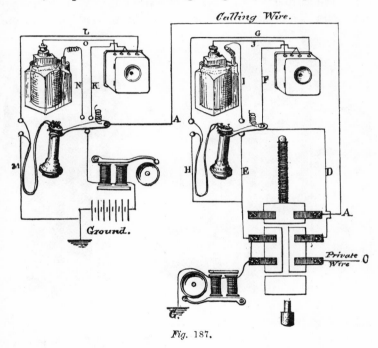

Fig. 187.

the push button, directly to the bell and the ground. The calling wire, entering at A, goes through the secondary coil of the transmitter, through the telephone and out at B, by way of the wires D, F, G and H; and the local battery is closed through the primary coil of the transmitter by way of the wires I, F and J. When the push button is released the calling wire again passes directly through the apparatus as in the first instance, but as the telephone is still removed from its hook, the circuit of the private wire is then by way of D, F, G and H, through transmitter, receiver and bell, to the ground.

Figure 187 shows how connections are made when calling wire is branched into subscriber's office and a bell and battery are placed in circuit at central office.

The connections in the subscriber's office are the same as when the calling wire is looped in, except that it does not go out again; and the wire E is connected to both of the con-

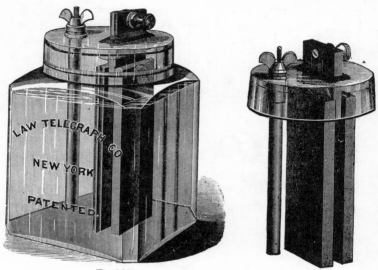

Fig. 188.　　　　　　　　*Fig.* 189.

tact springs nearest the bell. When the subscriber pushes in and holds his push button the battery at the central office is closed from the ground through the bell there—which should be a vibrator—the wires A, D and E to the bell and ground in the subscriber's office.

Figures 188 and 189 are cuts of the battery used by the Law Telegraph Company, which is claimed to be uniform in its action, and so constructed that the water cannot evaporate, nor the sal ammoniac creep out. To charge the battery, dissolve in the jar 6 ounces of best pure sal ammoniac with water, and fill so that when the carbons and zinc are inserted the water will rise to the shoulder, but no higher. The cover inside and outside, and its connections, must be kept perfectly dry and the carbons tightly bolted together. The circuit must stand open when the battery is not in use. No more sal ammoniac must be put in the jar than the water will dissolve. Many do this, under the belief that a deposit of sal ammoniac in the bottom of the jar serves as a reserve supply, on which the solution draws as required, which is not true—on the contrary, the deposit works. an absolute injury. By using hot instead of cold water and stirring it well, the sal ammoniac will dissolve quickly.

The round rod is the zinc and the flat plates the carbon element.

The following is a list of exchanges using the law telephone exchange system:

Philadelphia	Penn.	Columbia	S. C.
St. Louis	Mo.	Augusta	Ga
Kansas City	"	Savannah	"
Richmond	Va.	Macon	"
Norfolk	"	Columbus	"
Staunton	"	Atlanta	"
Selma	"	Rome	"
Danville	"	Athens	"
Lynchburg	"	Brunswick	"
Alexandria	"	Mobile	Ala.
Charleston	W. Va.	Montgomery	"
Raleigh	N. C.	Birmingham	"
Wilmington	"	Jacksonville	Fla.
Charleston	S. C.	Pensacola	"

The following abstract from the annual report of Mr. J. E. Zeublin, general manager of the Bell Telephone Company of Philadelphia, dated February 19, 1883, gives an interesting account of the change from the annunciator system to the law system by that company :

The fiscal year that has just closed has been a phenomenal one in the history of this company.

Last year's experience had demonstrated the necessity for more capacious quarters for the central exchange and prompted the executive officers to negotiate for accommodations in the new building on the southwest corner of Fourth and Chestnut streets. This resulted in giving to this company rooms and roof privileges exactly suited to our wire service. In order, therefore, to take advantage of all the progress that had been made in telephony, before making the removal it was deemed best to send Mr. Sargent, the general superintendent, upon a tour of inspection to all the prominent exchanges of the country. Mr. Sargent's large experience and progressive views especially fitted him for this mission, and resulted in his unwillingness to fetter this rapidly growing plant with the ordinary systems in use. He took advanced ground and boldly recommended the experiment of the law system of exchange service to secure rapid service between subscribers and to economize space in the operating room. These suggestions were adopted and four law switches were purchased.

In removing from the old to the new central exchange unforeseen difficulties were encountered, chiefly in the removal of such a mass of wires and the abrupt change from the old to the new system, and the necessarily temporary character of much of the construction. The public had to be personally taught to use the new system, and our operators had to be educated in its rapid use. This naturally caused dissatisfaction, and before the system was tried and the construction trouble eliminated, our subscribers, through misapprehension of the real purpose of the change, were invited to meet and form an association to protect their interests, and compel satisfactory and perfect service upon our part.

The officers of the company met this assault with kindness and individually and collectively labored to perfect the service in every manner possible, in all of which they were ably and industriously supported by Mr. Henry Bentley, of the Board of Directors. The work was performed so quietly and effectively that the officers of the association were soon without a following, the president himself being compelled to acknowledge the superiority of the new service over that of the old.

The loss of service was satisfactorily settled at a nominal expense, while the agitation convinced our patrons that the telephone was an indispensable business necessity, and has resulted in a greater increase of subscription in a given time than was ever before known in the history of the company, while the superior service rendered by the new and well-appointed exchange has called forth unstinted praise from the prominent telephonists of this country.

CHILD'S ANNUNCIATOR SYSTEM.

On the right, A, B, C, D and E (fig. 190), are table operators, each of whom has connected with his table, by an independent circuit, an indicator on the left of the switch board, correspondingly lettered.

Each table has also a specified number of wires arranged in pairs, each wire connecting with a horizontal bar on the switch board.

1, 2 and 3 are switch operators standing or sitting in front of the board, each with a telephone secured to his head and connected in an independent circuit with all the tables.

101 to 307 are subscribers' wires connecting with the vertical bars, which in turn connect with the subscribers' annunciators and then with the ground.

The operation is as follows: For example, 101 wishes to communicate with 307. 101 drops his annunciator; switch operator 1 withdraws the pin beneath it and sets the annunciator back. Glancing at the indicators, he observes that table operator A is disengaged and inserts the pin in the upper bar of any disengaged pair leading to his table, say pair No. 1, whereupon the current from the generator, shown on the left, closes indicator A, drops table annunciator 1 and rings subscriber 101. Thus the subscriber is answered, A is called, and all the switch operators are informed that A is busy.

A then moves the two-button switch from upper 1 to lower 1, switches his telephone into circuit with upper 1, receives his

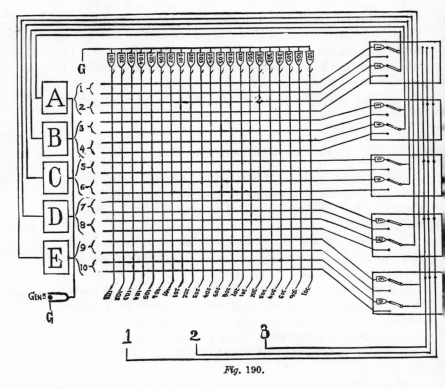

Fig. 190.

order 101–307, and records it either on ticket or in book, the latter preferred.

He now switches his telephone into circuit with switch operator 3, and gives the order 307–1.

3 withdraws pin 307, and inserts it in lower 1, whereupon the

current from the generator rings subscriber 307, who is then switched by A from the generator to 101.

The work completed, A touches a push button, which, by means of a circuit not shown, opens his indicator and notifies the switch operators that he is again disengaged.   Or, it can be arranged so that the act of A, in switching the two subscribers together, will open his indicator and thereby prevent his shirking work. · If a switch operator connects a subscriber with a bar already engaged, the fact is instantly made known to him by the proper indicator, which will refuse to close.

Disconnections are obtained by either subscriber dropping the table annunciator, whereupon table operator calls the numbers off by means of the proper circuit or circuits to the switch operators.

If, when called for, 307 were engaged, 3 would first answer A, engaged, and then hang a hard rubber ticket bearing the letter A on 307's pin, and, finally, on receipt of the order to disconnect 307, would connect 307 with A, who, from his record, would then find 101 wanted him, and make the connection.

Trunk lines to other central offices are connected with the board precisely as subscribers' lines, and if connection with a subscriber of another central office is desired, the table operator orders a trunk wire from the proper switch operator, drops an annunciator in the distant office, is switched to a table there, and calls for the party wanted.

Spring jacks and wedges are not used at the tables, but in their stead push-button switches, which are simple and perfect in their operation, and enable the operator, by merely passing his finger from one to another, to switch his telephone from wire to wire quickly and with ease.   The advantages claimed for this system are :

1. Each operator stands or sits in his place and does not move from it.

2. No time is lost at any point in filling an order, but every movement is quickly and easily made.

3. No matter how great the rush of business, it is impossible to confuse or delay the work, provided, of course, there are a sufficient number of operators, and this is not true of any other annunciator system.

4. The system is capable of expansion without limit, and will work just as well with 5,000 as with 500 subscribers; either when all are in one office or are divided among a number of offices

It is not claimed for this system that it is as good as the law system, in which annunciators are not used, and which for rapidity, uniformity, accuracy and cheapness is said to excel all other systems, but it is claimed that this system is superior to any other annunciator system.

THE CHINNOCK SYSTEM.

In 1880 the Metropolitan Telephone and Telegraph Company acquired the ownership of the Telephone Exchange in the City of New York and vicinity, of the Gold and Stock Telegraph Company, and of the Bell Telephone Company, and adopted in all the Exchanges the system invented by Mr. C. E. Chinnock, represented in figure 191, which had been in use by the latter company.

In the Central Telephone Office in New Street, New York, there are nine switch boards arranged side by side along one side of an oblong room, and eight annunciator cases arranged along the opposite side, while between the rows of switch boards and annunciator cases, in the middle of the room, are situated ten operating tables.

The switch boards are five feet in height by five feet in width, and are all of the same size and shape. Running horizontally across the front of the board are strips of brass, about half an inch in width, insulated from each other. There are one hundred of these strips, arranged in pairs, every alternate pair being stained black, while the intervening ones are of the natural color of the brass. Arranged in vertical lines, and about half an inch

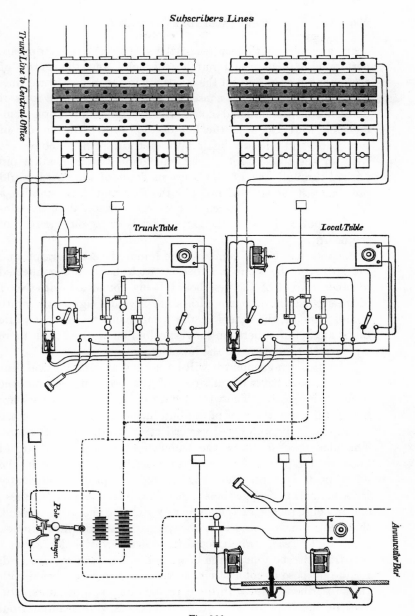

Subscribers Lines

Trunk Line to Central Office

Trunk Table

Local Table

Pole Changer.

Annunciator Bar

Fig. 191

apart, are holes in the centres of the strips. All the strips are perforated with an equal number of holes, and the centres of corresponding holes in all the strips are in the same vertical line. The strips are numbered consecutively, and the vertical rows of holes are also numbered consecutively, the numeration commencing with No. 1, at the left of the board. On the rear of the board, and directly behind the vertical rows of holes, are strips of sheet brass, set at such an angle that a metallic pin pushed through one of the holes in front of the board would press against the strip of brass in the rear, and thus establish a metallic connection between one of the horizontal brass strips on the front, and one of the vertical brass strips on the rear of the board.

Each switch board contains one hundred vertical strips, and the strips of the same number on each board are connected together; No. 1 of the first board being connected with No. 1 of the second, third, fourth, fifth, sixth, seventh, eighth, and ninth boards; and all the others in the same manner. So that while there are 900 numbers on the vertical strips of the board, there are only 100 numbers on the horizontal strips.

From this arrangement it will be seen that each vertical line may be connected with any one of the brass strips upon the front of the board. The wires from the various subscribers are brought through the roof of the building and are attached to the correspondingly numbered vertical strips on the switch board. The pins used to make the connections in the board are of brass, of a tapering form, to insure their fitting closely in the holes in the strips, and long enough to project sufficiently from the rear to engage the sheets of brass on the vertical lines; and in consequence of the angle at which the sheets are placed, they act as springs, and thus always insure a good, firm contact.

In front of each switch board there is a row of holes, about a foot from the bottom of the board, in which pins are inserted, for the purpose of connecting the vertical strips connected with the subscribers' lines with the corresponding annunciators, situated on the opposite side of the room. A wire leading from each vertical strip is connected to a piece of metal fastened to one side of each of the holes forming this row; and another wire, leading to each indicator, is connected to a piece of metal fastened to the opposite side of each of the holes above mentioned, in such a manner that when a pin is inserted into one of the holes, a metallic connection is formed between a subscriber's wire and the corresponding indicator.

The eight annunciator cases each contain one hundred annunciators, arranged in three rows, two rows each containing thirty-four, and one row containing thirty-three annunciators. The annunciator consists of a small disk, hinged on the under side, and so arranged as to drop of its own weight when released by a catch on the end of a lever, actuated by an electro-magnet. The number of each annunciator is painted directly over it, and corresponds to the number of each subscriber, in addition to which the name of each subscriber is written upon a card attached to the inside of each annunciator disk.

By inserting a pin in a hole in a brass strip under each annunciator, connection is made between the subscriber's wire and a telephone receiver and transmitter.

Over each of the operating tables, situated in the middle of the room, there are eight annunciators, the electro-magnet of each annunciator being connected by a wire to one of the horizontal strips running across the front of the switch board.

Upon the operating table there are eight brass spring jacks, about four inches long, rigidly fastened at one end, and resting on a small metallic plate at the other end. Each spring jack is connected by a wire with one terminus of an annunciator magnet, whose other terminus is connected to one of the horizontal strips of the switch board; and the small metallic plate of each spring jack is also connected with one end of an annunciator magnet, whose other end is connected to one of the horizontal strips of the switch board.

Thus there are eight spring jacks upon each table, connected with eight annunciators; that is to say, one spring jack for each annunciator, forming a connection with each of the horizontal strips for that table.

Upon each operating table there are also two keys, a transmitting and receiving telephone and a wedge, the latter instrument designed to be inserted between the spring jack and the small metallic plate; and to facilitate its passage, the end of the spring jack is curved upward. The wedge consists of an ebonite knife, whose blade is covered on each side with strips of brass insulated from each other, and from each strip a wire extends through the handle to the receiver and transmitter of the attendant operator.

When the wedge is inserted between the spring jack and the metallic plate, there is a metallic connection through the spring to the brass strip on the upper part of the wedge, through the wire in the handle to the transmitting and receiving instrument, thence back on the other wire to the lower plate of the wedge, and thence to the metallic plate connected with the annunciator magnet.

Having described the switch boards, annunciators, and operating tables, we will now follow the various operations which occur in the Central Office from the calling of a subscriber who wishes for a connection with another subscriber, to the completion of the conversation and the disconnection of the lines from the operating tables.

Let us, for example, suppose that Brown and Robinson, whose telephonic number is 1 New, desire to converse with Smith and Jones, whose telephonic number is 4 New. Subscriber No. 1 turns the crank of his magnet, which sends an electric current along his wire to the Central Office, where it enters the switch board by the vertical strip No. 1, passes down this wire to the pin which connects it with the annunciator wire, thence to the annunciator magnet No. 1 to the earth. As the current passes through the annunciator magnet the armature of the latter is attracted, thus raising the lever and detaching the catch which holds the shutter, and the latter falls by its own weight. The operator then inserts a pin in the hole under annunciator No. 1, which disconnects the annunciator from the earth direct, and connects it to earth through a telephone transmitter and receiver, and then asks the subscriber through the telephone, "What number?" and receiving the reply, "Number 4," writes the two numbers, 1 and 4, on a small slip of paper, and hands it to a boy, who carries the slip to a local table. The operator then removes the pin from the hole of No. 1 on the annunciator board, and replaces the shutter. The operator at the local table, after receiving the slip, tells the person whose duty it is to move the pins on the switch board as directed to connect Nos. 1 and 4. The switchman then removes the pin belonging to No. 1 from the lower hole, thus opening the circuit between No. 1 and the annunciator, and inserts it in the hole in horizontal strip No. 5, in the vertical line belonging to No. 1. He then moves the pin of No. 4 from the lower hole and places it in a hole on horizontal strip No. 6, and on the vertical line No. 4. The path for the current now passes from subscriber No. 1 through his vertical wire at the back of the switch board to the horizontal brass strip No. 5; thence to annunciator No. 5 on the local table; thence to the spring jack, on the local table, through the metallic plate to annunciator No. 6 on the local table; thence to the horizontal strip No. 6, to the pin inserted on the vertical wire of No. 4; thence out over the line wire to the office of subscriber No. 4, and through his instrument to the earth, thus placing the two subscribers in the same circuit.

The local table operator now notifies No. 4 that he is wanted, by ringing the alarm bell of the latter. Extending along the front part of the under side of the tables is a wire from a series of batteries placed in an adjoining room, the current from which is constantly reversed by an automatic pole changer, and when a subscriber's wire is connected with the battery wire, by pressing a key, the requisite intermittent current for ringing the subscriber's bell passes over it. In the present case the alarm in the office of No. 4 would be rung, while that in No. 1 would remain silent, as the latter had removed the hand telephone and opened the circuit to his own alarm, after he had called the Central Office, and is now waiting, with the receiving telephone at his ear, for the notice from his correspondents, Smith and Jones, that they are ready to talk with him.

The local table operator now inserts a wedge between the spring-jack and the metallic plate, and thus inserts in the circuit a telephone transmitter and receiver, in addition to the annunciator. As soon as the two subscribers, Nos. 1 and 4, finish their conversation, it is their duty to send to the Central Office a signal to that effect, by turning the crank of their magnets and dropping the annunciator shutters connected with their lines on the operating table; but in case they should forget or neglect to do so, the operator can ascertain when they have finished by listening occasionally at the telephone on his table.

The Metropolitan Company has divided the city into eight districts, and in each district established a central exchange. These exchanges are located as follows: New, Murray, Spring, Pearl, Nassau, Walker, Twenty-first and Twenty-second streets.

These exchanges are connected with each other by trunk lines, and also with exchanges in Harlem, Brooklyn, Flushing, Yonkers, Mount Vernon, White Plains, Sing Sing, and Portchester, N. Y., and Jersey City, Hoboken, Paterson, Passaic, Hackensack, Orange, Bloomfield, Montclair, Asbury Park, Elizabeth, Plainfield, New Brunswick, and Morristown, N. J.

When a subscriber connected with one exchange desires to be connected with a subscriber connected with another, the operations are as follows: A subscriber connecting with New Street office, say 280, who wishes to talk with a subscriber in Spring Street office, proceeds as follows: He turns his magnet crank, which throws down the annunciator drop No. 280 in New Street office. The operator in New Street office then inserts a pin connecting with a telephone, and asks what number. Subscriber replies: "250, Spring." These two numbers are then written on a slip of paper, and carried by a boy to an operator at a table having wires running to Spring Street office. This operator then tells the switchman to connect 280 with 18—the latter being the number of the trunk line to Spring Street office —and then depresses a key, which throws a battery current of the line and drops an annunciator disk on a similar table in Spring Street office, and says, through the telephone, "250." The operator at Spring Street then directs the switchman to connect 250, and then calls him by sending a battery current out on his wire, and at the same time rings bell of subscriber "280, New," who called for 250, Spring, and the connection is then completed between the two subscribers without saying a word to either. As soon as the subscribers have finished talking, one of them turns his magnet crank, which throws down an annunciator shutter, situated on a trunk line table, in each of the Central Offices, and the operator notifies the switchman to disconnect the wires from the table, and they are then restored to their normal position on the switch board.

There are in the New Street Central Office ten young women at the operating tables, seven young women at the annunciator cases, five switchmen, and one boy to pass the slips. The New Street Central Office has seven hundred aud thirty subscribers, ninety trunk lines running to different points, and averages six thousand five hundred connections each day, each connection being made, upon both trunk and local wires, on an average in thirty seconds.

The Metropolitan Telephone and Telegraph Company has 3,300 subscribers in the city of New York, and the Law Telephone Company 550; the suburban exchanges, working in connection with the above, have 3,800 subscribers, making a total of 7,650 subscribers in New York and vicinity, who can communicate with each other by telephone through the combination of the various exchanges.

The Metropolitan Telephone and Telegraph Company publishes a pamphlet containing a list of all the subscribers to its various exchanges, and to those of the suburban towns working in connection with them. This pamphlet contains, in addition to the subscribers' names, the name of the Central Office with which his wire connects, and the subscriber's number. The subscribers are only known to the operators by the name of the Central Office with which they are connected, and by the subscriber's number, and not by the subscriber's name.

The following instructions are given to the subscribers for communicating through the Central Offices:

Press in the button and turn the crank once only; unhook the listening telephone (receiver) and put it close to your ear, when Central Office will enquire: What number? Give Central Office and number of person wanted, and upon receiving the answer, all right, hang up the receiver, and wait till your bell rings, then place the receiver to your ear and address the person called. If you do not immediately hear his voice, the delay— except in rare cases—is owing to his failure to promptly answer the call. Therefore, hang up the receiver, press in the button and ring twice, then put the receiver again to your ear. Speak in a moderate, clear tone, with mouth three or four inches from transmitter. Loud speaking jars the mechanism of the instrument and produces a confused sound. When through, do not fail to hang up the receiver, and call off, pressing in button and turning crank once. If you wish to call for a subscriber before disconnection is made, hang up your receiver, press in button, and turn the crank once; then immediately place receiver to your ear and Central Office will answer.

If subscribers will respond quickly when their bells are rung, the service will be much improved.

If bell rings once, pay no attention—you are not wanted. If it rings twice you are wanted. Unhook receiver and speak immediately. The receiver, except when at your ear, must be always on the hook.

The spring-jacks on the trunk tables are similar to those on the local tables, and the application of the spring-jacks serves the same purpose. Immediately in the rear of the spring-jacks there are double switches with two arms swinging upon centres placed just behind three buttons. Over the switches are the annunciators.

On the switch board are certain strips, each one of which is directly connected with a trunk line from another exchange. Before considering this, we will take up the case of a call from another exchange—say Brooklyn. In order to receive a call, the arms of the switch are moved to the right. The trunk line from Brooklyn comes through the roof of the building to a button on the trunk table. The current passes thence through the arm to the brass spring, thence through the brass plate under the spring to the coil of the annunciator, and thence to the ground. The electro-magnet, being liberated, the shutter of the annunciator reveals the fact that Brooklyn is waiting. The attendant, having inserted the wedge in the spring-jack, inquires the number wanted, and, learning that No. 6 of New Street Exchange is wanted, she tells a switchman to connect No. 6 on the switch board with No. 50. He removes the pin from the bottom hole of vertical strip No. 6, and inserts it in the hole on strip No. 50. The arms of the switches are now moved to the left. The course of the current is now through the Brooklyn wire to the switch, thence to the annunciator, thence through the spring-jack and switch to the vertical strip of wire No. 6 on the switch board, and thence over the wire to the subscriber's office. When the conversation has ended, the switch is moved to its first position, and the exchange is ready for another signal from Brooklyn.

In calling up Brooklyn from the New Street exchange, the current from the batteries would pass to the trunk line leading to the Brooklyn exchange, when the New Street subscriber, having been connected with the Brooklyn strip on the switch board, would send his current through this exchange to Brooklyn, and from there to the number he called for.

In cases where all the wires leading from one exchange to another are in use, and yet calls are waiting, it becomes necessary to borrow a connection from a third office. If the wires from exchanges one and two are occupied, No. 1 will ask No. 3 if it can spare a line to No. 2. If the answer is affirmative, No. 1 connects with No. 3, thence to No. 2, and the subscribers belonging to Nos. 1 and 2 are placed in a circuit through No. 3.

THE HASKINS SYSTEM.

Figure 192 represents the Central Office system devised by H. C. Haskins, and in use in the Milwaukee Exchange.

By this system, talking in the office (except with subscribers)

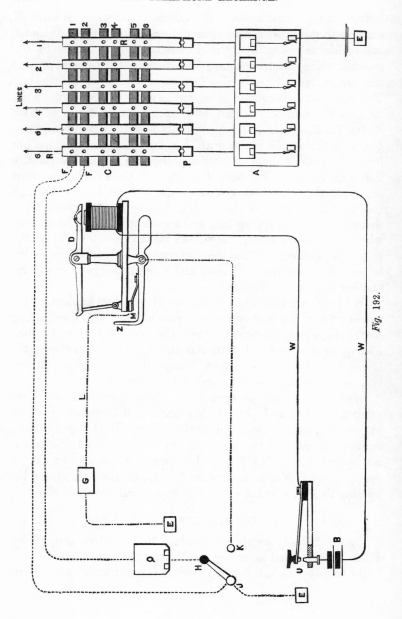

Fig. 192.

as well as the use of flexible cords, are dispensed with. No tickets are used, and connections and disconnections are made to and from the tables, silently and with great rapidity.

Two boards are used. All the lines are run to the perpendicular strips of the connecting board C, which are crossed by pairs of horizontal strips, with which connections are made.

The board A, on which the annunciators are placed, faces the connecting board situated five or six feet distant. The boards are of the Gilliland pattern. The course of the line wires is as follows:

From the tower to the top of the connecting board C, where they are attached to the perpendicular strips 1, 2, 3, 4, etc. By a plug inserted below at P, between a line strip and a brass plate, each line strip is connected with a wire which runs to the annunciator board A, thence through the annunciator B, and by a plug connection to the ground, E.

This is the ordinary path of the main circuit in the Gilliland board.

In the rear of the annunciator board A, are placed two or more listening or disconnecting tables. These tables may be placed in any convenient spot, even in an adjoining room if desired, as no conversation is necessary between the boards and the tables.

The horizontal strips on the connecting board are arranged in pairs, and wires from these strips lead to the tables; so that when two parties are connected, the circuit is through the loops to the tables, and back to the board.

A three point switch, H, is upon the table, for each pair of connecting strips on the board.

The lower strip, F', of the pair, is connected by its wire with the switch H, after passing through an annunciator drop Q, while the upper strip is connected to the plate J. To the other plate K, of the switch, is connected the wire L, from the power generator G.

The wire L, however, before reaching plate K, passes through the connecting points M, of the disconnecting drop D, so that when the drop D falls, it will break the wire L, at M.

The normal position of the switch H is on plate K. Thus the lower strip F' is connected with the generator, and if line I is connected by a plug inserted at R, the generator current will be thrown to that line, ringing the subscriber by the following circuit: G, L, M, K, H, annunciator Q, F', lower horizontal strip Z, R, and line I.

Hence the party desired is always put in the bottom horizontal strip, while the party calling (in this case No. 5) is plugged into the upper horizontal strip of any pair; and the insertion of the plug at the junction of a line and the bottom strip of a pair, not only rings the party wanted, but also drops the annunciator Q on the table, notifying the table operator of a connection.

It is evident that unless the switch H is moved, the generator current will continue to ring the party. Hence the table operator, as soon as the annunciator falls, moves the switch H, to plate J (to which the first party is already connected through the circuit J, F, and line 5) and restores the annunciator Q.

The answering ring of the party called passes through Q, dropping it again, and thence to the party asking the connection. Thus the answering ring notifies the table operator and the calling party at the same time.

Attached to plate J by a short wire, is a plate S, upon which the table operator can touch his telephone cord and listen.

Thus it will be seen that the duty of the answering operator is confined to answering the calls at board A, and plugging the two parties in a pair of strips at C, as described; and it is the duty of the table operators to see that the parties "get together." If the first call does not suffice, the table operator, by moving the switch H back to plate K, calls again.

When the parties have finished their conversation, they are disconnected, as follows:

Below the switch H, is a key, U, in the following circuit: Battery or power generator B, key U, wire W, disconnecting drop D, and wire W, back to B.

For each pair of connecting strips there is, in a frame near the board C, a disconnecting drop like D.

The table operator presses key U, dropping the disconnecting drop D, which notifies the disconnecting operator to take the parties out of the strips numbered the same as the drop.

At the same time, as before shown, the fall of the drop D having broken the generator circuit at M, by striking the lever Z, the table operator can at once restore the switch H to the point K, without ringing the second party again.

The disconnecting operator will not restore the drop D until he has disconnected the parties.

Notice of a desire to be disconnected may be given by a subscriber by ringing out, which will be received on annunciator Q by the table operator; or the latter may, by listening, ascertain when they have finished.

This system is also practical for exchanges which have several subscribers on each wire. At Milwaukee about twenty per cent. of the lines have more than one station, and the signalling is as perfect as though all were single wires.

Thus it will be seen that the operators are divided into three classes, answering, table, and disconnecting; and that all communications between them are by silent electric signals which cannot be misunderstood; and that except the low talking of the operators, answering the calls of the customers, not a word is spoken.

THE WILLIAMS APPARATUS.

Fig. 193 shows the form of the Williams switch board, with a hand telephone and Blake transmitter in position. It is composed of an upright and an inclined board, upon both of which are arranged connecting strips in series of four. Between the two boards are the annunciators.

The connections are made by inserting plugs into horizontal connecting bars studded with holes. These bars are divided into sections of four, and the bars of each section are connected with the corresponding bars of the other tables, and in this manner the connections between the different tables are provided for.

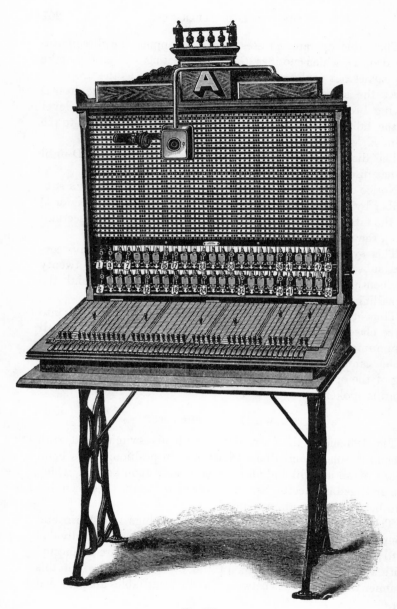

Fig. 193.

When a plug is inserted in one of the openings in the horizontal strips, its extremity forms a connection with a subscriber's line, whose course is vertical or at right angles to the horizontal strips. The point of the plug forms connection with the subscriber's line, not by entering a hole, but by entering between two springs, inclined toward each other in V fashion, and forming contact at their extremities; so that, instead of the line strips for the subscribers' lines, we have an arrangement resembling several letters V assembled together so as to come in contact at their outer margins, the apex of each V being in line with one of the plug holes on the horizontal or connecting strips.

Each vertical row of plug holes corresponds, therefore, to a subscriber's line, which enters the switch board through a spring jack placed on the lower margin of the table. The line divides into two branches there, one of which goes to the V shaped line of the upright portion of the switch board, while the other is connected to the inclined portion, first passing through its annunciator. A plug inserted in the lowest horizontal strip, which is connected to the ground, serves to ground each line.

When an annunciator drops, the operator loops her telephone into the circuit by inserting a jack knife with flexible cord connections. The number required being ascertained, the jack knife is inserted into the spring jack of that number, if it is on the same table. The jack knife is provided with a key and an extra line from the ground through the generator, so that on pressing the key the subscriber is called.

If the subscriber wanted is on another table, then the operator calls the operator of that table. This is done through a special circuit extending from a special spring jack on the under side of the margin of the table (not shown in the figure), which circuit includes an annunciator. Ordinarily this circuit is closed at the spring jacks of both tables. When the first operator inserts her jack knife into the special spring jack, she loops her telephone into this circuit. Now, by pressing the key on the jack knife, she closes the circuit through her generator, and the annunciator at the other operator's table is dropped. The latter loops her telephone in also, by inserting the jack knife into the special spring jack, and on ascertaining the number of the subscriber wanted, she signals him and then takes out the ground plug corresponding to his line, to insert in some one of the connecting bars which is in connection with a corresponding bar on the first operator's table.   If the first operator has not already inserted the ground plug of her subscriber into this bar, she proceeds to do so, and the communication is then established between the two subscribers.   The jack knife of the first operator is usually placed in the spring jack corresponding to the first subscriber, so that her telephone remains looped in, and she may listen until the conversation is ended, after which she disconnects.   It need scarcely be said that there are as many special spring jacks as are necessary to enable each operator to communicate with every other.

Fig. 194 is a sectional view, showing four connecting strips on each board.   Upon the back and under sides of the board are placed the line strips.   These are composed of metal springs arranged so as to normally press their free ends together as shown, and so form a continuous connection.   The spring jack, e', e', and wedge, H, shown on the front edge of board, are used to loop in an operator's telephone and transmitter, and also for signalling a subscriber.

The line circuit enters at L, connecting with spring jack, e' e', to line strip, C, on the upright board, a branch running through an annunciator, D, to the line strips on the inclined table, reaching the earth through the ground strip, f, by means of the plug, P, which normally rests therein, and connects the strip to the line.

To call up a subscriber, insert the wedge into the spring jack, and signal with the central office generator.   To connect two subscribers, the plugs, P, P, of the two lines which are withdrawn from the ground plate, f, are passed through the holes of a common connecting strip, B, pressing between the springs, d, of the line strip, C, and making electrical contacts therewith.   When the operator wishes to put the listening tele-

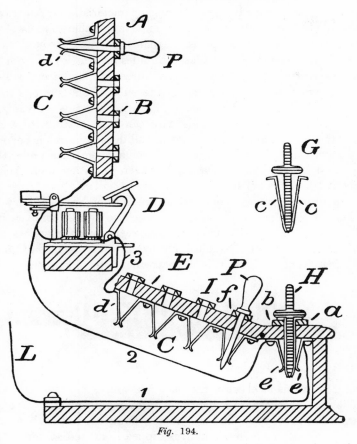

Fig. 194.

phone into any circuit, the wedge, H, is inserted in spring
jack, *e' e'.*

THE SWISS TELEPHONE SYSTEM.

The Swiss telephone system is patterned largely after American methods. The wires are run overhead, and issue from the top
of the central office building, generally through a kind of cupola,
around which, at a distance of a few inches, is built the large

frame studded with insulators that is characteristic of American exchanges. Sometimes in large exchanges, there are two or more of these wire cupolas. From the frame around each cupola the wires radiate in large bundles or arteries of from 30 to 120 wires, which take different directions, and from which the individual branches going to the subscribers' stations in a given district are given off. The wire used is galvanized steel, of No. 12 gauge. This wire can bear a strain of from 800 to 900 lbs., and can be twisted and does not stretch beyond two per cent. of its weight at the outside, even when under the greatest strain. Its resistance, however, is rather high, being about 100 ohms per mile.

In order to avoid kinks, some precautions are necessary in running the lines with this wire, because of its comparative rigidity. It is usually fed out from reels, and the splices are never made near any insulator, but usually at a distance of 25 or 30 feet from it. As it is not expedient to make the twist

Fig. 195.

joint with this steel wire, the English splice, fig. 195, is used. The end of each wire is bent at a right angle, and the two ends are made to overlap, and are then wound around with a soft iron wire, after which the joint is dipped in melted solder. The wires are never stretched beyond a strain of 125 lbs., the sag being purposely made so great on account of the severe climate of this Alpine country, which causes powerful contractions in the wires. The supports of the lines are placed at an average distance of 300 feet apart, though in some cases this distance may be reduced to 100 feet or extended to 1,000 feet or more. The supports are composed of vertical posts of quarter inch angle iron, two or three inches in width, between which the horizontal pieces that hold the insulators are disposed. There are usually six of these, made of T-iron of suitable size (about 2 x 3 in.), and each one carries from eight to ten porcelain insulators screwed into studs projecting from them at a distance apart varying from 12 to 20 inches, according to the length of spans, the latter separation being made when the span exceeds 600 feet.

The number of lines accommodated by each frame is, therefore, from 48 to 60. The vertical posts of the frame are each provided with two legs, which stride over the ridge of the roof

Fig. 196.

of the building in the well known manner. The frame is placed in a parallel line with the ridge of the house whenever it is possible, without deflecting the course of the lines too much, but the frame is sometimes placed obliquely over the roof, which can be done by a suitable change in the legs of the vertical posts. To protect the shingle or the slate covering the roof, a cushion of tarred cloth filled with mineral wool is interposed between the legs of the posts and the roof. Usually the legs are not made fast to the roof, the frame being preferably secured in place by means of stay ropes or wires fixed to the beams of the roof. This enables them to be taken away and placed in other locations with more ease and rapidity, while it also tends to irritate the proprietor of the house to a less degree than the American habit of driving long spikes or bolts through the roofing. The use of iron instead of wood for the frames is an advantage on the score of durability, but its weight appears to be objectionable. The weight of an iron structure like that just described is about half a ton, and when to this is added the weight of wires spanning 300 feet or more, besides the strain under which they are mounted, it looks as if it would be a less crushing imposition on the proprietor of the house to use a lighter material, as is generally done in America. However, if the Swiss houses and their owners can stand the load, our objections have no weight.

As the lines extend further and further from a central station, all the time giving off branches in all directions, they diminish in number, and then, instead of two vertical posts to support the cross beams, only one is used, which is fastened to the gable end of the house, or else a post may be used. The arrangement now becomes more nearly analogous to a telegraph line. In those parts where the wires are subject to annoyance from humming, devices are used to remedy the difficulty. The method of entering the subscriber's place recalls the way in which such installations are made in this country —that is to say, the line descends vertically from an insulator placed on top of the building, to a second insulator placed near the point of entrance. As each subscriber is placed on the end of his line, only one wire is thus laid instead of two, as in our American systems, where oftentimes two or more stations are looped in on the same circuit. Whenever it is possible, the entrance is effected from the rear of the building, so that the wires may be out of sight as much as possible. The rigid steel wire cannot be made to bend around cornices and other projections, and a soft iron wire is generally used for this portion of the circuit. The line properly ends at the subscriber's station, the return circuit being through the ground.

In every case, whenever the house on which a wire-supporting frame is placed is protected by a lightning rod, the frame is always placed in connection with this lightning rod. Where no lightning rods exist, the frame is provided with a suitable earth connection, and it thus becomes itself a lightning rod, which is all the more effectual from the fact that each wire it supports affords an avenue of escape to the lightning discharge, because a lightning arrester is placed in every subscriber's station. According to our observation, the cases of dangerous lightning discharge take place in the open country, and scarcely ever in cities, and lightning rods could as well be dispensed with. But

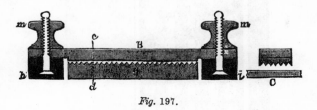

Fig. 197.

it is expedient to provide these precautions against lightning to satisfy public anxiety.

At the central office, the wires leading from the switch board to the wire cupola are provided with lightning arresters of a peculiar pattern, specially designed by M. Rothen, and shown in perspective in fig. 196, and in section in fig. 197. These lightning arresters are of the plate type used in Germany, but in this case they are arranged so as to accommodate several circuits, for the upper plate is replaced by a number of narrow blades, *b a*, fig. 196, B, fig. 197, which are firmly secured to pieces of insulating material *h i*, by nuts *m m*, each blade being about 4 inches long, half an inch wide and an eighth of an inch thick. Their lower surface is grooved lengthwise, as seen at C, fig. 197, so as to present a series of ridges. Each of these blades is in connection with one of the line wires, and the lower plate *g*, which is long enough to extend across the whole series of upper blades, is connected to the ground. The lightning discharge entering the central office on any wire would escape from the ridged surface of the blades *b a* connected with this wire, to the ground-plate *g*, whose surface is also grooved similarly, but at right angles to the grooves in the upper blades. The ridges of the blades, therefore, cross those of the ground-plate, and thus a large number of discharging points is produced, the separation between which is regulated by the nuts *m m*, that serve at the same time

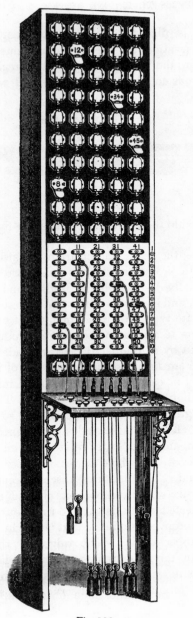

Fig. 198.

as binding posts. Usually, these lightning-arresters are placed in the dome and above the openings of the cupolas on top of the building, or else in the sides of the wire conduits leading to the operating room, when there is sufficient space to receive them. The wires leading from the lightning-arresters to the switch boards in the operating room are of copper of No. 18 gauge, with double paraffined cotton insulation, and are stretched parallel to each other, in layers of fifty, the number destined to each operating table. These layers of wire all run down a shaft which leads to the operating room, and generally enters it at the centre of the ceiling, from which point each set of fifty radiates in the direction of the operating table intended to accommodate it.

The Gilliland switch board is that adopted for the Swiss telephone service, each table (fig. 198) being arranged for fifty subscribers. It consists of a tall vertical stand. At the upper portion is a space occupied by the fifty annunciator dials, and immediately below is a space for the fifty switch openings that serve to make the connections between the subscribers' lines. The fifty annunciators and switch contacts are both disposed in ten horizontal rows of five each. Below these is a row of annunciators, like those above, but intended for a special function. Finally, below these there is a small table, on which are arranged two rows of contact-keys, one containing five keys, and the other containing ten. This table also supports ten movable plugs, whose connecting cords pass down below and are stretched by small weighted pulleys.

The annunciators (fig. 199) are arranged similarly to those of the Lartigue-Brown system of Paris. The disk a, which normally covers the annunciator number c, is held in its upright position by a horizontal arm b, moving with the armature of the magnet e in bell-crank fashion, on the pivotal joint l. When the subscriber signals, the current causes the electromagnet e to attract the armature, and the disk a being released, swings down until it strikes against a stop g, thus uncovering the annunciator number. In falling down the disk moves the spring f into contact with the end of the screw h, thereby closing a circuit through the signal bell that informs the operator of the call made by the subscriber. This bell is placed by the side of the switch board. Each of the plug holes

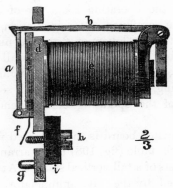

Fig. 199.

or switching openings of the switch board is so arranged that by inserting one of the ten plugs above mentioned, the circuit existing is broken, and a new one is closed simultaneously. Fig. 200 shows one of the plug holes in longitudinal section. From each plug hole a metallic stem extends through the switch board to a threaded portion, e, provided with two nuts $f\,g$, having contact washers between them, and which serve to establish connection with the subscriber's line. The nut f also serves to hold the end of a bent spring c, the free end of which normally bears against the point of a screw h, passing through a piece of ebonite. This screw is connected with the electro-magnet of the annunciator corresponding to this plug hole, the other end of the electro-magnet being connected with the ground. Thus it is seen that as long as there is no plug inserted in the plug hole, the annunciator is included in the circuit of the subscriber, the circuit from the line being through the spring c and screw h. But when a plug is inserted in the hole, as shown by the dotted lines, the spring is moved away from contact with h, while the plug itself forms a contact with the spring, and consequently with the line wire connected at fg. By means of the connecting cord attached to the plugs the line may be connected with another line by inserting a plug into the switching contact corresponding to the line in question, provided the two plugs are connected together.

The contact keys on the small table can be used for different purposes. After one of the plugs is inserted, the circuit of the subscriber is open, and the inner row of five keys is provided to enable the operator to temporarily close the circuit to the ground. The second row of ten keys is provided so that the circuit may be interrupted for the purpose of signalling to either of two subscribers connected together after their two switching contacts are connected together by two plugs and the connecting cords. The two upper portions of the switch board are entirely distinct from the two lower portions, but they become indirectly connected to them by the operation of connecting two subscribers together. The apparatus of the two lower portions is arranged into five sets, each of which forms a complete and distinct whole, and to which corresponds a telephone. Each set comprises the electro-magnet of one of the annunciators in the lower row, the two plugs which are nearest to this annunciator, besides the two outer contact buttons immediately in front and the single contact button behind and between them.

In order to explain the operation of the system, we will suppose that subscriber No. 12 (fig. 198) wishes to speak to subscriber No. 46. Subscriber 12 sends a signalling current (in some cases continuous and in other cases alternating), which drops the annunciator disk, and the operator, hearing the signal bell, immediately puts the plug of the second row into switching hole No. 12, which interrupts the signalling current. The operator's telephone at the same time becomes added to the circuit, and by pressing the second rear (from the left) contact button the circuit is closed, and the operator can ascertain the wants of subscriber 12. On being requested to connect with 46, she takes the next plug and puts it into switching hole No.

46. By pressing the right-hand one of the two front contact keys, she closes the circuit of subscriber 46 and rings his bell. A moment after she presses the rear contact button again, which establishes telephonic communication between her telephone and circuit of No. 46, so that she may inform him that No. 12 wishes to speak with him. As soon as the attention of the lat-

Fig. 200.

ter is secured, she releases the contact button, and the two subscribers can then speak together. When the conversation is ended, either subscriber sends a signalling current, which causes the annunciator of the lower row corresponding to the connection to drop and thus notify the operator to disconnect. Fig. 201 is a diagram of the circuits and their connections in the example just cited. The lines m_3 n_3 of the two subscribers enter at the back of the switch board by their connection with the spring of the plug hole m_2 n_2 touching the screw (fig. 200), which is joined to the annunciators m n, suitably connected to the ground. The signal circuit s, for calling the attention of the operator, is closed when the spring is pressed against the contacts m_1 n_1 (fig. 201). On inserting the plug c into m_2, the annunciator m is cut off and the line extended to e, and thence through one coil of the annunciator a of the lower row (fig. 198). On pressing the rear key or button b (fig. 201), the telephone T is brought into the circuit. On pressing the right-hand front key f after the plug d is inserted into n_2, the signal battery g is brought into play to signal the subscriber. It can be readily seen, also, that the annunciator a will be dropped with equal ease, whether the impulse of current is sent from m_3 or from n_3.

The switch board adopted by the Swiss service will accommodate fifty subscribers only. As the number of subscribers to the majority of the exchanges is greatly above fifty, it is necessary to use a large number of switch boards, and to provide means of communication between each. This is accomplished by the plug holes seen on the margin of the switch board stand at the right side of the middle portion. Each switch board is thus provided with a series of plug holes numbered from 1 to 10, and all the holes of the same number in all the switch boards are connected together by conductors. Consequently, in order to connect two switch boards together, it is only necessary to insert a plug into the hole of the same number at both switch boards. If, for in-

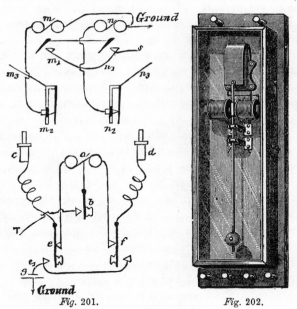

Fig. 201. Fig. 202.

stance, subscriber 39 is to be connected with 457; the operator of the switch board having the first fifty, places the plug in No. 39 and the other plug of the same set into a hole at the right hand side, we will say, No. 1. At the same time the operator of switch board 451–500 inserts a plug in No. 457 and the other plug of the same pair into the right hand hole No. 1. To simplify the operation, a connecting cord having a plug at both ends may be used at the second switch board to establish a direct connection between 1 and 457, and then the connection is the same as if the two subscribers were on the same switch board.

The signal bells ordinarily employed for the subscriber's station work with alternate currents, just like those used in American exchanges. In many American exchanges a large dynamo-electric generator which furnishes alternating currents is used. In other cases the current from a battery is rapidly reversed by an automatic contrivance. In Switzerland the latter method is used exclusively and the reverser used (fig. 202) is essentially the same as that to be seen in some of our American exchanges. To enable those not familiar with this apparatus to understand its operation more easily, we present a diagram (fig. 203), showing the arrangement of the circuits. It consists of a pendulum carrying an armature polarized by a permanent magnet above (fig. 202), which armature is alternately attracted by the electro-magnets placed on either side of it. The pendulum controls two sets of contacts which correspond to two distinct circuits, one of which includes a local battery and serves to cause the motion of the pendulum, the other being that of the battery whose current is to be reversed. In order to show the operation of each circuit more clearly the diagram is divided in two, the upper portion representing the local circuit and the lower portion the reversing apparatus proper. The current of the local battery c divides at b into two equal branches, passing through the electro-magnets i and k and going to springs $f g$ respectively, that rest against a fixed contact h, connected with the other pole of the battery. If the pendulum (shown in section at d) is swung either way, say to the right, it will move the spring g out of contact with h, and the whole current will now pass through the other magnet, i, whereby the pendulum will be moved in the opposite direction, only to cause the other spring, f, to move out of contact and to bring about a reciprocating action by the magnet k. In the second set of contacts the springs u n are also moved alternately away from r by the swinging pendulum c. The reversing function will be easily understood. Supposing b to be the positive pole of the battery, and the pendulum e to be at the right, then the positive pole is in connection with the line. When the pendulum swings to the left, on the con-

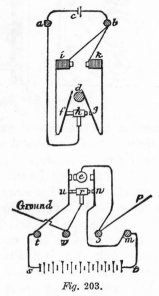

Fig. 203.

trary, the negative pole is to line, and the rapid reversal makes the current alternating. Let us follow the course of the current in both cases. In the first case the circuit is from b to m, to n e p, to and over the line (at e_1 fig. 201, the signal key e or f being depressed), returning through ground to v, and proceeding to r u t, and to the negative pole s. In the second case we have b m n r v, the ground, the line back to p, thence to e u t s. The batteries used are of the ordinary gravity type.

The telephone apparatus used by each operator in the central office requires no special description. It consists of a transmitter supported at a height convenient to the operator's mouth, and below this is a supporting device for the receiver, which is so disposed that it permits a large range of motion to adapt it to any position preferred by the operator.

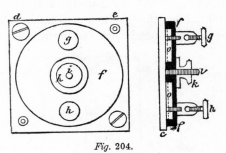

Fig. 204.

The apparatus used at the subscribers' stations is characteristically American, for it is nothing more than the familiar magneto box with automatic switches, worked by the weight of the telephone depending from a forked lever. The accompanying diagram (fig. 205) establishes this similarity. K is the fork of the lever *a*, which, when held down by the weight of the telephone, closes the line at *c* through the bell G and through the spring *w* (which short circuits the magneto-generator M I), and thence to the ground. The bell G is made so as to work generally with alternate currents, because it is then more sensitive, on long circuits, though sometimes it is constructed so as to work with continuous currents. In either case the resistance is about 100 ohms. The generators have a resistance of 500 ohms, and they give an electro-motive force of about 45 volts. When the magneto-electric generator is used, the spring *u* is depressed by the knob so as to open the shunt around the armature. This knob is now dispensed with, as a general rule, in the American magneto-generator.

When the telephone is taken off the hook K the lever *a* moves upward and comes against the contact strips *b*, whereby the local circuit through the battery, the primary coil of the inductorium,

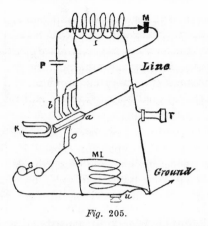

Fig. 205.

and the microphone transmitter M is closed, while the secondary coil I of the inductorium and the receiver T become included into the lines. The lightning arrester used at the subscriber's station is not of the serrated edge kind with which our
American apparatus is provided, but is of a special form, of
the plate description before referred to, and is shown in fig.
204.

The telephonic transmitters adopted by the Swiss service are
of various types, viz., the Blake, the Theiler, the Ader and the
Berliner. According to M. Rothen they each have their merits
and demerits. The Blake transmitters give purer and clearer
articulation, but they get out of order easily. They require only
one cell of Leclanche battery. The Theiler transmitter is less
delicate, and does not fry as readily as the Blake, but the voice
is not reproduced as clearly or as loudly, and two or three Leclanche cells are required. With the Ader transmitter, the voice
is weaker but distinct, and this transmitter is least subject to
frying. It requires four Leclanche cells connected in multiple
series of two. Finally, the Berliner transmitter, which requires
but one Leclanche cell, is very good, and while the voice is
not quite as clear and distinct as with the Blake transmitter, it
is much less liable to fry and get out of order.

In some cases the subscriber uses continuous currents to call the central office, and this requires a local battery of six cells or more. Owing to the cost and inconvenience of this arrangement, the magneto is preferred by the administration.

In special cases a station may be provided with accessory apparatus, such as additional bells, so that a call may be heard in different parts of a building or even outside. The form and function of the apparatus of course varies according to the purpose to which it is to be applied. One form of apparatus of this kind, the indicator bell, is worthy of special mention. It is used when the subscriber, a merchant, for instance, desires facilities such that he can be placed in connection with the central office or with his business establishment. The apparatus designed by M. Rothen (fig. 206) consists of a box provided with two annunciators, and a three-way switch to be operated

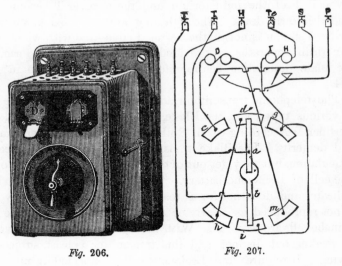

Fig. 206.   *Fig.* 207.

by hand. Fig. 207 is a diagram of the connections between the binding posts and the contact segments. The switch lever is composed of two pieces, *a b*, insulated from each other. The apparatus is placed near the telephone apparatus proper. Supposing the subscriber's house and place of business to be on the same line, when the switch is in the vertical position shown in the figure, the central station can call the intermediate station, and *vice versa.* In this situation the distant station can also call the intermediate station; the right-hand annunciator drops (I H), and closes a local circuit which rings a special bell. The midway station, by turning the switch on contact II (*g h,* fig. 207), reverses the connection, and it is then in connection with the distant station in the same manner as if the central station were not connected. If, now, the central station calls, the right-hand annunciator will again drop and cause the special bell to ring. When the remote station wishes to communicate with the central office, the midway station switch is placed on contact D, by which the apparatus of the midway station is excluded from the circuit, with the exception of the annunciator D, which is made to drop by an impulse of current when the conversation has ended. This switch system just described may be applied to multiple connections made from a midway station, just as if this station constituted a small central office, in which case there are as many annunciatiors as there are lines connected, and the switch is replaced by a Swiss switch board with connecting cords. The apparatus is modified to suit the convenience and wants of the subscribers, the government service being well disposed to favor its patrons in this respect, though of course, the expense is borne by the subscriber.

The Swiss system patterns after our methods in many respects. In many points we have progressed on this side of the Atlantic, particularly in the matter of switch boards, in which direction the efforts of inventors to improve never cease, and with the ultimate adoption of automatic exchange systems, toward which we are now progressing, the Swiss system would suffer greatly by contrast. The Swiss system has its advantages, and in a country where the patrons of the telephone are not so exacting and impatient as ours, it will, doubtless, give complete satisfaction, while it has the great merit of being uniform throughout the country.

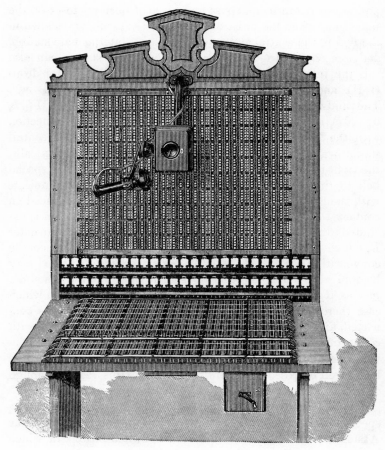

Fig. 208.

THE GILLILAND APPARATUS.

In the description of the Swiss Telephone system we have
illustrated (fig. 198) and described one of Gilliland's switch
boards. Fig. 208 is a general and fig. 209 a sectional view of
the Gilliland standard switch board, which is very extensively
used in America.

Fig. 209.

The crimped strips (fig. 209) extending from the front to the back in groups of ten, are line strips. Those running parallel with the front in groups of five are connecting loops. Loop strip B is used to ground all lines. Loop strip C is connected with the generator. Loop strip D is used for plugging into telephone strip. Line strip L is connected with the telephone. Group E is for making connections, which originate and end on the board. Plugs H and I show Nos. 4 and 7 as connected. Group F is for making connections which originate on this board and end on another. Plug G shows No. 9 as having called and connected with a number on another board. Groups A, 3, 4 and 5 are for making connections when a number on another board calls for a number on this board. Each group represents another board, but the connections of the board are so run that should more than five connecting loops be needed for one table, loops may be borrowed from another group. Plug N shows a call originating on another board connected with No. 5. The operator can always listen by plugging in on L at any loop desired. When not in use all lines should be grounded by plugging them on ground strip B.

Fig. 210.

Fig. 210 shows the Gilliland switch board for twenty wires, which constitutes a complete telephone exchange switch for a small number of wires, being designed for factories, charitable institutions, railroad offices and the club system of small towns and villages. The operation of the board consists simply in inserting plugs into the line and loop strips of those desiring to be connected, and whose wishes are made known by the fall of the annunciator drop.

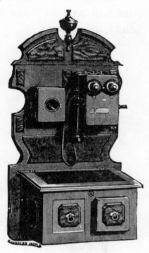

Fig. 211.

Fig. 211 represents Gilliland's cabinet set, designed for use in private residences. The cabinet is provided with drawers, in one of which the battery is placed, and is so arranged as to be of easy access for cleaning and replacement.

Fig. 212 represents the Gilliland standard bell. The generator has a powerful compound magnet and an armature of the Siemens form, wound with a fine silk covered wire, and is able to ring a bell or cause an annunciator drop to fall through 15,000 ohms resistance. The ringer has two helices, and a soft iron armature. To the latter is attached a small brass rod with a ball on the end, which is visible between the bells in the cut. When the current is generated from either end of the circuit, a vibratory motion is imparted to the armature and rod, causing the ringing of the bells by the motion of the ball. The automatic feature, which was designed by Mr. Gilliland to do away with the push button device, is a simple arrangement, consisting of an arm attached to the driving wheel of the generator, so that the current is shunted directly to the ringer instead of passing through the high resistance of the armature and generator, thus increasing the power of the latter and avoiding the necessity of the subscriber using both hands in calling.

Fig. 212.

When the telephone is not in use, it is hung between the forked end of a gravity switch, as seen in the cut. The weight of the telephone throws the lever upward to a contact with the flat spring connections, so as to cut it entirely out of circuit, leaving only the magneto engine and ringer or call bell in circuit. Attached to this telephone hook is a coil spring, which, when relieved of its tension, cuts out the engine and call bell, and thus leaves the telephone only in circuit. The magneto call bell is provided with an improved lightning arrester that has proven quite successful. The apparatus is so constructed that every part is in sight and can be readily removed and replaced; the engine being enclosed in the box, and the ringer and hook placed on the lid, which, on being opened, exposes the whole combination. The connections are composed of copper strips with soldered joints, with binding posts for line, microphone and ground on the top of the box, the connecting wires being run in grooves on the back side of the wall board.

Fig. 213.

Fig. 213 represents Gilliland's annunciator drop for switch boards. It is so constructed that it can be used on a closed or open circuit, and is capable of delicate adjustment. It is readily operated by a magneto generator through a resistance of several thousand ohms. The magnets are wound to a resistance suitable for both battery or magneto currents.

THE JONES APPARATUS.

The Jones apparatus is applicable to either magneto or battery signals. Every line has one terminal in a central or branch office. The lines are arranged in groups of fifty or more, and are brought to a separate operating table. Each table is in charge of an operator, who sits before it.

Fig. 214 shows one table complete with forty drops and a transfer arranged for four tables. The drops are fastened between the shelves by four screws, and any drop may be removed in an instant. New drops may be added at any time by simply screwing them on in position. The drop is very com-

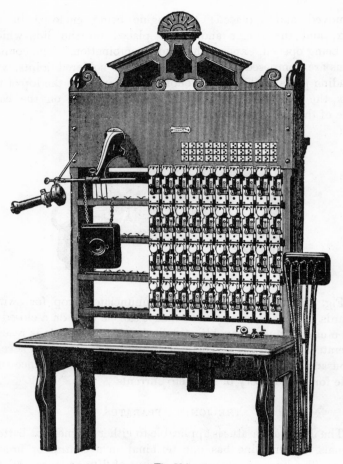

Fig. 214.

plete, containing all the apparatus employed between the line and the ground wire. At the right is the cord holder, where cords hang when not in use. F is a plug socket, to use by inserting a plug connector, instead of holding over the crank, when the operator wishes to hold a prolonged conversation or when he wishes to call or converse through the transfer. The spring

lever L, in its normal position, is in connection with the telephone. When pressed down, it is in connection with the generator.

Fig. 215 shows a side view of one of the drops fixed between
two shelves of the table. D being a target which falls when a
call comes in from a subscriber. The target is reset when the

Fig. 215.

crank is turned for telephoning by the aid of the brass slide and
the short arm on the right of the crank, as shown in cut. On
the top of each shelf three strips are fixed, which are permanently connected up as follows: G to the ground, E to one side

of generator, T to one side of telephone. The other sides of generator and telephone are connected to the ground. The incoming line is connected at the binding post C. The circuit passed thence through the coils of the metal work of the frame, thence by spring jack O to ground wire. All the movable parts about the frame have rubbing contact, insuring complete circuit. When a call comes in the crank is pressed to the right. A small eccentric on the same shaft with the crank lifts the spring jack O, breaks the ground connection and makes a new connection through wing S to the generator strip, and sends signal currents to the line in answer to the call.

The same operation is performed in calling a subscriber. Some exchanges do not have their subscribers wait for an answer to this call, but instruct them to take down their telephone, and listen after giving the signal, as the operators are supposed to be always on duty. In that case, the operator, after receiving a signal, simply places the crank N to left, thereby lifting spring jack O again, and making connections with the other wing, at S, to the telephone, and at once communicates with subscriber.

When the crank N is not pressed upon, it stands vertically, and the spring jack O contacts with the ground strip. A spring holds it in this position. If the plug of a connecting cord be inserted in the socket U, the plug will lift the spring jack from the ground strip, and the circuit will then be through the cord, whose other end may be plugged to another drop or to the transfer.

The drops are restored to their normal ground connection by simply pulling out the plugs. If the operator desires to listen, in order to test, when two drops are connected by a cord, he presses crank N of either drop to the left. This puts his telephone in connection with both parties.

Upon the top board of the table, transfer sockets are arranged in groups of nine, and numbered from one to nine, each group being designated by a color or a letter, as red, white, blue ; A, B, C, etc. These sockets are simply metal holes which receive the cord plugs, and each has a binding post behind the board.

Each plug socket in each group is connected to the corresponding socket in the corresponding group on each table in the exchange; for instance, No. 1 red socket is connected by wire with No. 1 red socket on each of the different tables.

THE MULTIPLE SWITCH BOARD SYSTEM.

The two most important requisites in switch boards for large telephone exchanges are speed and economy, and these go together; for whatever tends to reduce the amount of work to be done, also enables the operators to do it quickly, and therefore diminishes the cost of the work. This desirable result seems to be met with in a high degree in the multiple switch board, which is based upon the idea of having each operator reach all the subscribers' lines in an exchange with one motion for each line, and of having each operator do all the work involved in effecting the connecting and disconnecting of two subscribers; there being no repeating of orders, either by word of mouth or by tickets. An operator has a certain number of subscribers whose calls he answers. When one of these subscribers has called for a connection with any other subscriber of the exchange, the operator who takes the order makes the connection of the two lines instantly and rings the bell of the subscriber wanted. When the conversation is finished the same operator who connected them together receives the notice from the subscribers to disconnect, and then disconnects the lines. This is all done by the operator without moving more than a step, and it would be hard to imagine a system more simple or more easily manipulated.

One switch board of the multiple system is composed of— 1st. A certain number of spring jacks, one for each line, centring at the exchange. 2d. A number of annunciator drops. Two hundred is the number now commonly agreed upon as suitable for one board. Two operators are expected ordinarily to do all the work for two hundred subscribers. 3d. A number of pairs of connecting cords, each with suitable keys and connections for the operators' telephone, the apparatus for ringing subscribers' bells, and the clearing out drops. Fig. 216 represents one of these multiple switch boards for an exchange of 1,200 subscribers. It has 1,200 switch openings or spring jacks, one corresponding to each line. The connections between the spring jacks are made in a manner nearly identical to that of the switch board described on page 277. The connecting plugs are in pairs and hang down from the upper or projecting portion of the switch board, and the weighted pulleys which stretch the connecting cords are disposed above instead of below the spring jacks. The two plugs of each pair are placed in front of each other, so that only one is seen in the figure. It will be seen that there are thirty pairs, numbered from one to thirty, and to each pair corresponds a clearing out annunciator. Instead of pulling the plug up, it is pulled down, to make connection. Any pair may be used to make the connections. Thus, for instance, the pair No. 9 connects a spring jack in the second block of a hundred with a spring jack in the twelfth, as shown by the dark lines, which represent the connecting cords. For each pair of plugs there is a switch lever on the projecting table leaf below, and to each set of five pairs is a set of calling keys. Although each and every line centring in the exchange has a spring jack in the switch board, yet the two operators placed in charge of it are not expected to answer the calls for the whole 1,200 subscribers. Each switch board is intended to accommodate only 200 subscribers. In an exchange of 1,200, six switch boards like that shown in fig. 216 would be required.

The spring jacks, fig. 217, are of the ordinary description used in the standard switch board, except that the spring is insulated from the frame of the jack, and the connection is also made by inserting a plug which opens the connection between the phosphor bronze spring and the insulated screw. The spring jacks are mounted on bases, and form blocks or sections of one hundred (5×20), the section being 15 inches long and 5 inches wide. The sections may be removed independently of each other, and new ones may be added at the top as the exchange grows.

The spring jacks are numbered from 1 to 1,200 on each of the six switch boards, and all those of the same number are connected together.   Thus the line, A (fig. 218), passing through the lightning arrester, goes to the spring of the jack of the first switch board and from the insulated screw to the spring of the jack bearing the same number on the next switch board, and from this to the corresponding one on the next, and finally,

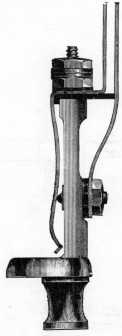

Fig. 217.

after passing through all of the same number at every switch board (three being shown in fig. 218), it goes to the annunciator and to the ground.

On the first switch board the annunciators corresponding to the first two hundred numbers are placed.   The next table receives the annunciators of Nos. 201 to 401, the next 401 to 601,

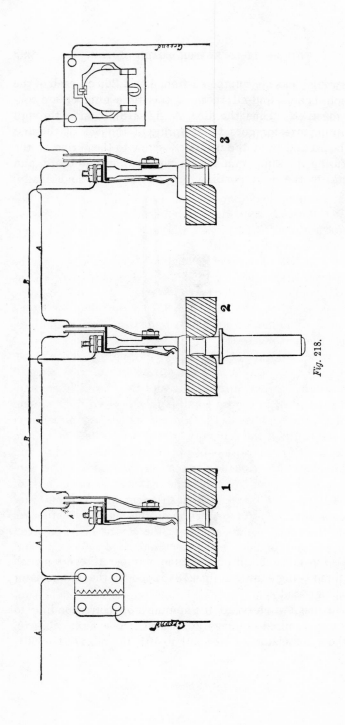

Fig. 218.

and so on. Thus the two operators at each switch board only become cognizant of calls made by 200 subscribers, corresponding to the annunciators on their switch board. It makes no difference on which switch board the annunciators are placed, provided they are placed between the last spring jack and the ground, because the subscriber's line affords practically six points of connection—one for each switch board—and the operator can evidently use the spring jack of the number corresponding to the annunciator, no matter at which switch board the latter is placed.

Each operator takes special charge of one half the switch board, or 100 of the annunciator numbers and their corresponding spring jacks. When the operator receives a call from any of the subscribers in his charge, he can connect them by using a pair of plugs, not only with any other on his section of spring jacks, but with any other of the 1,200 subscribers, without assistance, no matter on what table the latter may be specially accommodated; and likewise an operator on another switch board can connect with one of his subscribers without even his knowledge. This system dispenses with all necessity of repeating calls from one switch board to the other; but as several subscribers on different sections might desire to be connected with the same subscriber at the same time, it is necessary for each operator to have a means of determining whether any plug has been inserted in the spring jack of this number on any of the other six switch boards, and a special test is provided for the purpose.

It is for providing this test that the springs of the jacks are insulated from the frames, and that the frames themselves, moreover, are connected together, as shown in fig. 218, a line, B, passing from the frame of one spring to the frame of the corresponding jack on the other switch boards. Suppose that subscriber 205 on his section wants 673. As soon as the annunciator drops the operator pulls down the front plug of any pair and inserts it into the spring jack. By so doing he cuts off the annunciator and literally prolongs the subscriber's line into the connecting cord which completes a circuit to the other cord and to the rear plug of the same pair, whose upper end forms metallic connection with the ground strip. In passing from one cord to the other, however, the line may be made to include the operator's apparatus. The telephone apparatus is normally included in this loop whenever the switching lever corresponding to the pair of plugs is forward. The operator's telephone circuit also comprises a cell of battery for the test. Having ascertained the number required (673) by the calling subscriber (205), he takes down the rear plug of the same pair, thus opening the circuit between the first subscriber and his telephone, and while listening at the telephone he places the end of this plug in contact with the metallic portion of the spring jack 673, with which he is about to make connection.

The metallic portions of all spring jacks numbered 673 are connected together, and if this line is already in use by a prior connection with another line at one of the other six switch boards, the moment the operator at this table touches the metallic portion of 673 with the rear plug a cross is formed with the circuit already connected, and a click is produced in the telephone by the current of the single cell. In such a case the operator informs subscriber 205 that 673 is busy. If no click is heard by the operator, then he inserts the plug into spring jack 673 and depresses the right calling key, after which he throws the switch lever backward, whereby the telephone becomes cut out of circuit and the clearing out annunciator substituted. In case it becomes necessary to summon 205 again the left key may be depressed. When the conversation is ended either of the subscribers sends a momentary current and the clearing out annunciator is dropped, after which the plugs are pulled out and the switch lever turned forward. Fig. 219 is a diagram of the manner of making the connections of the telephone, the clearing out annunciators and the calling battery or generator. The two cords are connected to the calling keys, and the clearing out annunciator completes the circuit between the two upper contacts against which these keys normally rest,

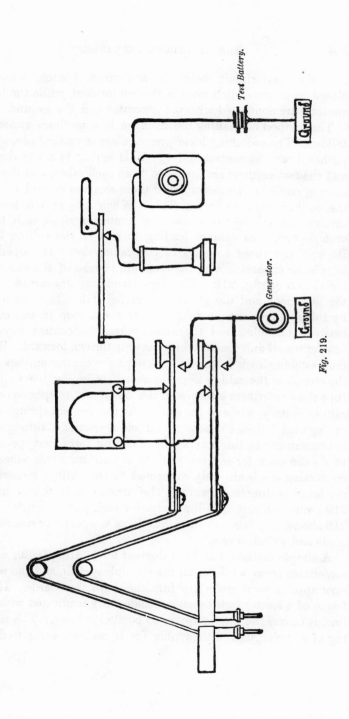

Fig. 219.

the telephone circuit being in a derived branch, which is closed when the switch lever is thrown forward, while the lower contacts are connected with the generator and the ground.

The method of making the changes is sometimes varied, as follows : The switching lever presses down a vertical pin, which pushes down the contact spring. This spring is made double, and the two sections are insulated from each other, and the connecting cords are connected with these sections instead of with the calling keys, as in fig. 219. When the switch lever is thrown forward the two sections of contact springs each touch on a contact, each contact leading to one of the calling keys. Between the upper contacts of the calling keys is looped the telephonic apparatus with the test cell, instead of the annunciator shown in fig. 219. The lower contacts are connected to the generator and the ground as in fig. 219. It is seen that by this arrangement the telephone forms a loop in the circuit between one plug and the other, when the contact keys are not depressed and the switching lever is thrown forward. When the switching lever is thrown backward the contact springs open the circuit to the calling keys, so that it is impossible to interrupt the subscribers either with the operator's telephone or the calling battery, while at the same time the contact springs come up against other contacts which close a circuit through the annunciator. In this way a pair of calling keys may be made to do the work for several pairs of connecting cords, since the connecting cords are only connected to the calling keys when the lever is thrown forward. The arrangement shown in fig. 219 requires a pair of calling keys for each pair of cords. Fig. 216 shows only one pair of calling keys to every five connecting cords and switch levers.

A simple method has been devised for locating faults which sometimes occur while using the multiple system, and the necessary appliances therefor are furnished with the boards. If the frame of a spring jack becomes accidentally connected with the line, it causes the line to appear to be always busy. The touching of a spring jack with a plug (as if making a test to determine whether the line is in use) serves to indicate the fact of the cross, and the jack at which the cross may be found is readily located by inserting a rubber plug at the first board and opening the connection of the spring at the first jack with the line ; this connection may be opened at any point, but preferably at the lightning arrester, thus avoiding tampering with the wires at the back of the board, the break at the lightning arrester serving the same purpose.

Fig. 220 shows the plug inserted in the second spring jack, and the line opened at the lightning arrester. The operator now tests as before to determine whether this cross exists at the first jack ; for if it does exist there, and nowhere else, the insertion of the rubber plug at the first board, and the breaking of the line connection, will clear the cross and show the line not busy. If, however, the cross is at some other jack, the test will still cause the line to appear busy. Upon removing the plug from the jack at the first board, and inserting it at the jack of the second board, a test with the telephone will determine whether the cross exists at the second board, the result being, if it does exist at the second board, that the line will test clear. By thus opening the line at the lightning arrester, and inserting the rubber plug at the jack to be tested, the point at which the cross exists may be located, as the insertion of the plug into the jack to be tested will cause the line to test clear. This test, however, only provides for discovering faulty insulation between the phosphor bronze spring and the frame. If a cross should exist in the bushing which insulates the contact point (against which the spring normally rests) from the frame, the fact can only be known by failure to find a cross between the spring and the frame. In this case it will be found in the bushing of the jack preceding the one in which the test located it. It is, however, exceedingly improbable that the fault will ever be found at this point, as it is entirely out of the way of harm from mechanical injury, and has never been found here in any of the boards thus far. This insulation is the same as that of the jack in the standard board, where it has always been found entirely reliable.

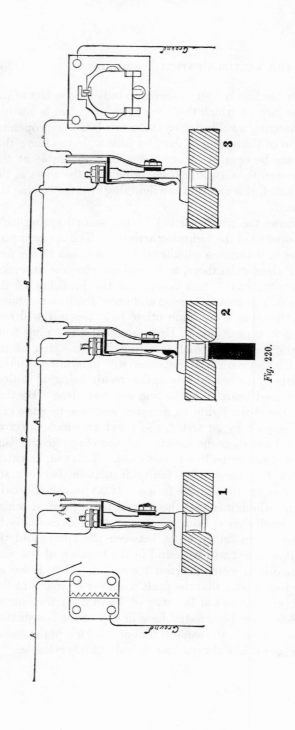

Fig. 220.

The only other fault which has thus far appeared in the multiple switch board system, is that a line has sometimes been found open in the spring jack connection, this being caused by an attempt to clean the contact points of the jack, and resulting in the crippling of the spring. This has been done by thrusting files into the jack from the front or back, in this way bending up the spring until it will no longer make contact with its point. The fact of such a break is determined by the failure of the annunciator to fall upon sending a current through the system. The jack at which the break occurs may be located by inserting the plug whose cord is connected with a calling generator, into the spring jacks successively, beginning at the first board, until the jack is reached at which, upon inserting the plug, the annunciator is caused to fall. When this jack is reached, it may be known that the fault exists in the jack immediately preceding the one where contact causes the annunciator to fall. The plug used to make this test is a special one, and does not, when inserted, occasion the usual break between the spring and its contact point. If the fault is at the last spring jack of the system, the insertion of the plug at any of the boards will fail to cause the annunciator to fall, and after the insertion of the plug at every jack of the line, the failure of the annunciator to fall is an indication that the fault is at the jack of the last board, it having been previously determined that the circuit from the last board and through the annunciator to ground is intact.

Another interesting feature of this switch board is the method of arranging the wires in cables. Behind these are vertical boards between the sections, and the cables, containing twenty wires, enter and leave through perforations in the boards. The first board has only one set of holes, through which the cables enter. Each cable gives off a wire to a spring jack, which, as we have seen in fig. 216, are arranged in rows of twenty. From each spring jack starts the test line which is destined to connect the frames of the corresponding jacks in all the switch boards, and the line out. These test lines are made of office wire of a uniform color and cabled together, and pass out through a hole in

the next vertical board, thence to the wire conduit leading to
the other switch boards. The line out from each spring jack is
cabled also with that of the others in the same row, and of another uniform color, and it also passes out through one of the
holes in the vertical board separating the sections of spring
jacks. The lines in of the same row of the next section enter in
cable form through an opening midway between the other two
cables. Thus a symmetry of disposition is obtained, which
economizes space and time and affords convenience and facility
in making connections.

POLICE TELEPHONE AND SIGNAL SYSTEM.

In every American city the police has employed the various
systems of electric communication in a greater or less degree
for the prevention or detection of crime; but the city of
Chicago occupies the front rank in the use of telegraphic and
telephonic communication, as one of the most essential factors
of the police system. The object of the system is twofold: to
increase, on the one hand, the rapidity and efficiency of police
assistance in cases of urgency, and to diminish, on the other
hand, the number of patrolmen, and, consequently, the expense
which they entail on account of the great number required to
be of service in time of need.

The urgent need of a policeman in one particular point in a
city is in general exceptional, and the actual tendency is to increase the territory placed under the surveillance of each one.
As a result, when an accident occurs, the policemen are nearly
always at a distance from the place where their co-operation is
necessary; and the thieves, who well know this peculiarity,
often take advantage of it to carry on their nefarious work. To
guard against these inconveniences, it is necessary to increase
very largely the number of policemen; but this process is much
less economical than that adopted in Chicago. This means consists in facilitating and rendering very rapid the movements of
the police force, so that each man on patrol or watch may be
placed in communication in an instant with the subdivision to

which he is attached, or, if that is necessary, with the police station of the district, and at the same time with the central station. Each principal citizen can also, in case of need, call instantly for the police and secure their presence in a very short time. In order to accomplish this in an efficient and practical manner, the police stations are established at certain points conveniently chosen in each district; to each station is assigned a horse and wagon and three men, always ready to start. The wagon carries a litter, bed, bed clothes and the necessary articles for receiving and taking care of a sick or injured person, to pick up a lost child, arrest persons accused of crime, etc. The police stations are in telephonic connection with the public alarm stations, which are similar to sentry boxes, and which are distributed along the streets at certain distances from each other. These sentry boxes are just large enough to contain a man and afford shelter for the occasion. They are opened by means of keys, which are given to all the principal people of the city, as well as to the police. In order to prevent their abuse, the locks of the alarm stations are made in such a manner that the key cannot be removed, when once placed in the lock, except by a policeman. As each key is numbered, and cannot be removed except by the co-operation of the police, the person who has given the alarm, on opening the sentry box, cannot prevent himself from being known. By this means all annoyance from unnecessary alarms are avoided, because the possessor of a key opens the box only when assistance is necessary, and is not lavish of his calls for fear of having to give up his key. It will thus be seen that each citizen co-operates by this means in the general surveillance, and that assistance is not unnecessarily delayed.

The series of manœuvres by which this is accomplished is as follows : As soon as an accident occurs, the citizen or nearest neighbor possessing a key proceeds to the alarm box nearest to him, opens it, and makes the signal indicated upon the apparatus. Immediately a squad of three men with a horse and wagon arrives at the point where the signal proceeds from. If a policeman is found near the sentry box, he opens the box and communicates with the police station by means of the telephone which is located therein. When the sentry box is opened by a private citizen, the latter works the call by means of the dial apparatus placed there for this purpose. This apparatus permits of the transmission of eleven different signals to the central station, by placing a pointer upon the number indicating the nature of the alarm to be given. The indications of the signals are as follows: 1. Police wagon. 2. Thieves. 3. Forgers. 4. Riot. 5. Drunkard. 6. Murder. 7. Accident. 8. Violation city ordinance. 9. Fighting. 10. Test of line. 11. Fire. In giving a signal the caller places the pointer upon the number corresponding to the signal required and presses upon a lever at the right of the dial. The movement of the lever causes the apparatus to convey to the police station a conventional despatch, indicating the number of the station calling and the nature of the appeal. The transmitter is auto kinetic, and the despatch is received in arbitrary characters, composed of dots and lines, upon a band of paper, by an ordinary Morse telegraph register, the instrument being put in motion automatically when the first signal is conveyed.

Fig. 221 represents the system in operation on the occurrence of an accident. The signal has been given and has been received and acted upon by the central office. Upon the left of the figure the relief wagon is seen arriving, while in the sentry alarm box a policeman is seen explaining through the telephone to the police station the nature of the accident, its importance, etc. Each hour, or each half hour, the officer on his round proceeds to one of the alarm stations and makes his report by telephone to the police station of his district, which much simplifies and facilitates the service. The chief officer of the station can then direct and regulate his service without difficulty. The system in Chicago allows also the installation of signal boxes analogous to those above described, in each house or office with or without telephone adjunction. In the latter case the indications are given upon the dial, as in the

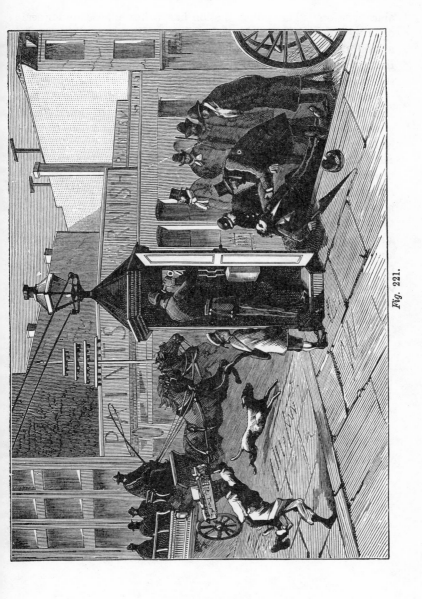

Fig. 221.

alarm station.   The police station has a key placed under seal
opening the house of each subscriber.   When a call is made
at night, for robbery with housebreaking, for example, a policeman responds to the call, taking the key of the house whence
the call came, and proceeds immediately to seize the robber.

The system practically operates in the most efficient and
satisfactory manner.   The number of arrests in the district
where it is applied has been largely increased, and has diminished the number of crimes in a corresponding proportion.   The
establishment is cheap, and its maintenance inexpensive.   It
proves useful more especially in the small cities, where the
number of policemen is relatively small.   By the aid of alarm
boxes, placed in particular houses, and of alarm stations in
the streets, they can call for assistance in a few moments,
and thus secure from a small number of policemen the same
amount of practical service·that they would ordinarily get only
from a numerous force.   We thus see by this brief description
of the alarm system of Chicago, that each individual plays a
part in the general security, and that every one contributes to
the repose of all.

CHAPTER IX.

VARIOUS MODIFICATIONS OF THE BELL TELEPHONE.

Since the discovery of the articulating telephone by Prof. Bell, the various modifications of the apparatus which have been devised are almost innumerable. We shall not attempt to give a description of any considerable number of these devices, but only refer to a few of the more important varieties.

BELL'S PHOTOPHONE.

The object of the photophone is the transmission of sounds, both musical and vocal, to a distance by the agency of a beam of light of varying intensity; and the first successful attempts made by Prof. Bell and his co-laborer, Mr. Samuel Tainter, were based upon the known property of the element selenium, the electric resistance of which varies with the degree of illumination to which it is exposed. Hence, given a transmitting instrument, such as a flexible mirror, by which the vibrations of a sound could throw into vibration a beam of light, a receiver, consisting of sensitive selenium, forming part of an electric circuit with a battery and a telephone, should suffice to translate the varying intensities of light into corresponding varying intensities of electric current, and finally into vibrations of the telephone disk audible once more as *sound*. This fundamental conception dates from 1878, when, in lecturing before the Royal Institution, Prof. Bell announced the possibility of hearing a shadow fall upon a piece of selenium included in a telephone circuit. The phototone, however, outgrew the particular electrical combination that suggested it; for not the least of the remarkable points in this research is the discovery that audible vibrations are set up in thin disks of almost every kind of material by merely throwing upon them an intermittent light. With the photophone, as with the telephone, there are instruments of

different degrees of perfection. The original telephone of
Philip Reis could only transmit musical tones, because it worked
by rapid abrupt interruptions of the electric current; while the
articulating telephone of Graham Bell is able to transmit speech,
since by its essential construction it is able to send undulating
currents to the distant receiving station.

We may in like manner classify the forms of photophones
under two heads, as (1) articulating photophones, and (2) musical photophones.

Up to the present time the simple receiving disk of ebonite or
hard rubber has only served for a musical photophone; the reproduction of the tones of the voice by its means has not yet been
demonstrated in practice. For while it produces unmistakable
musical tones by the direct action of an intermittent light, in the
experiments made hitherto with articulate speech, the instruments have by necessity been so near to one another that the
voice of the speaker was audible through the air. Under these
circumstances it is extremely difficult to say whether the sounds
that are heard proceed from the diaphragm, or whether they
merely come through the air to the ear, and if they come from
the diaphragm, whether they are really the result of the varying
light, and not mere sound vibrations taken up by the disk from
the speaker's voice crossing the air. Prof. Bell hopes soon to
settle this point, however, by appeal to experiments on a larger
scale with the receiving and transmitting instruments at greater
distances apart, and with glass windows in between to shut off all
sounds.

Fig. 222 illustrates the simple musical photophone of Bell and
Tainter. It might perhaps be described without injustice as an
optical siren, producing sounds from intermittent beams of light,
as the *siren* of Cagniard de Latour produces them from intermittent puffs of air. A beam of light from the sun or from a
powerful artificial source, such as an electric lamp, falls upon a
mirror, M, and is reflected through a large lens, L, which con-
centrates the rays to a focus. Just at the focus is interposed a
disk pierced with holes—forty or so in number—arranged in a

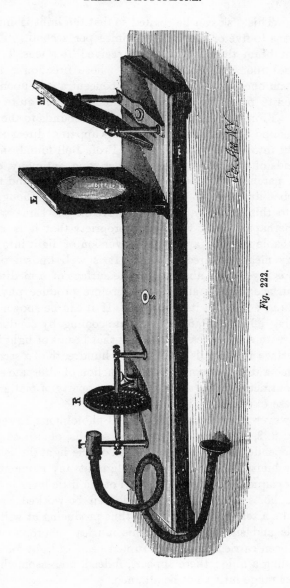

Fig. 222.

circle. This disk can be rotated so that the light is interrupted from one to five or six hundred times per second. The intermittent beam thus produced is received by a lens, T, or a pair of lenses upon a common support, whose function is to render the beam once more parallel, or to concentrate it upon the disk of ebonite placed immediately behind, but not quite touching them. From the disk a tube conveys the sounds to the ear. We may remind our readers here that this apparent direct conversion of light into sound takes place, as Prof. Bell found, in disks of all kinds of substances—hard rubber, zinc, antimony, selenium, ivory, parchment, wood—and that he has lately found that disks of carbon and of thin glass, which he formerly thought exceptions to this property, do also behave in the same way. We may perhaps remark without impropriety that it is extremely improbable that the apparent conversion of light into sound is by any means a direct process. It is well known that luminiferous rays, when absorbed at the surface of a medium, warm that surface slightly, and must therefore produce physical and molecular actions in its structure. If it can be shown that this warming effect and an intermediate cooling by conduction can go on with such excessive rapidity that beams of light falling on the surface at intervals less than the hundredth of a second apart produce a discontinuous molecular action of alternate expansion and contraction, then the mysterious property of matter revealed by these experiments is accounted for.

However this may be, the musical photophone, as represented in fig. 222, produces very distinct sounds, of whose existence and dependence for their production on the light the listener may satisfy himself by cutting off the light at any moment with the little opaque disk fixed on the end of the little lever just in front of the holes in disk, R, and which can be worked by a Morse key like a telegraph instrument, thus producing at will alternate sounds and silences. With this musical photophone sounds have been carried by an interrupted beam of light for a distance exceeding a mile ; there appears, indeed, no reason why a much greater range might not be attained.

The articulating photophone is that to which hitherto public attention has been most largely directed, and in which a selenium receiver plays a part. Fig. 223 gives in diagram form the essential parts of this arrangement. A mirror, M, reflects a beam of light as before through a lens, L, and (if desired for the purpose of experimentally cutting off the heat rays) through a cell, A, containing alum water, and casts it upon the transmitter, B. This transmitter, shown again in fig. 224, consists of a little disk of thin glass, silvered on the front, of about the size of the disk of an ordinary telephone, and mounted in a frame, with a flexible India rubber tube about sixteen inches long leading to a mouthpiece. A second lens, R, interposed in the beam of light

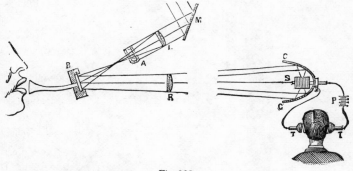

Fig. 223.

after reflection at the little mirror, renders the rays approximately parallel. The general view of the transmitting apparatus given in fig. 224 enables the relative sizes and positions of the various parts (minus the alum cell, which is omitted) to be seen. The screw adjustments of the support serve to direct the beam of light in the desired direction.

It may be well to explain once for all how the vibrations of the voice can affect the intensity of the reflected beam far away. The lenses are so adjusted that when the mirror, B, is flat (that is, when not vibrating) the beam projected from the apparatus to the distant station shall be nearly focused on the receiving

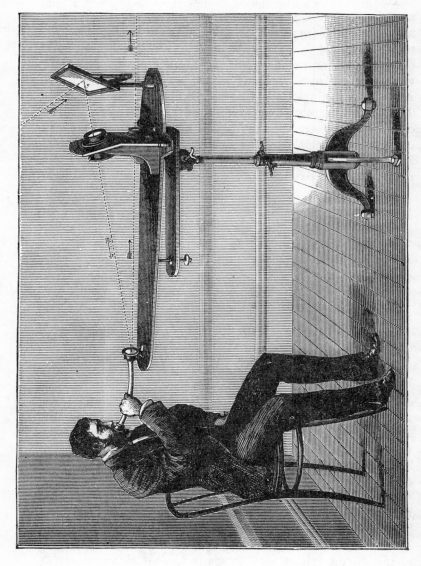

Fig. 224.

instrument. Owing to the optical difficulties of the problem it is impossible that the focusing can be more than approximate. Now, matters being thus arranged, when the speaker's voice is thrown against the disk, B, it is set into vibration, becomes alternately bulged out and in, and made slightly convex or concave, the degree of its alteration in form varying with every vibration of the voice. Suppose at any instant—say by a sudden displacement, such as takes place when the letter T is sounded —the disk becomes considerably convex ; the beam of light will no longer be concentrated upon the receiving instrument, but will cover a much wider area. Of the whole beam, therefore, only a relatively small portion will fall upon the receiving instrument; and it is therefore possible to conceive that, if perfectly adjusted, the illumination should be proportional to the displacement of the disk, and vary, therefore, with every vibration with the utmost fidelity. The receiver of the articulating photophone is shown on the right hand side of the diagram, fig. 223, sketched by Prof. Bell. A mirror of parabolic curve, C C, serves to concentrate the beam and to reflect it down upon the selenium cell, S, which is included in the circuit of a battery, P, along with a pair of telephones, T and T. Here again a general view, like that given in fig. 225, facilitates the comprehension of the principal parts of the apparatus. The sensitive selenium cell is seen in the hollow of the parabolic mirror, which is mounted so as to be turned in any desired direction. The battery standing upon the ground furnishes a current which flows through the selenium cell and through the telephones. When a ray of light falls on the selenium—be it for ever so short an instant— the selenium increases in conductivity, and instantly transmits a larger amount of electricity, and the observer with the telephones hears the ray, or the succession of them—hears, indeed, their every fluctuation in a series of sounds which, since each vibration corresponds to a vibration of the voice of the distant speaker, reproduce the speaker's tones.

The difficulty to be overcome in the use of the selenium as a working substance arose from its very high resistance. To

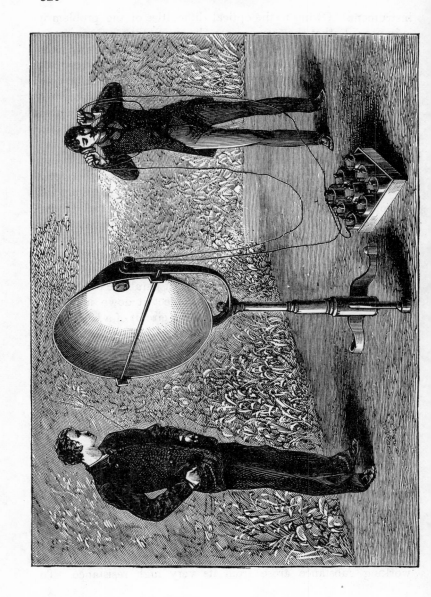

reduce this to the smallest possible quantity, and at the same time to use a sufficiently large surface whereon to receive the beam of light, was the problem to be solved before any practical result could be arrived at. After many preliminary trials with gratings and perforated disks of various kinds, Prof. Bell and Mr. Tainter finally settled upon the ingenious device to be described. A number of round brass disks, about two inches in diameter, and a number of mica disks of a diameter slightly less, were piled upon one another so as to form a cylinder about two and a half inches in length. They were clamped together from

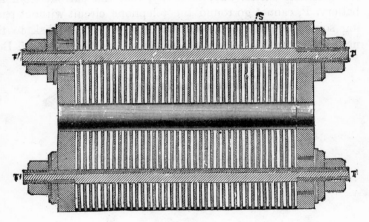

Fig. 226.

end to end, the clamping rods also serving to unite the disks of brass electrically in two sets, alternate disks being joined, the first, third, fifth, etc., being united together, and the second, fourth, sixth, etc., being united in another series. This done, the edges between the brass disks were next filled with selenium, which was rubbed in at a temperature sufficiently high to reach the melting point of selenium. After this the selenium was carefully annealed to bring it into the sensitive crystalline state. Then the cell is placed in a lathe and the superfluous selenium is turned off until the edges of the brass disks are bared. Fig. 226 shows,

in section, the construction of such a shell.   Prof. Bell has also
used cells in which the selenium filled only the alternate spaces
between disks, the intermediate spaces being occupied by mica
disks of equal diameter with the brass disks.   But this arrangement was in no way preferable, for in practice it was found that
moisture was apt to penetrate at the surface of the bare mica,
spoiling the effect.

   Fig. 227 is a diagram which simply illustrates the action of
the selenium receiver, and shows, first, the way of connecting
the alternate disks; and, secondly, that the current from the
battery, P, cannot go round the telephone circuit without passing somewhere through selenium from one brass disk to the
next.   The special advantages of the cell devised by Prof. Bell

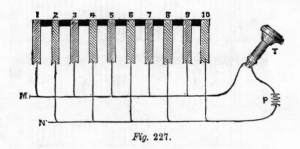

Fig. 227.

are that, in the first place, the thickness of the selenium that
the current must traverse is nowhere very great; that, in the
second, this photo electrical action of light on selenium being
almost entirely a *surface* action, the arrangement by which all
the selenium used is a thin surface film could hardly be improved upon; and that, thirdly, the symmetry of the cylindrical
cell specially adapts it for use in the parabolic mirror.   These
details will be of great interest, especially to those who desire
to repeat for themselves the experimental transmission of sound
by light.   The greatest distance to which articulate speech has
yet been transmitted by the selenium cell photophone is 233
yards.   When sunlight is not available recourse must be had to

an artificial source of sufficient power. During the experiments made by Prof. Bell the weather was adverse, and the electric light was called into requisition. The distance in these experiments between the transmitting diaphragm, B, and the parabolic reflector, C C, of the receiver was fifteen metres, the entire length of the room in which the experiments were made. Since at this distance the spoken words were themselves perfectly

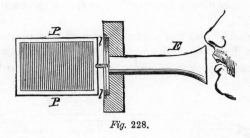

Fig. 228.

audible across the air, the telephones connected with the selenium cell were placed in another apartment, where voices were heard without difficulty and without doubt as to the means of transmission. The transmitter shown in fig. 228 consists of a fixed plate, P, provided with numerous slots, and of a like movable plate attached to a diaphragm, *l l*, mounted in a frame

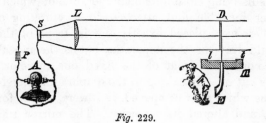

Fig. 229.

provided with a mouthpiece, E. The vibration of the movable plate varies the intensity of the light passing through it. In fig. 229 the transmitter is shown as used in combination with a col-

lecting lens, L, in place of the parabolic reflector.   In fig. 230 a
transmitter is shown which is based upon the effect of electricity
on polarized light.   A lens, L, throws the beam of a light, F, upon a
Nicol polarizing prism, R, and the polarized beams traverse an
analyzer, R.   A helix, B, is placed between the two prisms and
in the circuit of an ordinary microphone, M.   By speaking, the
intensity of the current traversing the helix is varied, and this
causes the plane of polarization of the rays to be turned more or
less, and consequently more or less rays are extinguished by the
analyzer, R'.

   Of the earlier and less perfect forms of the photophone little
need be said.   One device, which in Prof. Bell's hands worked
very successfully over a distance of eighty-six yards, consisted

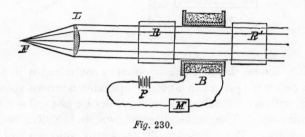

Fig. 230.

in letting the beam of light pass through a double grating of
parallel slits lying close to one another, one of which was fixed,
the other movable and attached to a vibrating diaphragm.
When these were placed exactly one in front of the other the
light could traverse the apparatus, but as the movable grating
slid more or less in front of the fixed one, more or less of the
light was cut off.   Speaking to the diaphragm, therefore, caused
vibrations which shut or opened, as it were, a door for the beam
of light, and altered its intensity.   The mirror transmitter of
thin glass silvered was, however, found superior to all others;
and it is hard to see how it could be improved upon, unless,
possibly, by the use of a thin disk of silver, itself accurately sur-
faced and polished.

Whatever be the future before the photophone, it assuredly deserves to rank in estimation beside the now familiar names of the telephone and the phonograph.

EDISON'S ELECTRO CHEMICAL TELEPHONE.

Mr. Edison has applied, with remarkable success, the principle of the electro motograph to the construction of a telephone receiver of extraordinary power and perfection.

This instrument consists in its simplest form of a diaphragm which is set into vibration by the variations of friction taking place between a metallic strip and a chemically prepared rotating cylinder, under variations of the strength of an electric current passing at the point of contact of the metallic strip and the cylinder. In its simplest form the apparatus consists of a cylinder composed of chalk and potassium hydrate with a small quantity of mercury acetate moulded round a flanged roller or reel of brass, which is lined with platinum on those surfaces which are in contact with the mixture, which is kept in a moistened condition. Upon the upper circumference of the cylinder, which is caused to revolve on a horizontal spindle, a metallic strip is caused to press with a firm and uniform pressure by means of an adjustable spring. The portion of the strip which bears upon the cylinder is lined with platinum, and the opposite end is attached to a diaphragm of mica, four inches in diameter, firmly fixed by its circumference. The cylinder is connected to the copper element of a battery, and the strip to the zinc pole, with a transmitting telephone included in the circuit. If, when no current is passing through the instrument, the cylinder be rotated at a uniform speed away from the diaphragm, the friction between the cylinder and the strip causes the diaphragm to be drawn inward—that is, toward the cylinder—and the diaphragm would take up a fixed position dependent upon its own rigidity and the friction between the cylinder and the strip.

The instant, however, that a current is transmitted through the instrument that friction is reduced, and the diaphragm flies back by its unopposed elasticity, the variation of friction being proportional to the variation of the strength of the electric current; and so marvellously sensitive is this combination, that the variations in the strength of the electric current caused by the human voice speaking against a carbon transmitting telephone instantly produce their corresponding variations of friction, and the diaphragm repeats the words, but very much louder than they were originally uttered at the distant station.

Fig. 231 is a perspective view of the apparatus, which is in reality three instruments in one, combining a transmitter, receiver, and call bell, and, therefore, has a somewhat complicated appearance. The whole of the upper portion, however, is the call bell and signalling apparatus, by which attention is attracted at the other station, and by which such calls are received; this differs in no respect from an ordinary electric bell, having a key and switch by which it is thrown into circuit. In front of the box, which is of cast iron, is seen the large diaphragm, but even this has a more complicated appearance, in consequence of the transmitting carbon telephone being fixed in front of and concentric with it. If the transmitter and call bell apparatus were removed, the external appearance of the receiver would resolve itself into a rectangular box, having a four inch hole in its front face glazed with mica, and a small winch handle projecting from the right hand side. The internal arrangements are shown in fig. 232, which is a back view of the interior. A is the chalk cylinder mounted on the horizontal shaft, B B, which, by a spur wheel and pinion, can be rotated at a moderate speed by turning the winch handle, W. The spindle, B, turns in, and is supported by the long boss bearing shown in the figure, and which forms part of the cast iron bracket, H H, to which every part of the apparatus, except the diaphragm and its connected strip, is attached. D is the diaphragm, which consists of a disk of thick mica, four inches in diameter, and C is a metallic strip attached to its centre, which is pressed tightly against the upper portion of the cylinder by means of the stiff spring, S, whose pressure can be regulated by the screw E. G is a counter shaft, which can be turned through a small angle by depressing a lever keyed on

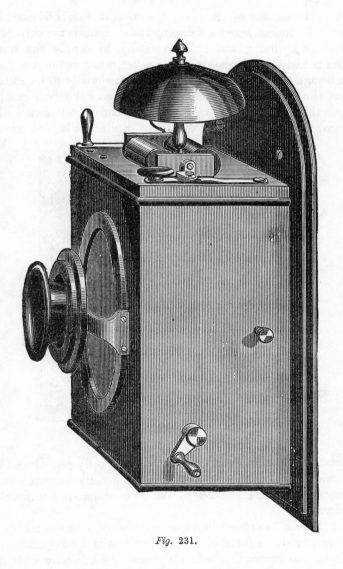

Fig. 231.

to it on the outside of the case; the effect of this is to raise, by means of a forked lever, a damping roller, against the surface of the chalk cylinder, and so occasionally to supply the water which is lost by evaporation. The roller, when not in use, rests in a trough of water, T, and has only occasionally to be raised, when the cylinder becomes too dry, to give the best results. When this instrument is connected to a carbon telephone, with no greater battery power than two Fuller cells, any sound

Fig. 232.

uttered in the transmitter is not only perfectly reproduced by the mica diaphragm, but its sound is so greatly increased as to constitute what in a speaker would be considered an unusually loud voice.

Mr. Edison has found that this instrument, like the magnetic receiver, produces far more satisfactory results when working on an induction circuit than when it is connected directly with the carbon transmitter. He therefore adopts the plan of placing the receiving instrument in circuit with the secondary wire of an induction coil, the transmitter and battery being on the primary circuit. The undulatory character which is given to the voltaic current by transmission through the carbon disk, whose resistance is continually varying under the influence of sonorous vibrations, produces by induction a correspondingly undulatory current in the secondary circuit of the induction coil, and this varying current being transmitted by the line wire to the receiving instrument, by varying the intensity of the electro chemical decomposition going on between the chalk cylinder and the platinum point which presses on it, causes a corresponding variation of the coefficient of friction between the two surfaces.

The secret of the great power of the instrument, by which it speaks with a voice to be distinctly heard all over a large room, is that the mechanical motion of the diaphragm is produced by local mechanical means, such as a train of clock work or rotation by hand, and not by the electric current, as in all other telephone receivers. The electric current merely controls the time when that mechanical force is exercised, and the amount which is brought into play. It may, mechanically, be compared to a frictional coupling or clutch through which a machine is driven by a steam engine, and which at any moment may be made to transmit the full power of the motor to the machine, or by varying the friction to transmit only a portion of that power.

BERLINER'S TELEPHONE TRANSMITTER.

Fig. 233 is a front view and fig. 234 a perspective view, showing the internal parts of the Berliner instrument. The principal feature of the invention is the disposition of the carbon contact surfaces, one being attached to the diaphragm, the other being supported by a metal socket attached to a hinged plate secured to an arm that projects from the back of the mouth piece downward over the diaphragm. This arm serves the double purpose of supporting the free carbon electrode and clamping the diaphragm in its place against the back of the iron mouth piece. The diaphragm is bound around the edges with soft rubber, and

Fig. 233.

Fig. 234.

is separated from the mouth piece by a ring of pasteboard. The iron mouth piece is hinged to a casting fastened to the circular box which contains the induction coil, and supports the binding screws for the battery, line, and ground wires. To the front of the induction coil is attached a plate connected with the battery wire, and carrying a spring having in its free end a screw which bears against a spring connected with the centre of the diaphragm, and acts as a dampener, as well as a conductor, through which the current passes to the carbon electrode at the centre of the diaphragm. The battery current enters at one of the binding screws, passes through the primary wire of the induction coil, through the spring and carbon electrode at the centre of the diaphragm, through the hinged electrode, metallic mouth piece and its hinge, and back through a binding screw to the battery. The variation of the current in the primary circuit occurs at the contact of the two carbon electrodes, the contact being varied by the vibration of the electrode attached to the diaphragm. When the transmitter is used for long distance telephony, the pendent carbon electrode is made heavier, to reduce resistance in the local current and to amplify the electrical undulations. The terminals of the secondary wire of the induction coil are connected with the two remaining binding screws, which are connected, one with the ground and the other with the line, in the usual way. The accessory devices connected with this transmitter may be of the usual character. It will operate well with any of the well known forms of receiver, and is easily managed and thoroughly efficient. This transmitter has been well introduced, and large numbers of them are being used in Europe. They have been adopted on several of the leading German railways, and are extensively used in the German postal service. The patent for this invention is owned and the instruments are made by the American Bell Telephone Company.

MAICHE'S TELEPHONIC IMPROVEMENTS.

Figs. 235 and 236 give a general and sectional view of an

improved Bell telephone receiver. The top or cup part of the case is made of brass, nickel plated, into the lower part of which the permanent magnet bar is screwed and rigidly held by means of a brass nut, as shown in the figure. The head of the magnet bar terminates in a little soft iron bar, which goes through and forms the core of the bobbin. The diaphragm is held, as usual, by the *cover*, and, lastly, the magnet bar is enclosed in the wooden handle, the expansion or contraction of which can in no way affect the adjustment of the instrument. This new disposition gives a well proportioned and handsome

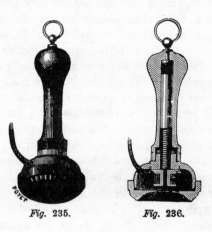

Fig. 235.   *Fig.* 236.

appearance to the telephone, assures a permanent adjustment and gives excellent results as a receiver.

Figs. 237 and 238 are front and side views of the microphonic transmitter of M. Maiche. The principle upon which it works is similar to that of the Crossley, Ader and other like telephones. The diaphragm is square in form and made of dry pine, on the under side of which is affixed the microphone. This consists of three pieces of carbon screwed crosswise on the diaphragm, and twelve little pencils of the same material. These latter are loosely laid in the holes previously pierced in the cross pieces, the whole resembling a sort of gridiron.

Fig. 239 shows the exterior view of what M. Maiche calls his electrophone. It is composed of a sort of frame into which is

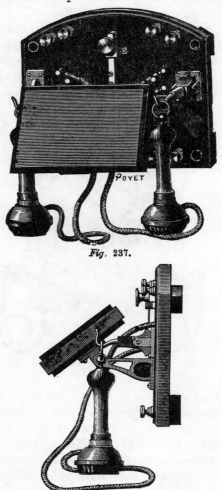

Fig. 237.

Fig. 238.

fixed the microphonic diaphragm, induction coil, etc., with two of the modified Bell receivers on the outside. The instrument

is intended for long line telephony.   It is said that conversation
between Paris and Nancy—a distance of 220 miles—has been
carried on through it with perfect satisfaction.

Of course the microphonic arrangement is the principal part.
It consists of three, four and sometimes six distinct microphones
fixed to the same diaphragm—a sort of compound microphone.
Each of these microphones is composed of a swinging armature,
on the end of which is a carbon ball.   This ball rests against a

Fig. 239.

thin pastil of carbon glued to the wooden diaphragm.   All the
pastils are connected together, as are also all the swinging armatures.

Fig. 240 gives a view of the Maiche battery.   It is well
known that the action of most batteries is limited, as to durability, by the coatings of salts and oxides which, in time, will
cover all metals attacked by acids, and therefore will offer
great resistance to the production and to the passage of the
current.   The resistance becomes so great that the battery in
time ceases to act.   In the new battery the simple action of the

air on the materials composing it suffices to cleanse them, so that the battery only ceases to work when the zinc is entirely consumed.

Another recent improvement consists in transforming the batteries known as the Leclanché peroxide of manganese batteries into accumulators of electricity. When one of these Leclanché batteries is worn out, it will suffice to send through its elements the current of a dynamo electric machine, such as the Gramme. This current reduces the oxide of zinc, leaving the

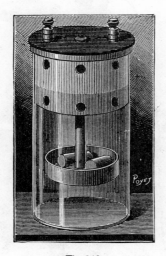

Fig. 240.

zinc in its former metallic state, and returning the oxygen taken from the zinc to the manganese; thus the battery is renewed and ready to work.

HOPKINS' TELEPHONIC TRANSMITTER.

Fig. 241 is a perspective view of the Hopkins transmitter, showing the relative arrangement of the transmitter and receiver; fig. 242 represents the arrangement of the local circuit and line, and fig. 243 is a vertical section of the transmitter.

The transmitter is fixed to the bracket and stands vertically, with its sound collecting mouth piece pointed in the direction whence the sound proceeds. The receiver, which is an ordinary Bell instrument, stands when not in use over a curved pendent resonator, the smaller end of which projects through the shelf of

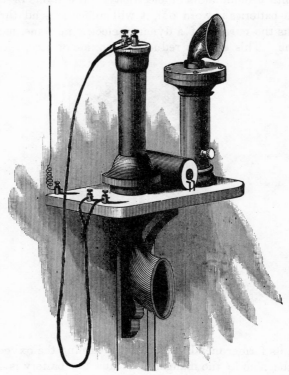

Fig. 241.

the bracket and just enters the hole in the centre of the receiver mouth piece. Between the transmitter and the receiver there is a small induction coil, whose primary wire is connected with the local battery and the transmitter. One terminal of the secondary wire of the coil is connected with the receiving instrument and line ; the other terminal is grounded.   These connections will be understood by reference to fig. 242.   *a* and *b* are the terminals of the primary wire of the induction coil, C.   The terminal, *a*, connects with the battery, B ; the terminal, *b*, runs to the transmitter, T, connected with the battery by the wire, *c.*   One terminal of the secondary wire of the coil, C, is grounded ; the other terminal, *d*, connects with one binding post of the receiver, R, the other binding post being in communication with the line wire,

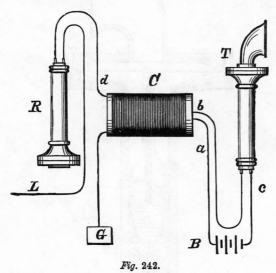

Fig. 242.

L.   This arrangement is adapted to a closed circuit, one or two cells of gravity battery being connected with the transmitter.   If an open circuit battery is used, a switch is placed in one of the wires, *a, b, c,* so that the local circuit may be left open when the talking is done.

The construction of the transmitter will be seen in the vertical section, fig. 243.   The diaphragm, A, has attached to its centre a small brass cup, B, containing a button of ordinary battery carbon three sixteenths of an inch in diameter and about the same thickness.   This carbon projects beyond the brass cup,

and is surrounded by a short paper tube, which projects beyond
the face of the carbon one eighth inch.   A piece of copper foil
placed between the brass cup, B, and the diaphragm extends to

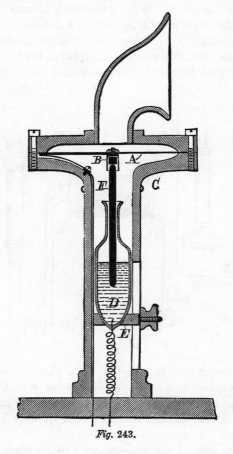

Fig. 243.

the edge of the diaphragm, where it is pressed by a spring in
the cell, C, which is in metallic contact with a wire extending
downward through the lower end of the instrument.

The standard supporting the diaphragm cell is hollow, about

five eighths inch internal diameter, and the height of the diaphragm above the bracket is four inches.

In the standard there is a bottle, D, of special form, supported
by a ring, E, having a threaded stud extending through a slot
in the standard, and provided with a milled thumb nut, by
which it may be clamped at any desired height. The bottle,
D, has a long, narrow neck, about three sixteenths inch internal
diameter, and a platinum wire blown in the lower end connects
with the local circuit wire, which is coiled to admit of moving
the bottle up or down. This wire extends through the base of
the instrument, and is connected as shown in fig. 242. The
bottle, D, is partly filled with mercury, in which floats a pencil,
F, of carbon of the kind used for electric lighting by incandescence. This pencil is one eighth inch in diameter, two and one
eighth inches long, and is made slightly convex and very smooth
at the ends. The mercury buoys the carbon up so that it is
always kept in light and uniform contact with the carbon button,
while it also forms part of the conductor in the local circuit.
The carbon attached to the diaphragm is perfectly plain on its
contact surface, and as smooth as it can be made by means of a
fine file. The diaphragm, which is of mica, has one and three
fourths inches free to vibrate. It is rather stiff, and is clamped
firmly in its cell. The surfaces between which the diaphragm
is clamped are perfectly true, and made of material not liable to
warp. Wood well soaked in paraffine answers a good purpose,
but vulcanite is far better. The induction coil used with the instrument is of the ordinary form, two inches long, one inch in
diameter, with a three eighths inch core of No. 18 soft iron
wires. The primary coil consists of three layers of No. 18 silk
covered copper wire, and the secondary of No. 36 in sufficient
quantity to fill the spool. One cell of Leclanché or Fuller battery will work the transmitter, but two will augment the volume
of sound. As to the efficiency of this instrument, it will bear
comparison with other transmitters, and in one or two points it
seems to have an advantage. It will transmit speech clearly,
whether the speaker is within ten inches or as many feet of the

instrument. Although a call bell may be used in connection with it, generally none will be required, as by saying o-o-o-o loudly in the mouth piece a trumpet like sound is heard in the receiver at the other end of the line, which, although not very loud, is sufficient to attract attention in a measurably quiet room.

THORNBERRY'S TELEPHONE RECEIVER.

Fig. 244 represents the Thornberry telephone receiver, the action of which is due to the contraction of a spiral magnet core under the influence of the current traversing the bobbin. The spiral core is attached at one end to the diaphragm, and is con-

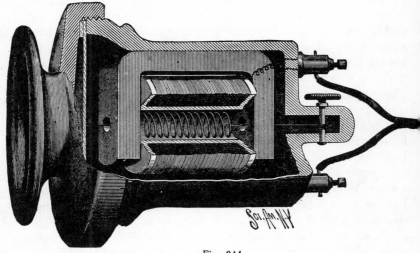

Fig. 244.

nected at the other end with an adjusting screw. The spiral core is perfectly free to work in the helix, and the contraction or expansion of the spiral under the influence of the current from the transmitter acts on the diaphragm in much the same manner as though it were attracted by a magnet, the results being the same as in other forms of the Bell telephone.

A permanent magnet placed outside the bobbin magnetizes the spiral core by induction, so that the spiral is very sensitive, thereby making it sensitive to the influence of currents passing in the bobbin.

The construction of the telephone will be readily understood by reference to the engraving, in which a portion of the instrument is broken away to show the internal parts. The diaphragm is mounted on a mouth piece of the usual description, and the permanent magnet and bobbin with the enclosed spiral is placed in a small casing attached to the mouth piece. The instrument is provided with the usual binding posts and flexible connections.

HUGHES' MICROPHONE.

Fig. 245 represents the Hughes microphone, which consists of a carbon pencil, A, terminating in a point at each end ; the

Fig. 245.

two ends rest lightly between two small circular holes of two pieces of carbon, C C¹, and the carbon pencil has a vertical position; C and C¹ are fixed to a thin sounding board, which is placed on a solid block. The pieces C and C¹ are connected by wires with the battery and receiving telephone. This instrument is of such marvellous delicacy as to convert into sonorous vibrations the slightest movement, and even a fly walking on the block, D, will cause a vibration which can be heard in a Bell telephone receiver at a distance of a mile from the transmitter.

Fig. 246 represents another form of the Hughes microphone. A small pencil, C, of gas carbon, pointed at its extremities, is maintained in a vertical position between two carbons, D D¹

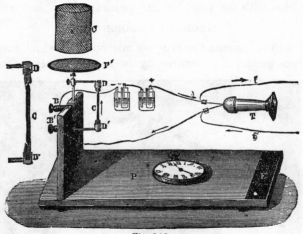

Fig. 246.

The support of the upper carbon is arranged in such a way that the equilibrium and play of the pencil between the two carbons, and consequently the sensitiveness of the microphone, can easily be regulated at any moment. The two carbons are in direct communication with the two terminals, B B¹. The whole is fixed on a small board and a wooden block, P. Two rubber legs insulate the block from extraneous vibrations. The slight frictions produced on the rough surface, E, of a band of emery paper are transmitted by the apparatus. A battery of two Leclanché cells, and a Bell telephone receiver placed at a distance, form a complete circuit, comprising the carbon pencil, C, with imperfect contacts.

ADER'S MICROPHONE.

Fig. 247 represents the Ader transmitter, which is now the most extensively used in France. It consists of ten small carbons, A A, arranged in two rows of five, and resting their extremities on three cross bars of carbon, B C D, fixed to a

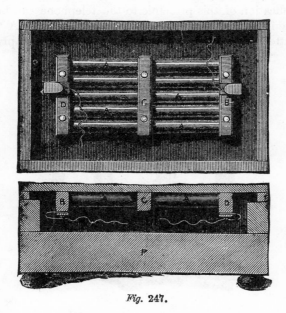

Fig. 247.

small deal board, which receives the vibrations and serves at the same time as a cover to the apparatus. It is fastened to a leaden socket, P, supported by five rubber legs, in order to prevent the concussions of the floor from reaching the transmitter.

D'ARSONVAL'S TELEPHONE.

Fig. 248 represents the D'Arsonval telephone, which is based upon experiments proving that the power of the telephone is greatly increased by bringing both poles of the magnet near the vibrating plate, while considerable advantage is also obtained by having them provided with flat bobbins very close together. By this means any too strong magnetic induction is prevented, the magnets, on the contrary, being somewhat weaker when encircled with thin and flat bobbins. The experiment of Marcel Deprez, in constructing his galvanometer, showed that the only active part of the circuit lies between the poles of the magnets. The application of this principle to the telephone can be easily and practically proved in the following manner: A magnet with flattened poles is brought under the vibrating plate of a

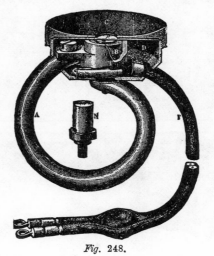

Fig. 248.

telephone, and a wire, conveying an interrupted current, placed between, but in such a way that it can be also placed outside the poles when required. It will be found that the plate will vibrate strongly when the wire is between the poles, and that the vibrations, when the wire is in any other position, will be either very weak or altogether absent. In double poled telephones, therefore, such as Gower's, Siemens', Ader's, the parts of the coil circuits which are not between the poles may be considered as simply useless. D'Arsonval has therefore selected the ring shape for the magnetic field, so as to submit the whole circuit to its influence—an arrangement that has been adopted by Klés for his electro magnets. One of the poles has a cylindrical core and carries the bobbin ; the second has a ring shape and envelops the first, so that the whole bobbin is within the influence of the magnetic field. All the lines of force of the field are perpendicular to the wire coils, and consequently experience the maximum action of the current.

The telephone is thus made in the simplest and most effective form. The magnet has the form of a spiral, which has the advantage of uniting the lines of force in a closed circuit. The two ends of the magnet hoop carry the cylindrical core—that is, the ring—and between these ends the bobbin is carried and enclosed, while the flat ends are brought as close as possible to the vibrating plate. The arrangement of the plate is very simple ; the metal case containing it is placed between the cylindrical core and the corresponding end of the magnet. The whole apparatus weighs only one pound, but despite these small dimensions, it repeats vocal sounds with great exactness, and so clearly that the tones can be heard throughout a room when the instrument is provided with a speaking tube.

GOLOUBITZKY'S TELEPHONE.

Fig. 249 represents Goloubitzky's telephone, which is based upon the idea that several magnets, acting at the same time on the same diaphragm, would produce more energetic sounds, provided that the vibrations produced were concordant. The poles of two horseshoe magnets crossing each other at right angles are placed in front of the diaphragm, in the annular region corresponding to the centres of vibration ; the four poles of the two magnets form the four angles of a square, two poles of the same name being placed alongside each other. For the purpose of magnetization, they need only be held for five minutes against the poles of the magnetizing electro magnet. The diaphragm is separated from the cylindrical box of the telephone by a small copper ring surrounding the border. It is stretched and held in convenient distance from the four magetic poles by the cover

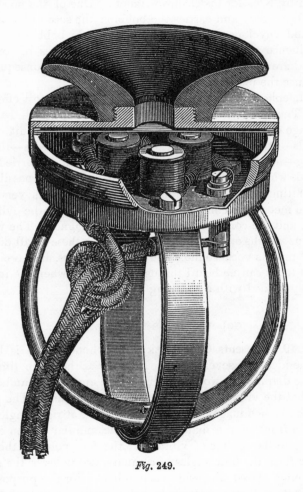

Fig. 249.

carrying the telephonic mouth piece. If a hollow sound is produced by tapping on the diaphragm through the opening of the

mouth piece, the adjustment is complete. The coils of the magnet are first of all connected so as to correspond to the two
different poles of the same magnet, and the two pairs of helices
are subsequently joined for tension. Goloubitzky asserts that
the power of his apparatus is four times greater than that of any
other.

DOLBEAR'S TELEPHONES.

Fig. 250 represents an apparatus which differs only slightly
in form from one of the instruments shown in Prof. Bell's patent

Fig. 250.   *Fig.* 251.

of January 30, 1877, but which Pröf. Dolbear, of Tufts College,
claims to have conceived of as early as September 20, 1876, and
a week or two later to have employed a student named Stetson
to make. Failing to do so, however, he personally began the
construction of a pair, which were finished and tested in January
or February, 1877. The instrument consists of a horseshoe
permanent magnet, mounted upon a block fastened to a base;
upon each pole is fitted a spool of wire, and a square piece of
sheet iron, fastened to a wooden upright provided with a round
hole or aperture in the centre, fig. 251, is arranged in front of
and in proximity to both poles.

The special object which Prof. Dolbear had in view when the construction of these instruments was begun, was the obtaining of a patent, which, however, was not applied for until October 31, 1877.   On March 26, 1878, the patent office declared Dolbear's application in interference with Bell's patent of January 30, 1877, and on July 21, 1883, the examiner of interferences awarded the priority of invention to Bell, saying that "Dolbear's testimony that at some time during the month of October, 1876, he concluded to try a sheet iron diaphragm for his telephone, is insufficient to overcome Bell's evidence of completion in October, 1876, and possibly earlier."

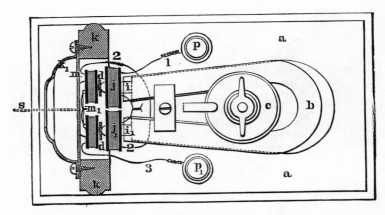

Fig. 252.

Fig. 252 represents another modification of the Bell telephone, made by Prof. Dolbear, in which he employs a paper diaphragm with an electro magnet armature.

Fig. 253 shows Prof. Dolbear's battery telephone, in which plates of two different metals are separated by a non-conductor in such a way as to make a shallow cell.   When a sound is made against one of these, as at I, the current from the cell is broken up into waves precisely like the movements of the sound waves, and speech is rendered remarkably distinct from the employment of such a sounder.

Fig. 254 represents a form of microphone transmitter devised by Prof. Dolbear. In this instrument a ring of wood, *a a*, has a plate of iron, *p*, screwed to one side of it, the plate being in metallic connection with a screw cup leading to a battery. Upon the opposite side of the ring is a cross arm, *b*, through which passes a screw, *s*, carrying a point which may be adjusted at any

Fig. 253.

required distance from the plate, *p*. This screw, *s*, is also in metallic connection with the other terminal cup.

If a battery of two gravity cells be put in circuit with this, together with a receiving telephone, and the point be screwed down so as to touch the plate, and a sound be made in the cavity in front of the plate, *p*, the circuit will be made and broken the number of times per second due to the pitch of that sound, and the

like pitch will be given out by the receiving telephone; the loudness of this sound will depend upon the ability of the receiver
to respond to the pulsations.   If the point be drawn back, so as
not to touch the plate at all, and a drop of water be inserted between the point and the plate, the articulation becomes remarkably good, though the sound is not very loud.

꜀ If a strong battery of fifty cells, or more, be put in circuit, and
the screw be turned down so as to have a jumping spark between
the point and the plate, the vibrations of the latter introduce a
variable resistance in the air.   If at the same time there is a

Fig. 254.

strong current, the result will be very loud talking.   In this device it is found best not to use a very sharp point, but one having
a surface like a sewing needle, with about one eighth of an inch
broken off from the point.   Such a one gives much better results
than a sharp point, for the obvious reason that a greater quantity
of electricity can pass from such a surface than from a fine
point.

Fig. 255 represents a modified form of the Edison transmitter
devised by Prof. Dolbear.

This transmitter is attached to the door of a box containing a battery and induction coil. The diaphragm, A, is horizontal, and carries a carbon electrode, upon which rests a movable carbon electrode connected by an arm with a delicately pivoted bar

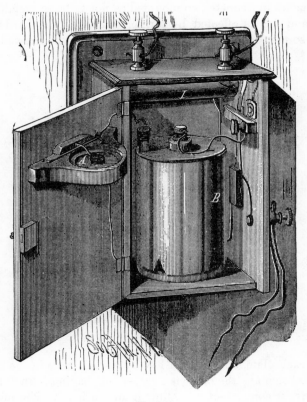

Fig. 255.

supported by the diaphragm cell. The local circuit is from the battery, B, through the carbon electrodes, and through the primary of the induction coil, I.

THE CONDENSER TELEPHONE.

On page 146 we have given a description of Edison's condenser telephones. Fig. 256 represents a form devised and described by Prof. Dolbear.

This consists, in its simplest form, of two metallic disks about two inches in diameter, so mounted as not to be in metallic contact, and this is effected by turning a flange in a hard rubber case, so they may be kept apart by it. A cap is screwed down

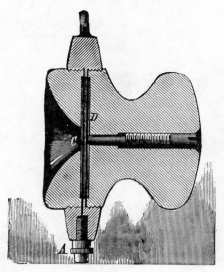

Fig. 256.

upon each plate, one of them having a small hole in the middle of it to listen at; the other is a larger one, having a knob turned upon it for conveniently holding it in the hand. Through the middle of the knob a screw is sunk which touches the back plate and serves to adjust it to the best position relative to the front or vibrating plate. The back plate is thus fastened at both edge and middle, which prevents it from vibrating, while the front plate is only fast at its edge, leaving the middle free to vibrate. Each of these plates, A B, fig. 257, is in metallic connection with the induction coil so as to be its terminals. When thus connected, and one makes and breaks connection in the primary circuit, a click may be heard by holding the receiver near to the ear. If a Helmholtz interrupter be employed to

Fig. 257.

make and break the primary circuit, the pitch of the fork can easily be heard, and with an Edison transmitter in the same place any kind of a sound will be reproduced.

The explanation of this is easily understood. The electro

motive force generated by induction in the coil changes the two terminals in the receiver, one positively, the other negatively; they therefore attract each other. One of them is free to move, while the other is rigid. The middle of the free plate consequently moves slightly toward the other whenever they are electrified, and in so doing spends the energy of the electricity, while its elasticity brings it back to its place. It is not essential, however, that both of these terminal plates should be connected to the induction coil, for if only one is connected the recurring charges will cause the free plate to vibrate, for a charged body

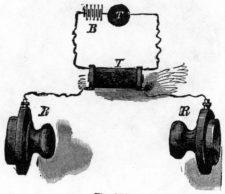

Fig. 258.

will attract any other body; so if the connection be to the back plate it will attract the front one and make it move, and if the connection be to the front plate it will attract the back plate and approach it. The effect will be increased by putting the finger upon the terminal that is free; not because it makes a ground, or completes an electrical circuit, for if the individual listening be as perfectly insulated as glass or hard rubber can make him, the sound is as loud as if he stood on the ground; but the individual becomes electrified by induction, which has the same effect as enlarging the terminal. Consequently receivers are made having only one terminal wire (fig. 258), the other plate being connected by a conductor to a metallic ring upon the knob, and this receiver is as efficient as the other.

This structure is technically known as the air condenser, and the mutual attraction of the two plates has been employed as a means of measuring electric potential. In this case one of the plates is suspended from one arm of a balance, while the other is fixed underneath it at a short distance. The attraction of the plates when they are electrified requires an extra weight to keep them apart, and the weight needed is the measure of the

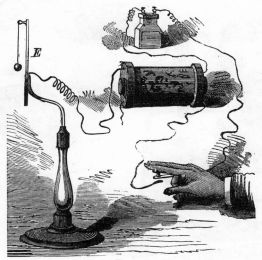

Fig. 259.

attractive force. But the plates will attract each other when glass or mica or any other non-conducting substance is placed between them in the place of the air; and one might expect that if such an air condenser would give sonorous results, other forms of condensers would do so likewise, which is true. Indeed, whoever has charged a Leyden jar has probably noticed the sounds coming from it when it is nearly saturated.

When the two plates of Epinus' condenser, E, fig. 259, are in metallic contact, no sounds can be produced by it; but if they are separated by a thin film of air, they will reproduce speech (fig. 260). In the first case the electricity passes from one plate to the other without doing work or changing its form; while in the latter, its form is changed and work is done, and between the best conductors, such as silver and copper and the perfect non-conductor air, there are all degrees of conductibility, and whenever electricity spends its energy upon an imperfect

Fig. 260.

conductor it results in heating it; that is, in molecular and atomic vibrations. Consequently an undulatory current from an ordinary transmitter, when sent through an imperfect conductor, will set up sound vibrations in it which may be appreciated by the ear. Let, then, any poor conductor, like a disk of carbon, a sheet of paper or of gelatine, or such chemical substances as ammonium chloride, be placed between the terminal plates, and an undulatory current sent through them will result in sound, and speech may be reproduced.

When a non-conductor, such as air, or vulcanite, or mica, separates the two plates, there is a complete transformation of the electricity at the limiting surfaces, and with small condensers the efficiency depends upon the electro motive force employed. For low electro motive forces, such as common batteries of a few cells can give, the effect is almost inappreciable, and for this reason such a receiver as this is quite free from the disturbance known as induction, which is so troublesome in

Fig. 261.

the magneto telephone, such induced currents being generally of low electro motive force.

Among the earliest experiments made by Prof. Dolbear while developing this method, was to attach one terminal wire from an induction coil to the outer coating of a Leyden jar, taking the other wire from the coil in one hand, and applying one ear to the knob of the jar. Every word spoken at the transmitter was distinctly heard, but the prickly sensation due to the electricity was rather disagreeable. Another receiver, not less curious than the Leyden jar, was found in a pair of insulating handles made for the medical application of electricity (fig. 261). When these were connected to the coil wires, and one held in each hand by the wooden part, while the metallic ends were placed at the ears, any kind of a sound at the transmitter could be

Fig. 262.

heard without any difficulty, but of course they were accompanied by the same sensations as were felt with the jar. Many forms of condensers have been employed with capacities too small to measure up to two micro farads, and these in all sorts of relations, such as charging the plates from batteries, from Holtz machines, and also by charging the line as in cable works, etc., all of which give results that differ only in degree.

Fig. 262 shows the condenser telephone in actual use, the transmitter being secured to the wall and the battery and induction coil being placed on a box on the floor or in a convenient closet. Fig. 263 is a perspective view of the new receiver. Fig. 257 is a face view of the instrument, with a portion of the casing broken away to show the connection of the two binding

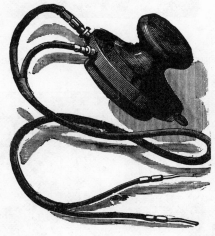

Fig. 263.

posts, A, B, with the diaphragms, C, D. The adjusting screws by which the distance between the diaphragms is regulated are shown in the sectional view, fig. 256. Fig. 259 illustrates the principle of electrical attraction upon which the action of the new receiver is based; the electro static charge received by the plate, E, from the induction coil, attracts the pith ball suspended in front of the plate. Fig. 264 shows an induction machine with a separable primary coil, such as is used in the Edison transmitter and its various modifications.

Fig. 258 illustrates the essential features of Dolbear's telephonic system. I being the induction coil, whose primary is in circuit with the battery, B, and transmitter, T, the receivers, R,

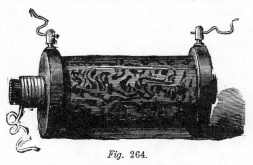

Fig. 264.

are each connected with a single terminal of the secondary wire of the coil, I.

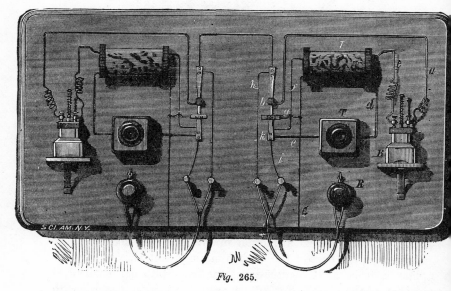

Fig. 265.

Fig. 265 shows the Dolbear exhibit prepared for the Paris Electrical Exhibition, representing two similar instruments,

which in practice are placed at opposite ends of the telephone
line. T is the transmitter; B the battery, I the induction coil,
R the receiver, and G the ground. b is a key for cutting out
the receiver when it is desired to talk. $d\ e$ are the primary
wires, f the secondary wire leading to the key, h the line connection of the receiver, and i is the ground connection of the
receiver.

PROF. DOLBEAR'S LECTURE BEFORE THE SOCIETY OF TELEGRAPH ENGINEERS.

In March, 1882, Prof. Dolbear lectured before the above
named society on the development of a new telephonic system.
He began his lecture with a brief description of Dr. Page's
attempt to transmit sound through the agency of electricity in
1837, and then described Farrar's proposal to transmit sounds
of different pitches by the use of the vibrating armature of

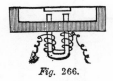

Fig. 266.

an electro magnet (fig. 266) and a make and break transmitter,
made of the reeds of a melodeon and operated by piano keys.
After describing Helmholtz's telephonic experiments, in which
he used tuning forks in connection with electro magnets to reproduce sound at a distance, he referred to the operation of the
earliest musical telephone, which he described as the attempts of
Philip Reis to solve the problem of transmitting articulate
speech. In this connection he exhibited the diagram shown
in fig. 267, as representing an instrument similar to the typical
Reis transmitter, but having a shallower chamber, and stated
that it was made by Albert, who was the instrument maker for
Reis in 1863, and that it, along with many other forms which
he made, was exhibited at the Paris Exhibition.

He said that Reis invented a transmitter which would vary a

current of electricity, depending altogether upon the varying pressure brought about between two conducting surfaces when the surfaces were vibrated, and whether or not there was a break of contact depended upon the amplitude of vibration of the membrane; and that from many experiments made by himself, he could testify that such an instrument will talk, thus proving that the Reis transmitter will transmit. He also said that the Reis' receivers would receive. The failure of Reis to make them receive "was due to the absence of the boxing up, and not to any defect in principle."

We think Prof. Dolbear allowed his wishes to run away with his judgment in this matter. He would like to be able to prove that Reis' apparatus was arranged to transmit undulatory

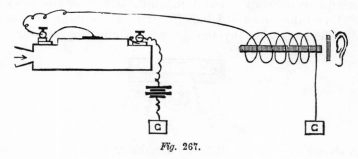

Fig. 267.

currents—an absolute requisite for the electric transmission of speech—and consequently that it did actually talk, for by this means he could perhaps get around the Bell patents and operate his "new system."

But there is not a particle of evidence that the Reis apparatus was arranged to transmit undulatory currents, or ever transmitted articulate speech, before Mr. Bell showed how to do it. More than that, none of the Reis machines can be made to talk now, unless some new device, involving Mr. Bell's invention, is added to them. Of course his transmitters can be easily modified so as to transmit undulatory currents. In our work on the telephone, published four years ago, we said, "If we place two common nails in a telephonic circuit and insulate them from each other, and then place a third nail upon them so as to close the circuit, a capital transmitter is at once made. The sonorous vibrations, falling on the nail, will be reproduced in the telephone with startling distinctness." But while you can now talk with the assistance of three nails, thanks to Mr. Bell's discovery, it would be folly to pretend that it had been done before. But after all, what better evidence is needed to prove that the Reis telephone never did talk, than that it ever ceased talking? We are not adding to the list of lost arts in the nineteenth century. When we discover a good thing we keep it and make the most of it. Imagine the discovery of the art of transmitting speech in Germany in 1863, and then its entire loss and rediscovery in America a dozen years afterward!

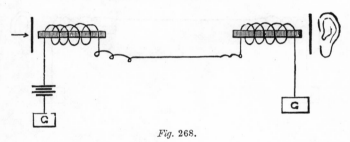

Fig. 268.

Prof. Dolbear next describes Prof. Bell's invention of the speaking telephone as follows: "In 1876 Prof. Bell put forward another system, quite distinct from the Reis. He proposed, and I think he was the first one in the world to propose it, to speak to the armature of a magnet with the expectation that somebody else listening at the armature of another magnet in the same circuit might be able to hear what was said. His device you are all acquainted with. Fig. 268 contains an illustration of this arrangement. (In the figure the electro magnets are shaded, and the permanent magnets are indicated by poles.) But the principle involved in Prof. Bell's arrangement is altogether different from that involved in the Reis arrangement. In this case, when two electro magnets are included in the same circuit with a battery, any motion of the armature of one will vary the current that is upon the line, because an electro motive force will be induced upon that line which will traverse the circuit to or fro, according to the direction of motion of the armature, and so will increase or decrease the attractive strength of the other magnet, causing vibration of its armature. I say that this was a new system, entirely distinct from the other.

"An improvement on that was to dispense with the battery and electro magnets, and employ permanent magnets in their place, and that condition is represented in fig. 269. This was an invention of my own in 1876. [This claim Prof. Dolbear has been wholly unable to substantiate.] But though the instrument could be used for 15 or 20 miles under certain condi-

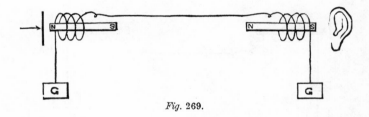

Fig. 269.

tions, its action was not reliable for long lines, and it became necessary, therefore, to find some means for making the telephone a more practical instrument. It did not seem possible to make the permanent magnet arrangement or the electro magnet arrangement any more efficient than it was. If the magnet was enlarged, no increased effect occurred, and if the size of the diaphragm was increased, a maximum was very soon reached; if it was made thicker it would not move so freely, and so on. Attention reverted to the original Reis device, and many attempts were made to improve his transmitter, or find a substitute for it. Platinum was often tried, but was generally not very efficient, on account of its liability to break on the one hand, and to fuse on the other. Mr. Edison proposed to use plumbago, and afterward lampblack encased in a short cylinder, and the vibratory movement of a diaphragm upon them was to subject either the plumbago or the lampblack to varying degrees of pressure, and he found, or thought he found, that subjecting them to a pressure in that way would increase and decrease their resistance. Afterward Prof. Hughes discovered that gas carbon, when in an unconstrained state, was as efficient or more efficient than any other substance that had hitherto been appropriated to that use; and now when gas carbon is made to take the place of platinum in the Reis instrument, we have one of the most efficient transmitters that has yet been invented. This is shown in fig. 270, in which appears the identical instrument invented by Reis, in all of its features, excepting

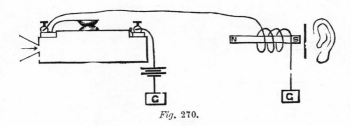

Fig. 270.

that carbon is used as a substitute for the platinum. Furthermore, it is coupled up with a magneto telephone known as the Bell, and the arrangement is the original Reis system, plus the permanent magnet."

That is to say, if we take a Reis transmitter and make an Edison microphone of it, by removing the platinum make and break contact points and substituting carbon therefor, " we have one of the most efficient transmitters that has ever been invented!" Unquestionably. But if we couple an Edison transmitter and a Bell receiver, and employ Bell's undulatory current, it strikes us that we have something more than " the original Reis system, plus the permanent magnet." We have the original Bell telephone, plus Edison's improvements.

After describing various other telephonic devices and experiments, Prof. Dolbear exhibited what he called his own system, and explained it as follows:

"In this case I shall have the device represented in fig. 271, in which I have a Reis transmitter, *plus the carbon points, with a secondary coil,* connected to one of the plates of my receiver. The *undulatory current* in the primary coil sets up varying electro motive forces in the secondary coil sufficient to work the instrument, and as the electro motive force is high, external resistance is a very small factor indeed, and the length of wire through which it will work is almost unlimited."

It will be observed that Prof. Dolbear included in "his own system" not only an Edison carbon transmitter with induction

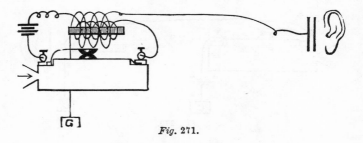

Fig. 271.

coils, under the guise of a Reis transmitter, but the vibrating diaphragm of Bell's receiver, and actuated the whole by the employment of Bell's undulatory current!

At the conclusion of the lecture, Mr. Preece, who always has something interesting or amusing to tell on all occasions, said:

"There is nothing more marvellous than the wonderful universality of this power which electricity possesses of making everything reproduce speech. Now that we know what electricity can do, the difficulty appears to be, not so much how to make apparatus speak, but how to prevent it from speaking. A very curious instance came beneath my notice in the very early days of telephony, some four years ago, when two men in a carpenter shop (I think it was at Worcester) heard a conversation, and those who were conversing by telephone were certainly 100 yards away from the carpenter's shop, and out of earshot. The only connection between those who spoke and the carpenter's shop was the fact that the wire connecting the telephones rested upon the carpenter's bench, and upon that very spot there happened to be a bad joint, and there is no doubt whatever in my mind that that bad joint was a good telephone, and it repeated the words that were spoken at the other end."

If all the "bad joints" in the telegraph lines in this country should make up their minds to talk, there would be a worse

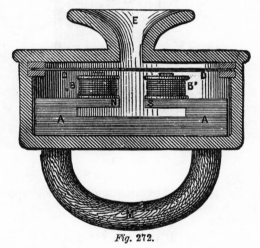

Fig. 272.

gabbling going on than was ever heard, even in a telephone exchange. We trust this innovation won't cross the water.

KOTYRA'S TELEPHONE.

Fig. 272 presents a sectional view of Kotyra's modification of Bell's receiver. The core of the electro magnet is formed of a large number of small thin plates of tempered steel, cut out of the same bar and joined in the form of a horseshoe, M. Two bundles of plates, A A, of different lengths, are placed above, and over these two similar plates, N S, to which are attached two iron cores forming the prolongation of the poles. The two coils, B B', the diaphragm D, and mouthpiece, E, are of the usual Bell type.

Fig. 273 shows the arrangement of the Kotyra system, in which the switch for placing the line in communication with the call bell or the telephone is enclosed in the box containing the

Fig. 273.

transmitter, the outer end terminating in a hook upon which the receiving telephones are hung.

THE BLAKE TRANSMITTER.

This apparatus, which is an improvement upon the Edison transmitter, and has practically supplanted it in this country, is represented in fig. 274. The contact of the two carbons, instead of being effected by the pressure of two pieces, one of which is stationary and the other movable, which renders the apparatus impressionable to exterior physical actions, is composed of two movable organs which are always in slight contact with each other, and entirely independent of the diaphragm. To obtain this effect, the piece d, which is not in direct contact with the diaphragm, and which serves as carbon holder, is arranged in such a manner as to present at its extremity a heavy mass, *g h*, in which inertia takes the place of rigidity, which is obtained in the Edison instrument by attaching the carbon to the frame. As this piece, *d*, on the side of its point of attachment, is terminated by a spring, the contact is always effected under the same conditions of pressure.

Fig. 274.

To regulate the pressure of the system with reference to the diaphragm, Mr. Blake fastened the spring of the contact piece, *g h*, upon a metallic plate, F, arranged vertically, and itself sustained by a spring plate, *j*, and as it carries at its lower part an inclined plane upon which rests the point, G, of a screw, *l*, it becomes easy, by means of this screw, to conveniently regulate the pressure with reference to the diaphragm.

The second contact, on the side of the diaphragm, has itself a particular arrangement; that is, a little grain of platina, one twenty-fifth of an inch in diameter by one sixteenth in length, which a spring, c, presses lightly against the carbon, h, and it is upon this grain that the diaphragm rests for the proper regulation of the apparatus. The carbon itself is composed of a particular substance not yet made public, but which it is thought to have for base lampblack. With this arrangement it is easy to comprehend that the disagreeable cracklings of the ordinary microphones are partially eliminated, since the pressure of the two contact pieces always remains the same, even though the diaphragm does not touch at all. Naturally, the current comes to this interruption by the suspension springs of the metallic grain and the carbon mass. The apparatus is, besides, arranged vertically, and has in front of the diaphragm a mouth piece, E, as in the ordinary telephones, and the current which actuates the telephone is supplied, as in the Edison transmitter, by an induction coil, I, animated by a voltaic cell.

POLLARD'S TELEPHONE.

Fig. 275 represents Pollard's modification of the Bell telephone, of which the upper part alone is shown in section.

A is a very powerful horseshoe magnet, made of from two to three pieces, according to the dimensions of the instrument. These pieces are separated from one another, in the middle and at the extremities, by soft iron wedges. To the two outer ones is riveted the piece that carries the eye, m, by means of which the telephone is suspended, and to the middle one are screwed the soft iron polar appendages, f f, which serve as a cover to two flat bobbins placed opposite each other, as in the Siemens, Gower and Ader telephones.

The two branches of the magnet enter a cylindrical block of wood, B, in which they are firmly held by the tightening up of a brass cross piece by means of a screw, V, in the interior. The instrument is capable of being taken apart and put together very easily. The vibrating plate, L, of tin, is held by a box, made of wood, in two parts, which is movable. One of these latter, C, is screwed to the block, B, and the other, E, is fixed to the former by screws and serves as a mouth piece.

Regulation is affected by revolving the movable box with the

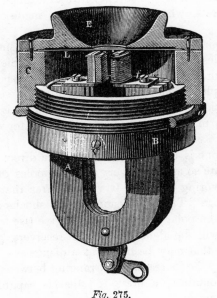

Fig. 275.

hand, and consequently screwing it on to the fixed block. A metallic threaded ring, *a*, plays the role of a set screw and permits of fixing accurately the position of the vibrating plate after regulation. Under these circumstances the regulating is easily performed and is very precise, and, moreover, an inspection of the instrument may be made immediately by unscrewing the movable box.

In the large size the vibrating plate is about one fiftieth of an inch in thickness, and about three inches in diameter. The bobbins are of fine wire (No. 40) and possess, together, a resistance of 300 to 400 ohms. The wires are attached by means of bolts traversing the fixed block and having pliable cords connected with their extremities.

In a smaller size the vibrating plate is only two and a half inches in diameter and one seventy-fifth of an inch in thickness; and the magnets, which are smaller, are made of two pieces only.

The large size constitutes an energetic transmitter and receiver. It is less sonorous, less noisy than the Siemens apparatus, but it is intense and remarkably clear. It has been advantageously employed as the sole apparatus in several of the telephone stations of the naval arsenals, and is destined to render service in laboratories as an apparatus for study and demonstration.

This telephone is capable of furnishing a direct call by regulating the plate so as to be very near the poles of the magnet, and by endeavoring to make it vibrate after the manner of a Reis transmitter. The succession of the shocks of the membrane against the polar appendages will give rise to intense currents, which will be denoted by the receivers giving out a musical sound that may be heard at a distance. The intensity of this call may be increased by arranging between the bobbins a small tube containing a brass rod that is capable of moving freely in the interior.

When the telephone is held in the hand for listening or speaking, the small mass of metal rests naturally at the bottom of the tube at the side of the block of wood and proves no obstacle to the working of the instrument. At rest, the telephone being suspended by the eye, m, and its mouth piece pointing downward, the metal then falls, and, while still remaining in the tube, rests upon the centre of the membrane.

The regulation of the apparatus is performed, as in all magnetic telephones, with great accuracy by endeavoring to get the plate as near as possible to the magnet, without, however, having it beat against the polar extremities.

BŒTTCHER'S TELEPHONE.

Fig. 276 represents Bœttcher's modification of Bell's magneto telephone, arranged as a transmitter. This instrument is said to

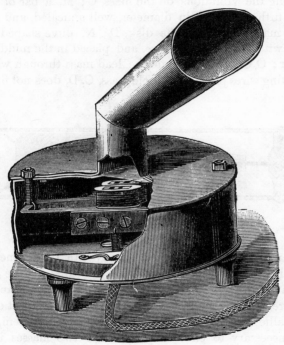

Fig. 276.

be not inferior to the best carbon transmitters, and is especially recommended for use in mines, where it is said the ordinary carbon telephones cannot resist, for any length of time, the disturbing influences of these localities, and are continually getting out of order. The ordinary Bell receiver is employed with the Bœttcher transmitter.

ADER'S TELEPHONE WITHOUT A DIAPHRAGM.

In fig. 277, which represents a longitudinal section of this instrument, A is the ear piece; B, the outer case; C, mass of lead; D, copper disk, soldered on the lead; E, copper mass; F, India rubber mass; H, flexible envelope of India rubber for insulating the vibrations of the mass, C; M, a bar of iron one twenty-fifth of an inch in diameter, well annealed, and soldered to the mass, E, and to the disk, D; N, olive shaped bobbin wound with fine insulated wire, and placed in the middle of the iron bar; O O, holes through the lead mass through which the conducting wires pass. The whole mass, C, D, does not fit tightly

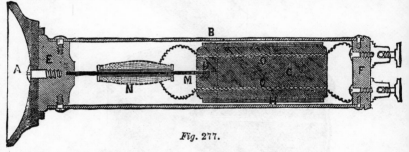

Fig. 277.

in the case, B, but has about a twenty-fifth of an inch space around it. The difficulty which was presented in the first experiments with this apparatus was that of acoustically insulating two extremities of the iron wire, which is terminated at each end by metallic masses. In order to solve this problem, it was found necessary to envelop one of the two masses in India rubber, so that this mass could be placed in a metallic case fitted to the other mass, thereby preventing any confusion of vibrations.

When simple voltaic currents are employed to work the instrument, a well annealed iron wire must be employed; but if induction currents are used, as in the Edison system, which allows the apparatus to work over long distances, the iron wire should be replaced by a strongly magnetized needle. The induced currents cannot work telephones constructed with a simple iron wire.

The telephone is extremely portable and efficient, and, moreover, is, in outward appearance, similar to the ordinary Bell telephone.

ADER'S TELEPHONE RECEIVER.

In order to render the receiving telephone of Mr. Bell more powerful, Mr. Ader has sought to greatly increase the magnetic force by the reaction of an iron armature, and the results achieved satisfactorily show the advantageous effects which can be obtained by this kind of reaction.

Suppose that before the poles of a horseshoe magnet, N S, fig. 278, is placed between two small columns, C C, a spring

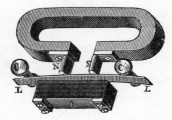

Fig. 278.

plate, L L, sufficiently distant from the poles, N S, to be unattracted by them; if we move toward this plate, L L, a massive iron armature, A, we shall immediately see that the plate, L L, is attracted by the magnet, and that it returns to its normal position as soon as we remove the armature. There is then produced under the influence of the armature, A, an excessive excitement of the magnet, which has rendered it qualified to attract the plate. Let us try to ascertain the cause of this action.

We know that the conditions of the maximum force of magnets in the reactions exchanged between them and their armatures, carry, in proportion to their respective dimensions, the equality of mass between these two organs. Consequently, the plate, L L, acting alone, has too small a mass to completely utilize the magnetism of the magnet, and the armature, A, being more massive, ought to produce a much greater reaction ; but if we consider that the plate, L L, being intermediate between the

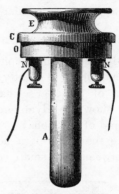

Fig. 279.

armature, A, and the magnet, could, to a certain extent, serve as a screen in the reactions exchanged between these two magnetic pieces, then we must examine and discover how the

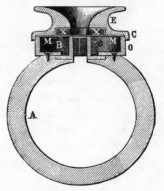

Fig. 280.

magnetism is distributed upon the plate. In ordinary conditions, with a thick plate, the inverse effect to that previously established ought evidently to be produced, for there should have been developed between the armature, A, and the plate, polarities of contrary names. But in the present conditions the polarities developed upon the plate, L L, opposite the poles, N S, being of contrary names to these poles, and penetrating the plate through and through, by reason of its small mass, cannot oppose themselves to the polarities developed upon the armature, A, on the side of N S, to make them different from those that they would be without the intervention of the plate, L L.

Fig. 281.

If we study the magnetic image of such a system without the interposed bar, we find exactly the same disposition of the lines of magnetic force, which clearly proves that they cross through the blade. The result then is, that on this side there are face to face polarities of the same name, which tend to exert a repulsion and to augment, consequently, the effect produced on the

Fig. 282.

opposite side. With this system there is then not only excessive excitement produced by the enlargement of the mass of the armature, but besides a tendency to facilitate the vibratory movements by the arrangement of the polarities developed. Such is the principle upon which Mr. Ader has established his receiving telephone, which is represented in figs. 279 to 282. In this telephone the magnet is circular, as in the pony crown of Mr. Phelps; but Mr. Ader utilizes the two magnetic poles, to which are added oblong polar appendices of soft iron, and upon which are placed the helices of fine wire, B B. These helices occupy the centre of a small circular resonant drum, M M, formed by the diaphragm, and it is above this diaphragm that is placed the exciting armature made by a ring of soft iron, X X, placed at the base of the mouth piece, E, fig. 280. This mouth piece is made of ebonite and all the metallic pieces are nickel plated. In fig. 281 is seen, from the top, two oblong poles of the magnet, and in fig. 282 the diaphragm with the ring of iron, X, which surmounts it. This is the most popular telephone receiver in Paris, and is the one used at all the telephonic theatrical representations which were organized at the electrical exhibition, and which were heard at the office of the minister of the posts and telegraphs, and at the residence of the President of the Republic. It is competent to act as a Bell telephone transmitter as well as receiver, but it is with a microphonic transmitter, arranged by Mr. Ader, that it furnishes the best results.

THE ADER TRANSMITTER.

In the beginning Mr. Ader had fully appreciated the importance of the action of the weight employed as an antagonistic force to the effect of vibration, but he then constructed his transmitter with a single contact. At present there remains only the exterior arrangements of the original apparatus, which is represented in fig. 283, and the horizontal spruce board. The form of the transmitter has been changed from round to square. On the under side of a horizontal spruce board, D, fig. 284, has been placed the microphonic system, which is composed of a sort of double grating, with 24 carbon contacts, as shown in fig. 285, the bottom of the board being elevated to show the parts.

This double grating is composed, as we see from the figure, of three traverses of carbon, *a*, *b*, *c*, upon which pivot 12 sticks of the same substance, E, E, forming at their extremities small trunnions adapted to freely turn in the holes made in the traverses; there are then 24 turns and consequently 24 contacts, coupled by 12 in quantity, and each corresponding with two carbons united in tension. The induction coil is in B, and the suspension hook serving as a commutator for the bell circuit and the telephone circuit, is seen at C. The bell call button is in M, and in P, in the interior of the wood of the desk, is a small lightning arrester.

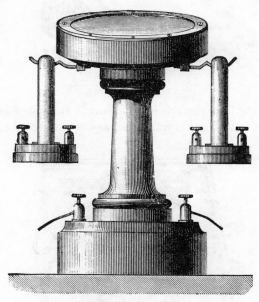

Fig. 283.

These were the transmitters which were installed on the stages of the opera, of the Opera Comique, and of the Theatre Français, during the continuance of the Electrical Exhibition of 1881, and which furnished the marvellous results so much admired. In order to satisfy the demands of a numerous public, very eager for this sort of experience, they were obliged to install these telephonic transmitters in such a manner as to operate a great number of telephones; and as they were willing that the

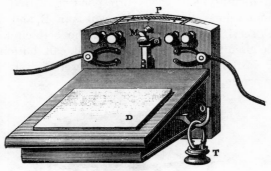

Fig. 284.

public should hear the opera by means of two telephones placed separately at each ear, it was necessary to arrange the transmit-

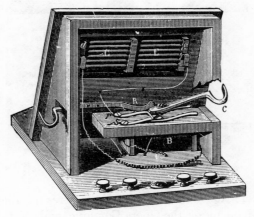

Fig. 285.

ters for a great number of double telephones. Naturally the receivers corresponding to these transmitters were those with

excessive excitement devised by Mr. Ader, which we have just described.

THE TELEPHONE AT THE PARIS OPERA.

One of the most popular attractions at the Paris Electrical Exhibition of 1881 was the demonstration of the marvellous powers of the Bell telephone, by its transmission of the singing on the stage and the music in the orchestra of the Grand Opera, to a suite of four rooms reserved for the purpose in one of the galleries of the Palais de l'Industrie, fig. 286. This demonstration was given nightly between eight and eleven o'clock, and the enormous number of people who crowded the entrance to the building before the doors were open to the evening visitors rapidly resolved themselves into patient queques as soon as they could obtain access to the gallery adjoining the telephone rooms. There they patiently awaited their time for admission, and the privilege of hearing for a few minutes whatever might be going on at the opera—solo, chorus, instrumental music, or possibly all three, until the allotted time had expired, and the listeners had to give way for a fresh instalment from the outside. In this way eighty telephones were constantly at work at the same time, the communication being shifted at short intervals to another set of eighty similar instruments in two other rooms. It may be remarked in passing that this distant audience of the performance at the opera enjoyed their allotted moments of actual transmission and that interludes did not count. Certainly nothing has ever been done before so effectually to popularize science, and to render the masses familiar with the effect, however ignorant they may be of the cause, of this marvellous invention, the first feeble voice of which was heard in the Centennial Exhibition at Philadelphia, in 1876.

The transmitters were microphones of the Ader system, placed in front of the opera stage, close to the footlights and behind them. Figs. 287 and 288 are a plan and longitudinal section of one of these transmitters. Each consists of ten small carbon pencils, A A, arranged in two series of five each, and

supported by three cross pieces, B C D, fixed to a small pine
board, which receives the vibration and serves as a cover to the
instrument. This board rests, as shown, in a massive block of
lead, P, which in its turn is supported by four blocks of soft
rubber. This arrangement is found to prevent any vibrations
of the stage from being transmitted to the microphone, and the
only movements taken up by the instrument are the sonorous

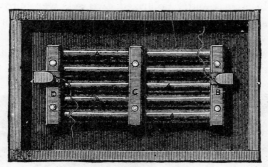

Fig. 287.

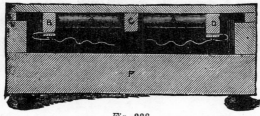

Fig. 288.

vibrations of the air. The microphone is in connection with a
Leclanché battery and the wire of a small induction coil, similar
to those found inside the Blake transmitter, and were mounted
upon a small pine base, with the ends of the primary coil terminating at one end of the base and the ends of the secondary
coil at the other. The line, laid in double wire, is connected
on the one hand with the induction coil, and on the other with
a series of telephone receivers placed in the rooms at the Palais

de l'Industrie. There are eight receivers thus coupled to each transmitter. The undulatory induction currents developed in the fine wire of the induction coil by the variation in intensity of the current traversing the induction wire react on the receiver. There were ten such installations as we have just described on the stage of the opera, each with its own battery and induction coil and double line to the exhibition. As the batteries became rapidly polarized, two sets were provided for each transmitter, and the batteries were shifted every fifteen minutes by a commutator.

The transmitters were arranged along the front of the stage, on each side of the prompter's box, as shown in fig. 289, and

Fig. 289.

were connected by double subterranean wires placed apart in the sewers, with five rooms arranged for this purpose in the exhibition building.

Fig. 290 is a diagram showing the complete arrangement for one circuit from the transmitter placed at the opera to the receivers placed at the concert room. T, T, are the transmitters, S, S, are the commutators or switches for changing the circuit of the receivers from chamber No. 1 to chamber No. 2, for changing the transmitter batteries at the opera house every fifteen minutes, and for cutting off the wires for the night which are

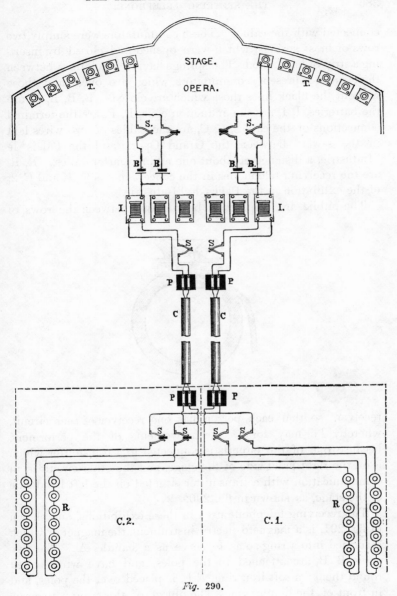

Fig. 290.

connected with the cables. These commutators were simply two rows of brass springs, which were opened and closed by inserting a strip of hard wood. The springs having black lines between their ends represent commutators which are open, and those without the black lines those which are closed. B, B, B, B, are the batteries, I, I, are the induction coils, P, P, are the terminal connections of the cables, C, C, are the cables of two wires laid in the sewers between the Grand Opera and the Palais de l'Industrie, a distance of about one and a quarter miles. R, R. are the receiving telephones in the concert rooms C, 1, and C, 2, of the exhibition in the Palais de l'Industrie.

The public are supposed to be standing between the rows of

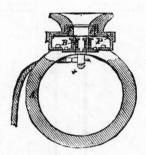

Fig. 291.

receivers, so that each person has one receiver of each circuit, whereby he may follow the movements of the performers, because one of the circuits is connected to a transmitter which is on the right hand side of the stage, and the other circuit is in communication with a transmitter situated on the left hand side of the stage, as shown in fig. 290.

The receiving telephone used in these exhibitions, and shown in fig. 291, is a magneto electric instrument, the magnet of which is formed into a ring so as to serve as a handle, A. The two cores, B B, are attached to the poles, and have wires coiled round them; a soft iron ring, F F, is placed over the poles, and in front of the diaphragm. The object of this ring is to serve as a supplementary exciter, and give to the lines of magnetic force a direction perpendicular, instead of divergent, to the diaphragm ; by this arrangement the variations produced in the magnet by the induction currents of the coils have a maximum effect on the diaphragm, and greatly add to the clearness of the telephone.

A new acoustic effect was discovered by Mr. Ader, and applied for the first time in the telephonic transmission at the Electrical Exhibition. Every one who was fortunate enough to hear the telephones at the Palais de l'Industrie has remarked that in listening with both ears at the two telephones, the sound took a special character of relief and localization which a single receiver could not produce. It is a common experience that, in listening at a telephone, it is practically impossible to have even a vague idea of the distance at which the person at the other end of the line appears to be. To some listeners this distance seems to be only a few yards, to others the voice apparently proceeds out of a great depth of the earth. In this case there was nothing of the kind. As soon as the experiment commenced the singers placed themselves, in the mind of the listener, at a fixed distance, some to the right and others to the left. It was easy to follow their movements, and to indicate exactly, each time that they changed their position, the imaginary distance at which they appeared to be. This phenomenon, which was very curious, approximated to the theory of binauricular audition, and has never been applied, we believe, before to produce this remarkable illusion, to which may almost be given the name of auditive perspective. The cause of this phenomenon, however, is a very simple one. In order to realize it, we may recall the stereoscope, which allows us to see objects in their natural relief. A similar effect is produced to the ear, and may be explained by referring to fig. 292. Each person is placed in front of a transmitter with two telephones, which receive the impression from two distinct transmitters, placed a certain distance apart. These transmitters are grouped in pairs, 1 and 6, 2 and 7, 3 and 8, 4 and 9, and 5 and 10. Fig. 292 shows the arrangement for group

1 and 6.   This group supplies sixteen telephones, adapted for
eight listeners, but the transmitter T serves the eight telephones
on the left, R, and the transmitter T′, the eight telephones on the
right, R′, of the eight listeners.   When the singer is at the
point A, the transmitter T is more strongly influenced than the
transmitter T′; the left ear is, therefore, more deeply impressed
than the right ear, and the singer appears to be on the left to the
eight listeners of the group.   When the singer is at A′ the trans-

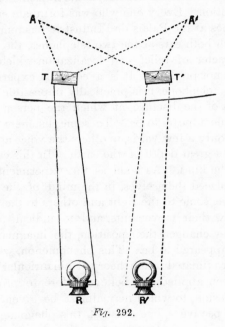

Fig. 292.

mitter T′, is more affected than the transmitter T, and the singer
appears to the right of the audience ; these aural impressions
change with the relative positions of the singers, and their movements can in this way be followed.   The use of the double conducting wire has been necessary to obviate the effect of induction, and in this respect it has been entirely successful, although
of course it increases the cost.

Another interesting experiment was performed recently between the Hippodrome and the offices of the International Telephone Company, 15 Place Vendome. The orchestra of the Hippodrome, which plays during the day and evening for the two daily performances, was heard distinctly by numerous invited guests assembled at the Place Vendome. There were ninety-six telephone receivers, and, each auditor having two of them, forty-eight persons were enabled to hear at the same time. Owing to the fact that one of the two wires that usually serve for the direction of the Hippodrome was in use, only one wire was disposable for the experiment. The apparatus was arranged at the Hippodrome as follows : There were twenty-five microphone transmitters mounted on a single board, which was inclined slightly from the horizontal over the leader of the orchestra. The microphones were placed above the board and protected from dust by a light box. The board itself was supported by four cords. The battery consisted at the beginning of three Reynier-Faure accumulators. The intensity of the current was indicated by a Deprez galvanometer placed in the circuit, and was kept sensibly constant by adding to these three accumulators another, then another, until the total number was nine. The current of the battery was branched between the twenty-five microphones, then into the twenty-four primary wires of twenty-four induction coils that were mounted by twos in series of twelve on a derived circuit. The intensity of the current was twelve ampères. The twenty-four secondary circuits of the twenty-four induction coils were grouped by fours in series, and six on a derived circuit. The resistance of each was 300 ohms, or, altogether, 1,200 ohms. The line from the Hippodrome, two miles in length, ended in one of the offices of the General Society of Telephones, Rue Petits-Champs, where also ended the line from the Place Vendome, which was a very short one. The receivers, which were of the Ader type, were grouped by sixteens in series, and six on a derived circuit. The clearness with which the music was heard was perfect, and all the auditors were perfectly satisfied with the result. In the arrangements just noted, which were said to be an improvement over those employed at the Electrical Exhibition, the principal novelty consisted in the association of the twenty-five microphones on a derived circuit, and in the association of the twenty-four secondary wires of the induction coils for tension and quantity, as is done with voltaic battery elements.

IMPROVED FORM OF EDISON'S CHEMICAL TELEPHONE.

We have described on page 325 Edison's electro chemical telephone as it first appeared in practical shape; since then it has passed through a succession of changes, until it has finally assumed the compact and convenient form shown in fig. 293. The form, however, is not the only change. In the first electro chemical telephone, the chalk cylinder was supplied with moisture by a movable roller which dipped in the exciting fluid and supplied it with moisture. This movable roller is now dispensed with, and the chalk cylinder is inclosed in a vulcanite box, seen at the end of the movable arm. The cylinder, when once moistened, remains in that condition for an indefinite period, as the box is practically air tight.

The small shaft that runs parallel with the iron arm extends through the side of the box and carries the chalk cylinder. Upon the opposite end there is a small pinion moved by a worm, the crank of which is turned by the finger. The diaphragm of the receiving instrument is covered by the front of the box, excepting a small central portion, which is quite sufficient for the exit of the sound.

The arm which supports the receiving instrument is jointed, so that it may be raised vertically out of the way when the telephone is not in use.

The transmitter is contained in the stationary rectangular box; its mouth piece projects slightly, and the diaphragm, which is of mica, is supported by a metal frame and springs inside the box cover. This transmitter is quite different from the carbon transmitters now so largely in use in this country. It is exceedingly simple, and does not require frequent adjustment, while it is equally as sensitive as existing forms of transmitters.

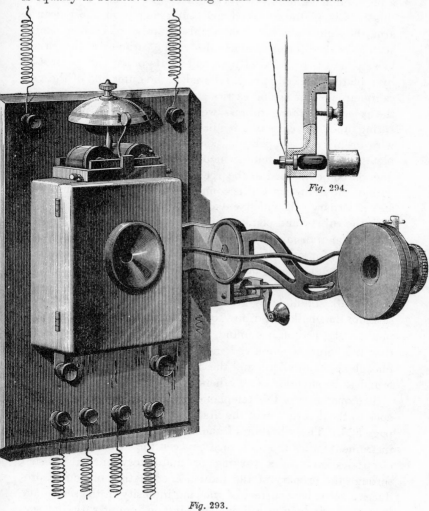

Fig. 294.

Fig. 293.

Fig. 294 shows the details of its construction.   A vulcanite arm is secured to the centre of the mica diaphragm by means of a small bolt, which is connected with one pole of the battery by a piece of metallic foil or very thin copper wire. The head of this bolt is platinum faced, and sunk deeply in the vulcanite arm, the same cavity containing also a piece of carbon pencil, such as is used for electric candles. The carbon fits the cavity loosely, and is rounded at both ends. Its outer end is pressed by a platinum faced spring, secured to the outer end of the vulcanite arm. The spring carries at its free end, exactly opposite the piece of carbon, a brass weight, and the pressure of the spring upon the carbon is regulated by the small set screw. A wire or piece of copper foil, connecting with the spring, completes an electrical circuit, which includes the primary of an induction coil contained in the rectangular box. The secondary wire of the induction coil is connected with the telephonic line, and a tertiary coil which envelops the secondary is connected with the rubber and chalk cylinder of the receiving instrument. Below the transmitter box are two keys, the right hand one being used for signalling, the left hand one for completing the tertiary circuit when a message is received.

The cylinder of the receiving instrument is made of precipitated chalk solidified by great pressure. The fluid now used to saturate the chalk is a dilute solution of hydrogen disodic phosphate. Mr. Edison has found, by a long series of experiments, that the solution employed must be that of an alkali or the phosphate of an alkali, and the hydrogen disodic phosphate is found to be superior to all others.

The operation of this telephone will be understood by reference to the description of the first electro chemical telephone, on page 326. The vibration of the diaphragm of the transmitting instrument varies the resistance between the carbon and the two electrodes, so that a varying or undulatory current is sent through the primary of the induction coil ; this, of course, produces a secondary current of varying intensity in the secondary wire of the induction coil, which being in circuit with the secondary wire of the induction coil of a distant instrument, produces a current in the tertiary wire wound around the secondary coil. The tertiary current passes through the chalk cylinder and the platinum faced rubber, and as the chalk cylinder revolves, the friction of the rubber is varied according to the variation of the primary, secondary and tertiary currents. The

Fig. 295.

platinum faced rubber is connected with the diaphragm, and the friction of the rubber is sufficient, when only a slight current passes, to pull the diaphragm forward as the cylinder is turned ;

but when the slightest increase of current is sent through the primary coil, the induced tertiary current transforms the frictional surface of the chalk into a frictionless surface, and the diaphragm springs back.   All this is necessary to describe a single vibration of the diaphragm, thousands of which are required for the utterance of a single sentence.   It is not necessary that the current should be broken to produce the desired effect in the receiver.   Indeed, it is probable that an absolute break never occurs in the ordinary use of the telephone.   An ordinary call bell is adopted in this system as a means of giving an

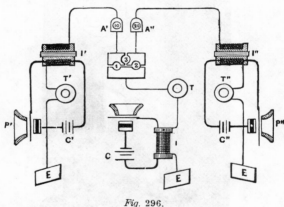

Fig. 296.

alarm.   This telephone is unrivalled for loudness of speech, and an electro magnet is not required in its construction.   The system is covered by the Bell patent, and Edison's improvements belong to the American Bell Telephone Company.

Fig. 295 shows a call box containing an Edison transmitter and a Gray bipolar receiver.   This instrument was one of the most effective modifications of the Bell telephone brought out in this country.

Fig. 296 represents the arrangement of the circuits with the Edison system.

GRAY'S BATTERY TELEPHONE.

Fig. 297 represents a modification of the Bell telephone devised by Mr. Gray, in which no permanent steel magnet is used; nor is there connected with it a battery current flowing through the main line. Instead of a permanent steel magnet, such as is more commonly used in speaking telephones, Gray used an electro magnet, B, which is held permanently charged by a local battery. The electro magnet C, which is next to the diaphragm, and which connects with the line and ground, and a corresponding magnet at the other end of the line, are charged by induction from the core of the magnet, B, which is charged from the local battery.

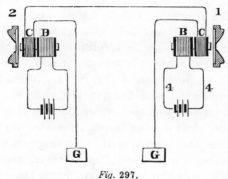

Fig. 297.

Before a battery current had been passed through the coils, and while the cores were perfectly neutral, Mr. Gray made the following experiment: he connected the telephones to the two ends of the line, as shown in fig. 297, and put on a local battery at station No. 1, shown at the right hand of the diagram, connecting the battery with magnet B, through the wires 4 4. The local battery at station No. 2, at the left of the diagram, was for the time left unconnected, so that the core of the magnet B, and also that of C, were both in a neutral state. He now placed his ear to the telephone at station No. 2, and had his assistant speak in a loud tone into the instrument at station No. 1, which had the local battery attached, and was therefore in condition to transmit the electrical vibrations produced by the motions of the diaphragm acting inductively upon the then magnetized electro magnet C. Although the vibrations were passing through the circuit, and consequently through the coils of magnet C, at station 2, he could get no audible effect until he put on the local battery and charged the cores of the magnet at the receiving end of the line. Immediately after this was done he could hear every word loudly and distinctly. He then threw off the battery at station 2, when he could hear the words very faintly, and he was able then to transmit very faint sounds, due wholly to the residual charge left in the iron after the battery was taken off. It is easy to see why no sound could be transmitted from the apparatus before it had been charged by the battery, because there was neither electricity nor magnetism present, nor had we any of the conditions necessary to produce either of these forces by simply speaking against the diaphragm. This was not true, however, of the No. 1 station, because the battery was connected and the magnet charged. No doubt there was some effect produced upon the receiving magnet, for the electrical impulses passing through the line must have been the same whether the magnets at the receiving end were charged or in a neutral condition. This one fact, however, was prominently brought out, that in order to make an electro magnet, which is the receiver of rapid vibrations (such as will copy all the motions made in the air when an articulate word is uttered), sensitive to all the changes necessary in receiving sounds of varying quality, it must be constantly charged by some force exterior to the electrical vibrations sent through the wire from the transmitting station. We were well aware that this condition is unnecessary where the force transmitted is of sufficient magnitude, or where the signals are of sufficiently long duration. Mr. Gray's experiments led him to the conclusion that a soft iron core is far more susceptible to the slight changes in the electrical conditions of the wire surrounding it when it is already in a high state of magnetic tension.

BREGUET'S TELEPHONE.

Fig. 298 represents M. Breguet's modification of the Bell telephone. The transmitter and receiver are alike, and consist simply of a glass vessel containing a layer of mercury, over which floats a layer of acidulated water. Into this water dips the point of a glass tube containing mercury.

The upper part of the glass tube contains air, and may be open to the atmosphere or closed by a vibrating diaphragm. The circuit is formed by connecting the mercury in the tube and vessel of the transmitter with that in the receiver. When one speaks over the top of the tube of the transmitter, the vibrations of the air are transmitted through the mercury to the point of the tube where the mercury makes contact with the acidulated water of the vessel by the fine capillary bore of the tube. Here

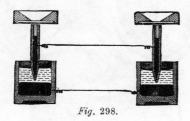

Fig. 298.

the electro capillary action takes place, the vibratory motions of the mercury generating electro capillary currents, which traverse the circuit to the receiver, and by a reverse process reproduce the air vibrations at the top of the tube of the receiver.

Mr. Breguet claims that this telephone will act through submarine cables with instantaneous effect, because it will only establish variations of potential at the sending end of the line, and, unlike other telephones, will not generate currents to flow through the line. But this claim does not appear to us to be justifiable, since currents must result in the line from the variations of potential set up; and, if there is to be any communication at all, they must travel throughout the length of the cable from end to end.

A VIBRATING BELL TELEPHONE SIGNAL.

Colonel Jacobi's telephone call, in which the bell is set free by the motions of the diaphragm, is based upon the same principle as the Ader signal. Fig. 299 shows how the apparatus is constructed. Beneath a telephone, A, of the Siemens system, there is adapted a spring bell arrangement, operating in such a way that when the lever, C, is depressed the bell rings, and when

Fig. 299.

it again assumes its position of equilibrium the ringing ceases. The mouth piece of the telephone is provided with a groove in the middle, which serves as a point of suspension for a small plate, E, carrying at its extremity an insignificant weight. When the diaphragm vibrates strongly, its vibrations cause the fall of plate, E, which acts upon the lever, C, and sets the bell free. The latter then continues to ring as long as the lever, C, remains down.

The vibrations necessary to effect the ungearing of the bell are produced at the transmitting station by means of an ordinary Siemens whistle. When the two persons who wish to converse have exchanged their call signals, they each lock their levers by means of the rod, F, lower their plates, E, and begin their conversation. The talk finished, each one puts his apparatus in its former position. The fall of the plate, B, may also be employed for closing the circuit of an electric bell connected with a local battery.

CHAPTER X.

Before entering upon the history of the invention of the electric speaking telephone, we will present a condensed statement from the able and exhaustive report of the examiner of interferences in the United States Patent Office, on the state of the art at the time when Mr. Bell's great discovery was publicly announced.

The word telephone, although popularly employed to designate an apparatus for the electrical transmission and reproduction of articulate speech, has no such limited meaning, comprehending equally any device for conveying sounds to a distance. There are two classes of electric telephones now recognized, the musical or harmonic and the articulating, the capacity of the former being limited to the production, and of the latter to the reproduction, of sounds. The first class embraces those instruments wherein the electric current operates in part as a regulator and in part as a producer. By virtue of the electrical impulses created, the sounding devices are caused to vibrate at their normal rate, or at a rate determined by the number of pulsations, and thus *produce* a musical tone, which is the exponent of their normal rate, or of the electrical pulsations, however the latter may have been created. The second class embraces all instruments wherein the electric current, operating as a motor, is controlled by and acts upon the sounding device to *reproduce* an original tone. The two classes differ from each other in that the one *produces*, whereas the other *reproduces*, sound vibrations.

All sound results from vibrational motions communicated to the air, and possesses three characteristics, *i. e.*, pitch, loudness, and timbre, or quality, which are dependent upon the rate, amplitude, and form of vibration. To produce a given sound it is only necessary to establish its characteristic vibration ; to reproduce a sound it is necessary to repeat the original vibrations in all their parts.

In the electric current is found a medium capable of receiving, transmitting, and rendering into audible vibrations, pulsations, or impressions, in all respects the equivalents of sound waves. But as sound waves possess three characteristics, it is obvious that to *reproduce* any given series of acoustic vibrations it is essential that the impressions shall be produced in the first place by that series. If, on the other hand, electrical pulsations are created in imitation of those which would result from the direct action of sound waves, audible vibrations will be *produced* which are the expression of the electrical pulsation, but not of original sounds.

Pure musical tones, being devoid of quality, or timbre, may be produced by imitating their constituents—rate and amplitude ; and, as vibrational or pendulous motions may be effected by the intermittent application of force, it is not essential that the intermediate periods should be controlled. Not so, however, with sounds possessing quality, or timbre, the distinguishing feature of articulate speech ; here the form of vibration— the motion of the air particles between the extremes of condensation and rarefaction — determines the character of the sound, and, as they never cease, they must at all times find expression in and become a constituent part of the impressed current.

A wide distinction exists between the transmission and production or reproduction of musical tones, and the transmission and reproduction of articulate speech, as well as between the instruments for effecting these operations. To transmit electrical impulses bearing the impress of musical tones, it is only necessary to establish the same rate of vibration. If we do this, and nothing more, the receiving instrument will give a tone whose pitch is represented by the number of vibrations, modified by the normal tone of the receiver. Such a tone is without quality or timbre other than that supplied by the instrument itself, and it makes no difference how the pulsations are produced so long as they possess the necessary rate. This may be effected by periodically interrupting, augmenting, diminishing or reversing the electric current.

Inasmuch as articulate speech and all sounds having quality possess, over and above rate and amplitude, what is termed " form of vibration," it is apparent that before we can transmit we must first impress their characteristics upon the current. To do this the current must be constantly and uniformly controlled during the entire interval between the succeeding impulses which serve to establish the rate (pitch) and amplitude (loudness) of the sound vibration.

The irregular motions incident to "quality" must in some way be impressed upon and expressed by the current. If, during any portion of the vibration, these "quality" producing motions are not registered, to that extent is the sound lost or mutilated. The same is true of the receiving instrument. It must be so constructed and controlled in its motions by the current as to lose none of its impressions.

THE INVENTION OF THE MUSICAL OR HARMONIC TELEPHONE.

The production of musical tones by the electric current was first observed by Page in 1837, who noticed that a ringing sound—which he called galvanic music—proceeded from a horseshoe magnet when it was brought within the influence of a coil of insulated wire through which an interrupted current passed ; and he also found the same result could be produced by rapidly rotating an electro magnet in front of the poles of a horseshoe magnet. These phenomena were afterwards made the subject of investigation and experiment by a number of scientists, with a view to determining the probable cause. The sounding media included bars, rods and wires of iron and steel ; wires stretched on sounding boards; bars free and clamped at one or both ends. Those magnetized by induction

gave louder tones.   Stretched wires gave forth sounds when the
interrupted current was passed through them without the use of
a helix ; in this case the sound could be reinforced by the
simultaneous passage of a continuous current.   The rheotomes
generally employed gave no tones, but De la Rive used one
wherein a spring vibrated by a toothed wheel (fig. 300) broke
the current and emitted a musical tone.

As the result of all these investigations, the conclusion was
reached that the sound was due to molecular changes, produced
by the alternate magnetization and demagnetization of the metal,
and that these motions were isochronous with the interruptions.
For the production of the interrupted currents universally employed in these experiments, it was customary to use rheotomes or
circuit breakers, some of which were operated by hand, others by

   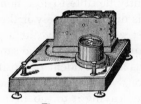

Fig. 300.   *Fig.* 301.

clock work (fig. 301), and others by the current itself, being entirely automatic in their action.   The springs or armatures of many of
these automatic circuit breakers produced musical tones by virtue of their rapid vibrations, and although no importance had
been attached to this circumstance as influencing the sounds
produced by the current, it had been proposed that this principle
might be employed in constructing musical instruments.

While these investigations were progressing respecting Page's
galvanic music, Bourseul was speculating upon the possibility
of transmitting and reproducing speech by means of the electric
current ; but it was from the wonders of telegraphy, and not
from galvanic music, that he drew his inspiration, and prophe-
sied the transmission of speech by electricity, an announcement
so novel and incomprehensible at the time that Du Moncel, by

whom the account was first published, pronounced it a fantastic idea.

·Although Bourseul is entitled to the credit of first suggesting the possibility of transmitting sounds by electricity, and of the operations necessary to the accomplishment of such result, he fails to disclose any means for performing the described operations or of producing the desired result. His mode of reasoning and the conclusions deduced therefrom are as follows : We know that sounds are made by vibration, and are adapted to the ear by the same vibrations which are reproduced by the intervening medium. But the intensity of the vibrations diminishes very rapidly with the distance, so that it is, even with the aid of speaking tubes and trumpets, impossible to exceed somewhat narrow limits. Suppose that a man speaks near a movable disk, sufficiently flexible to lose none of the vibrations of the voice ; that this disk alternately makes and breaks the currents from a battery ; you may have at a distance another disk which will simultaneously execute the same vibrations.

It was a self evident proposition that to reproduce the sound vibrations was to reproduce the sounds. He suggests what is to be done, leaving it to the inventor to supply the means. The circuit breaking transmitter proposed, he acknowledges, will not reproduce the variable motions of the sound waves ; and although he considers this of slight consequence, it is obviously of vital importance. Not only is the described transmitter defective, but the manner of constructing and operating the receiver is left to the imagination.

The value of many alleged conceptions and disclosures is typified in this description. Presuming that certain results will follow the establishment of certain conditions, they suggest generally a method for bringing about those conditions. The conception is inadequate and the mechanism insufficient, but after trial and experiment they, or some more successful inventor managed to supply or interject the vitalizing element by addition, subtraction or entire change in principle and structure ; and although the later period marks the first stage of actual invention, they seek to establish the earlier date, simply because they then commenced to speculate upon the subject.

But it is obvious, as in the present case, that the invention—the production of a given result by specified means—had not been conceived or accomplished. However suggestive this apparatus of Bourseul's, it was never developed by him, for the probable reason that he did not have the requisite knowledge. The approximations obtained, he says, promise a favorable result, but no further information is furnished, and the presumption is that if he made additional effort he failed.

Helmholtz had established the existence of three distinct properties or characteristics of sound vibrations, namely, pitch, loudness and quality or timbre. The pitch of a sound, as determined by the number of vibrations executed in a given time; the loudness, by the amplitude of the vibrations; and the quality or timbre, whereby tones of the same pitch and amplitude, given by different instruments, are distinguished from one another by character or form of vibration. Articulate speech is dependent upon the co-existence of all three of these constituents for the vibrations incident to pitch and loudness, and unless modified by those which go to establish the form of vibration, will be devoid of quality, and produce only that succession of musical tones incident to the number and amplitude of the vibrations. It is apparent that Helmholtz's researches, while confirming Bourseul's anticipations as to the necessity of reproducing all the vibrations imparted to the transmitter, magnified the apparent difficulties, and rendered more speculative and uncertain the agencies to be employed. The only method known to the art at this time for producing electrical impulses such as would develop the motive power at a distance, were the interrupted voltaic and the magneto electric current. The former we have considered; the latter, though in its infancy, was understood, and had been practically applied in operating instruments.

Prescott, in his work on The Electric Telegraph (1860), referring to the instantaneous magnetization and demagnetization of iron cores by the interrupted current, mentions the facility with which the current may be interrupted and re-established hundreds and even thousands of times a second, producing pulsations that, acting through an electro magnet upon an oscillating lever, produced musical notes, and confidently asserts that the adaptation of this power to the production of music upon telegraphic piano fortes, at any distance which may be desired, is a matter of the utmost simplicity, capable of being successfully carried into practice by any one who has the money and taste for the experiment. Even this method of producing musical sound by the rapid oscillations of an armature was dependent upon pulsating currents due to interruptions. To these instances may be added the observations of Noad in 1857, that the sounds produced by an interrupted current acting through a helix upon an iron core varied with the velocity of the interruptions, and that different sounds could be produced by the employment of toned wires and rods.

Thus the art stood when Reis presented to the world his telephone. The idea of causing sounds to produce sounds at a distance through the intervention of the electric current was both novel and captivating. Had the proposition not been supplemented by demonstration, it would, no doubt, have shared the fate of Bourseul's. Tangible evidences were, however, furnished in the form of working instruments; and although it nowhere appears that they satisfied the conditions prescribed for the reproduction of sounds having quality—that is, the vibrational curves produced were not the same as those of the inducing sound waves—sounds were in fact produced bearing a resemblance to the originals. The characteristics of these sounds and their relations to the vibrations from which they were derived is not clearly evidenced. Not only do they suffer by translation, but upon comparison it will be found that the earlier authors are much more sanguine as to its future, give more credit to its productions, and show they are more or less influenced by the novelty of the performance. It was at first regarded as opening a new field for the application of electricity

to the useful arts, and was looked upon as an invention of value
in the hands of improvers ; but as its capacity became better
understood, and as such improvements as were added did not
materially change the results, its reputation began to wane, until
in the course of a few years it was mentioned only as an interesting philosophical apparatus—a scientific toy—and thus it remained, well known, but to all intents and purposes dead, until
resurrected for the purpose of belittling subsequent inventions.

The striking similarity existing between the method and apparatus suggested by Bourseul and those described by Reis
would seem to indicate that the latter was but an imitator, his
first description occurring seven years after the former's announcement.

No less than four distinct varieties of telephones are attributed
to Reis.   The first is described by the inventor, in 1861, and
by Dingler, in 1863 ; the second by Legat, in 1862 ; the third by
Cosmos, in 1864 ; Koenig, in 1865 ; and Van der Weyde, in
1869 ; and the fourth by Pisco, in 1865 ; Hessler, in 1866 ; and
Ferguson, in 1867.   As determined by the earliest date of publication, he is thus accredited with a different apparatus in each
of the years 1861, 1862, 1864 and 1865, and, with the exception
of the 1862 devices, two or more descriptions of each instrument
have been produced.

The four transmitters were without exception so designed and
operated that the diaphragm, when set in motion by sound
waves, should sever or break the electric circuit at each vibration.   Of this fact there can be no doubt.   Not only do all the
writers on the subject agree in so stating, plainly and unequivo-
cally, but judging from the receiver employed and its supposed
capacity, it could not have been otherwise.   This receiver, which
Reis himself says is one of the well known instruments for producing galvanic sound, is almost identical with that described
by Noad in 1857, and it had been determined by Poggendorf
and others that such sounds could only be produced by an
interrupted current—a proposition neither questioned nor modified by Reis.

The apparatus of the first, third and fourth periods were identical in principle and mode of operation, differing from each other only in details of construction.

The first transmitter consisted of a cubical block of wood having a conical perforation, the smaller end closed by a membrane diaphragm. A thin strip of platina was fastened to the centre of the diaphragm, and upon this rested a platina point carried by a strip of thin metal. The point and strip of platina constituted the terminals of the circuit.

The third transmitter, fig. 302, differed from the first by the substitution of a box for the cube, the addition of a mouth piece or tube to the side, and the arrangement of the diaphragm on the top.

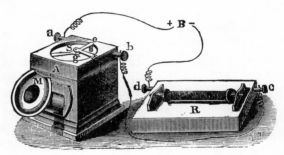

Fig. 302.

The fourth was the same as the third, with the exception of the method of fastening the diaphragm and the arrangement of the contact piece. The diaphragm was stretched over a ring and held by a thread, the ring being placed in the top of the box. The thin strip carrying the point was replaced by a right angled strip—one end perforated and passed over a pin to retain it in place, the other carrying a point dipping into a cup of mercury, while the contact point, which rests upon the platina disk, was situated at the angle.

This instrument, fig. 303, represents the last and most improved form of the Reis telephone, and is provided with a Morse telegraph key and sounder for signalling.

The receivers for all three of these are the same.   It consists of a knitting needle or wire passing through a helix and resting upon bridges fastened to a resonant case.

The second instrument, described by Legat, fig. 304, differs from the others in structure, but not in mode of operation.   In

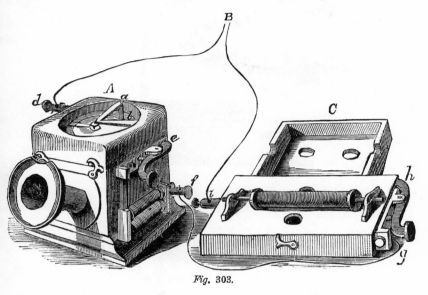

Fig. 303.

this apparatus the diaphragm was fastened to the smaller end of a metal cone.   A delicately pivoted lever was held in contact with the centre of the diaphragm by a light spring, the other end of the lever making contact with an adjustable spring.

The receiver consisted of an electro magnet and a long and broad metal plate, resting on pivots near the centre and carrying at its lower end an armature.

The manner in which these instruments were constructed and used would seem to preclude the reproduction of the quality of sounds, whatever they may have accomplished in the way of pitch and amplitude, and none of the publications referred to show the contrary. If we follow the directions given, the contact point must be so arranged and disposed that, not being

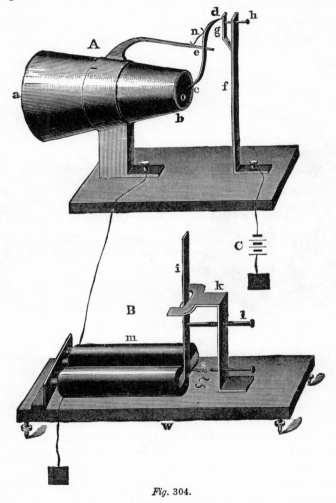

Fig. 304.

able to follow the retreating membrane, but lagging behind, it shall be struck, and its inward course intercepted by the next outward movement of the diaphragm. Under such conditions it is obvious that the form of vibration of the sound wave cannot be maintained or impressed upon the current. During part of a vibration the two electrodes are approaching each other, impelled by dissimilar forces, move together, separate, and then move in the same direction, but not together. Such was their described action, and any alteration or change which involves a departure therefrom is not the same invention.

A great diversity of opinion is manifested by the authors referred to, as to the capacity of the apparatus to reproduce sounds, which can be explained in no other way than upon the hypothesis that as the subject became better known there was a truer appreciation of the performances of the apparatus.

Taking the authorities in the order of publication, and without regard to the special devices employed, we find the following statements: *Reis:* Melodies sung not very loud were rendered "audible." Complete chords of three notes of a piano, upon which the transmitter was placed, were "reproduced;" also the "sound" of other instruments; not possible to reproduce human speech with a distinctness sufficient for every one; consonants for the most part reproduced pretty distinctly; vowels not in an equal degree. *Legat* (three different translations): Chords and melodies transmitted with marvellous accuracy; vowel sounds more or less indistinct; single words indistinctly recognizable, though inflection clearly reproduced. *Dingler:* Melodies "heard;" "if we are not so far advanced that we can converse with a friend a hundred miles away and yet recognize his voice as though he were sitting alongside of us, the *impossibility* of attaining this result can no more be claimed." *Cosmos:* "Fantastic minds have singularly exalted the qualities of this apparatus; they have undertaken to indicate for it at once an office which it is far from being able to fill. When one sings the musical scale at the transmitter, there needs an ear well trained to distinguish the sound repeated by the receiver in the midst of the vibrations which agitate it." Only able to recognize the successive rise and pitch. " The electrical transmission of musical sounds is therefore a problem of which the true solution has not been found ; and all the magnificent promises which have been made and published on the subject of acoustic telegraphy seem to us still to belong to the region of illusions." *Koenig :* Intended to transmit " sounds" to a distance. "Sounds" produced a continuous "sound," not of good quality, and cease from time to time. Transmitter far from perfect. *Pisco :* "In my experiments with the telephone, the rod never changed its pitch, even with the most different tones and sounds, and always produced only the rhythm of the words sung or spoken. The aria of the song sung into the instrument could generally be recognized *from the rhythm.* The apparatus of Reis is indeed a ' telephone,' but not a ' phonic telegraph,' and may be classed with the most beautiful and interesting of school experiments." Tones and melodies sung into the transmitter always effect a " sounding" of the rod, "*without a change of pitch,* simply with the reproduction of the rhythm of the respective song or words." *Hessler :* Sufficiently strong tones from organ or voice produce tones and combinations of tones. The telephone is yet in its infancy, it is true, but even now, by employing powerful currents, it transmits at a distance not only solitary tones, but even tunes, consisting of slow consecutive tones, quite perceptibly and distinctly. *Ferguson :* An instrument for telegraphing notes of the same pitch ; note weak, and in quality resembles the sound of a toy trumpet. *Van der Weyde* (1869) : "An instrument which transmits directly the pitch of a sound by means of a telegraph wire." In its present state has no practical application, but is a mere scientific, though highly interesting, curiosity. " No quality of tone can be transmitted, much less can articulate words be sent, notwithstanding the enthusiastic prediction of some persons who, when they first beheld this apparatus in operation, exclaimed that now we would talk directly through the wire. It is from its nature able to transmit only pitch and rhythm—consequently melody, and nothing more. No harmony, no different degrees of strength or other qualities of tone, can be transmitted. The receiving instrument, in fact, sings the melodies transmitted, as it were, with its own voice, resembling the humming of an insect, regardless of the quality of the tone which produces the original tune at the other end of the wire."

Experience demonstrates that inventions and discoveries involving novel principles of construction and operation are, as a rule, developed and enlarged upon in the hands of skilled operators, and unless overestimated by unskilled or incompetent judges, their first performances are improved upon, or at least equalled, the capacity of the apparatus enlarged, and the range of application increased ; and this in proportion as they become better known and understood.

With Reis' invention the contrary appears to be the case. The best results are accredited to the first and crudest instruments ; later improvements, added by the inventor himself, diminished its capacity, until finally, after years of experience and trial, it had so far degenerated as to be incapable of more than approximating its traditional performances. Is it not much more probable that time developed , and demonstrated its weakness, and that the later, rather than the earlier, observations are the more reliable ? There is every reason to believe this supposition to be correct. It cannot be said of the invention that it was so much in advance of the art that it had to wait until the public were educated before it could be appreciated or understood. It was at the outset given a fictitious value, as possessing qualities now sought to be established, but which fifteen years of trial failed to develop or make known.

It is difficult, nay impossible, to conceive how an instrument operating as described could impress upon the current the minor vibrations incident to and productive of quality. That it might to a certain extent mark the succession of larger vibrations is obvious, but the separation of the electrodes would seem to prevent further influence until they again came into contact. The transmitter was, in fact, a rheotome or circuit breaker, whose vibrations were occasioned by and varied with those of the sound waves, instead of being confined to a fixed and predetermined series, as in other rheotomes. In this way some, but not all, of the constituent parts of the sounds were impressed upon and transmitted by the current.

Another source of interference was the receiver. Even had the current transmitted been properly impressed, this instrument was unfitted for manifesting the changes.

Other articles referring to the Reis instrument, which appeared from time to time, confirm the conclusions arrived at, and conclusively disprove the proposition sought to be established, that the instruments either transmitted or reproduced sound vibrations.

ORIGINALITY OF THE INVENTION OF THE ELECTRIC SPEAKING TELEPHONE.

James Watt said that the maker of a great invention must pass through three stages in the estimation of the great mass of the public: first, it would be said it was impossible; next, it would be said that he had not done it; finally, it would be asserted that it had long been known. It may be added that when an inventor has reached this last stage of attack he may be certain that both the novelty and the value of his work has become assured. To this habit Mr. Bell is no exception.

In the modest account of his invention which Mr. Bell gave in his lecture before the Society of Telegraph Engineers, in London, in 1877, and which we have reproduced in the second chapter of our work, he has not indicated the various successive steps which led to this invention. No claim of priority having at that time been put forth—except that of Prof. Dolbear of having suggested the idea of maintaining the cores in the telephone in a permanently magnetic or polarized state by the inductive influence of a permanent magnet instead of by a voltaic current, which Mr. Bell alludes to as an example of the independent discoveries which naturally followed the investigation of the subject after the first published accounts of the operation of the telephone—he did not think it necessary to enter into these details, and his extremely reserved character did not prompt him to do so; but when a horde of pretenders arose to put forth their claims to this discovery, and a score of lawsuits occurred on this account, these details were no longer useless, and it became necessary not only to furnish them, but to fully investigate the subject in all its bearings and in all directions. As the result of these investigations, which have been made during the trial of these various suits, as well as in the controversies carried on in the Patent Office, a great mass of documentary evidence, of great value to the history of this invention, has been produced, which we believe worthy of reproduction here, as showing by what difficult and tortuous roads a great discovery must pass before arriving at the important results which it is destined to realize.

THE ANNOUNCEMENT OF THE INVENTION OF THE SPEAKING TELEPHONE.

When it was announced that the electric transmission and reproduction of articulate speech had been accomplished, the novelty and utility of the invention elicited the wonder and admiration of the world. It first engaged the attention of the scientists, by whom it was unqualifiedly accepted as a novelty and a wonder. There was no suggestion or intimation that it was a mere improvement; that it permitted a conversation to be carried on at a greater distance with greater facility or better than something else. It was accepted at the outset as the unrivalled discovery of a new art.

Having passed the crucial test of scientific investigation, it rapidly acquired a commercial standing by reason of its great utility. It did not supplant other devices of a similar nature, but took possession of a field theretofore unoccupied.

It is an historical fact that the introduction of valuable and important inventions is productive of a host of rival claimants; and so the steady growth and assured success of the articulating telephone as a commercial venture had the usual effect of developing, reviving, and resurrecting all manner of inventions and contrivances, both near and remote, upon which the shadow of a claim to priority could possibly be based. Stimulated by visions of glory and profit, all manner of incomplete, dormant, unsuccessful, and abandoned inventions and devices have been brought to light, polished, and made to resemble as much as possible the real article, in order that their projectors might obtain the profits.

The electrical transmission and reproduction of sounds possessing quality was unknown to the public prior to the year 1876. It had never been asserted, explained or demonstrated, and the means and method were alike undetermined. It is true there were those who undertook to predict its ultimate accomplishment, to advance theories, construct apparatus, and make experiments with that object in view ; but it is equally true that in every such instance their efforts resulted in complete and entire failure until Alexander Graham Bell, on the 8th of May, 1876, and again on the twenty-fifth of June, 1876, for the first time in the history of the art, publicly explained a method and exhibited an apparatus, not only designed and constructed for reproducing, but practically operating to reproduce, at a distance, through the agency of the electric current, sound waves whose form and characteristics were sensibly the equivalents of those transmitted. From that time the success of the articulating telephone became an established fact, and from the circumstance that Bell was the first to explain and demonstrate its operation, he was publicly accredited with its discovery and invention.

The disclosures thus made, together with the stimulus given by the approval and adoption of the invention by the public, afforded an opportunity and inducement for the revival of antiquated ideas and experiments which in themselves possessed no advantage in point of utility over the inventions of Bourseul and Reis, and would possibly have resulted the same ; but being further prosecuted and conducted in accordance with the principles thus announced, were readily made to develop those properties essential to the transmission of articulate speech, the existence of which was before unknown.

But the knowledge thus obtained and applied constituted the gist of the invention. It was the key to the mystery which had baffled prior investigators. When once discovered and placed in the hands of intelligent and experienced inventors, its application in a variety of forms was not difficult so long as the principle was preserved. These persons, totally oblivious to the insidious influences produced by the knowledge of a practical method and apparatus, undoubtedly imagined they were independently pursuing and developing their original ideas. The absence of success before, and its immediate accomplishment after, the introduction of the Bell telephone is a circumstance worthy of notice. Like persons to whom a problem is submitted, but before it is fully comprehended the solution is explained, they are loath to admit that they might not have proceeded in the right direction and have produced the correct result. It is almost impossible to ascertain the effect produced upon mental processes by such information. The merits and demerits of an instrument are determined by its results, and are the best evidences of intelligent design and purpose.

Prior to 1876, the instruments tested were not thought capable of and never did transmit and reproduce sounds possessing quality—an essential component of articulate speech. Since then, the same, or what are alleged to be similar devices, have been made to accomplish that operation. If the capacity was inherent, but dormant, some one must have discovered it; if the device was altered, or its mode of operation changed, some one invented or discovered the change. In either case, an invention was made, for new and useful results were produced. It is this discovery or invention which rendered possible and practicable the electrical transmission and reproduction of sounds in their entirety that forms the most important element of this inquiry.

MR. BELL'S FIRST CONCEPTION OF THE SPEAKING TELEPHONE.

As a result of the legal investigations and the proofs which have been produced, it appears that, from 1874, Mr. Bell devoted himself to the solution of the problem of the electrical transmission and reproduction of articulate speech, his first researches to this end going as far back, in fact, as July, 1874. But it was not till October of that year that his ideas may be said to have taken a definite form. After having studied the beautiful works of Mr. Helmholtz upon the combinations of sounds, he thought that if two electro magnets placed at the two ends of a circuit had for an armature a series of iron reeds of different lengths and placed in exactly the same conditions at the two stations, the sound of the voice would be able to impress such of these reeds as harmonized with their fundamental sound, and that the result of the vibration of these reeds at the transmitting station would be the creation of induction currents capable of reproducing parallel vibrations upon the reeds of corresponding length at the receiving station. In October, 1874, he commu-

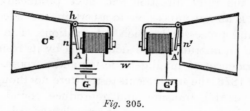

Fig. 305.

nicated a part of his ideas to Dr. Clarence J. Blake, of Boston, and described and illustrated by drawings made on the spot an apparatus in which one metal reed was substituted for the several reeds in the apparatus described above, this one reed being actuated by a membrane to which it was to be attached, and the membrane was to be set in motion by the human voice. Mr. Bell suggested that if the simple pendulous vibrations of a metal reed could be communicated to a second reed electrically connected with the first, then the more complicated vibrations of the human voice communicated to the metal reed, through the medium of the air, could also be electrically transmitted. To accomplish this purpose, he thought it advisable to attach the metal reed to a membrane which would reproduce the aerial vibrations produced by the human voice. Fig. 305 represents this apparatus, which is the same as that shown in fig. 7 of Bell's patent of March 7, 1876. He did not construct the apparatus at that time, because he was not sure that the currents generated by that method would be strong enough to be of practical utility; and, fearing that they would not be, he conceived that a proper way to obtain the desired effects would be to use the constant power of a strong battery, and utilize the vibrations given to the transmitter by the voice to vary the resistance of the circuit through which the current from the battery passed. With reference to this plan, he wrote Gardiner G. Hubbard, May 4, 1875, that if this turns out to be the case, the oscillations of the current should correspond in amplitude, as well as in the rate of movement, to the vibrations given to the transmitter by the voice, one consequence of which would be that the timbre of a sound could be transmitted. The plan for transmitting timbre—which, of course, means the transmission of speech—by causing permanent magnets to vibrate in front of electro magnets, being, in his estimation, chiefly defective on account of the feebleness of the induced currents ; and if the other plan were successful, the strength of the current could be increased ad libitum without destroying the relative intensities of the vibrations.

In the last of February, or early part of March, 1875, Mr. Bell had an interview with Prof. Henry, which is described in a letter which he wrote to his father and mother, dated March 18, 1875. He described to Prof. Henry certain experiments in the production of sound by electricity which excited Prof. Henry's interest, and induced him to ask Mr. Bell to repeat them in his presence, and appointed noon of the next day for the experiment. Mr. Bell set the instrument working, and Prof. Henry sat at a table for a long time with the empty coil of wire against his ear, listening to the sound. Feeling so much encouraged by the interest manifested by the great scientist, Mr. Bell determined to ask his advice about the apparatus he had designed for the electric transmission of the human voice, and, after explaining the idea, asked what he would advise him to do—

publish it and let others work it out, or attempt to solve the problem himself? Prof. Henry said he thought it was the germ of a great invention, and advised him to work at it himself, instead of publishing. Mr. Bell said that he recognized the fact that there were mechanical difficulties in the way that rendered the plan impracticable at the present time, and added that he felt that he had not the electrical knowledge necessary to overcome the difficulties. Prof. Henry's laconic answer was, "Get it."

In a letter to his parents dated May 24, 1875, Mr. Bell says that every moment of his time is devoted to study of electricity and to experiments; that the subject broadens, and he thinks that the transmission of the human voice is much more nearly at hand then he had supposed. He modestly adds that his inexperience in such matters is a great drawback, but that Morse conquered his electrical difficulties, though he was only a painter; and he does not intend to give in till all is completed.

Before this time Bell satisfied himself that the true and only method for the electrical transmission of vocal sounds involved as its fundamental element an apparatus which should transmit amplitude or intensity as well as pitch—for quality or *timbre* or articulation were ultimately resolvable into these two characteristics of vibration—and therefore that the electrical transmission of speech depended upon producing upon the line wire electrical undulations or variations which should correspond in form to the aerial vibrations which constituted the sound to be transmitted; and he perceived that a circuit breaking apparatus (such, for example, as the Reis transmitter) was necessarily totally inadequate to do this, because it merely tended to intermit the current, and not to control it—to govern its changes as to frequency, but not as to intensity or form or character. Bell was aiming to perfect an apparatus which should carry out his method in two ways: one by varying the electro motive force in a circuit of constant resistance, and the other by varying the resistance in a circuit supplied with a constant electro motive force. He intended to do both of these by means of the vibrational movement taken up by stretched membranes or elastic metals when spoken to.

In the description given to Dr. Clarence J. Blake, in October, 1874, Bell had described a working apparatus intended to produce these electrical undulations when spoken to, by varying the electro motive force. His only doubt about this apparatus was purely electrical and practical, viz., whether currents generated by such slight movements of a thin armature would be sufficiently strong to produce audible effects at the receiving station. On June 2, 1875, in the course of some experiments, he discovered that slight movements of a thin armature would produce currents of available strength. This at once removed the last supposed difficulty from his mind, and the electrical speaking telephone became to him a completed discovery and a fixed fact. He announced this in a letter to Mr. Hubbard written the same day, in which he used the following language: "I have succeeded to-day in transmitting signals *without any battery whatever!* The musical note produced at the receiving end was sensibly the equivalent of that at the transmitting end in *loudness* as well as pitch."

This discovery was the result of accident rather than design. Mr. Bell was engaged at the time in conducting experiments relating to his harmonic telegraph, in which he was assisted by Thos. A. Watson. A series of interrupters or circuit breakers, with separate keys for connecting them with the main line at one station, and a series of harmonic receivers, were stationed at two points on the line. Each receiver consisted of a horseshoe electro magnet, with a reed (corresponding in pitch to one of the interrupters) fastened to one leg and a coil of insulated wire surrounding the other. It was the design that one of the receivers at each station should respond when the interrupter, whose rate of vibration corresponded to that of the reed, should be connected by depressing its key. In testing the apparatus, one of the reeds at Watson's station failing to respond, he was directed to pluck it, as that means was sometimes adopted for starting a reed when it had become attached to the pole of the magnet. He did so, and Bell observed that the corresponding reed at his station was thrown into vibration, though he had not depressed the key of the transmitter. He was at a loss to understand where the current came from to operate the reed; and to make sure that it was not derived from the transmitters, he cut them out entirely and connected the two receivers upon a circuit without a battery. He then proceeded to test the receivers and discovered that, when a reed was plucked at one station, by placing his ear against any one of the reeds at the other station he could distinguish the tone, and comprehended at once that the *timbre* of the plucked reed was reproduced. The

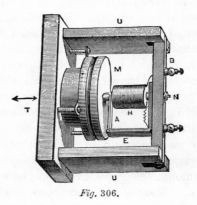

Fig. 306.

experiment was repeated with a single receiver at each end, the result being more marked, and still more so when the reeds were in unison. By placing a battery in circuit, better results seemed to be obtained.

These experiments led him to believe that the reeds and cores of the electro magnets had been rendered slightly magnetic by the passage of the battery currents, and that the plucking of a reed induced a magneto electric current in the helices in line, which manifested itself by influencing the reeds of the receivers.

He had by accident made a discovery which demonstrated, as he thought, the incorrectness of his conclusions as to the efficiency of a magneto electric current, generated by the vibrations of an armature, to produce practical results, and his hypothetical instrument of 1874 at once occurred to him. He became as sanguine as he had before been doubtful, and expressed the belief that by this discovery he had solved the problem of the transmission of speech by electricity. Wishing to avail himself of this discovery, which removed the only difficulty he had foreseen, he at once began preparations for testing his theoretical instruments of 1874. Accordingly Watson was instructed on the 2d of June, 1875, to make the first instrument, which was completed on or before the 5th. Fig. 306 represents a plan and 307 a sectional view of this instrument.

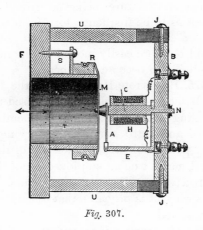

Fig. 307.

The membrane, M, of gold beater's skin, is attached to a ring and stretched over the end of a short wooden tube, T, three or three and a half inches in diameter, by means of three screws, S, passing through lugs on the ring. The electro magnet is supported on an adjustable cross piece, B, above the membrane. The uncovered leg of the electro magnet, H, is hinged to a steel reed, A E, the free end being attached to the centre of the membrane diaphragm a little beyond the covered pole of the electro magnet.

It was Bell's intention that Watson should have used a light armature and hinge it differently; and in the course of a day or two the armature and uncovered leg of the electro magnet were removed and others substituted, wherein the end of the leg was filed to an edge and a thinner steel reed was hinged to it by means of a strip of leather. Although a duplicate was to have been constructed as a receiver, Bell was so anxious to try the instrument that he could not wait, and so immediately attempted to use it with one of his harmonic receivers. The first test was with a battery, which at once tore the membrane, but at a subsequent trial the results obtained were such that Bell was encouraged by them to reconstruct the instrument with a lighter armature, the heavier armature being so strongly attracted by the electro magnet as to be frequently torn from the membrane; hence he thought a lighter armature would not only be less attracted, but would be more easily moved by the membrane, and would not be so liable to become detached.

On July 1, 1875, Bell wrote Hubbard that the experiment to which he alluded when he saw him last promised to be a grand success. On singing in front of a stretched membrane attached to the armature of an electro magnet, the varying pitch of the voice was plainly perceptible at the other end of the line, no battery or permanent magnet being employed; and that when the vibrations are received upon another stretched membrane in place of a steel spring, it is probable that the "timbre" of the sound will be perceived.

For the purpose of carrying into execution the design of a membrane receiver, expressed in this letter, he, on the same day —July 1, 1875—instructed Watson to make a second membrane telephone, and it was completed a day or two later. Fig. 308 represents a plan, and fig. 309 a sectional view of this second instrument, which is substantially the same as the first instrument. During all of his experiments in June and July, 1875, Bell used gold beater's skin in single or double thickness for the diaphragm.

At the trial of these two instruments they were connected on the same line upon which the first membrane transmitter and harmonic receiver had been used. Bell was at one end, Watson at the other. Whether a battery was used or not does not appear, but presumably one was used, for both had electro magnets, and, unless charged in some way, could not have been expected to work unless residual magnetism was relied upon. They alternately spoke and listened. Bell does not remember with any great distinctness the details of the experiment, but has a distinct recollection that during the course of the experiments Mr. Watson rushed up to the room at the top of the building where he was, and informed him that he could

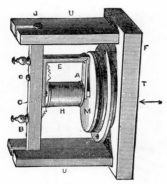

Fig. 308.

distinctly hear him speaking, although he could not quite make out what was said. He had satisfied himself that the sounds he heard had been produced by the membrane telephone to which he had been listening; but all that Watson remembers of this trial is, that the results were a slight improvement on what they had previously obtained, which were faint sounds.

So far as the actual transmission of speech was concerned, the results he then obtained were trivial. But they were significant.

For the first time, so far as was known, the voice of the speaker, by means of the true kind of a current, had produced a sound, and the experiments demonstrated the practicability of

transmitting articulate speech by instruments having the same
mode of operation and principle as these stretched membrane
instruments; it was only necessary to make further experiments
to ascertain the best arrangements of the parts.

The discovery of America and the consequences which have
followed from it, cannot be more surely traced to the voyage of
Columbus than the speaking telephone can be to what Mr. Bell
had thought out and done that summer and during the preceding
year. If he had instantly published a description of the instruments he had made, and the way in which he intended them to
operate, the world would have had the speaking telephone.

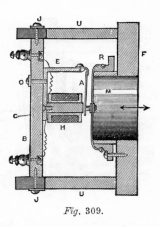

Fig. 309.

If Philip Reis had published an account of these instruments
and the way they were intended to work, instead of what he did
publish, the world would have had the speaking telephone fifteen
years earlier than it did, for the description in Bell's patent of
March 7, 1876, of the instruments which he had then made, could
not have been put into the hands of skilled workmen without
producing telephones which would have " talked, and in the way
pointed out."

It is now known why he did not obtain better results. All the
important parts of these instruments remain, and the apparatus

has been reconstructed in exact accordance with them.   This is not a case where, as with the circuit breaker and the microphone, a slight change can alter the whole character of the instrument. The reconstructions *cannot* differ, unless in mere workmanship. In 1879 the reconstructed instruments were taken by a number· of witnesses to the precise place in the workshop where Mr. Bell tried the originals in 1875, and no words could be made out. They were immediately taken to a quiet place and conversation was carried on.   In the Drawbaugh case two sets of them were made, and newspaper paragraphs were read through them in the presence of the defendants' counsel and expert witnesses.

On the 14th of August, 1875, Mr. Bell wrote a letter showing that he believed that he had made an invention involving a great principle, and although he had not developed it to the point needed for commercial use—or, as he expressed it, use on "actual telegraph lines"—he thought he had gone far enough to patent it.   The invention consisted in the creation and employment of electrical undulations similar in form to sound waves, and he insisted that whatever sounds could be transmitted by the air, including "spoken utterances," could be transmitted by these undulations, and he believed that his apparatus was sufficient to accomplish it.   In September, 1875, while in Canada, he had a talk with his father, of which the latter made the following note: "Sunday, September 12, 1875.   Telephone talk; wonderful!"   His invention of the speaking telephone is one in which the purely intellectual part, the conception of a new principle and mode of operation, of a new relation of means to an end, was the great step.   With the conception once fully formed and believed in as the solution of the problem, the construction became easy, and sank into insignificance as a part of the work of invention.   It reduced the problem of the commercial transmission of speech to a mere question of mechanical improvement, and it declared the precise direction and limitations under which all these improvements must be made.   It brought the problem from the domain of the originator to the domain of a mere improver. It is worth noting, also, that the improver, who very speedily carried this art and the instruments for practicing it up to the point of their successful commercial use, was the originator, Mr. Bell himself.

INTRODUCTION OF THE SPEAKING TELEPHONE TO PUBLIC NOTICE AND USE, AND ITS RECEPTION.

On May 10, 1876, a description by Mr. Bell of his researches in telephony was read before the American Academy of Arts and Sciences, at Boston. This paper was published soon after-

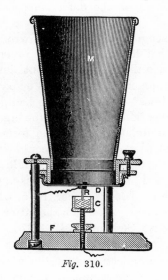

Fig. 310.

ward, and contained a description of his electrical speaking telephone, as shown in fig. 7 of his patent of March 7, 1876, and described the transmission of speech by it. It also contained a description of an electrical speaking telephone made upon the plan of varying the resistance of an electrical circuit supplied with a constant electro motive force from a battery ; the particular form indicated was that known as the liquid transmitter, referred to in the patent, and described as follows : A platinum

wire, attached to a stretched membrane, completed a voltaic circuit by dipping into water.   Upon speaking to the membrane,
articulate sounds proceeded from the telephone in the distant room.   The sounds produced by the telephone became
louder when dilute sulphuric acid or a saturated solution of salt
was substituted for the water.   Audible effects were also produced by the vibration of plumbago in mercury, in a solution of
bichromate of potash, in salt and water, in dilute sulphuric acid,
and in pure water.

Fig. 310 represents this liquid transmitter, which consists of
a membrane diaphragm, D, arranged horizontally and carrying

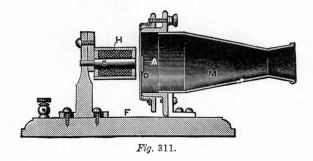

Fig. 311.

a wire, R, which is dipped into a liquid held in a cup, C, located
beneath it.

EXHIBITION AND USE AT THE CENTENNIAL, JUNE, 1876.

Two sets of Mr. Bell's speaking telephones were made by Mr.
Watson for exhibition at the Centennial Exhibition in Philadelphia, and were exhibited there in June, 1876, before the judges
of the group and many other persons.   They consisted of a
magneto transmitter and receiver and of a liquid transmitter.

Fig. 311 shows a sectional view of the single pole centennial
membrane telephone, which consists of a single pole electro
magnet, H, with a gold beater's skin diaphragm, D, with a means
for regulating the tension by a screw seen at the top, and a clock
spring armature, A, glued to the diaphragm.

Fig. 312 represents Bell's double pole centennial membrane telephone, which is substantially the same as fig. 311, a double pole being substituted for the single pole electro magnet.

Fig. 313 is a sectional view of the centennial iron box magnet receiving telephone, which consists of a single pole electro magnet, H, situated within a tubular iron casing, E, upon the top of

Fig. 312.

which rested a soft iron diaphragm, D. The electro magnets in all of the above were adjustable toward and from the armatures.

Bell's centennial liquid transmitter was the same instrument shown in fig. 310.

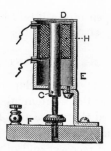

Fig. 313.

On the 25th of June, 1876, all of these instruments, with the exception of the liquid transmitter, were successfully operated at the Centennial Exhibition, and were exhibited, explained to

and tested by the judges on that and the following days. Two
reports were made upon Mr. Bell's invention. One, by Prof.
Joseph Henry, describes the apparatus and the transmission of
speech by it as follows:

"The telephone of Mr. Bell aims at a still more remarkable
result—that of transmitting audible speech through long telegraphic lines. In the improved instrument the result is produced with striking effect, without the employment of an electrical current other than that produced by the mechanical action
of the impulse of the breath as it issues from the lungs in producing articulate sounds. To understand this wonderful result,
suppose a plate of sheet iron, about five inches square, suspended vertically before the mouth of the speaker so as to vibrate
freely by the motion of the air due to the speech, and suppose
also another iron plate, of the like dimensions, similarly suspended before the ear of the hearer of the sound, and between
these, but not in contact with them, is stretched the long telegraphic wire. Each end of this wire is attached to two coils of
insulated wire surrounding a core of soft iron, the ends of which
are placed near the middle of the plate, but not in contact with
it. These four cores are kept in a magnetic condition by being
attached at each end of the line to the two poles of a permanent magnet. Now it is evident that in this arrangement any
disturbance of the magnetism of one of the permanent magnets,
increasing or diminishing it, will induce electrical currents,
which, traversing the long wire, will produce a similar disturbance of the magnetism of the arrangement at the other end of
the wire. Such a disturbance will be produced by the vibration of the plate of soft iron due to the words of the speaker,
and the current thus produced, changing the magnetism of the
soft iron cores, will by reaction produce corresponding vibrations
in the iron plate suspended before the ear of the hearer. The
vibrations of the second plate, being similar to those of the first,
will produce the same sounds. Audible speech has, in this way,
been transmitted to a distance of three hundred miles, perfectly
intelligible to those who have become accustomed to the pecu-

liarities of certain of the sounds. All parts of a tune are transmitted with great distinctness and with magical effect.

"·This telephone was exhibited in operation at the Centennial Exhibition, and was considered by the judges the greatest marvel hitherto achieved by the telegraph. The invention is yet in its infancy, and is susceptible of great improvements."

The other report was made by Sir William Thomson, and is reproduced on page 92.

After the successful use of his instruments on June 25, 1876, Bell proceeded at once to develop and improve them; the experiments were carefully noted down, beginning June 30, and concluding November 12, 1876. The memorandum of June 30, 1876, illustrates two instruments in circuit with a battery; one of them is referred to as an ordinary telephone, and resembles fig. 312, while the other consists of an electro magnet with a flat disk or diaphragm of very thin sheet iron. This is the first use of a metallic diaphragm clamped at the edges. The instrument was made by Watson, who used it as a transmitter about the 1st of July, 1876.

On the 2d of July, 1876, Bell writes Hubbard about an experiment he is making preparatory to the transmission of sounds between Boston and Philadelphia. Electro magnets of high resistance had been constructed for the purpose, and he mentions having discovered that the apparatus could be worked with one cell of battery, and says he is sure that by substituting a *permanent magnet* for the pole of the electro magnet, he could work it *without a battery at all.* This was in accordance with his original ideas of 1874, which embraced, as applied to the transmission of speech, the membrane diaphragm, hinged armature and electro magnet.

An experiment made on July 3, 1876, seems to have had reference to resistance; the receiver was like fig. 313. On the 6th and 7th of July the experiment was continued, *sounds* being repeated when the resistance was increased or the battery reduced or disconnected. July 11 the transmitter was improved by increasing the size of the armature; instead of a strip of iron, a disk almost as large as the membrane diaphragm was attached thereto, and greatly improved articulation was the result. A battery was employed.

Heretofore electro magnets alone had been actually employed in the instrument, although the suggestion is contained in the letter of July 2 as to the possibility of dispensing with a battery and employing permanent magnets instead. It was during the month of July, 1876, that the first apparatus was constructed having a single permanent magnet and a single induction plate. It was used without a battery, and at one end of the line only.

In August, 1876, an iron diaphragm with a case or mouth-piece was first used. On the 7th of October, 1876, the experiment of July 11, which had shown such good results, was repeated ; a large disk of thin steel was substituted for the smaller one, the articulation being the most distinct yet attained. From the sketches and notes it is inferred that it was customary to have one of the instruments with a membrane and the other similar to fig. 313, a metallic diaphragm, and with battery in circuit. Electro magnets were employed, with the exception of the experiment of July, with the permanent magnet at one end of the line. Having found that by increasing the size of the armature attached to the membrane of the transmitter, articulation was rendered more distinct, Bell concluded to try dispensing with the membrane altogether, and to that end he fastened by its lower edge a disk of thin steel in front of an electro magnet, using the old form of receiver like fig. 313, it is presumed, as no other is mentioned. A battery was employed, and improved articulation was the result. It was during this period also that the results of experiments with the October 7 instrument were noted.

On the 19th or 20th of October the next, and so late as the 12th of November the preferred form of instrument was constructed. The electro magnet was mounted within a box, on one end of which a sheet of thin steel was fastened by screws, forming the armature or diaphragm. A hole was formed in the top of the box for the purpose of speaking into it. Two such

instruments were employed in a circuit with a battery. It is
noted that when speaking into the hole the sounds reproduced
were loud, but indistinct, and that they were rendered more distinct by speaking directly against the plate or diaphragm, and
by condensing the air against the plate by means of the hand its
utterance was perfectly distinct and quite as loud as when the
hole was spoken into. An experiment took place November
10, 1876, with instruments like those last described, on a line
between Boston and Cambridge. The articulation was perfectly
distinct, and even a whisper was intelligible, although the resistance on the line was equal to fifteen or sixteen miles. The bat-

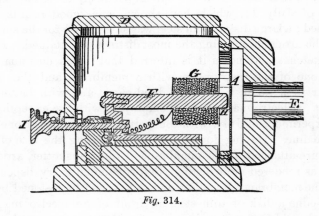

Fig. 314.

tery was then cut out, and the tones of Mr. Watson's voice,
singing one of Moody and Sankey's hymns, could be distinctly
heard without any battery at all. Bell now became convinced
of the practicability of using permanent magnets on a real line
of considerable resistance without a battery.

The box telephones constructed in October, 1876, form the
basis of figures 2 and 3 of Bell's patent of January 30, 1877.
Fig. 314 is a vertical section of this instrument. A is a plate
of iron or steel, which is fastened to the cover or sounding box,
D. F is a bar of soft iron. G is a coil of insulated copper wire,

placed around the extremity of the end, H, of the bar, F.   I is
an adjusting screw, whereby the distance of the end, H, from the
plate, A, may be regulated.   The hole in the top, being found
disadvantageous, is closed, and instead of condensing the air
under the hand, a speaking tube or mouth piece, E, communicates with an air space in front of the diaphragm.   It was not
until about the latter part of November or the first of December,
1876, that the battery was discarded entirely and permanent
magnets employed.

Fig. 315 represents fig. 4 of Bell's patent of January 30, 1877,
and is thus described :   " Whatever sound is made in the neighborhood of any telephone is echoed in fac simile by the
telephones of all the other stations upon the circuit; hence this
plan is also adapted for the use of the transmitting intelligibly the

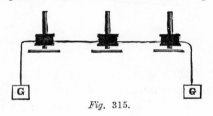

Fig. 315.

exact sounds of articulate speech.   To convey an articulate message it is only necessary for an operator to speak in the
neighborhood of his telephone, preferably through the tube, E,
and for another operator at a distant station upon the same
circuit to listen to the telephone at that station.   If two persons
speak simultaneously in the neighborhood of the same or different telephones, the utterances of the two speakers are reproduced
simultaneously by all the other telephones on the same circuit;
hence, by this plan a number of vocal messages may be
transmitted simultaneously on the same circuit in either or both
directions.   All the effects noted above may be produced by
the same instruments without a battery by rendering the central
bar permanently magnetic."   Another form of telephone, for
use without a battery, is shown in fig. 316 (fig. 5 of the patent),

in which to the poles of a compound permanent magnet are affixed pole pieces of soft iron, G Q, surrounded by helices of insulated wire.

Fig. 317 (fig. 6 of the patent) illustrates the arrangement upon circuits of similar instruments to that shown above: "In lieu of the plate, A, iron or steel reeds of definite pitch may be

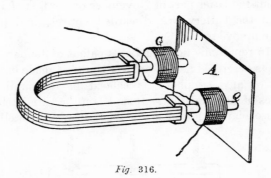

Fig. 316.

placed in front of the electro magnet, O, and, in connection with a series of such instruments of different pitches, an arrangement upon circuit may be employed similar to that shown in my patent No. 174,465, and illustrated in fig. 6 of sheet 2 in the patent. The battery, of course, may be omitted."

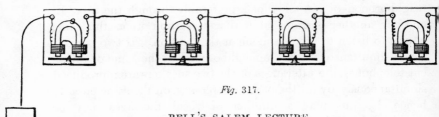

Fig. 317.

BELL'S SALEM LECTURE.

Fig. 318 represents Mr. Bell lecturing on his electric speaking telephone, at Salem, on the 12th of February, 1877, and fig. 319 represents the group in the inventor's study, in Exeter place, Boston, receiving his communications during the course of the

Fig. 318.

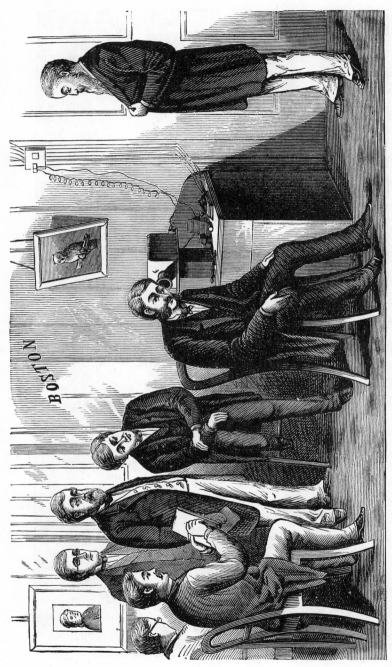

BOSTON

Fig. 319.

lecture. The apparatus, an exterior view of which is given in fig. 320, was all contained in an oblong box about 7 inches high and wide, and 12 inches long. This is all there was visible of the instrument, which during the lecture was placed on a desk at the front of the stage, with its mouth piece toward the audience. Not only was the conversation and singing of the people at the Boston end distinctly audible in the Salem hall, fourteen miles away, but Mr. Bell's lecture was plainly heard and applause sent over the wires by the listeners in Boston.

PUBLIC AND COMMERCIAL USE OF TELEPHONES WITH METALLIC DIAPHRAGMS.

Mr. Bell's magnet receiver, used as part of his speaking telephone apparatus, exhibited and used at the Centennial Exposi-

Fig. 320.

tion, had a diaphragm entirely of soft iron. One like it, with a soft iron diaphragm, was given by him to Sir William Thomson, and described by that gentleman in his address before the British Association in August, 1876. This thin metallic iron disk, in combination with the electro magnet, which is shown in fig. 59 on page 93, is also described as the receiver used at the Centennial in the official report on awards, prepared by Sir William Thomson.

Metallic diaphragms were also employed in the telephones used between Boston and Cambridge in October, 1876.

The diaphragms in all instruments furnished after January 1, 1877, were composed entirely of soft iron.

Mr. Bell and his associates made an arrangement with Charles Williams, Jr., of Boston, for the manufacture of his telephones with metallic diaphragms for general commercial use some time previous to April 1, 1877. An arrangement was made prior to April 1, 1877, by which Mr. Williams also obtained the right to supply the public with telephones made under Bell's patents for "private lines." He was to be allowed a commission on all he leased. Before April, 1877, a line of wire was built from Boston to Somerville, for the purpose of being used with telephones, and is described in the Boston *Advertiser* of April 5, 1877, as follows : "The first telephone line that was ever established has just been constructed between the office of Mr. Charles Williams, electrician, in this city, and his house in Somerville, and a conversation can be carried on with perfect

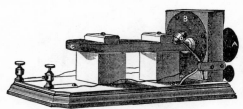

Fig. 321.

distinctness. Mr. Bell was in New York on Tuesday evening, and conversed readily over the regular wires with parties in this city. He lectures in Providence this evening on telephones."

The telephone used on that occasion was what was called a box telephone, consisting essentially of a large permanent magnet, with coils of wire on its ends and a diaphragm of soft iron, fastened on a wooden block behind a mouth piece, and the whole covered with a thin wooden box. It is essentially like fig. 321. That drawing, however, shows the instrument with its cover off, in order to exhibit its interior. In practice, a wooden cover like a box went over the whole interior part, which was screwed on to the base, and this is what gave it the name of box telephone. As they progressed, the telephones were gradually made neater

and smaller.   The box telephone, shown in fig. 322, was made
in June, 1877.   In this the cores of the coils are prolongations
of the magnet.   They were afterward placed on the side of the

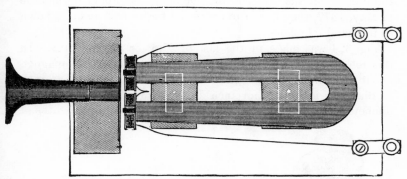

Fig. 322.

magnet, and the position of the diaphragm and mouth piece
changed, so as to occupy the same position in relation to the
cores as in fig. 322.   This much reduced the size of the instru-

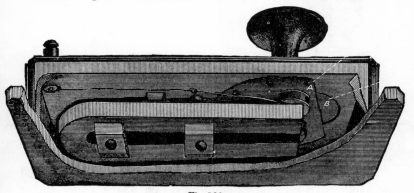

Fig. 323.

ment and allowed it to be screwed directly to the wall.   The
change was made about August 1, 1877.   The box telephone,
illustrated in fig. 323, shows this change.

Those used at the lectures in the spring of 1877 were substantially like this, but were much larger. The first modification was to reduce the size of the box and magnet; then to change the position of the cores on the magnet; and about the middle of May, 1877, they began to make the form of telephone known as the hand telephone.

Fig. 324 was made in the last of May or first of June. In this telephone the magnet is a solid single pole steel magnet, about four inches long. The core is about a quarter of an inch in diameter and half an inch long, formed by reducing the diameter of the steel magnet with a coil about three eighths of

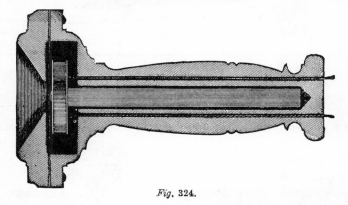

Fig. 324.

an inch long and one and a quarter in diameter of insulated wire. Resistance, sixty-five ohms. The diaphragm is of thin soft iron, about two inches in diameter. The whole is mounted in a wooden handle, similar in shape to a butter stamp, so that it can be easily handled.

After this form the shape of the hand telephone was modified by making it a little larger and of a plainer shape, with a rather deeper flare at the mouth piece. This change was made early in June, 1877. Fig. 325 shows one of this form.

About the middle of December, 1877, Bell gave up wood as a material for the handles of hand telephones, and adopted hard

rubber of substantially the form now in use, which is shown in
fig. 326.

About the middle of August, 1877, they changed from single
bar magnets to compound bar magnets made up of several

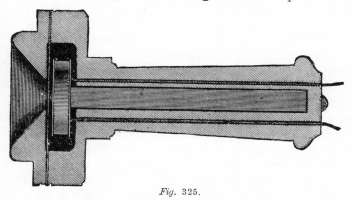

Fig. 325.

layers of magnetized steel, which was stronger and easier to
magnetize than the single bar magnet.

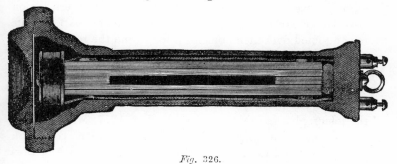

Fig. 326.

FIRST APPEARANCE OF RIVAL CLAIMANTS TO BELL'S INVENTIONS.

It is a curious fact that no rival claims of priority to the invention of the electric speaking telephone were made in any

quarter until more than a year after the descriptions of the experiments of Mr. Bell had been published by the journals of the entire world, which would seem to show that the authors of these claims had not, in the origin of the discovery, attached much importance to the invention, and it had been necessary for success to crown the work of Mr. Bell in order to incite them to undertake it. These claims were first put forth in the interests of the Western Union and Gold and Stock Telegraph Companies. The history of this controversy shows how great results sometimes follow insignificant causes. In the summer of 1875 Mr. Bell asked permission of the Western Union Telegraph Company to conduct experiments in the office of their electrician at New York. This was granted, but shortly after Mr. Bell began his experiments there, Mr. Orton, the president of the company, learned that Mr. Gardiner G. Hubbard, who was personally obnoxious to him, was pecuniarily interested in Mr. Bell's inventions, and immediately directed that the permission to conduct his experiments should be withdrawn. After Mr. Bell had brought his invention before the public, and was endeavoring to perfect it by experimenting over actual telegraph lines, orders were given to exclude him from the Western Union wires. In spite of these orders, however, telephone experiments were conducted over them, but for a long time the results, while regarded with interest, were looked upon as possessing little practical value, and it was not until the summer of 1877 that the progress of Mr. Bell's invention was deemed to have arrived at such a state of efficiency as to threaten to be a serious competitor of the telegraph. At this juncture, August, 1877, Mr. Frank L. Pope, the electrical expert of the Western Union Telegraph Company, saw and talked through a speaking telephone in Boston for the first time, and soon after mentioned the fact to Mr. Orton, who said: "I have been looking into this matter of the telephone somewhat, and regard it as a matter likely to be of considerable future importance. If this proves to be the case, it is very necessary that we should have the right to use it; therefore I wish you to make a careful and thorough investigation of the whole subject, and ascertain what are the fundamental principles of the invention, and what inventions or patents it will be desirable or necessary for us to acquire the control of, in order to be able to use the invention in connection with our business." Learning about this time that Prof. Dolbear, of Tufts College, claimed priority to some portion of the Bell telephone, Mr. Orton, who was also president of the Gold and Stock Company, requested Mr. Prescott, one of the vice-presidents of the latter company, to visit Prof. Dolbear and ascertain the character and extent of his claims. This visit was made during the month of August, 1877, and resulted in an agreement between the Gold and Stock Company and Prof. Dolbear, by which the company acquired the ownership of and agreed to exploit his telephonic inventions.

About the first of December, 1877, the Gold and Stock Telegraph Company made an arrangement with the Harmonic Telegraph Company, by which Mr. Gray's inventions in harmonic telegraphy, in so far as they might be found applicable to the transmission of articulate speech, were also acquired, and, united with those belonging to the Gold and Stock Telegraph Company, formed the basis of a new organization called the American Speaking Telephone Company. This company was to own all the patents and profits of the business, but its management was to remain with the Gold and Stock Telegraph Company, who made active preparations to go extensively into the manufacture of electric speaking telephones.

The telephones which were first made were exclusively of the Bell magneto type, the form being changed from the rubber hand telephone, shown in fig. 326, to the oval form, devised by Phelps, and shown on page 23, and the two forms devised by Gray, which are shown on pages 31 and 33. In the early part of the summer of 1878, Mr. Edison's carbon telephone, which the Gold and Stock Company had also acquired for the American Speaking Telephone Company, was perfected and rapidly put into use in connection with the various modified forms of Bell's magneto receiver.

SUITS BROUGHT AGAINST INFRINGERS OF BELL'S PATENTS.

In the meantime suits were brought under Mr. Bell's patents against those who used the telephones of this company, and one of them, in the United States Circuit Court at Boston, was vigorously pushed for trial. That suit was defended by the Gold and Stock Telegraph Company, who employed as counsel Mr. George Gifford, Mr. Causten Browne and Mr. W. D. Baldwin ; and as experts Mr. Edward S. Renwick and Mr. Frank L. Pope. The answer set up a great variety of defences. Among others, the European publications relating to Reis' invention were relied upon, and it was alleged that Bell's telephone, as described in his patent of March 7, 1876, was not capable of talking.

Mr. Edward S. Renwick produced a pair of telephones which he said were made in exact accordance with the patent, and which he said would not talk. Whereupon the Bell Company caused to be constructed twelve pairs, all of which did talk with practical success, and all of which exactly conformed to the description in the patent; the largest had diaphragms three and three eighths inches in diameter ; the smallest had them one inch in diameter, which is the exact size of fig. 7 of the drawing filed by Mr. Bell in the Patent Office, Washington, February 14, 1876.

These were constructed by different persons in different shops; two pairs were made by Mr. Georges d'Infréville in his own laboratory. They were tried by many independent persons, among whom were Prof. Cross, Professor of Physics at the Massachusetts Institute of Technology, and his assistant, Mr. J. B. Henck, Jr.; Prof. Clarence J. Blake, Mr. Georges d'Infréville, and Mr. Henry B. Renwick. One pair of these were constructed of a pair of "lovers' telegraph" string telephones, purchased in the street, and mounted with magnets. One pair was an exact copy of those exhibited by Mr. Edward S. Renwick, except that the membranes were stretched in the proper and usual way.

NOVELTY OF BELL'S INVENTIONS PROVED BY INFRINGERS' EXPERTS.

Regarding the novelty of Mr. Bell's invention, the Bell Company brought out the following acknowledgments, on cross-examination, from the Gold and Stock Company's experts: Mr. Edward S. Renwick testified that the first knowledge he had of the speaking telephone was through printed descriptions in 1877, and that his impression was that they spoke of the telephone as a new invention, and attributed it to Prof. Bell.

Mr. Frank L. Pope testified that in the summer of 1877 he saw used in Boston a pair of telephones which were identified as Bell telephones; that he had never before heard articulate speech transmitted over a telegraph wire by means of electricity ; that he first learned by actual observation and study the interior construction of a speaking telephone about the first of August, 1877, and that the telephone he then examined was marked and stamped as made under the Bell patents.

Mr. Elisha Gray testified that he listened at the receiver of Mr. Bell's telephone when it was exhibited to the judges at the Centennial, June 25, 1876, and heard words, and that it was the first time he had ever listened at a speaking telephone apparatus for the purpose of hearing what it would do.

After a very vigorous defence had been made by the Gold and Stock Telegraph Company, and testimony at great length and great expense had been taken in support of the answer, and the testimony was substantially closed on both sides, Mr. Gifford became convinced that Bell was the first inventor of the telephone, and that his patent had been infringed by the use of telephones in which carbon transmitters and microphones were elements, and that none of the defences which had been set up could prevail against him, and advised the company to that effect, and suggested that the best policy for them was to make some settlement with the Bell Company.

For the purpose of effecting such a settlement, the position of the Gold and Stock Company was very strong. They controlled, through the Western Union Telegraph Company, the celebrated Page patent, which covered the "induction coil" used in the transmitters of the telephone, and was of great importance to them, and which the Bell Company were using.

VALIDITY OF BELL'S PATENT ACKNOWLEDGED BY INFRINGERS' COUNSEL.

Under Mr. Gifford's advice a negotiation was opened with the Bell Company on the basis of the claims· which the Western Union Telegraph Company made, that the telephone used by the Bell Company was an infringement of the patents and applications for patents owned or controlled by the Western Union Telegraph Company. Mr. Gifford met Mr. Chauncey Smith, counsel for the Bell Telephone Company, by arrangement, at the White Mountains, where they remained for a week in negotiation. Mr. Gifford opened the negotiations by admitting that Bell's patent was valid, and that the Gold and Stock Company infringed it, and these questions formed no part of any discussion between them, but claimed, on the part of the Gold and Stock Company, in view of their patents, that all the patents should be put together, and that they should have one half in the joint property. This claim was refused by Mr. Smith, and the negotiations failed at that time. After Mr. Gifford's return, Mr. Prescott, the vice-president of the Gold and Stock Telegraph Company, then in charge, had an interview with Mr. Causten Browne, who coincided in Mr. Gifford's views, and said that the court would undoubtedly sustain the Bell patent of March 7, 1876, the fifth claim of which, viz.: "The method of, and apparatus for, transmitting vocal or other sounds telegraphically, as herein described, by causing electrical undulations, similar in form to the vibrations of the air accompanying the said vocal or other sounds, substantially as set forth," covered all electric speaking telephones in use. Upon the receipt of this advice, negotiations were immediately reopened with the Bell Company, and soon resulted in a contract, in which, instead of the Gold and Stock Company and its associates getting one half of the joint property for the inventions which they contributed, and which were essential for the satisfactory operation of the best telephone system, they got only twenty per cent. of the earnings, and agreed to go out of the business and never to make use of any telephones, excepting such as they should acquire the right to use from the Bell Company and pay them the market price for, the same as other people have to do. They transferred to the Bell Company their exchanges for cost and sold them their instruments at twenty-five per cent. less than cost, and thus ended the first attack on Mr. Bell's invention of the electric speaking telephone.

Let us now briefly examine the evidence presented by and in behalf of the several parties for whom claims to priority have been made, or are now being made, together with the decisions of the courts in such suits as have been adjudicated.

THE VOELKER CLAIMS.

On the 19th of May and the 26th of September, 1879, William L. Voelker filed applications for improvements in speaking telephones, at the expense and in the interest of John H. Irwin, an experimenter in and patentee of telephones, in whose employ Voelker had been engaged since January, 1878. Although familiar alike with the telephone and the experiments of Voelker for more than a year prior to that time, it was not until advised of an interference investigation, involving the broad principles of the electric speaking telephone, that he was put forward as a competitor, and his claims as the inventor of one of the greatest achievements of science published.

Voelker's attention was first directed to the subject of the electrical transmission of sound by a conversation had with Irwin in November or December, 1875, when he visited the latter at Morton, Pa., for the purpose of shaving him — for Voelker was a barber by profession—and began his first experiments during the Christmas holidays of 1875 on the transmission of light and sound through pneumatic tubes. Nothing new was accomplished, however, until his attention was called to the now well known toy called the lovers' telegraph, consisting of two small tin cylinders, over one end of which was stretched a piece of sheep skin, and a cord attached to the centre connected the two. Voelker says in his preliminary statement that he completed his first telephone in March, 1876. In his deposition he says : " I conceived the idea, which is the point of this controversy, during the month of January, 1876. I carried it into practical shape the latter part of February or beginning of March of the same year." Mr. Bell's patent shows that his completed specification was signed Jan. 20, 1876, and filed Feb. 14, 1876. If the instrument constructed by Voelker were a speaking telephone, the dates he names would not anticipate Mr. Bell. It was, however, expressly adjudged by experts who examined it for Mr. Voelker at the time, to be not distinguishable from the Reis circuit breaker, and Mr. Voelker has so testified in terms.

THE GRAY CLAIMS.

In 1867, while experimenting upon an improvement in telegraphic relays, Gray made his first observation relating to the electric transmission and production of musical sounds. The instruments then used were an induction coil with a vibrating electrotome, and a polarized relay in the secondary circuit, sounds being heard at the relay when the primary circuit was closed. He does not appear to have considered the matter further until 1874, when his attention was again accidentally called to the subject. While taking shocks from an induction coil connected with the zinc lining of a bath tub, Gray noticed, upon rubbing the lining to complete the circuit, fig. 327, that a sound proceeded from the hand at the point of contact, apparently of the same pitch and quality as that of the electrotome of the induction coil ; and that by rubbing hard and rapidly he could amplify the sound, and that by changing the rate of vibration of the electrotome a corresponding change was effected in the pitch. Experiments were continued during February and March, when he says he conceived the idea of transmitting

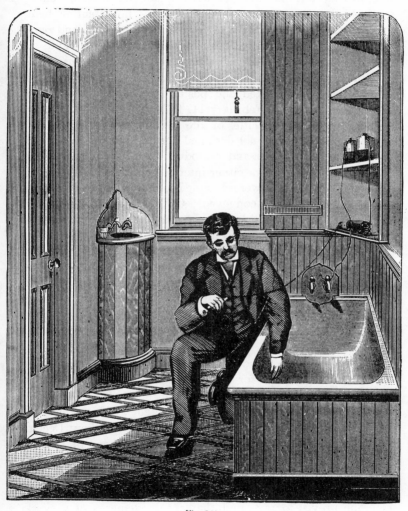

Fig. 327.

musical compositions and sounds of all kinds, including articulate speech, but his energies were apparently directed exclusively to the transmission of musical tones, no attention being given to instruments for the *reception*, transmission, and *reproduction* of articulate speech until February, 1876; and, although he claims to have had some conception of the *possibilities* late in the fall of 1875, he neither disclosed them to others nor clothed them in any fixed and positive form until he made the sketch for his caveat, February 11, 1876. Whatever may have been the inherent capacities of the instruments constructed in the interim, they were not designed for nor known to be capable of the transmission and reproduction of articulate speech, nor were his transmitters either intended or adapted for the reception of sounds, but were designed to create and originate the particular sounds to be conveyed. Gray was led to *believe* that the receivers constructed by him in the winter of 1874–5 were adapted to reproduce the sounds of the human voice, if they could be properly impressed upon and transmitted by the electric current, but he was totally unaware of any transmitter capable of performing this highly important and essential task, and it was not until he had witnessed the successful operation of Bell's telephone at the Centennial that the possibility of using his receiver as a transmitter was suggested to his mind, as he frankly admits.

Like Voelker, Gray seems to have been indebted to the so called lovers' telegraph for suggestions as to the construction of an instrument for electrically transmitting speech. In December, 1875, he saw in the streets of Milwaukee a string telephone. He does not exactly recollect the date, but places it about December, 1875. It has been established by the testimony of another witness, a dealer in toys in Chicago, that these instruments were first made in the United States at that time, and reached Chicago during the first week in December, 1875. "The lovers' telegraph proved to my mind that the movements of a single point on the diaphragm corresponded accurately with the movements of the air produced by any spoken word or sound. I saw that if I could reproduce electrically the same motions that were made mechanically at the centre of the diaphragm by speaking upon it, such electrical vibrations would be reproduced upon a common receiver in the same manner that musical tones were; and from the fact that the electrical vibrations were the same in respect to rate, amplitude, and form or complexity, as the motions made in the air by uttering words or sounds, it followed that the receiving diaphragm would be thrown into mechanical vibration or motion of a corresponding character, and consequently reproduce the same word or sound. The fact that the longitudinal movement (in water or other fluid of poor conducting quality) of a wire or some good conductor of electricity, with reference to another wire or metal conductor, produced variations in the resistance of an electric circuit proportional to the amplitude of movement, was old in the art of that time; so that the last link of knowledge necessary to solve the problem in my mind was furnished in the capabilities of the longitudinal vibrations of the string in the before mentioned so called lovers' telegraph." This knowledge does not seem to have been disclosed to others, nor to have been reduced to form until February 11, 1876, when the sketch for the caveat, fig. 327, was made. This date is therefore the earliest that can be accorded Gray for the conception of his first instrument organized designedly for the transmission of articulate speech.

At the time of filing his caveat, February 14, 1876, he was unaware of the existence of any apparatus for the telephonic transmission of speech, and his affirmance of this fact was made with a knowledge of the Reis transmitter. He sets forth in said caveat that he has "invented a new art of transmitting vocal sounds telegraphically."

The object of the invention is said to be "to transmit the tones of the human voice through a telegraphic circuit and reproduce them at the receiving end of the line, so that actual conversations can be carried on by persons at long distances apart;" to which end he had "devised an instrument capable of vibrating responsively to all the tones of the human voice, and by which they are rendered audible." He very accurately outlined, in a general way, what has since been demonstrated as the essentials of the modern telephone. These are a diaphragm at the transmitter station, "carrying an apparatus for producing fluctuations in the potential of the electric current, and consequently varying its power," and a diaphragm at the receiving station acted upon by the current, and thus "thrown into vibrations corresponding with those at the transmitting end" (A and F, fig. 328). Both the transmitter and receiver are provided with a "vocalizing chamber," and the diaphragm is described as "of some thin substance, such as parchment or gold beater's skin, capable of responding to all the vibrations of the human voice, whether simple or complex." Considering the events which immediately preceded the conception of the apparatus described, as narrated by Gray himself, it seems apparent that this description of the new art and the characteristics thereof are derived from the lovers' telegraph, and not from any of his harmonic systems of telegraphy. It was the first instrument of its kind that had been brought to his notice; articulate sounds were to be transmitted and reproduced at a distance; the instrumentalities employed for the purpose were the vocalizing chambers, diaphragms "capable of responding to all the vibrations of the human voice," and a means for transmitting such vibrations from one diaphragm to the other.

He had undoubtedly previously speculated upon the possibilities of electrically transmitting articulate speech; had advanced "some idea or plan by which it could or might be done." He claims, moreover, to have become convinced from experiments with the "mechanical transmitter" that not only could his receivers render articulate speech, "but that such speech could be transmitted through or from a single point;" but as this instrument, though operating by variation of pressure and friction to transmit sounds resembling the human voice, did not receive its impressions from any sound, and, as he testifies to having first obtained the idea of a single vibrating point capable of responding to the vibrations produced by the voice from the lovers'

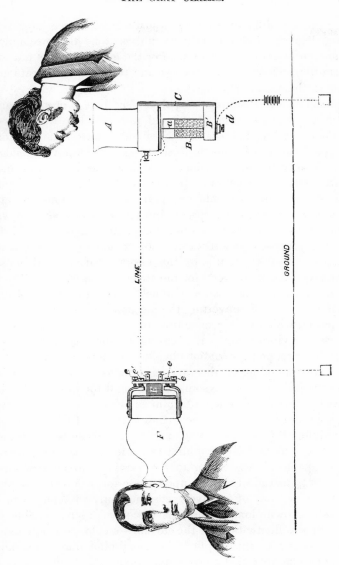

Fig. 328

telegraph, it is difficult to perceive just what idea was suggested by the "mechanical transmitter," unless it be the mechanical production of articulate sounds after the manner of his musical transmitters, which do not receive and transmit, but create and transmit, the sounds produced.

His mode of reasoning was, that *if* he had a proper transmitter his receiver *might* be caused to respond to the tones of the human voice, because it did, when certain manipulations were performed, produce musical tones and tones *resembling* the human voice, all of which was mere speculation and conjecture, and not invention. In the lovers' telegraph he found combined all the elements essential to the transmission and reproduction of articulate speech, but its range of operation was restricted by the nature of the conducting medium, and he therefore proposed to substitute " an apparatus for producing fluctuations in the potential of the electric current, and consequently varying its power," for the string which was acted upon mechanically in the same manner; and, to that end, he conceived a plan of converting the mechanical vibrations of the diaphragm, which were transmitted to the string, into electrical impulses or vibrations, by interposing in the electric circuit a device for producing variations in the conducting power of the circuit corresponding to the varying motions of the diaphragm under the influence of the sound waves, and for this purpose he adapted a device well known to him as possessing this property, viz.: a wire or some other good conductor vibrated in water or other fluid of poor conducting quality in proximity to another wire or electrode. He had already made and patented instruments capable of responding to the varying impulses of electricity, but, instead of relying upon these for receivers, he contrived a new form of receiver, retaining only that part which was well known, long before his discovery, to be capable of responding to fluctuations in the current—an electro magnet and armature—and to this applied the membrane diaphragm and vocalizing chamber of the lovers' telegraph.

These circumstances lead to the conclusion that the invention of the art of transmitting and *reproducing* articulate speech, and the means therefor, was not contemporaneous with nor the natural outgrowth of the transmission and production of musical tones, as previously practiced by him, but was anterior to and derived from the so called lovers' telegraph.

The filing of the caveat was presumptive evidence that the invention had not been perfected; but, aside from this, there is testimony tending to prove that it was not until June, 1876, that the first transmitter was made, and even then it was not used as shown in the caveat, but with a different receiver, and the apparatus as a whole was found to be inoperative. It was not until November, 1877, that he made such a receiver as is described in the caveat, but with a metallic instead of a membrane diaphragm; and it does not appear that his transmitter was ever successfully used. If Gray had entertained any confidence in the operation of the devices described in his caveat, he was guilty of great negligence in not promptly demonstrating their capacity. The caveat was filed February 14, 1876, and five days later he was notified that an interfering application had been filed which seemed to conflict with his claims. On the 7th of March, 1876, Bell's patent issued, and Gray became aware that this was the application referred to in his notice. On the 10th of May, 1876, the Centennial Exhibition opened, and Bell exhibited his articulating telephone, and Gray his harmonic system of telegraphy. Gray witnessed and tested the performance of Bell's telephone, and received a copy of his lecture. After being thus fully notified of Bell's claims, what did Gray do? He made a transmitter copied after the description given in his caveat, and "experimented with it in the Centennial building, in connection with a wooden sounding box magnet receiver. The results were not satisfactory, owing, I believe, to the fact that the receiver that I used was not adapted for reproducing vibrations of such feeble character as are transmitted by the aerial vibrations of the human voice. *If I had had* with me the magnet receiver in either of these forms, viz., the concave metallic diaphragm magnet receiver (fig. 329), the diaphragm box magnet receiver, or the resonant box magnet receiver, I *believe* the experiment *would have been* a success."

There is nothing, however, to indicate that his transmitter was designed for use with any of these receivers, nor that his experiments at that time related to the transmission of articulate speech, and, from the fact that he did not test it for that purpose, because he only had the wooden sounding box receiver, but did, in fact, use it with the latter, we may conclude he was following out some other idea that proved unsuccessful.

Fig. 329.

In addition, we have the direct admissions of Gray, in lectures, publications and letters to Bell, acknowledging that the latter was the first inventor of the apparatus for transmitting vocal sounds. In a letter to Bell, dated March 5, 1877, Gray says, referring to the matter of transmitting vocal sounds: "I do not, however, claim even the credit of inventing it, as I do not believe a mere description of an idea that has never been *reduced to practice*—in the *strict sense* of that phrase—should be dignified

with the name of invention." It is clear, therefore, that Gray
cannot be regarded as the inventor of the articulating telephone.

THE EDISON CLAIM.

In July, 1876, Edison learned of Bell's centennial exhibition
of the articulating telephone, and in the same month the first
evidence is disclosed of a distinct effort being made on his
part to construct an instrument designed for the transmission
of articulate speech. It also appears that during this same
month, as if under the spur of Bell's success, his experiments
with the Reis transmitter, described in Chapter V., were again
taken up and pursued in a variety of forms, as if for the purpose of satisfying himself that it had failed because it broke
the circuit, and could be made to transmit articulate speech by
the interposition of a liquid for varying the resistance by the
vibration of the diaphragm. From July, 1876, Edison appears
to have actively pursued the subject of the speaking telephone.
Two lines of experiments seem to have been followed—the first
designated as the "water telephone," wherein the tension of the
current in a closed circuit was to be varied by the movement of
electrodes with reference to an interposed liquid; and the second,
wherein the vibration of a diaphragm imparted motion to several
contact points and cut in and out resistance.

Throughout all of his experiments on the speaking telephone
Edison maintained the principle of varying the resistance in a
closed circuit; and something having occurred which recalled to
his mind the defective "carbon rheostat" of 1873, he proposed
to turn to advantage that feature of the rheostat which constituted the chief obstacle to its successful use, and which was first
discovered upon the trial of the instrument. In January, 1877,
he made the earliest experiments with this material, and the result illustrates the first attempt to apply the peculiar property
possessed by carbon of varying its resistance by pressure. After
a year or more of further experiment, Edison's efforts culminated in the production of his celebrated carbon transmitter,

which, under this name or that of the microphone, is used in some form as an important adjunct of the Bell telephone throughout the world. As Edison's experiments with this apparatus were not begun until long after Bell had invented and patented the electric speaking telephone, and as he testified in the interference cases before the patent office that "he never conceived the possibility of transmitting articulated speech by talking against a diaphragm in front of an electro magnet," and that he "did most emphatically give Mr. Bell the credit of the discovery of the transmission of articulated speech by that principle," and as articulate speech was never electrically transmitted by any other means before Mr. Bell discovered that principle, it is clearly evident that Mr. Edison was not the inventor of the electric speaking telephone, but he is entitled to the great credit of having vastly increased its practical value by his improvements.

THE DOLBEAR CLAIMS.

At the time Dolbear claims to have first turned his attention to the subject of telephony, August, 1876, he was a professor at Tufts College. He began with Page's experiments, using a Helmholtz automatic interrupter in circuit with an electro magnet; this would produce a sound, but did not transmit and reproduce. He apparently recognized the necessity of controlling the current by the sound waves uttered at the transmitting station and to be reproduced at the receiver. Accordingly he proposed to utilize the vibrations of the membrane of an instrument designed by him, and which he named an opeidoscope, as a substitute for the interrupter of Helmholtz, and thus cause the vibrations of the membrane to break the current the number of times per second due to the pitch of the voice. To this end he bent a wire at right angles and fastened it to the middle of the membrane, the end of the wire being so arranged as to complete the circuit when touching a globule of mercury. Subsequently he substituted for the wire a conical piece of iron, with the expectation that its motion into and out of the mercury would change the cross section without breaking the circuit, and thus vary the resistance. He found upon testing the conical point that the mercury was caused to bound away, and instead of partially interrupting the current, as he supposed it would, it interrupted it entirely, and the sounds transmitted were the pitch of the voice, and not articulate speech.

The next step taken seems to have been the making of a memorandum and sketch in a diary, under date of September 20, 1876. The memorandum is as follows: "Let a coil of wire be about the pole of a permanent magnet, and the terminals be attached to a galvanometer, then when a piece of iron approaches the magnet a current is induced; suppose that the wires connect with another coil about a permanent magnet, then the current will affect a piece of iron in front of the poles in the same way as the first is affected; in this way a telephone may be constructed by making a sound to vibrate a piece of sheet iron in front of one magnet; the ear applied to the other magnet should hear the kind of sound made at the first." The sketch accompanying this description shows two straight bars with a coil of wire about one end of each, the two coils being connected by two wires; above that end of the bar upon which the wire is wound is a line representing the piece of sheet iron.

It is clear that this memorandum contains a general description of a magneto telephone, substantially like that shown in Bell's patent No. 186,787, of January 30, 1877, except that there is nothing to indicate the manner of supporting the "piece of sheet iron" whose vibrations, under the influence of the sound, are to induce a current in the wire. His subsequent proceedings, however, furnish the necessary evidence on this point. Within a week or two after the making of the memorandum, a student, Mr. Stetson, who only came on Saturdays to work, was employed to make a pair of telephones after the plan there indicated. The instructions, given by the aid of drawings on the blackboard, were to take two permanent straight bar magnets belonging to the college collection, wind a coil of wire about one pole or end of each, and for vibrating armatures to take two opeidoscope tubes and fasten a piece of sheet iron to the middle of the thin rubber diaphragm stretched across the end of each. Only one instrument was completed on that day, and it was coupled up with a small model telegraph register, with the expectation that some audible results might be manifest. It was used but a moment or two, as Mr. Stetson had to go away. It is presumed no encouraging results were obtained, or the fact would have been mentioned. Stetson came only on Saturdays, and September 20, 1876, was Wednesday; hence it must have been the 7th or 14th of October that this work was begun.

According to Dolbear's testimony, he determined before Stetson's next visit that it would probably be better to make the entire diaphragm of sheet iron, and proposed that the pair should be constructed in that way. This was in October, 1876. Accordingly, when Stetson came again, he was instructed to work on this plan, employing some wooden spouts about three or three and a half inches in diameter, the sheet iron diaphragm to be fastened on one end. Stetson did some work on this—how much we are not informed—and did not return for several weeks; and even then, it seems, he did not renew his efforts. The excuse offered by Dolbear for not giving the matter his personal attention was the expectation that Stetson would finish it, his time being devoted to his profession and in writing a book.

In the latter part of December, however, he personally began the construction of a pair of telephones, which were finished and tested the latter part of January or first part of February, 1877. One of these instruments is shown and described on page 347.

The special object had in view when the construction of these instruments was begun was the obtaining of a patent, and the delay in their completion was not from lack of time, as he frankly admits, but because of information obtained from Mr. Richards, about January 6, 1877, to the effect that Bell claimed to have patented the same thing two or three years prior. Without further investigation on his part as to the truth of this report, he seems to have at once abandoned all expectation of obtaining the patent himself until the last of February, 1877, when he discovered that Bell's patent was applied for and obtained in January. Prior to this discovery of the date of Bell's patent, he visited Bell's room and was shown his telephone by Watson. The instrument exhibited at that time consisted of a U shaped permanent magnet, with coils of wire on the poles and an iron diaphragm in front : a short speaking tube or air chamber was also provided. On the 16th of that month he addressed a letter to Bell, wherein he referred to the latter's " very great invention," and congratulated him thereon, having been led to believe, as he says, that Bell had patented the same two or three years prior. Dolbear's testimony as to what Bell said to Richards or somebody else is mere hearsay, and no effort was made to prove that Dolbear's instrument or invention was at the time explained to Bell by Richards or others. After learning the date of Bell's patent, in the latter part of February, 1877, he says he began to take steps to procure a patent ; made an unsuccessful attempt to enlist friends, and sought the advice of counsel, and was discouraged upon learning the probable cost. When these efforts were made is not stated, and we can only locate them as between the first of March and the filing of the application, October 31, 1877.

During February and March, 1877, he seems to have conducted a number of experiments, for he testifies to having made an instrument employing an electro magnet, as distinguished from a permanent magnet, with an iron diaphragm fastened at the edge ; also one having a permanent magnet with *iron* poles, another having a permanent magnet with *conical* or *rounded* iron poles ; and a fourth employing a signalling fork for a call.

Dolbear attended a lecture given by Bell in Music Hall, Boston, and a few days later addressed the latter a letter, dated May 6, 1877, wherein he enters a protest against Bell's claim to be without a competitor as to his latest form of telephone. In this letter Dolbear lays claim to having invented " substantially this present arrangement" in June, 1864, but abandoned it for want of means. He acknowledges that he was led to take up the subject again in the fall of 1876, by reading Sir William Thomson's remarks concerning Bell's invention, and that he then began experiments " which resulted," early in December, 1876, " in the present form of the telephone, such as you use ; that is, the inducing permanent magnet and the vibrating plate." He denies all knowledge of Bell's work *in this line* and says : "After I had succeeded in this I thought of *visiting you, and saying to you, what you were doing with a battery* could be as well done without a battery, but my friends persuaded me to keep away from you, to perfect a pair of instruments, and obtain a patent for them. This I was doing when your invention of the same thing was made public. I have looked over the patent files and noted that your application dates January 15, and that the patent was granted on the 30th of that month. To me it appears that I had invented this form while you were yet experimenting with the battery, as, for instance, between Cambridgeport and Boston, Malden and B., etc. There are plenty of persons here who know about these things, and can testify that they all preceded any mention of your experiments in the same direction. This, I think, entitles me to at least an equal claim with yourself to this latest form of the telephone."

In order to reconcile the statements contained in this letter with the evidence, we must credit him with referring to the sketch, memorandum, and incomplete instruments made by Stetson, as the "experiments which resulted in this present form of the telephone " with inducing permanent magnet and vibrating plate, and that he had not " succeeded," in the sense of having completed or tested the invention, when he proposed to visit Bell and suggest that the latter could do without a battery ; for he says he was persuaded to keep away from Bell, perfect a pair of instruments, and obtain a patent for them, *which he was doing* when Bell's invention became public, and these instruments were not commenced until the latter part of December, 1876, and finished in the latter part of January or first part of February, 1877.

He also says in the same letter : " I did at one time seriously think of contesting your patent, but I learned that it was always a costly thing, and I hadn't a cent to spend for any such purpose; therefore I beg you not to be uneasy in the slightest degree as to your claim. *I shall not interfere.* All I would ask of you will be that while giving the work of others upon the subject, you will not entirely ignore me."

This was after Dolbear had inspected the files of Bell's patent of January 30, 1877, and knew not only what it contained, but the date of the application also, January 15, which was earlier than the construction and trial of any of his instruments. Bell did not, however, accord him the credit which he demanded, but, as Dolbear testifies, "reiterated his former statement concerning the matter of competition in invention, and my only chance of recognition was to maintain my rights in this way. In a very few weeks, when the reports of Prof. Bell's utterances reached me, I made up my mind to apply for a patent."

In September, 1877, Prof. Dolbear entered into a contract with the Gold and Stock Telegraph Company for patenting and exploiting his inventions, and soon after an application for a patent was filed for the device in controversy, which was refused on the ground that "Dolbear's testimony that at some time during the month of October, 1876, he concluded to try a sheet iron diaphragm, for his telephone, is insufficient to overcome Bell's evidence of completion in October, 1876, and possibly earlier."

THE REIS CLAIM.

In 1861, and subsequently, Philip Reis, in Germany, made an electrical instrument to be operated by the voice. It was known as an instrument which could transmit the pitch of a sound, but which did not transmit speech. About 1863, Reis began to make his apparatus for sale, and continued to do so until his death, in 1873, but he never offered it as an instrument that could transmit speech, and no man ever bought it for that purpose. Prof. Henry had the Reis apparatus at the Smithsonian as early as 1874. It was with full and recent knowledge of this instrument, therefore, that Prof. Henry, in his official report as one of the judges of the Centennial Exhibition, declared Mr. Bell's speaking telephone to be the greatest marvel hitherto achieved by the telegraph. Reis' efforts, well and widely known, had never given a speaking telephone to the community. The publications by and about Reis state that his apparatus was one which interrupted the circuit at each principal vibration of the transmitting membrane.

In Spencer's case, it was shown that the Reis transmitter, if connected with the most improved form of the Bell receiver, could be so managed that it would not perform the circuit breaking operation of Reis, but would produce, though imperfectly, an undulatory current, resembling in form the sound waves, and that this current would cause a modern receiver to give forth, to some extent, the same words spoken into the transmittter. But the defendant's witness in that case, Prof. Morton, said that he had not been able to obtain speech by the Reis apparatus as a whole, and had not been able to obtain speech by the Reis apparatus when it made and broke the circuit, as stated in all the Reis publications. The court thereupon held and decided that nothing that Reis did anticipated Mr. Bell's patent, or limited its scope, remarking:

" Reis appears to have been a man of learning and ingenuity. He used a membrane and electrodes for transmitting sounds, and his apparatus was well known to curious inquirers. The regret of all his admirers was that articulate speech could not be sent and received by it. The deficiency was inherent in the principle of the machine. It can transmit electrical waves along a wire, under very favorable circumstances, not in the mode intended by the inventor, but one suggested by Bell's discovery; but it cannot transmute them into articulate sounds at the other end, because it is constructed on a false theory, and the delicacy of use required to make it perform part of the operation is fatal to its possible performance of the other part. *   *   *   A century of Reis would never have produced a speaking telephone by mere improvement in construction."

In Dolbear's case the work of Reis was put forward again with very great elaboration and with an exhaustive collection of publications relating to Reis. It was asserted that Reis' apparatus as a whole, when spoken to so as to produce no separation of the electrodes, and not to perform the operation described by Reis, but to produce the current specified in Mr. Bell's claim, could transmit speech to some extent; but the cross-examination of the defendants' witnesses and a public trial of the instruments showed that only a word or two could be transmitted in this way, and that the apparatus, even with the knowledge imparted by Mr. Bell and subsequent inventors, was practically worthless. It is further proved by the same public trial that the Reis transmitter, when coupled with the modern improved coils and receivers, could transmit sentences. The court still held that this neither anticipated Mr. Bell's invention nor limited the scope of his patent. Neither that apparatus nor any other can transmit speech when operating in the way in which Reis specially directed it to be operated, and declared that it did operate. That is enough to destroy the value of it as an anticipation. The man who did not know how to transmit speech does not supersede the need for one who does.

The Reis apparatus, when spoken to in the ordinary way, and as Reis contemplated, does not, in fact, transmit speech. If it were true that in the course of a year's use of it Reis had occasionally unwittingly produced Mr. Bell's currents, and transmitted a word or two without recognizing how he had transmitted it, and without knowing how to reproduce that phenomenon, it would not make of his apparatus a speaking telephone.

In addition to this it is a fact that writers after the date of Mr. Bell's patent, as well as before, declared that the Reis apparatus could not transmit speech. The notion that any part of it can be used for that purpose is one which has arisen within the last three or four years in consequence of the great development which has been given to Mr. Bell's invention, and because it has been found that the rudest and most imperfect instruments enable it to be practised to some extent by those who are fully instructed in it. Thus a Morse key and sounder can, under proper conditions, be made to transmit speech.

Professors Brackett and Young have testified that, with the Reis transmitter and the modern improved Bell receiver, or with what they call the McDonough receiver, they can transmit speech. They do not venture to say that they can do this by the method and kind of operation described by Reis. They do not venture to refer to the Reis publications or to say that any man, doing what is there laid down, can transmit speech. They further state in terms that they did not test the Reis apparatus as a whole, consisting of the Reis transmitter and receiver, because such a test, in their judgment, would "have no particular bearing in this case."

William J. Green, connected with the Smithsonian Institution, says that two years and a half ago he, in company with a person who does not testify, heard speech transmitted with the Reis transmitter and receiver. Considering how glibly witnesses in the Dolbear case swore that they could do this, and how completely they broke down when a suitable test was applied to their story, it is plain that the testimony of Mr. Green alone, to an experiment which Professors Young and Brackett were brought face to face to, but did not try, is worthless. It is virtually destroyed by the testimony of E. W. Smith, who says that with a Reis instrument made by him he "found that he could *hear* words spoken, but very indistinctly;" that when he connected the transmitter with a modern receiver he "found that he could *distinguish* words and sentences."

Sylvanus P. Thompson has written a book, in which he states that Reis employed a variable contact as distinguished from a making and breaking contact. Considering that every publication made by or about Reis before 1878 described his telephone as a make and break contact instrument, it would be difficult to characterize this assertion in strong enough language. It appears, however, that Sylvanus P. Thompson published a book on electricity in 1881, and in that he said that the operation of the Reis apparatus consisted in "making and breaking contact," and that "the utterance of speech cannot be transmitted by abrupt interruptions of the current. They require gentle undulations, sometimes simple, sometimes complex, according to the nature of the sound." In 1882 Mr. Thompson became expert witness in a suit of the United Telephone Company, Limited, against Harrison, Cox, Walker & Company, which involved the question of the microphone and its operation, and testified as an expert for the defence. He then had got along to the point of saying : " Reis' transmitter was intended by the inventor to work as a make and break contact instrument, and the inventor expected it to produce articulate speech by this action. He was not aware that prior to Bell's patent anybody had written to the effect that Reis' transmitter acted in any other way than as a make and break instrument." He asserted that " as a matter of fact Reis did obtain articulate sounds, but this was when the instrument worked in a manner which it was not intended it should."

Mr. Thompson's book purports to have been written with the assistance of Mr. Albert Stetson, of Boston, and the Dolbear Telephone Company, who communicated to him a large portion of the Reis publications, which are more or less correctly copied. Mr. Stetson has long been associated with Mr. Dolbear and the Dolbear Telephone Company, and the publications procured by him in Germany were procured for and used by the Dolbear Company in the suit brought against them and decided in 1883. It also appears that Sylvanus P. Thompson has patented in England certain improvements in speaking telephones, which he asserts to be improvements on the principle of variable resistance between two contact pieces, alleged by him to have been discovered by Reis. He has, therefore, a direct personal interest to have it believed that the Reis apparatus was a speaking telephone.

As a specimen of the shallow and sophistical arguments which Mr. Thompson brings forward in support of his new theory that Reis' apparatus was a speaking telephone, we reproduce the following communication :

REIS' TELEPHONE.

It may, perhaps, interest the readers of *The Electrician* to read the *prospectus* which Reis issued with his telephones in August, 1863, of which I enclose for your inspection an original print, together with the accompanying translation. I may add that a copy of the prospectus (reprinted in Pisko's "Recent Apparatus of Acoustics") has been in the British Museum for the last dozen years, and another copy in my own possession for seven years. Written one month later than the letter to Mr. Ladd,

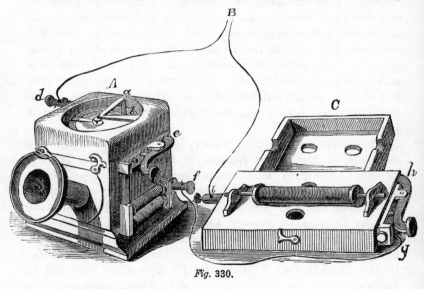

Fig. 330.

which has so lately been reprinted in your columns, it explains several of the obscurities in that letter. It is valuable also as showing, among other things, the function of the auxiliary apparatus which Reis used as a call signal, and *which in his letter to Mr. Ladd he had styled the "complementary telegraph."*

The question raised by the letter of Mr. Farquhar in your columns as to whether the existence of this telegraphic signalling apparatus did not show that the instrument was intended only to transmit music, is most satisfactorily answered by the prospectus and by the figure. In the first place, had the "complementary telegraph" been intended to make up for supposed deficiency of the telephone, it would have been placed at the side of the receiving, not of the transmitting, part of the apparatus. *Its position at the side of the transmitter shows that it was put there to enable the person who was listening at the receiving end to telegraph back to the person who was singing or talking at the transmitter.*

Further, the instructions given for signalling are a sufficient reply in themselves to the question raised by Mr. Farquhar. If the person who is listening to the receiver wants the person at the transmitting end to *talk*, he signals *two* strokes; if he is to *sing*, *one* stroke is signalled.

Lastly, a most curious commentary on Reis' utter unfamiliarity with the technicalities of telegraphy is afforded by the code which he suggests for the use of the person who wants to signal through the "complementary telegraph." Yet the Morse code was known in Germany long before 1863.

Yours, etc.,

SYLVANUS P. THOMPSON.

April 21, 1883.

REIS' PROSPECTUS.

Telephone.

Each apparatus consists, as is seen from the illustration (fig. 330), of two parts: the telephone proper, A, and the reproduction apparatus [receiver], C. These two parts are placed at such a distance from each other that singing or the tones of a musical instrument can be heard from one station to the other in no way except through the apparatus itself.

Both parts are connected with each other, and with the battery, B, like ordinary telegraphs. The battery must be capable of effecting the attraction of the armature of the electro magnet, placed at the side at station A (3 to 4 6 in. Bunsen elements suffice for several hundred feet distance).

The galvanic current goes then from B to the screw, *d*, thence through the copper strip to the little platinum plate at the middle of the membrane, then through the foot, *c*, of the angular piece to the screw, *b*, *in whose little concavity a drop of quicksilver is put.* From here the current then goes through the little telegraph apparatus, *e f*, then to the key of station C, and through the spiral past *i* back to B.

If now sufficiently strong tones are produced before the sound aperture, S, the membrane and the angle shaped little hammer lying upon it are set in motion by the vibrations, the circuit will be once opened and again closed for each full vibration, and thereby there will be produced in the iron wire of the spiral at station C the same number of vibrations which there are perceived as a tone or combinations of tones (chord). By imposing the little upper case [oberkästchen] firmly upon the axis of the spiral, the tones at C are greatly strengthened.

Besides the human voice (according to my experience), there can also be reproduced the tones of good organ pipes from F to $\equiv$ C, and those of a piano. For the latter purpose A is placed upon the sounding board of the piano (of thirteen triads, a skilled experimenter could with all exactness recognize ten).

As regards the telegraph apparatus placed at the side, it is clearly unnecessary for the reproduction of tones, but it forms a very agreeable addition for convenient experimenting. By means of the same it is possible to make one's self understood right well, and certainly by the other party. This takes place somewhat in the following manner. After the apparatus has been completely arranged, one convinces one's self of the completeness of the connection and the strength of the battery by opening and closing the circuit, whereby at A the stroke of the armature, and at C a very distinct ticking, is heard.

By rapid alternate opening and closing at A, it is asked at C whether one is ready for experimenting, whereupon C answers in the same manner.

Simple signals can, by agreement, be given from both stations by opening and closing the circuit one, two, three, or four times. For example,

> 1 beat = sing.
> 2 beats = speak, etc.

In telegraphing words thus I number the letters of the alphabet, and then transmit their numbers:

> 1 beat = A,
> 2 beats = B,
> 3 "   = C,
> 4 "   = D,
> 5 "   = E, etc.

Z would accordingly be designated by 25 beats.

This number of beats would, however, appear wasteful of time, and would be uncertain, wherefore I employ for every five beats a dactyl beat (dactylusschlag), and there results:

> — ∪∪ for E,
> — ∪∪ and 1 beat for F, etc.

Z = — ∪∪ — ∪∪, — ∪∪ — ∪∪ — ∪∪, which is more quickly and easily executed, and easier to understand.

It is still better if the letters are represented by numbers which are in inverse proportion to the frequency of their occurrence.

PHIL. REIS,
Teacher at L. F. Garnier's Institute for Boys.

Friedrichsdorf, near Homburg-by-the-Height, *Aug.*, 1863.

Mr. Thompson's three reasons why Reis' "complementary telegraph" did not show that his "telephone" was not a speaking telephone are:

1. Because, "had the complementary telegraph been intended to make up for the supposed deficiency of the telephone, it would have been placed at the side of the *receiving*, not of the *transmitting*, part of the apparatus."

Reis did place a part of the supplementary telegraph apparatus —viz., the key—at the side of the receiving part of the apparatus; but why should he place a sounder there? If the receiving part of the Reis apparatus was competent to reproduce musical tones, was it not competent to reproduce the simple making and breaking of the current representing the dots of Reis' telegraph signals? Reis placed a key upon the *telephone transmitter* to send make and break signals which were reproduced upon the *telephone receiver;* and he placed a key upon the telephone *receiver* to send make and break signals to the Morse *sounder* placed upon the telephone *transmitter.* This constituted a complete telegraphic system by which the experimenters with the telephone could communicate with each other, and make themselves " understood right well."

Mr. Thompson cannot be so dull as not to comprehend this, and we cannot imagine why he should believe anybody else to be.

2. " The instructions given for signalling are a sufficient reply in themselves to the question raised by Mr. Farquhar. If the person who is listening at the receiver wants the person at the transmitting end to *talk,* he signals *two* strokes; if he is to *sing, one* stroke is signalled."

Now this was an experimental apparatus by which certain sounds were transmitted and reproduced with more or less accuracy. The transmitter was sung, shouted or talked into, and the experimenters amused themselves by listening at the receiver for what might come out. The imagination helped some to hear a good deal more than came, as it did the drunken man who, on falling into a frog pond, heard in the croaking of the frogs, " Abrams got drunk; how much did he drink? Half a pint!"

To argue that Reis' apparatus could transmit articulate speech, because he had provided in his code of signals that two beats should stand for speak, is more absurd than it would be to argue that Mrs. Toodles had a son-in-law by the name of Thompson, because she had bought a door plate with that name upon it, in the possibility that " she might have a daughter who

might grow up and marry a man by the name of Thompson."
All of these events, although improbable, might have happened
in the course of twenty or thirty years of Mrs. Toodles' existence ; but twenty, thirty or a hundred years of Reis' could not
have produced a speaking telephone, because his apparatus did
not contain the latent possibilities of such a result.

3. "Lastly, a most curious commentary on Reis' utter unfamiliarity with the technicalities of telegraphy is afforded by
the code which he suggests for the use of the person who wants
to signal through the complementary telegraph. Yet the Morse
code was known in Germany long before 1863."

We venture to say that Reis knew as much about the Morse
code as Thompson does—and a good deal more about the telegraph system, if the latter's knowledge is to be measured by his
apparent or assumed ignorance of the function of Reis' complementary telegraph. The reason why Reis used his own code
was because it required no effort to learn it, and was better
adapted to be used in connection with his telephone by the
inexperienced people who experimented with it; but suppose
he had not been familiar with the technicalities of telegraphy,
would that fact increase the probabilities that his telephone
could transmit and reproduce articulate speech ?

But why waste words on such a perfectly simple matter ?
If Reis' telephone could transmit speech, why did he not provide both a transmitter and receiver at each end of his line, and
rely wholly upon the telephone for communication, instead of
employing an auxiliary telegraph apparatus for the purpose ?
People gifted with the faculties of hearing and speaking are
not in the habit of acquiring a knowledge of the deaf and dumb
alphabet for the purpose of making themselves "understood
right well, and certainly by the other party"!

A great many articles have appeared in support of the new
Reis claims, but most, if not all of them, have been written by
interested parties, one of these parties being Mr. Buck, assistant
to Mr. Dolbear and the Dolbear Telephone Company, and witness for the defence in the Dolbear suit. One of Mr. Buck's

articles states that he can say that he has often reproduced speech, including both words and unexpected sentences, using a Reis transmitter to transmit and a Reis receiver to receive. He was called as a witness in the Dolbear case to support that assertion, and both he and his assistants utterly failed to transmit anything beyond three or four detached words in the course of rather long trials on two different days.

DR. VAN DER WEYDE AND HIS REIS APPARATUS.

In 1869 Dr. Van der Weyde had read a description of the Reis apparatus in Hassler's "Technical Physics," and constructed and exhibited one in which he introduced some slight modifications of detail which are not intended to, and did not, change the nature of the operations performed or of the results produced. He exhibited it at the Cooper Institute, January 7, 1869, and a report of the exhibition was published in the New York "Tribune" of the next day. In the "Manufacturer and Builder," of which he was editor, he published, in May, 1869, an account of his apparatus, the character of its operation, and its result. He describes it as a current interrupter, and says of it: "It is clear from the foregoing explanations that no quality of tone can be transmitted, much less can articulate words be sent, notwithstanding the enthusiastic predictions of some persons who, when they first beheld this apparatus in operation, exclaimed that now we would talk directly through the wire. It is, from its nature, able to transmit only pitch and rhythm—consequently melody and nothing more. No harmony nor different degrees of strength or other qualities of tone can be transmitted. The receiving instrument, in fact, sings the melodies transmitted, as it were, with its own voice, resembling the humming of an insect, regardless of the quality of the tone which produces the original tune at the other end of the wire."

In the "Scientific American" of March 4, 1876 (three days before the date of Mr. Bell's patent), he redescribed what he and Reis had done, and claimed no greater capacity for the apparatus.

In 1880 he made an affidavit, in which he testified: "I think that I was, and down to the time of Mr. Bell's patent 174,465, March 7, 1876, continued to be, familiar with all that was publicly known on the subject. I have reason to believe that the instruments I constructed were the most perfect known before Mr. Bell's patent, in which any sound was produced at a distant station by the voice of the speaker at the transmitting station. But neither the instruments then made, nor any other that were known before Mr. Bell's invention, were capable of transmitting articulate speech."

He then repeated the paragraph already quoted from the "Manufacturer and Builder," and testified that it expressed his opinion and the opinion of scientific men generally at the time. He added: "I have read Mr. Bell's patent of March 7, 1876, and understand it. The apparatus there shown I believe to be new, but the invention therein described consists chiefly in the introduction and use of an entirely new method and mode of operation. This I believe to be the opinion of the scientific world."

He has since made an affidavit, in which he says that in 1880 he still believed that the Reis apparatus would not transmit speech, but *now* thinks it can. But he does not pretend that it can do so when performing the circuit breaking operation, which, according to all the descriptions, was the only operation it did perform, or was intended to perform, in the hands of Reis or of himself.

It is also alleged that he constructed a receiver, consisting of an electro magnet placed near to, but not touching a diaphragm, as a means of converting intermittent currents into musical sounds. Unfortunately for him, the printed publications of the period, made by and about his instruments, describe various receivers, but they do not describe this, and the descriptions they give are totally inconsistent with his present pretensions. The statements in his affidavit, that he disclosed such a contrivance so operating to the Bell counsel, they pronounce entirely untrue.

McDONOUGH'S CLAIMS.

There are two answers to the pretensions put forward on be-half of McDonough. One is, that he never made and never knew how to make a speaking telephone; the other is, that what he did was later than Mr. Bell's invention. McDonough was a wholesale furniture manufacturer of ample means, and had taken out several patents on matters relating to his business. In April, 1875, he read in a Chicago newspaper an account of Gray's musical telephone, and told Mr. Eastman that he could make an instrument that would carry speech from one place to another in place of musical sounds. In the latter part of May, 1875, he began the construction of his first instruments designed for the electrical transmission and reproduction of articulate speech. For this purpose he procured two tin cans, and over one end of each stretched a piece of parchment, pasting it to the tin as well as tying it with a string. A screw fastened to the side of one of these cans served to fasten it to a base, and a piece of tinned iron pasted near the centre of the parchment diaphragm served as an armature for an electro magnet mounted upon a block, which latter was so pivoted to the base as to permit of an adjustment of the electro magnet toward or from the diaphragm. This constituted the receiver. The other tin can formed part of the transmitter and was a duplicate of that above described, ex-cept that in place of the tinned iron a piece of thin German sil-ver was attached to the diaphragm. The can was placed on end, the diaphragm being horizontal, and immediately above the piece of German silver projected an arm carrying a small glass tube, through which passed a needle. This needle was free to move up and down in the glass tube, and one end rested upon the German silver, while the other was connected to a binding post by a thread of tin foil.

The transmitter and receiver were connected with a battery, the circuit being from the battery, through the coils of the electro magnet, to the piece of German silver, through the needle, and back to battery. When completed the instruments were tested, and the mode of operation and results obtained were in kind the same as had been described by Reis, as will be apparent from McDonough's own statement, who says: "This set of instruments was operated by singing upon the diaphragm of the transmitter, the vibrations produced by the voice causing the diaphragm to vibrate, making and breaking the electric current at the point of contact between the needle and the piece of metal upon which it rested. This breaking of the current caused an alternate magnetization and demagnetization of the magnet of the receiver, attracting the piece of metal fastened to the membrane of the receiver and releasing it, causing it to vibrate together with the membrane, thereby producing sound which could be heard by the one at the receiver. This instrument was used and operated by myself and Mr. Eastman. We could recognize tunes, but no words." Eastman, who assisted, says: "The results from these experiments, as heard at the other end, or in the receiver, was a variation of rattling sound and musical tones;" and again: "We made many experiments with this machine, and at times we could distinguish the tune that was sung."

Without apparently understanding the cause of his failure, or, at least, without any express purpose to depart from the general principles embodied in these first instruments, McDonough constructed a new transmitter and receiver, which he tested in June, 1875. He took two iron hoops, twelve inches in diameter, and fastened upon them parchment diaphragms, by first winding cotton cloth around the hoops and then pasting the parchment to it. Near the centre of one of the diaphragms he pasted a piece of tinned iron, and mounted the hoop upon a base in front of the electro magnet used in his previous experiment. This constituted the receiver. The other hoop he used in the transmitter. Near the centre of the diaphragm two pieces of thin German silver were pasted, about an inch and a half apart, with a wire attached to each. A bridge or arch shaped piece of thin German silver rested loosely upon the pieces of German silver on the diaphragm; the circuit was from one of the pieces, through the bridge to the other piece, thence through the coil of the receiver back to the battery.

When these devices were tested the bridge piece was shaken off from the contact pieces by the vibrations of the diaphragm; and to remedy this, he sought to maintain the bridge piece in place by passing a thread through it and the diaphragm, tying a knot above the former and one below the latter. With these instruments, McDonough says, " we could distinguish tunes and some words distinctly." He then substituted for the thread a screw threaded pin, fastening it to the diaphragm by two nuts— one above and the other below—and placed another nut above the bridge piece.

This constitutes the extent of his invention and most perfectly constructed form of his apparatus. As to the results obtained, McDonough says : " Clearly recognizable tunes and entire sentences of clearly understood words were transmitted through the instruments and heard at the receiver," and when asked to specify the tunes or spoken words, he says : " To my knowledge the tunes were ' Swanee River,' ' Muffin Man,' ' Shoo Fly,' and some others. The words which impressed themselves upon me more particularly were, ' Way down upon the Swanee Ribber, far, far away,' which I heard consecutively and clearly, noticing the elision at the beginning of the word ' 'way,' and the change of ' v ' to ' b ' in the word ' river.' The words of other tunes were distinct when the instruments were properly regulated. I could distinguish peculiarities of voice in those speaking or singing."

Eastman says : " I assisted Mr. McDonough in operating the machine whenever I had time and we were home together— generally every evening—and I guess we exhausted all the songs we ever heard. I can give you the names of a few of them; others I don't remember. They were 'Swanee River,' ' Down in a Coal Mine,' ' Old Zip Coon,' and others that I have forgotten. I heard many of the words of these songs; exactly which words I can't remember. I also heard Mr. Mc-Donough say, 'Halloo, Frank,' and other words that I can't remember now.'

Wilsey, McDonough's step father, says: "It was in the latter part of June—the exact date I can't recollect—1875, at 72 Warren Avenue, Chicago, I asked Mr. McDonough what results he was getting. He told me he was pretty well satisfied. I requested him to let me listen, in order to hear whether I could hear anything or not. I listened at it. At first I heard nothing. I concluded that I was a little too far from the machine. By getting very close to it I could hear singing; I was able to determine what tune he was singing; I also was able to catch now and then a word; that is all."

J. E. McDonough, the applicant's brother, says: "It was at 72 Warren Avenue, in the latter part of June or near the first of July, 1875. I was called to listen by my brother one evening while my mother was singing in the parlor of the house, and I heard the singing; and slapping my brother on the back and saying, 'By George, Jimmie, you've got it, after all!' I heard 'Down come uncle and aunt, down come sister Caturah.' That's about all that I can recollect at the time of hearing." The words referred to above were the words of a song he had often heard his mother sing.

This is the mere unaided memory of the applicant and his household, the only parties who testify of their own knowledge as to the working of the device, testifying six years after the experiments. When it is considered that an instrument operating as his contemporaneous and uncontradicted sworn and written statement—his application—stated that it did operate, cannot transmit speech, no doubt is left as to what was heard and was not heard.

With respect to the construction and mode of operation of the several devices, the examiner of interferences says: "Evidence of two kinds is presented from which, and the surrounding circumstances, to determine the nature and extent of McDonough's invention. The two kinds of evidence are the testimony of witnesses as to transactions occurring a number of years previous, and the description of the apparatus as contained in the application. With respect to the first of these, it would seem, upon a careful examination, to be insufficient to establish beyond doubt or question the successful reduction to practice of an articulating telephone, whatever else it may prove. Not a single witness describes, nor does it appear that he was conversant with, the conditions necessary to render the instruments capable of transmitting and reproducing articulate speech. It is not pretended that, prior to the last of June, 1875, any instrument had reproduced a single articulate sound, and this was due, it would seem, to the fact that the transmitter broke the circuit instead of maintaining a constant control over it. Without designing, so far as the record shows, to depart from the principles underlying previous constructions, he made an instrument such as is embodied in his application, obviously capable of operating in the same manner as those that preceded it, and with it obtained the results stated. Conversation was not carried on with it, but tunes were recognized, together with some words of the tune. A sound approximating to a familiar tune naturally suggests to the mind the words; it is frequently a mental deception, as observation teaches. That his experiments amounted to more than this has not been satisfactorily proved. He may have advanced a little beyond Reis, but it is not certain. Not having fully realized his expectations, he attempted to improve not alone the loudness, as he would have us understand, but the distinctness also; in this he failed. Fearful lest others should outstrip him in the accomplishment of that for which he was seeking, but had not found, he concluded to file an application for a patent. This application, then, must be presumed to contain the best explanation of his invention that he could furnish to the public; it forms the standard with which his invention must be compared and measured. Further progress was abandoned, the instruments neglected or destroyed, and, except as described in the application, not a single person, including himself, knew how to construct and operate the devices for the accomplishment of the end in view. The invention, which is called a teleloge, is thus described in the application: 'The object of my invention is to provide a means for transmitting articulate sounds from one place to another through the medium of electricity, and it consists in the combination with an electrical battery, circuit wires, armature, magnet and a *circuit breaker* of a transmitting and a receiving membrane or sounding apparatus, so constructed as to vibrate in accord with the vibrations of articulate sound, and so arranged relative to the magnet and *circuit breaker* that the vibrations of the transmitting membrane or apparatus, produced by articulate sounds, are transmitted by the electrical current to the receiving membrane or apparatus, and so as to cause a like vibration of the receiving membrane or apparatus, and it to produce the articulate sounds transmitted from and by the transmitting membrane or apparatus. My invention also consists in the novel construction of the *circuit breaker*, as hereinafter more fully described.' "

Then follows a description of the apparatus made the last of June, 1875, the bridge piece being referred to as the *circuit breaker*, and is thus described : "D is the circuit breaker, which consists of an arch shaped piece of metal *loosely* secured at its centre upon the bolt, D, and is bent upward at each end, and from the membrane, A, as shown in fig. 3, so as to form independent V-shaped points adapted to rest upon the respective plates, C C. The circuit breaker, D, is so fitted upon the bolt, D, as to admit of a free and easy ascending and descending movement, *the limit of its ascending movement being determined by its contact with the nut, E, on the bolt, and the descending movement being limited by its contact with the plates, C C.*"

The bridge or contact piece, through which the current passes, is to have a free and easy ascending and descending movement, limited only by contact with the plates on the one hand and the nut on the other. It has been argued that this may be interpreted to mean a tendency to move which is resisted by the plates and nut; and thus he may have expressed constant contact with variation in pressure. Such, however, cannot be accepted as the reasonable interpretation of his language. To limit the motion of a body between two objects is essentially different from restraining or resisting the tendency to move. Then, again, he denominates it a " circuit breaker," a technical name for an instrument adapted to break or sever the contact, and hence totally interrupt the passage of electricity. If he purposed maintaining the bridge piece in constant contact with the metal plates, he could not have selected a more inaccurate title, for it represents exactly the opposite. But all doubt, if any there be, upon this point is set at rest by the description of the operation of the devices as he designed they should be used.

" The operation of my said teleloge is as follows : The transmitting membrane, A, being sensitive to the vibrations of articulate sounds produced thereon, is caused to vibrate in sympathy therewith, thereby imparting an upward movement to the circuit breaker at each vibration, and disconnecting it from the plates, C C, and alternately breaking and closing the circuit, when the intermittent current alternately magnetizes and demagnetizes the magnet, G," etc.

The examiner of interferences says : " There cannot be the shadow of a doubt but that he claimed to have invented an instrument which should operate to transmit articulate speech by opening and closing, or, as he says, ' breaking and closing,' an electric circuit. It is the judgment of all the experts examined in this case, as well as of the office, that articulate speech cannot be transmitted by such an instrument. Had a patent been granted upon this application as it stands, it would undoubtedly be void as for an inoperative device.

" As opposed to this proposition, what do we find tending to establish the contrary ? Only the testimony of three or four witnesses that they recognized the words of some familiar tunes, and the allegation contained in the application that a device constructed as described will transmit and reproduce articulate speech. This, it is submitted, is not sufficient proof of the fact; the only inference that can be drawn from the record is that the witnesses are either mistaken or he operated the device in a manner different from that set forth in his application, and unknown to him.

" But these are not the only circumstances from which such a conclusion can be drawn. He describes in his application an alternative form of transmitter, which must be presumed to operate upon the same principle and with the same results as the one illustrated. *It is the instrument made in May*, 1875, with which they could 'recognize tunes, *but no words*,' and is thus described : ' I do not limit myself to the construction and arrangement of the circuit breaker, D', as shown and described, as other means may be employed, as, for example, only one of the plates, C, may be attached to the membrane and the other made either in the form of a plate or *needle* and attached directly to the connecting wire, and adjusted to rest upon the plate *so as to break the connection by the vibration of the membrane, which will accomplish the same result.*'

" The only instrument that he testifies to having tried was that of May, 1875, which he knew would not transmit articulate speech, or at least never had, yet he says it will do it as well as his latest instrument. This would seem to furnish conclusive evidence that he was seeking to patent an instrument which, while he may have assumed it to be theoretically sufficient, he had demonstrated to be practically inoperative, and outweighs any evidence produced tending to prove that the instrument of June, 1875, did operate to transmit words.

" Three claims were filed with the application, as follows :

" ' 1. The combination with the battery, circuit wires, magnet, armature, and circuit breaker of the transmitting membrane, A, and receiving membrane, F, substantially as and for the purpose specified.

" ' 2. The combination with the plates, C C, of the *circuit breaker*, D', whereby the circuit is alternately *opened* and *closed* by the vibrations of the membrane, A, substantially as specified.

" ' 3. The combination of the bolt, D, and adjusting nut, E, of the circuit breaker, D', substantially as and for the purpose specified.'

" When the application came up for examination in the patent office on the 28th of April, 1876, the claims were rejected because, in the opinion of the examiner, the transmitter was substantially anticipated by the Reis telephone.

" Nothing further was done, either with respect to the alleged invention or application, until March 4, 1878, when he filed an amendment, wherein he sought to introduce what was clearly new matter, and was so decided by the examiner, at the same time erasing all of the claims and substituting the following restricted claim : ' The combination with the membrane, A, plates C C, the circuit breaker, D', of the bolt, D, and adjusting nut, E, for confining the vibrations of the membrane against the circuit breaker, substantially as specified.'

" Between the rejection of April 28, 1876, and the amendment filed March 4, 1878, not a thing was done toward prosecuting, perfecting, introducing or even claiming the alleged invention, although, as shown by the numerous publications in evidence, the speaking telephone was being largely introduced and heralded throughout the world as a new discovery.

" Perhaps it would be incorrect to say that nothing was done during this interval, for McDonough says that in 1876 or 1877, from the book in which the sketch of August 26, 1871, is found, he ' copied what I thought worth preserving into another book, and threw this aside as no value,' and it does not appear that this sketch was included among those he thought worth preserving."

In March, 1878, McDonough was put in interference in the patent office—not on any broad claim to the electric speaking telephone—but as defined by the examiner of interferences, it turns upon the construction of a receiver alone, though its constructor had neither invented nor possessed a speaking telephone. He awarded this to McDonough. That decision has been appealed from, and the appeal has been argued and is now held under advisement.

THE DRAWBAUGH CLAIMS.

If there be any truth in the favorite Southern maxim, that " the longest pole brings down the persimmons," Daniel Drawbaugh, of Eberly's Mill, stands the best chance of winning the prize, for of all the claimants who have entered the field, none has brought so long a pole as he. While Gray and Voelker were claiming the stem, McDonough the pucker, Dolbear the rind and Edison the improved flavor, Drawbaugh was calmly and patiently waiting for the fruit to fully ripen and then claim the whole persimmon—stem, pucker, rind, flavor and all!

Although it was more than four years after Bell's first patent was granted; more than four years after his invention had electrified the world by its exhibition at the centennial; and more than a year since the greatest telegraph corporation in existence had been advised by its counsel that it must cease infringing Bell's patents, before Daniel Drawbaugh, of Eberly's Mill, first "put in an appearance" as a claimant, yet when he did appear it was with no feeble and uncertain claim of having discovered some part of Bell's invention, but as the inventor of the whole of it, including even the subsequent improvements of Peirce, Edison and Blake! His advent was heralded by the following glowing proclamation, which appeared in the Cincinnati "Commercial" of July 22, 1880: "Telephone Combination. Washington, D. C., July 21. An application for a patent was filed to-day that in consequence of its vastness of interest, as well as wealth of prospect, renders it a subject of national interest. A company of leading business men has been formed that has bought up all the telephone patents antedating those now in use, and known as the Bell, Gray, and Edison patents. The company is composed of leading business men from all parts of the country, Cincinnati being largely represented and interested. The cash capital of the company is $5,000,000, with headquarters in New York, and in about sixty days they will open the telephone, which will certainly result in the driving out of all telephones in the market, save the ones they hold, or else the compelling of the Gray, Bell, and Edison lines to pay the new company a munificent royalty. It appears from the testimony now on file and in the possession of the new company, which is conclusive and exhaustive, that the inventor of the telephone is a poor mechanic, living near Harrisburg, Pa., named Daniel Draw-baugh. Owing to his poverty, he was unable to push his patent on the market. The new company have secured and are sole possessors of this invention, antedating those now in use. They are also owners of four patents for telephones issued to Mr. Klemm, of New York. A large number of capitalists were here to-day to see the filing of the application, and they assert, with a positiveness which is almost convincing, that it will not be long till they have entire charge of the telephones, not only in this country, but in the world, and that they will be able to establish lines by which messages can be transmitted for almost a song."

A PICKWICKIAN EPISODE.

When Sam Weller was reading his celebrated " walentine " to his father, and had got along to—

" ' Feel myself ashamed, and completely cir—— ' I forget what this here word is," said Sam, scratching his head with the pen, in vain attempts to remember.

" Why don't you look at it, then?" inquired Mr. Weller.

" So I *am* a lookin' at it," replied Sam, " but there's another blot. Here's a ' c,' and a ' i,' and a ' d.' "

" Circumwented, p'r'aps," suggested Mr. Weller.

" No, it ain't that," said Sam ; " circumscribed ; that's it."

" That ain't as good a word as circumwented, Sammy," said Mr. Weller, gravely.

" Think not?" said Sam.

" Nothin' like it," replied his father.

" But don't you think it means more?" inquired Sam.

" *Vell, p'r'aps it is a more tenderer word*," said Mr. Weller, after a few moments' reflection.

But, although Mr. Samuel Weller, of the George and Vulture, felt " himself ashamed, and completely circumscribed " in addressing himself to the conquest of a sweetheart, Mr. Daniel Drawbaugh, of Eberly's Mill, evidently did not feel himself either ashamed, or in the least circumscribed, in addressing himself to the conquest of Bell's speaking telephone. Whether the elderly Weller's word, if less " tenderer," would not more accurately characterize the methods by which this latter conquest was to be effected, can be best determined after an examination of the facts.

DESCRIPTION OF DRAWBAUGH'S ALLEGED TELEPHONIC INVENTIONS.

The following particulars are condensed from an illustrated article published in the " Graphic," of January 21, 1884. We omit the illustrations, as the instruments are so similar to those of Bell, Edison and Blake as to render them unnecessary :

" Drawbaugh's early transmitter, made in 1866, is made of an ordinary china tea cup, with a piece of flexible material like membrane stretched over the top. A metal rod extends down from the membrane and has at its lower end a plate, which rests on a mass of powdered material, under which again is another metal plate. The current from an electric battery enters by the wire, passes to the lower plate, then through the powdered substance, then to the upper plate and the rod, and finally to the line wire. For the powdered material many substances were used, but ultimately he fixed on plumbago, pulverized charcoal and other forms of carbon as giving the best result. The instrument is operated by speaking before the membrane. This in vibrating produces variations in pressure on the carbon powder, and the current passing through the powder is then modified in accordance with these variations."

Drawbaugh's early receiver, made also in 1866, is composed of " an old mustard can made of tin, and fastened on its side to a board, and an electro magnet, consisting of a coil of insulated wire wrapped around a bent piece of iron. In front of the coil is the armature, supported on a spring. A string from this armature led to a membrane, which was stretched across the end of the can.

" It is one of the most singular facts in the history of Drawbaugh's progress with the telephone, that he simultaneously maintained two distinct lines of invention. *The receiver above described is substantially the same in form, and identically the same in principle and mode of operation, as the apparatus which Bell constructed.* On the other hand, the transmitter operates on a different and converse principle, *and works exactly the same as the apparatus which Edison and Hughes disputed over when they brought it out in 1878—when it was hailed as a new and wonderful discovery!*

"During the following year, 1867, or in the beginning of 1868, Drawbaugh improved his apparatus," as follows : The transmitter "is made out of a jelly tumbler. It has a wooden mouth piece, which every one will recognize as similar to that on the receiver in common use, and the carbon powder, instead of resting on a plate in the bottom of the vessel, is supported in a suspended tray. This identical apparatus, though not in complete form, still exists. The receiver was modified by the suppression of the string and the direct attachment of the armature plate to the membrane. It is identical in all essential particulars of form with one of the instruments which Bell exhibited at the centennial nine years later. This instrument also, in incomplete condition, still exists. In 1870 Drawbaugh had found out that the telephone could be made to operate without a battery. He discovered that the battery served no purpose except to convert the iron core within the coil of his receiver into a magnet, and this might as well be done once for all by putting in a permanently magnetized core. He found also that a plate metal diaphragm was better than one of membrane.

" The apparatus consists of a permanent horseshoe magnet, fastened with its poles in contact with the core of the electro magnets, thus permanently magnetizing these cores. The mouth piece is a cylindrical box, held in a support and having a plate diaphragm, to which the armature is fastened. This instrument transmits and receives speech equally well without a battery, *and is nearly identical in construction with the telephone patented to Bell in January,* 1877, *and the same in all important particulars.*

" The form of this instrument, still in existence in incomplete form, is large and cumbrous, and within a year Drawbaugh had improved it very materially, producing an apparatus in which, instead of leaving the diaphragm exposed on one side, he enclosed it and all the working parts of the instrument in a cylindrical box about five inches in diameter. He made the whole diaphragm out of very thin iron plate and reduced the size and shape of the permanent magnets. This instrument also exists in incomplete form.

"The efforts of the inventor for the next two years seem mainly, so far as the magneto telephone is concerned, to have been directed to reducing the size of the instrument and rendering it more compact in arrangement and delicate in adjustment. In 1873 or the beginning of 1874 he produced a receiver intended for use with a battery, as it has no permanent magnet. It is of flat cylindrical shape, about five inches in diameter, and contains means of adjusting the electro magnet with nicety. It has frequently been used on telephone lines within the last two years. Thus, nearly three years before Bell had produced his instrument Drawbaugh had completed a telephone which could to-day be successfully used anywhere.

"In January of 1875, Drawbaugh reached a form for his magnet instrument which seems to be as compact as that device can be made. He made two instruments, each about three inches in diameter by an inch and a half thick, and each is for all practical purposes *identically the telephonic receiving instrument now in common use*. Instead of a bar magnet, which is used in the ordinary so-called Bell instrument, Drawbaugh has a magnet curled flatly against the back of the case, and he has an adjustable core which Bell does not use. It is small, compact and in every respect an excellent working instrument, which could to-day successfully compete, if the market were open, with any known form of telephone of its class.

"Having thus reduced his magneto telephone in point of size and compactness to the smallest and most convenient form, Drawbaugh turned his attention more particularly to his carbon instrument, in which in the meanwhile he had made numerous important improvements, and finally, early in 1876, he produced an exceedingly compact device wherein a plate diaphragm is used, and instead of loose carbon powder, blocks of hard gas carbon held normally in contact by spring pressure are employed. This is an exceedingly sensitive transmitting apparatus, and in its essential features still exists.

" Finding out, however, that there was no very material advantage to be gained in making a transmitter of light and portable form—as it could as well be fastened to a wall instead of being movable—Drawbaugh made another apparatus which he had completed and in practical use before August of 1876. This instrument is in every essential particular and almost identically in form the so-called Blake transmitter, now in common use. The carbons are held together by spring pressure, and the instrument contains the induction coil. It exists in perfectly operative condition and is sensitive to a remarkable degree. It has recently transmitted speech uttered in an ordinary tone twenty-three feet away from it. This was the transmitter which Drawbaugh had in actual practical operation when Bell exhibited his crude contrivances at the centennial, and when the distinguished scientists who witnessed his trials pronounced them a marvel of the age. The transmitter of the present day in almost identical form—and the identical receiver—were there in Eberly's Mill, transmitting speech whenever Drawbaugh used them or showed them to his neighbors, and doing it as well as the instruments at this moment in use in this city and throughout the country.

" The reader who has followed this recital may well stop here and demand the proof of assertions so sweeping and startling. All of the proof stands filed as sworn evidence in the United States Circuit Court for the Southern District of New York, and the foregoing article, where it is not based directly upon that evidence, is founded upon actual trials conducted under the most severe conditions by expert electricians of the identical instruments made by Drawbaugh, or of instruments whereon the missing parts of those still existing in incomplete form are supplied in accordance with his sworn testimony."

THE BAD BOY'S STORY.

Everybody knows how the Harvard professor explained the bad boy's impossible story, and Dickerson, who also has a blunt way of telling disagreeable truths, explains Drawbaugh's story in the same manner. There has sometimes arisen a question as to whether there was any difference between a discovery and an invention, which would receive an additional illustration, as showing that both terms are sometimes applicable to the same thing, if Dickerson's solution of the Drawbaugh problem should prove to be true; for in that case Drawbaugh would be shown to have *invented* a Munchausen tale and Dickerson to have *discovered* it. It would be so much easier to copy Bell's, Edison's, and Blake's apparatus than to invent them, that nothing but the most implicit faith in the honesty and integrity of Drawbaugh, and in the intelligence and veracity of the witnesses who corroborate his statements could make them believed. But at the same time, those who do believe that Drawbaugh, like Washington, "could not tell a lie," would not doubt his statement, even if he were to assert that he invented these telephones not only ten years before Bell did, but ten years before Bell was born. Now, these inventions do not surprise us in the least. The only thing we are surprised at is that he did not invent more while he was about it. Why did he not, for example, invent the Ader, Pollard and Crossly telephones which are now so popular in Europe? It cannot, of course, be owing to the fact that hitherto descriptions of these instruments have not been accessible in English, or because the inventors are French, for a genius of his grade must naturally be familiar with all languages; and as to the nationality of the inventors, we take it that he would not stand upon any more ceremony about anticipating a party of Frenchmen a dozen years or so in the discovery or improvement of a great invention, than he did in the case of Bell, Edison and Blake, who were allowed to spend so many tedious years in the discovery and development of this great invention, when he had it "on hand, ready made," all the while at Eberly's Mill!

Perhaps Drawbaugh has invented these new telephones, how-ever, and is waiting, as he did in the case of Bell, until there is a demand for them, before bringing them out.

When Barnum had shown Clark the wonders of his museum, the latter inquired with much interest if he could show him the club that Capt. Cook was killed with, which, of course, Barnum promptly produced. With a gleam of delight Clark gazed upon the sacred relic and enthusiastically exclaimed, "I was sure you had it. I never visited a museum so well organized as yours that was without it." Now no inventor, so thor-oughly organized as Drawbaugh, ought ever to be without a good supply of all the latest telephonic inventions, of his own discovery, ready for any call. We suppose it would be asking too much to suggest that he invent a telephone, by way of a novelty, which nobody else had invented. It would be amaz-ingly odd, though!

GREAT ANTIQUITY OF DRAWBAUGH'S INVENTIONS.

In the olden times, every event of any great importance was always authentically established as occurring at or about the be-ginning of the world, or intimately associated therewith; and great families often had an equally remote origin. Thus it is related that a distinguished member of the Weed family in America traced his pedigree back to the oldest Weeds in Eng-land, and from them to the Counts de Grass, of France, and thence in a direct line to Nebuchadnezzar, who went out to grass. Now, in the same manner the celebrated Daniel Draw-baugh, of Eberly's Mill, traces his inventions back, not only to the beginning, but long before the beginning, of the telephonic world. He made the first telephone eight years before Bell had conceived of it even, and employed in his transmitter, in 1866, the principle of the varying pressure of carbon to produce changes in the strength of current—*a principle which was not discovered* until 1873, seven years afterward, and which Edison, who was the first to use it for any purpose, did not employ in the construction of his famous carbon transmitter until **1877,** four years later still. Drawbaugh was also so lavish and fruitful in his inventions that in 1867, he even took the trouble to invent the very mouth piece invented ten years afterward by Prof. Peirce, of Brown University (see fig. 60, page 103), and, moreover, made it in exactly the same form—as near like it, in fact, as Drawbaugh could have made it if he had copied the very apparatus itself. If Prof. Peirce had only known that Drawbaugh was going to antedate him in this device by a whole decade, he doubtless would have felt less sensitive about Bell's stinted acknowledgment in his London lecture! But there is nothing stingy, mean or "narrer contracted" about Drawbaugh. When he makes an invention, he makes the whole of it. He doesn't call on Professors Henry, Blake, Channing, Peirce, or any other distinguished scientist for advice and assistance in surmounting the difficulties in his path, but goes it alone, asking no odds of anybody!

There is another strong contrast between the methods of the slow plodding Bell and Edison and the brilliant genius of Drawbaugh. The former create their great works by the slow and tedious process of evolution. Thus it was four years from Bell's discovery of the telephone in 1874, with its membrane diaphragm and hinged armature, working entirely by induction, and capable of talking only in the feeblest of tones, to the completion of the instrument with its carbon transmitter energized by a voltaic battery and capable of being audibly heard by a whole congregation; but Drawbaugh does not employ any such slow coach arrangements. When he wants a thing he invents it out of hand and off hand, like a genie of the Arabian Nights.

FACTS INCONSISTENT WITH DRAWBAUGH'S PRETENSIONS.

But we regret to say there is another side to this picture. It must be confessed that the facts in Drawbaugh's history are inconsistent with the pretensions put forth in his behalf. When we are groping in the dark with little more than the feeble light which comes from the memory of Pennsylvania farmers and farm laborers to find the history of this man and of his work for fifteen years before 1880, we meet the facts, admitted at the outset, that the alleged possessor of this most wonderful invention of our generation produced instruments which for some reason or other never excited in the breasts of any of the hundred persons who knew of them the desire to possess them and apply them to use; that, for some reason or other, though more than a hundred people knew what he had done, and knowledge of what he had done "was freely communicated to the public," yet no knowledge derived from him ever led the community to make or use speaking telephones; but the world waited for this until Mr. Bell appeared, and then seized upon them with an avidity at once remarkable and natural. We have the further fact that this man, having been an inventor and patentee from his youth upward, having taken out a dozen patents before 1876, never filed an application or caveat for this.

There is one cause which would account for this condition of facts, and that is, that his instruments, if he had any, were not of a good enough character to excite anybody's desire, or to make him think they were fit to patent.

Excuses for His Failure.—The Drawbaugh party have felt the great weight of this consideration, and they have sought to meet it by the statement that Drawbaugh, for more than ten years prior to the year 1880, was miserably poor, in debt, with a large and helpless family dependent upon his daily labor for support, and was, from such cause and his utter want of proper mechanical tools, materials, and appliances to conduct such work, utterly unable to patent or caveat his invention or manufacture and introduce it upon the market, and that the reason why other persons, who had full knowledge of his invention, refrained from making and using it, was because of their conscientious, scrupulous regard during all these years for his supposed equitable rights, though he neither patented it nor took any steps toward that end.

There is something in the invention given to the world by Mr. Bell and those around him which makes other persons extremely desirous to use it in spite of Mr. Bell's patents, if they only think they can escape the strong arm of the law. A scrupulous tenderness of conscience of all the hundred persons who knew of Mr. Drawbaugh's invention was, however, quite sufficient to prevent them from using anything which they found in his instruments, though he had never patented them.

The Drawbaugh party produced some instruments, and a number of their witnesses testified that at Drawbaugh's shop on various occasions, the dates of which they stated or attempted to fix as before the summer of 1876, they heard speech transmitted by them.

The instruments named are: F and B.—F is made of a broken glass tumbler, and B of an old tin can, once used as a paint pot and smeared with green paint, attached to a piece of board. C and I.—C is made of a rough board, and bears every mark of being a rude and temporary instrument. Some of its most essential parts no longer exist. I, when produced and sworn to by the first witnesses called, consisted of a box roughly turned out of black walnut, about four inches in diameter and about four inches deep. The interior works, consisting of diaphragm and magnets, have been added while the testimony has been in progress. The diaphragm is new, and supplied from recollection. The magnet is alleged to be old. It is said to have been found in the garret some time after the defendants had produced the instrument in that cause. A is a highly organized magneto receiver, with a neutral magnet. The case is of black walnut, nicely turned, and furnished with screw cups to attach the line wires to. D and E are a pair of magneto instruments with permanent magnets. They are highly organized, enclosed in turned black walnut cases, and with most of the refined improvements of detail found in the best commercial instruments of to-day, though they are rather feeble.

It is alleged that F and B were made and used about 1867–8 and since. That C and I were made and used about 1869–70, and since. Drawbaugh attempts to fix the date by an association of memory with the painting of a certain wagon, which they attempt to show was in the spring of 1870. A is alleged to have been made about November, 1874; a witness, Smith, says that he saw Drawbaugh making it then. A witness, U. R. Nichols, alleges that he visited Drawbaugh in January, 1875, saw A, and was told by Drawbaugh that he had it about sixty days. D and E are alleged to have been made in the spring of 1875.

Alleged Capacity of the Alleged Instruments.—Drawbaugh testifies that he made C before the spring of 1870, and made F and B "two or three years before that." Of the capacity of F and B he was asked: "During that time and before you made 'C,' what results had you been able to get with the instruments 'B and F'?" and replied: "Sufficiently good to be heard distinctly; there were even words that were whispered. You couldn't just hear the words exactly, but could hear the whispering. I did that often; spoken words you could hear the whole sentences— I mean words spoken out loud and not whispering many. I would have persons in the cellar reading printed matter—some advertisement or something—and I could hear the words that were read; and at other times I would go down into the cellar and read something, and coming up they would repeat to me the words that I read."

That is an assertion of instruments abundantly fit for commercial use, and so perfectly reliable that they would produce these results habitually without trouble when the transmitter "F" was put into the hands of any chance comer, and Drawbaugh was at the other end of the line listening.

One witness, Samuel Snell, reports that he heard good speech at "B" in the summer of 1867. No man except Drawbaugh swears to reading through them. Drawbaugh testifies that the results with F and C were still better; that C and I gave better results than F and C; "much more satisfactory—louder—entirely better." Under examination by his own counsel he testified:

"Were the instruments 'C' and 'I' an improvement in respect to loudness?

" Yes, sir; loudness and plainness, too.

" Were they an improvement or not in respect to adjustment?

" Yes, sir."

He says that "A" was rather better; it apparently should be; and that D and E were better than either. Moreover, C and I and D and E, formed couples of magneto instruments which in their nature, if able to talk at all, would talk both ways and need no battery nor nice adjustment. If they talked at all they would be always ready.

This, then, is their story which they ask the court to believe: that F and B were practical instruments fit to be operated by any one, transmitting conversation and newspaper extracts in a perfectly intelligible manner; that this point was reached in 1867-8-9 , and that every succeeding set of instruments was an improvement on this first set.

They have produced about forty witnesses who swear that they heard perfectly clear, distinct, and intelligible speech through these various instruments before the summer of 1876, hearing and understanding all that was said. Half of these witnesses swear to such results with F and B. Their proof (whatever it may be worth) is stronger for F and B than for any other couple. About a dozen assert that they got these results with F and B before 1872. More than twenty assert such results from F and B, and one other instrument (most of them with F and B), before midsummer, 1873. Twenty-eight out of the forty assert such results before midsummer, 1874. Not far from seventy-five more witnesses assert that they saw these instruments at various times before the summer of 1876. Most of them swear to " F " and " B," and at dates distributed substantially like those given by the persons who say they heard. This is their story. If their proofs are worth anything they prove all this. It is all true, or none of it is. It all rests on recollections—word of mouth. Compare it with the certain facts of Drawbaugh's history, drawn from the depositions of himself and his own witnesses, and from contemporaneous writings. We are to begin with the facts, that he never prepared or filed a caveat or application until 1880; that he never put any telephone to any practical use; that no one ever obtained one from him for use, nor tried to; that the community acquired its telephones from Mr. Bell, and not by reason of any information drawn from Drawbaugh; and that the moment Mr. Bell communicated the information *he* had, the public seized upon it with avidity. We are to take along with it the *facts* that Drawbaugh lived within three miles of Harrisburg; was known and favored as an inventor of various contrivances; a patentee many times as to other matters; advertised before Mr. Bell's patent as the inventor of telegraph apparatus and the constructor of other electrical machines—but not of telephones; and possessed of the means and resources actual and potential, now to be mentioned:

Drawbaugh's Inventions and Dates of Patents.—Stave jointer, November 11, 1851; stave machine, May 22, 1855; improvement in mill stones, April 28, 1863; mill tram, May 12, 1863: nail plate feeder, December 12, 1865; faucets, November 20, 1866; faucets, November 20, 1866; nail plate feeders, November 19, 1867; improvement in magnetic clocks, applied for May, 1878; improvement in earth batteries for magnetic clocks, applied for May, 1878.

Drawbaugh's Finances.—When asked: "What is the actual cost of procuring an ordinary patent, including attorney fees?" Drawbaugh answered: "I have paid as high as sixty-five or seventy dollars." He held himself out, and advertised himself in print, as a solicitor of patents.

His specific cash receipts—that is, the actual cash which came into his hands—as specifically admitted by him, from 1867 to 1876, nine years, was $10,612.91. This was merely the cash which came into his hands from specific property sold or rented, from one loan of $400, and about one year's wages. In addition to this was all he earned for about five years' work as a jobbing machinist. He owned his house, and had to pay interest only on an incumbrance of about $300 for part of the time. It was worth $2,300. He had the use of a power driven machine shop rent free. These receipts appear from Drawbaugh's testimony and the papers put into the case. Drawbaugh undertook to meet this by very elaborately showing that he had spent the money—and so he did, but not on telephones. He bought himself a house; he furnished it; he provided himself with a parlor organ; he paid into the Drawbaugh Manufacturing Co., of which he was a member, $1,200 in cash toward its capital, and also paid in about $1,000 of his wages, which we have not reckoned among his receipts. But this created property which gave him some borrowing power; he gave his father $1,400; he spent a good deal of his time in constructing instruments and machinery which he had devised for other purposes; he made before 1878, at his own cost and charge, several large and handsome electric clocks; one of them was in a carved black walnut case six feet high; one of them, less expensive than the rest and less elaborate, was made before April, 1876.

The best proof of his resources in the way of tools and machinery suitable for the construction of small electrical machines is found in his advertising bill head, viz.: "Bought of Daniel Drawbaugh, practical machinist. *Small machinery, patent office models, electric machines, etc., a specialty.*"

It was expressly admitted that model making was one of his occupations. He did a great deal of jobbing work. He gives a list of so much of the machinery as he could remember off hand, and it includes two bench vises, tools of a hand lathe, general tools for a drill press or drilling machine, and general wood working tools, five engine lathes, two small or hand lathes, a machine for drilling faucets, a drill press, a grindstone, and a wood turning lathe. All this he owned or had the use of.

Readiness with which money was obtained from his friends for the inventions of himself and others, as shown by the amount actually raised and expended in Drawbaugh's shop:

In 1865–1872 he invented and built a nail plate feeder, for which he received several hundred dollars, largely in supplies, from Eberly, a mill owner.

In 1865–6, he got up a measuring faucet for molasses. It was invented at the request of the local store keeper, Crull, who, for a half interest, agreed to pay all expenses, including Drawbaugh's time and labor. Then Drawbaugh sold the other half to Gardner, who also bought Crull's interest under the contract, and continued to pay expenses. Gardner agreed to pay Drawbaugh $1,000 for this half, and gave him a note for it in April, 1867. Afterward Drawbaugh indorsed the note and got it discounted April, 1869. The patents were dated November 20, 1866.

The invention covered by them was really a kind of chambered rotary pump. Drawbaugh had sold to Crull & Gardner the right to use it for measuring ; he now sold to another concern the right to use it for pumps. This concern was organized as an association in 1867, known as the Drawbaugh Pump Company. It soon bought the faucet right, and in 1870 was reorganized as a corporation under the name of the " Drawbaugh Manufacturing Company." It paid him $6,000 for the patent, and raised not far from $20,000 more in cash, with which it fitted up and stocked the machine shop, of which they made him master mechanic, and which he has since occupied rent free. Drawbaugh owned from one sixth to one ninth of it. This appears from the depositions of John B. Drawbaugh, who states the story succinctly, and of W. L. Gorgas, the treasurer, and of D. Drawbaugh. John B. Drawbaugh, brother and next door neighbor of the claimant, says : " Daniel sold the right of the faucet to a company by the name of Gardner & Crull for $1,000, for which he took Mr. Gardner's paper with Jacob Coover's name as security. Then Daniel turned the faucet into a pump, or rather made a pump on the same principle as the faucet ; on that they formed a company in the names of Mr. Gorgas, Musser, Hursh and others. They were to pay him a consideration of $6,000, as I have heard ; that company established a machine shop at Eberly's Mill, which some of the company told me cost them from $20,000 to $25,000 ; after manufacturing the pump for about one year they found the pump to be a failure ; the pump company then purchased the Drawbaugh rotary molasses faucet from Mr. Gardner and others."

In July, 1873, D. A. and S. F. Hauck raised $7,000 in cash and paid it to the "Drawbaugh Manufacturing Co" for the Drawbaugh faucet patents and machinery. A concern called the Millbush Co. was formed about 1868 upon the invention of a neighbor, and raised and expended about $1,500 cash in machinery constructed at the shop according to Drawbaugh's designs and under his supervision. The axle company, formed early in 1875, upon the invention of another neighbor, had their work done at Drawbaugh's shop by Drawbaugh personally, and he designed and constructed special tools for them. They also purchased at least $1,000 worth of new machinery, and paid Drawbaugh about $425 for services in the course of a year. They raised and used at least $1,500. The clock company, got up in 1878, paid Drawbaugh $500 in cash; were to give him part of the profit; and bought more machinery. They put in about $1,000.

Thus, in nine years before the date of Mr. Bell's patents, Drawbaugh's friends raised and invested nearly $35,000 in his machine shop on the faith of his inventions and his skill as a designer. Yet he would have us believe, that during this time he could not find $15 for a caveat to cover the greatest invention of modern times, embodied in instruments which he had made, and could make in a day, at a cost of a dollar or two.

The Drawbaugh Pump Company at least was anxious to devote their capital and machinery to exploit some other invention of Drawbaugh's, if they could find one. In 1869 they proposed to manufacture his improved gas governor. They had a special meeting at the shop. He constructed a new one on purpose to exhibit. He fitted up a contrivance to make gas, and run a pipe from his forge into the second story of the machine shop, and arranged one or more burners. They did not take it up, but not for want of faith in him, for their next proposition was that he should invent screw machinery—as if he then had no inventions worth touching. This story is told by Drawbaugh.

Drawbaugh testified: "I made the second (gas governor) more complete, in order to show it to the Drawbaugh Pump

Company for the purpose of illustrating it to them, for the purpose of getting them to take an interest in it. There were some inquiries made about the machine, and it was found that the gas company would not allow it to be attached to the meter. I guess for that reason there was nothing done. They didn't take an interest in it."

The minutes of the *Drawbaugh Pump Company* contain the following: January 29, 1869. "Daniel Drawbaugh agreed to give his gas governor that he is now preparing to secure a patent for, to the company, for the company's use and benefit, the conditions to be agreed upon hereafter." March 26, 1869. "On motion of Henry S. Rupp and Daniel Drawbaugh, it was agreed that Daniel Drawbaugh shall, as speedily as possible, not to interfere with other necessary work, get up and make a screw machine for the use of the shop and its benefit."

A year later the association reorganized as a corporation, with a capital of $20,000. Its purpose is stated in its bill head of 1870, to be the manufacture of "Drawbaugh's rotary power pump, for mining and factory use; Drawbaugh's self measuring faucet, for drawing and measuring molasses, honey, tar, and all viscid liquids. Also stave cutters, stave jointers, mill trams, hydraulic rams, etc. All kinds of job work and building of special machinery solicited and attended to promptly."

Drawbaugh was the master mechanic it employed to design all special machinery. It sent him to the State fairs of 1868 and 1869 to exhibit the machinery he had invented and it manufactured. In 1874-5-6 he told various people that he proposed to exhibit an electric clock at the centennial. But he neither exhibited nor undertook to exhibit a talking machine. Will anybody believe that in 1868-9, and from that time forward, he had "full sized operative practical speaking telephones," and that work upon them was the absorbing occupation of his life?

The list of inventions printed and published by Drawbaugh in 1874 does not contain the telephone.

In June, 1874, Drawbaugh published a card, of which the following is a photo-electrotype copy:

Daniel Drawbaugh.

INVENTOR, DESIGNER

and

SOLICITOR-PATENTS.

☞ Also Models Neatly Made To Order.

Eberly's Mills,

Cumberland County, Pennsylvania.

[See Other Side.]

Dan'l Drawbaugh

INVENTOR OF
THE FOLLOWING PATENTS.

Stave, Heading & Shingle Cutter.
Barrel Machinery.

STAVE JOINTING MACHINE, Many in use.
Fram & Bed-staff for leveling face of Millstone.
Rine and Driver for running Millstone.
Nail Machinery for feeding Nail Plates.

PUMPS, ROTARAY & OTHERS.
Hydraulic Ram.
THE DRAWBAUGH Rotary Measure-
ing Faucet. very extensivly used.

CARPET RAG LOOPER -- A little
device by which rags are looped quick and firm,
without Needle or Thread.

ELLECTRIC CLOCK.

MAGNETO ELECTRIC MACHINE,

For short line Telegraphing. Fire Alarm.
and Propelling Electric Clocks. It can be
applied to any form of Electric movement.
Gives entire satisfaction USEING NO
GALVANIC BATTERY.
☞ For SIMPLICITY it has NO RIVAL.

In the above list of inventions, which are called "patents," it will be seen by comparison with the list of his patented inventions, that only part of them (not more than seven) had been patented, so that the list was not restricted to *patented* inventions. It was an announcement of works on which his title to advertise himself as an "inventor" was to rest. *It does not mention the telephone.* This published list is a conclusive proof which no ingenuity can explain away that he did not have "good full sized practical working speaking telephones" in 1874.

In 1876, or earlier, came his advertising bill head. "Daniel Drawbaugh, Practical Machinist. *Small machinery, patent office models, electric machines, etc., a specialty.*" And before and after 1876 were the other publications quoted, none of which asserted that he was the first inventor of the telephone.

The Drawbaugh answer admits that he made no use of telephones beyond experimental use; that the public never transmitted speech by reason of any information derived from him, and that he filed no caveat nor application until he was produced by others as a defence in 1880. It attempts to account for this state of facts only on two grounds: First, that Drawbaugh for more than ten years prior to the year 1880, was miserably poor, in debt, with a large and helpless family dependent upon his daily labor for support, and was, from such cause alone, utterly unable to patent his said invention, or caveat it or manufacture and introduce it upon the market." And second: "IIis utter want of proper mechanical tools, materials, and appliances."

It will be seen that the facts do not correspond in the slightest degree with those assertions. The *facts* now rehearsed are part of Drawbaugh's history. If, during all those years he had had practical speaking telephones, knowledge whereof he "freely communicated to the public"—and his answer and witnesses allege that whatever he did in that regard was freely communicated to the public—they would have borne some fruit, and his history would not have been what it is.

Finally, we have the fact, virtually admitted by him under oath in 1879, and proved by a test of his instruments in 1881, that the apparatus his party relies on is not a practically operative apparatus.

RECAPITULATION.

Drawbaugh's claims were first made public in 1880—when Bell's patent was four years old—and thousands of telephones made under it were in public use. Although Drawbaugh claims to have had operative speaking telephones as early as 1867, no patent was applied for, nor caveat filed, until 1880; nor was his alleged invention used except in his own shop, and experimentally. Bell's invention was given to the world in 1876, and before the close of that year had attained world wide notoriety. Before another year had gone by the invention was in extensive public use. This was known to Drawbaugh; yet he made no sign, even in the public prints. Such silence, under such circumstances, is irreconcilable with the truth of his present story. He was not a man unnoticed nor unknown. He had kept himself before the eyes of his community as an inventor. He exhibited at public exhibitions. He was mentioned in the newspapers. He had occasion both before and after Bell's patent to enumerate the works on which he rested his claim to be an inventor. But the invention of the speaking telephone was not among those alleged creations which he enumerated or which others attributed to him. The proofs show that the allegations as to Drawbaugh's abject poverty and lack of means and facilities for experimenting, are essentially untrue, and that, on the contrary, during all these years in which he now claims to have been in possession of the invention, his situation and opportunities for developing it—if he had had it—were exceptionally favorable. During that very time he was holding himself out to the public as a machinist whose specialty was "electrical" machinery, and as a solicitor of patents; and it appears that he had, in fact, all the mechanical skill, and all the tools and appliances for making that skill available for the ready production of speaking telephones—if only he had possessed the invention. That he did not give the speaking telephone to the world was *not* owing either to poverty or to lack of mechanical skill or appliances. Nor was it owing to lack of moneyed persons willing to interest themselves in such an invention. The proofs show that Drawbaugh's neighbors were only too ready to invest their means in schemes of his devising, and the inference is irresistible that if he did not interest moneyed neighbors in a "talking machine" it must have been either because he did not seek to do so, or, more probably, he had no "talking machine" fit to attract their attention.

———

CIRCUIT COURT OF THE UNITED STATES, DISTRICT OF MASSA-CHUSETTS.—AMERICAN BELL TELEPHONE COMPANY ET AL. *v.* ALBERT SPENCER ET AL.—OPINION OF THE COURT.—JUNE 27, 1881.

LOWELL, *J.*: The bill alleges an infringement of two patents, granted to Alexander Graham Bell. The defendants admit that they have infringed some valid claims of the second patent, but the plaintiffs are not content with this admission; they rely besides upon the fifth claim of the first patent, which is much more comprehensive in its scope.

Patent No. 174,465, issued to Bell, dated March 7, 1876, is entitled "Improvement in Telegraphy," and is said in the specification to consist in "the employment of a vibratory or undulatory current of electricity in contradistinction to a merely intermittent or pulsatory current, and of a method of and apparatus for producing electrical undulations upon the line wire." The patentee mentions several advantages which may be derived by the use of this undulatory current, instead of the intermittent current, which continually makes and breaks contact, in its application to multiple telegraphy, that is, sending several messages, or strains of music, at once over the same wire; and the possibility of conveying sounds, other than musical notes. This latter application is not the most prominent in the specification, though, as often happens, it has proved to be of surpassing value. This part of the invention is shown in figure 7 of the drawings, and is thus described in the text:

"The armature, *c*, fig. 7, is fastened loosely by one extremity to the uncovered leg, *d*, of the electro magnet, *b*, and its other extremity is attached to the centre of a stretched membrane, *a*. A cone, A, is used to convey sound vibrations upon the membrane. When a sound is uttered in the cone, the membrane, *a*, is set in vibration, the armature, c, is forced to partake of the motion, and thus electrical undulations are created upon the circuit E, b, e, f, g. These undulations are similar in form to the air vibrations caused by the sound; that is, they are represented graphically by similar curves. The undulatory current passing through the electro magnet, f, influences its armature, h, to copy the motions of the armature, c. A similar sound to that uttered in A is then heard to proceed from L."

With the figure 7 before us, this description is readily understood. A cone of pasteboard or other suitable material has a membrane stretched over its smaller end; at a little distance is a piece of iron magnetized by a coil through which is passing a current of electricity. When sounds are made at the mouth of cone, A, the membrane vibrates like the drum of a human ear; and the armature, which is directly in front of the magnet, vibrates with the membrane, and its movements cause pulsations of electricity, like those of the air which excited the membrane, to pass over the wire; and the wire stretches to another similar magnet and cone with its membrane and armature. The second armature and membrane take up the vibrations and make them audible by repeating them into the condensing cone, L, which translates them into vibrations of the air.

The defendants insist that the instrument represented in figure 7 will not transmit articulate speech; that this great result has been reached by Mr. Bell entirely through the improvements described in his second patent, such as the substitution of a metal plate for the stretched membrane, and some others.

The importance of the point is, that if Bell, who is admitted in this case to be the original and first inventor of any mode of transmitting speech, had not completed his method and put it into a working form when he took his first patent, he may lose the benefit of his invention; because, in his second patent, he made no broad claim to the method or process, but only to the improvements upon a process assumed to have been sufficiently described in his first patent.

There is some evidence that Bell's experiments with the instruments described in fig. 7, before he took out his patent, were not entirely successful; but this is now immaterial, for it is proved that the instrument will do the work, whether the inventor knew it or not, and in the mode pointed out by the specification.

The fifth claim of this patent is for—

"The method and apparatus for transmitting vocal or other sounds, telegraphically, by causing electrical undulations, similar in form to the vibrations of the air accompanying the said vocal or other sounds, substantially as set forth."

The defendants use a method and apparatus for transmitting vocal sounds, which resemble those of the plaintiffs in producing electrical undulations copied from the vibrations of a diaphragm, and sending them along a wire to a similar receiver at the other end. The specific method of producing the electrical undulations is different. It is made on the principle of the microphone, which has been very much improved since the date of the first Bell patent.

If the Bell patent were for a mere arrangement, or combination of old devices, to produce a somewhat better result in a known art, then, no doubt, a person who substituted a new element not known at the date of the patent might escape the charge of infringement. But Bell discovered a new art—that of transmitting speech by electricity—and has a right to hold the broadest claim for it which can be permitted in any case; not to the abstract right of sending sounds by telegraph, without any regard to means, but to all means and processes which he has both invented and claimed.

The invention is nothing less than the transfer to a wire of electrical vibrations like those which a sound has produced in the air. The claim is not so broad as the invention. It was, undoubtedly, drawn somewhat carefully in view of the decision in *O'Reilly* v. *Morse*, 15 How. 62, and covers the method and apparatus—that is, any process and any apparatus of substantially similar character to those described. The patent points out distinctly that the undulations may be produced in other modes beside the vibration of an armature in front of a magnet; and the defendants make use of a mode not wholly unknown at that time, though much improved, in creating their undulations.

It seems to me that the defendants use both the method and the apparatus of Bell. The essential elements of the method are the production of what the patent calls undulatory vibrations of electricity to correspond with those of the air, and transmitting them to a receiving instrument capable of echoing them. Granting that the defendants' instrument for converting the vibrations of the diaphragm into vibrations of electricity is an improvement upon that of the plaintiffs, still it does the same sort of work, and does it in a mode not wholly unknown at the date of the patent, though I do not consider that material.

An apparatus made by Reis, of Germany, in 1860, and described in several publications before 1876, is relied on to limit the scope of Bell's invention. Reis appears to have been a man of learning and ingenuity. He used a membrane and electrodes for transmitting sounds, and his apparatus was well known to curious inquirers. The regret of all its admirers was, that articulate speech could not be sent and received by it. The deficiency was inherent in the principle of the machine. It can transmit electrical waves along a wire, under very favorable circumstances, not in the mode intended by the inventor, but one suggested by Bell's discovery, but it cannot transmute them into articulate sounds at the other end, because it is constructed on a false theory, and the delicacy of use required to make it perform part of the operation is fatal to its possible performance of the other part. A Bell receiver must be used to gather up the sound before the instrument can even now be adopted to a limited practical use. It was like those deaf and dumb pupils of Prof. Bell, who could be taught to speak, but not to hear. That was all, but it was enough. A century of Reis would never have produced a speaking telephone by mere improvement in construction.

I am of opinion that the fifth claim of patent No. 174,465 is valid, and has been infringed.

The statute declares that if a patentee has claimed too much in any part of his patent he shall not recover costs, and it has been argued that certain claims of these patents, not relied on by the plaintiffs, are too broad. In this stage of the case the question of costs does not arise ; but I may as well say, that there is not sufficient evidence in the record to enable me to find whether these claims are valid or not, and that the statute does not mean that claims not in issue should be contested for the mere purpose of settling the costs. More expense might be incurred in such a mode of trial than depended upon the main issue. *Decree for the complainants.*

CIRCUIT COURT OF THE UNITED STATES, DISTRICT OF MASSACHUSETTS. — IN EQUITY. — AMERICAN BELL TELEPHONE COMPANY ET AL. *v.* ALBERT L. SPENCER ET AL.

DECREE.—This cause came to be heard upon the bill, answer, replication and proofs, and was argued by counsel and considered by the court, whereupon it is now, to wit, Aug. 27, 1881, ordered, adjudged and decreed that Alexander Graham Bell is the original and first inventor of the invention specified in the fifth claim of the patent numbered 174,465, granted to said Bell March 7, A. D. 1876, and the fifth, sixth and eighth claims of the patent numbered 186,787, granted to said Bell, Jan. 30, 1877, being the claims in respect of which the proofs were taken ; that the said patents are good and valid patents therefor ; and the complainants waiving a reference to a master to ascertain profits and damages, and accepting nominal damages, it is further ordered that the defendants pay to the plaintiff the sum of one dollar as profits and damages, and also costs taxed at　　　　, and that they be perpetually enjoined from further infringing the said patents.

By the Court,　　　　　ALEX. H. TROWBRIDGE,
　　　　　　　　　　　　　　　　　　Deputy Clerk.

　　Attest: ALEX. H. TROWBRIDGE,
　　　　　　　　Deputy Clerk.

CIRCUIT COURT OF THE UNITED STATES, DISTRICT OF MASSA-
CHUSETTS. — AMERICAN BELL TELEPHONE COMPANY *v.*
AMOS E. DOLBEAR ET AL.—BEFORE GRAY AND LOWELL,
JJ.—OPINION OF THE COURT.—JANUARY 24, 1883.

GRAY, *J.:* Few legal rules have been oftener misunderstood
and misapplied than the maxim that you cannot patent a principle. But the confusion on this subject has been so effectually
cleared up by the recent judgment of the Supreme Court, delivered by Mr. Justice Bradley, in *Tilghman* v. *Proctor,* 102
U. S. 707, that it will be sufficient for the purposes of this case
to state the conclusion there announced.

There can be no patent for a mere principle. The discoverer
of a natural force or a scientific fact cannot have a patent for
that. But if he invents for the first time a process by which a
certain effect of one of the forces of nature is made useful to
mankind, and fully describes and claims that process, and also
describes a mode or apparatus by which it may be usefully applied, he is, within the meaning, and the very words, of the
patent law, " a person who has invented or discovered any new
and useful art;" and he is entitled to a patent for the process
of which he is the first inventor, and is not restricted to the
particular form of mechanism or apparatus by which he carries
out that process. Another person, who afterward invents an
improved form of apparatus, embodying the same process, may
indeed obtain a patent for his improvement; but he has no
right to use the process, in his own or any other form of
apparatus, without the consent of the first inventor of the
process.

It was decided by this court in *American Bell Telephone Co.* v.
Spencer, 8 Fed. Rep. 509, and is not denied by present defendant, that Bell is the first inventor of a speaking telephone. The
only controversy is of the extent of his patent.

The draughtsman of the specification has exhibited as clear
and accurate a comprehension of the rules of the patent law, as
the inventor has of the force of nature with which he was

dealing, and of the means by which he reduced that force to a practical use.

The patent is clearly not intended to be limited to a form of apparatus, but embraces a method or process. This is apparent upon the face of the specification.

The inventor begins by saying: "My present invention consists in the employment of a vibratory or undulatory current of electricity in contradistinction to a merely intermittent or pulsatory current, and of a method of and apparatus for producing electrical undulations upon the line wire."

After describing the advantages of an undulatory current, resulting from gradual changes of intensity, over a pulsatory current caused by sudden changes of intensity, he says: "It has long been known that when a permanent magnet is caused to approach the pole of an electro magnet, a current of electricity is induced in the coils of the latter, and that, when it is made to recede, a current of opposite polarity to the first appears upon the wire. When, therefore, a permanent magnet is caused to vibrate in front of the pole of an electro magnet, an undulatory current of electricity is induced in the coils of the electro magnet, the undulations of which correspond, in rapidity of succession, to the vibrations of the magnet, in polarity to the direction of its motion, and in intensity to the amplitude of its vibration;" or, as he afterward repeats in fuller language: "Electrical undulations, induced by the vibration of a body capable of inductive action, can be represented graphically without error, by the same sinusoidal curve which expresses the vibration of the inducing body itself, and the effect of its vibration upon the air; or, as above stated, the rate of oscillation in the electrical current corresponds to the rate of vibration of the inducing body—that is, to the pitch of sound produced; the intensity of the current varies with the amplitude of the vibration—that is, with the loudness of the sound; and the polarity of the current corresponds to the direction of the vibrating body—that is, to the condensations and rarefactions of air produced by the vibration."

He further says : " There are many ways of producing undulatory currents of electricity, dependent for effect upon the vibrations or motions of bodies capable of inductive action. A
few of the methods that may be employed I shall here specify.
When a wire, through which a continuous current of electricity
is passing, is caused to vibrate in the neighborhood of another
wire, an undulatory current of electricity is induced in the latter. When a cylinder, upon which are arranged bar magnets, is
made to rotate in front of the pole of an electro magnet, an undulatory current of electricity is induced in the coils of the electro magnet.

" Undulations are caused in a continuous voltaic current by
the vibration or motion of bodies capable of inductive action, or
by the vibration of the conducting wire itself in the neighborhood of such bodies. Electrical undulations may also be caused
by alternately increasing and diminishing the resistance of the
circuit, or by alternately increasing and diminishing the power of
the battery. The internal resistance of a battery is diminished
by bringing the voltaic elements nearer together, and increased
by placing them farther apart. The reciprocal vibration of the
elements of a battery, therefore, occasions an undulatory action
in the voltaic current. The external resistance may also be
varied. For instance, let mercury or some other liquid form
part of a voltaic circuit, then the more deeply the conducting
wire is immersed in the mercury or other liquid the less resistance does the liquid offer to the passage of the current. Hence
the vibration of the conducting wire in mercury or other liquid
included in the circuit occasions undulations in the current. The
vertical vibration of the elements of a battery in the liquid in
which they are immersed produces an undulatory action in the
current by alternately increasing and diminishing the power of
the battery.

" In illustration of the method of creating electrical undulations, I shall show and describe one form of apparatus for producing the effect. I prefer to employ for this purpose an electro magnet, A, fig. 5, having a coil upon only one of its legs, b.

A steel spring armature, c, is firmly clamped by one extremity to the uncovered leg, d, of the magnet, and its free end is allowed to project above the pole of the covered leg. The armature, c, can be set in vibration in a variety of ways, one of which is by wind, and, in vibrating, it produces a musical note of a certain definite pitch. When the instrument, A, is placed in a voltaic circuit, $g\ b\ e f g$ " (in which b represents the covered leg of the first electro magnet ; f represents the covered leg of another similar electro magnet, I, whose uncovered leg is marked h ; and g and e represent the two points of the voltaic circuit midway of the wire connecting the two magnets), "the armature, c, becomes magnetic, and the polarity of its free end is opposed to that of the magnet underneath. So long as the armature, c, remains at rest, no effect is produced upon the voltaic current ; but the moment it is set in vibration to produce its musical note, a powerful inductive action takes place, and electrical undulations traverse the circuit, $g\ b\ e f g$. The vibratory current passing through the coil of the electro magnet, f, causes vibration in its armature, h, when the armatures, $c\ h$, of the two instruments A, I, are normally in unison with one another ; but the armature, h, is unaffected by the passage of the undulatory current when the pitches of the two instruments are different."

Then, after showing how two or more telegraphic signals or messages may be sent simultaneously over the same circuit without interfering with one another, he adds : "I desire here to remark that there are many other uses to which these instruments may be put, such as the simultaneous transmission of musical notes, differing in loudness as well as in pitch, and the telegraphic transmission of noises or sounds of any kind.

"When the armature, c, fig. 5, is set in vibration, the armature, h, responds not only in pitch, but in loudness. Thus, when c vibrates with little amplitude, a very soft musical note proceeds from h ; and when c vibrates forcibly, the amplitude of the vibration of h is considerably increased, and the resulting sound becomes louder."

He proceeds to say : " One of the ways in which the armature, *c*, fig. 5, may be set in vibration has been stated above to be by wind. Another mode is shown in fig. 7, whereby motion can be imparted to the armature by the human voice or by means of a musical instrument.

"The armature, *c*, fig. 7, is fastened loosely by one extremity to the uncovered leg, *d*, of the electro magnet, *b*, and its other extremity is attached to the centre of a stretched membrane, *a*. A cone, A, is used to converge sound vibrations upon the membrane. When a sound is uttered in the cone, the membrane, *a*, is set in vibration, the armature, *c*, is forced to partake of the motion, and thus electrical undulations are created upon the circuit, E *b e f g*. These undulations are similar in form to the air vibrations caused by the sound—that is, they are represented graphically by similar curves. The undulatory current passing through the electro magnet, *f*, influences its armature, *h*, to copy the motion of the armature, *c*. A similar sound to that uttered into A is then heard to proceed from L."

The reference to fig. 7 will be better understood by repeating, slightly amplified, Judge Lowell's explanation in *Spencer's case*. A cone of pasteboard or other suitable material, A, has a membrane, *a*, stretched over its smaller end; at a little distance is the armature, *c*, consisting of a piece of iron magnetized by the coil of the electro magnet, *b*, through which is passing a current of electricity. When sounds are made at the mouth of the cone, A, the membrane, *a*, vibrates like the drum of the human ear; and the armature, *c*, which is directly in front of the magnet, *b*, vibrates with this membrane, and its movements cause pulsations of electricity like those of the air which excited the membrane to pass over the wire, *e*, which stretches to another similar magnet, *f*, and cone, L, with its membrane, and its armature, *h*. The second armature and membrane take up the vibrations and make them audible by repeating them into the second cone, L, which translates them into vibrations of the air. In practice, a metallic diaphragm or disk is often substituted for each membrane.

The inventor adds this explanation: "In this specification

the three words 'oscillation,' 'vibration' and 'undulation' are used synonymously, and in contradistinction to the terms 'intermittent' and 'pulsatory.' By the term 'body capable of inductive action,' I mean a body which, when in motion, produces dynamical electricity. I include in the category of bodies capable of inductive action brass, copper and other metals, as well as iron and steel."

His fifth and final claim is of "the method of and apparatus for transmitting vocal or other sounds telegraphically, as herein described, by causing electrical undulations, similar in form to the vibrations of the air accompanying the said vocal or other sounds, substantially as set forth."

In this claim, as throughout the specification, the word "method" is evidently used, not as synonymous with "mode" or "apparatus," but as equivalent to "process;" just as it was used by Chief Justice Taney, delivering the judgment of the majority of the court, in *Morse* v. *O'Reilly*, 15 How. 62, 117, as well by Mr. Justice Grier (who dissented in *Morse* v. *O'Reilly*), in delivering the unanimous judgment in *Corning* v. *Burden*, 15 How. 252, 267. And the invention claimed is not merely the apparatus described, but also the general process or method by which the wind, or a musical instrument or the human voice, produces in a current of electricity a succession of electrical disturbances, not sudden and intermittent or pulsatory, but gradual, oscillatory, vibratory or undulatory, so as to give out at the farther end of the conducting wire sounds exactly corresponding in loudness, in pitch, and in tone, character or quality, to the sounds committed to it at the nearer end.

The opinion in *Spencer's case* clearly points out that "Bell discovered a new art—that of transmitting speech by electricity—and has a right to hold the broadest claim for it which can be permitted in any case," and "the invention is nothing less than the transfer to a wire of electrical vibrations like those which a sound has produced in the air;" and that his patent, while not covering the abstract principle, without regard to means, of transmitting speech by electricity, yet is not limited to a particular form of apparatus, but includes the process or method (using the two words as equivalent), the essential elements of which are "the production of what the patent calls undulatory vibrations of electricity to correspond with those of the air, and transmitting them to a receiving instrument capable of echoing them."

The evidence in this case clearly shows that Bell discovered that articulate sounds could be transmitted by undulatory vibrations of electricity, and invented the art or process of transmitting such sounds by means of such vibrations. If that art or process is (as the witnesses called by the defendants say it is) the only way by which speech can be transmitted by electricity, that fact does not lessen the merit of his invention, or the protection which the law will give to it.

The mode or apparatus by which Bell effects his purpose is, by using an electro magnet in the transmitter, and another electro magnet in the receiver. But the essence of his invention consists not merely in the form of apparatus which he uses, but in the general process or method of which that apparatus is the embodiment.

Dolbear likewise uses an electro magnet in the transmitter; and both his method and his apparatus, as is admitted in his own affidavit, are substantially like Bell's, until he comes to the receiver. For the magneto receiver, Dolbear substitutes a condenser receiver, consisting of two thin metal diaphragms or disks, of about the size and thickness of those used in an ordinary Bell telephone, separated by a very thin air space, one or both disks connected with the conducting wire, and the speaking disk, if not so connected, otherwise charged with electricity; so that, as the varying currents flow into and out of this condenser, the two disks attract one another more or less strongly, and thereby vibrations are set up which correspond to the vibrations of the original sound.

The main difference on which the defendants rely is, that Bell uses what is called dynamic electricity, producing by its motion an electric current; while Dolbear, in his receiver, uses what is called static electricity, producing, while at rest, electrical attraction. And the learned counsel for the defendants illustrate the distinction thus : " It was known, long before Bell's method, that electricity had two properties, very much as water has two properties, namely, first, pressure or head, or that property which tends to make it flow, and which can exist by itself only in the case of an insulated and charged body, or a reservoir of water ; and, secondly, that dynamic property arising from its motion, and which never can exist by itself, but depends upon the quantity in motion and the rate of motion. This is not an absolutely exact way of expressing it, for the reason that electricity is not a fluid ; but, were it a fluid, the statement would be entirely exact."

It does not appear to us to be important to determine whether, in scientific exactness, the varying influences of static electricity may properly be called currents ; or whether the two properties of electricity differ in kind and in substance, or only in degree, or in the form of manifestation and application ; or whether the force of the property which tends to make a fluid, when stationary, change its place and flow, is different in kind from that which it exerts, when changing its place and flowing—in short, whether the power of the pressure of water in a reservoir is different in kind from water power in a stream or current.

Whatever name be given to the property, or the manifestation of the electricity in the defendants' receiver, the facts remain that they avail themselves of Bell's discovery that undulatory vibrations of electricity can intelligibly and accurately transmit articulate speech, as well as of the process which Bell invented, and by which he reduced his discovery to practical use ; that they also copy the mode and apparatus by which he creates and transmits the undulatory electrical vibrations, corresponding to those of the air ; and that in the plate charged with electricity, which they have substituted for the magnetic coil in the receiver, the charge constantly varies in accordance with the principle which Bell discovered, and by means of the undulatory current caused by the process and in the mode which he invented and patented.

The defendants have therefore infringed Bell's patent by using his general process or method, and should be restrained by injunction from continuing to do so ; and it is unnecessary, for the purposes of this decision, to consider whether the defendants' apparatus is a substantial equivalent of the plaintiff's, or whether it is an improvement for which Dolbear might himself be entitled to a patent. *Temporary injunction ordered.*

CIRCUIT COURT OF THE UNITED STATES, DISTRICT OF MASSA-
CHUSETTS, AMERICAN BELL TELEPHONE COMPANY *v.* AMOS
E. DOLBEAR ET AL.—OPINION OF THE COURT, AUGUST 25,
1883.

LOWELL, *J.:* The final hearing in this case was hardly more than a form, because the two questions which are raised by the record have been decided in favor of the plaintiff on motions for preliminary injunction, which were prepared and argued with unusual thoroughness. These questions are : " Whether the telephone described by Reis anticipates the Bell telephone ?" and, " Whether Dolbear's apparatus infringes Bell's patent ?"

1. I decided in *American Bell Telephone Co.* v. *Spencer*, 8 Fed. Rep. 509, that Reis had not described a telephone which anticipated Bell's invention. The same point has since been decided in the same way in England. (*United Telephone Co.* v. *Harrison*, 21 Ch. D. 720.) It is admitted in the present case that the Reis instrument, if used as he intended to use it, can never serve as a speaking telephone, because the current of electricity is constantly broken ; and it is essential for the transmission of speech that the current should not be broken. The defendant now testifies that the Reis instrument can be made to transmit speech, under some circumstances, if operated in the way which Bell has shown to be necessary. In 1877 he several times expressed the opinion that Bell made the invention, and that Reis did not make it. The experiment made in the presence of counsel,

which was intended to prove the correctness of the defendants' present opinion, was an utter failure. But if it be admitted that the Reis instrument is capable of such use, to a very limited extent, and after a change in its proportions, and when used in a way which the inventor did not intend, still, I am of opinion that it was not an anticipation of Bell. The case of *Clough* v. *Barker*, 106 U. S. 166, would apply to such a state of facts. That case, undoubtedly, is an exceptional one, and its doctrine must be applied with much reserve ; but when so applied, it will occasionally be useful. It is, that if a certain machine or organization is capable of a certain use only under unusual, and, as I may say, abnormal conditions, so that a person of skill and knowledge in the art to which it relates, or a person using the machine, would not, unless by accident, discover that it was capable of such a mode of operation, it shall not be considered an anticipation of a machine or organization which is founded upon such mode of operation.

2. At the former hearing in this case, before Mr. Justice Gray and me, we decided that the defendant, whatever the merits of his telephone may be, employs in it a part, at least, of Bell's process. No additional evidence has been given at the final hearing, unless a further explanation of that already given may be called additional ; and I remain of the opinion expressed by the presiding justice at that time : *American Bell Telephone Co.* v. *Dolbear et al.*, 15 Fed. Rep. 448. *Decree for the complainant.*

CIRCUIT COURT OF THE UNITED STATES, DISTRICT OF MASSACHUSETTS.—MAY TERM, 1883, TO WIT, SEPT. 8, 1883.— IN EQUITY.—AMERICAN BELL TELEPHONE CO., COMPLAINANT, *v.* AMOS E. DOLBEAR ET AL., DEFENDANTS.—FINAL DECREE FOR PERPETUAL INJUNCTION.

This cause came on to be heard at this present term upon the pleadings and proofs, and was argued by counsel for the respective parties, and now, upon consideration thereof, to wit,

Sept. 8, 1883, it is ordered, adjudged and decreed as follows, viz. : that the Letters Patent referred to in the complainant's bill, being Letters Patent of the United States granted unto Alexander Graham Bell, No. 174,465, for improvement in telegraphy, dated March 7, 1876, is a good and valid patent, and that the said Alexander Graham Bell was the original and first inventor of the improvement described and claimed therein, and that the said defendants have infringed the fifth claim of said patent, and upon the exclusive rights of the complainants under the same.

And it appearing to the court that the complainants waive a reference to a master, to take an account of the profits and damages, and that the parties agree that the amount of profits and damages to be recovered by the complainants be fixed at the sum of one hundred dollars, it is further ordered that the complainants recover the said sum of one hundred dollars accordingly.

And it is further ordered, adjudged and decreed that a perpetual injunction be issued under said patent No. 174,465 against the defendants, according to the prayer of the bill.

The court has not considered Letters Patent No. 186,787, dated Jan. 30, 1877, in the bill mentioned.

And it is further ordered, adjudged and decreed that the complainant recover of the defendants its costs of suit.

By the Court,

John G. Stetson, Clerk.

STATISTICS OF THE AMERICAN BELL TELEPHONE COMPANY.

The number of telephones in the hands of Bell licensees in the United States on February 20, 1880, was 60,873 ; 1881, 132,692 ; 1882, 189,374 ; 1883, 249,711 ; 1884, 307,010 ; showing an increase of each year over the preceding of : 71,819 in 1881 (this number including 20,885 taken over from the Gold and Stock Telegraph Company, and in use by the Bell licensees; deducting these, the increase was 50,934 in 1881), 56,682 in 1882 ;

60,337 in 1883 ; and 57,299 in 1884. The total increase is 246,137, or four hundred per cent.

The number of telephone exchanges in operation in the United States on the 1st of March, 1880, was 138 ; 1881, 408 ; 1882, 592 ; 1883, 735 ; 1884, 890 ; showing an increase each year over the preceding of 270 in 1880 ; 184 in 1881 ; 143 in 1882 ; and 165 in 1883. The total increase for the four years was 752, or 544 per cent.

The earnings from rentals of telephones for the year ending February 28, 1881, were $535,754.84 ; 1882, $885,312.92 ; 1883, $1,257,054.58 ; 1884, $1,695,678.58. Total increase for the four years, $1,159,923.74, or 216 per cent.

INDEX.

————•••————

TECHNOLOGY AND SOCIETY

An Arno Press Collection

Ardrey, R[obert] L. **American Agricultural Implements.** In two parts. 1894

Arnold, Horace Lucien and Fay Leone Faurote. **Ford Methods and the Ford Shops.** 1915

Baron, Stanley [Wade]. **Brewed in America:** A History of Beer and Ale in the United States. 1962

Bathe, Greville and Dorothy. **Oliver Evans:** A Chronicle of Early American Engineering. 1935

Bendure, Zelma and Gladys Pfeiffer. **America's Fabrics:** Origin and History, Manufacture, Characteristics and Uses. 1946

Bichowsky, F. Russell. **Industrial Research.** 1942

Bigelow, Jacob. **The Useful Arts:** Considered in Connexion with the Applications of Science. 1840. Two volumes in one

Birkmire, William H. **Skeleton Construction in Buildings.** 1894

Boyd, T[homas] A[lvin]. **Professional Amateur:** The Biography of Charles Franklin Kettering. 1957

Bright, Arthur A[aron], Jr. **The Electric-Lamp Industry:** Technological Change and Economic Development from 1800 to 1947. 1949

Bruce, Alfred and Harold Sandbank. **The History of Prefabrication.** 1943

Carr, Charles C[arl]. **Alcoa, An American Enterprise.** 1952

Cooley, Mortimer E. **Scientific Blacksmith.** 1947

Davis, Charles Thomas. **The Manufacture of Paper.** 1886

Deane, Samuel. **The New-England Farmer,** or Georgical Dictionary. 1822

Dyer, Henry. **The Evolution of Industry.** 1895

Epstein, Ralph C. **The Automobile Industry:** Its Economic and Commercial Development. 1928

Ericsson, Henry. **Sixty Years a Builder:** The Autobiography of Henry Ericsson. 1942

Evans, Oliver. **The Young Mill-Wright and Miller's Guide.** 1850

Ewbank, Thomas. **A Descriptive and Historical Account of Hydraulic and Other Machines for Raising Water,** Ancient and Modern. 1842

Field, Henry M. **The Story of the Atlantic Telegraph.** 1893

Fleming, A. P. M. **Industrial Research in the United States of America.** 1917

Van Gelder, Arthur Pine and Hugo Schlatter. **History of the Explosives Industry in America.** 1927

Hall, Courtney Robert. **History of American Industrial Science.** 1954

Hungerford, Edward. **The Story of Public Utilities.** 1928

Hungerford, Edward. **The Story of the Baltimore and Ohio Railroad, 1827-1927.** 1928

Husband, Joseph. **The Story of the Pullman Car.** 1917

Ingels, Margaret. **Willis Haviland Carrier, Father of Air Conditioning.** 1952

Kingsbury, J[ohn] E. **The Telephone and Telephone Exchanges:** Their Invention and Development. 1915

Labatut, Jean and Wheaton J. Lane, eds. **Highways in Our National Life:** A Symposium. 1950

Lathrop, William G[ilbert]. **The Brass Industry in the United States.** 1926

Lesley, Robert W., John B. Lober and George S. Bartlett. **History of the Portland Cement Industry in the United States.** 1924

Marcosson, Isaac F. **Wherever Men Trade:** The Romance of the Cash Register. 1945

Miles, Henry A[dolphus]. **Lowell, As It Was, and As It Is.** 1845

Morison, George S. **The New Epoch:** As Developed by the Manufacture of Power. 1903

Olmsted, Denison. **Memoir of Eli Whitney, Esq.** 1846

Passer, Harold C. **The Electrical Manufacturers, 1875-1900.** 1953

Prescott, George B[artlett]. **Bell's Electric Speaking Telephone.** 1884

Prout, Henry G. **A Life of George Westinghouse.** 1921

Randall, Frank A. **History of the Development of Building Construction in Chicago.** 1949

Riley, John J. **A History of the American Soft Drink Industry:** Bottled Carbonated Beverages, 1807-1957. 1958

Salem, F[rederick] W[illiam]. **Beer, Its History and Its Economic Value as a National Beverage.** 1880

Smith, Edgar F. **Chemistry in America.** 1914

Steinman, D[avid] B[arnard]. **The Builders of the Bridge:** The Story of John Roebling and His Son. 1950

Taylor, F[rank] Sherwood. **A History of Industrial Chemistry.** 1957

Technological Trends and National Policy, Including the Social Implications of New Inventions. Report of the Subcommittee on Technology to the National Resources Committee. 1937

Thompson, John S. **History of Composing Machines.** 1904

Thompson, Robert Luther. **Wiring a Continent:** The History of the Telegraph Industry in the United States, 1832-1866. 1947

Tilley, Nannie May. **The Bright-Tobacco Industry, 1860-1929.** 1948

Tooker, Elva. **Nathan Trotter:** Philadelphia Merchant, 1787-1853. 1955

Turck, J. A. V. **Origin of Modern Calculating Machines.** 1921

Tyler, David Budlong. **Steam Conquers the Atlantic.** 1939

Wheeler, Gervase. **Homes for the People,** In Suburb and Country. 1855